D0241526

HISTORICAL GERMAN SYNTAX

HISTORICAL GERMAN SYNTAX

W. B. LOCKWOOD
M.A., D.LITT.
PROFESSOR OF GERMANIC AND
INDO-EUROPEAN PHILOLOGY,
UNIVERSITY OF READING

OXFORD
AT THE CLARENDON PRESS
1968

Oxford University Press, Ely House, London W. I
GLASGOW NEW YORK TORONTO MELBOURNE WELLINGTON
CAPE TOWN SALISBURY IBADAN NAIROBI LUSAKA ADDIS ABABA
BOMBAY CALCUTTA MADRAS KARACHI LAHORE DACCA
KUALA LUMPUR HONG KONG TOKYO

PRINTED IN GREAT BRITAIN

CONTENTS

III · ADVERBS

IV · PRONOUNS

V · ARTICLES

VI · VERBS

PREFACE

None of the departments of historical grammar is so extensive or so intricate as that of syntax; indeed, the field often seems inexhaustible. There is no standard method of analysis and no recognized pattern of presentation.

In compiling the present introduction to historical German syntax, I have endeavoured to select such materials as will be most useful for English-speaking students of the language, and it will therefore be found that emphasis tends to be upon those aspects in which German usage differs from our own. A fair knowledge of modern German has been assumed, so that examples of recent German have not usually been translated. On the other hand, translations of medieval German have been supplied in every case, usually into English, but into modern German if an aspect of syntax could be economically illustrated in this way.

Quotations from the older and classical stages of the language are accompanied by the name of the author or text. But for the most recent period this generally seemed unnecessary. The majority of the examples are in any case from ephemeral sources, but all are thoroughly typical of the language of today. Luther's Bible has been the main source for Early New High German, and is quoted in the form in which it is usually read today, i.e. with modernized spelling but otherwise (as a rule) in the original idiom. Middle High German quotations are naturally in the standard normalized orthography. Old High German examples have frequently been normalized, too, especially with regard to vowel length and the distinction between *z* and *ʒ*, but dialect differences in these texts are so marked that orthographical uniformity is out of the question. One needs to know, for instance, that *th* occurs in some texts, but becomes *d* or even *t* in others, thus Otfrid *ther*, Notker *der*, *ter*.

Reference has sometimes been made to English usage, though not in any systematic way, since that would have altered the character of the book. But points have been taken up here and there where they seemed to have practical relevance. For guidance in this respect I have found Leon Kellner's old book, *Historical Outlines of English Syntax*, 1892, as handy as any.

The writer on German syntax has the good fortune of being able to draw upon the copious materials assembled in Grimm's monumental *Deutsches Wörterbuch* and in such standard works of reference as Wunderlich-Reis, Paul, and especially Behaghel, and for the critical Early NHG period, Johannes Erben, *Grundzüge einer Syntax der Sprache Luthers*, 1954. In attempting a concise statement of essentials, one can scarcely fail to be under an obligation to Ingerid Dal, *Kurze deutsche Syntax*², 1966. I take this opportunity, too, of drawing attention to Fritz Tschirch, *1200 Jahre deutsche Sprache*, 1955, a work which illustrates the evolution of German style by means of biblical extracts from all periods of the language.

Professor C. T. Carr, who invited me to contribute the present volume, has my best thanks for important suggestions made during the preparation of the work and for assistance in proof reading. I am happy to acknowledge a long-standing debt of gratitude to my wife for unfailing advice on the most diverse problems of German usage. To my daughter I am indebted for a number of trenchant examples, especially from current speech.

W. B. LOCKWOOD

I · NOUNS

NOMINATIVE

THE nominative is the case of the subject. It is also the case of the predicative noun referring to the subject: *er ist ein Narr* (*geworden, geblieben*), *er scheint ein Meister seines Faches.* This construction was more widespread in the older language and was used with other verbs where today (if the idiom survives) *als* or *wie* is found: OHG (Ludwigslied) *kind warth er faterlôs* 'als Kind wurde er vaterlos', MHG (Walther) *dâ wart ich enpfangen / hêre frouwe, / daȥ ich bin sælic iemer mê* 'dort wurde ich wie eine vornehme Dame empfangen, daß ich für immer glücklich bin', NHG (Luther) *es ist dir besser, daß du zum Leben lahm oder ein Krüppel eingehest,* (Schiller) *ein Rebell kämpft mein Fiesko.* There are survivals today in a few fixed expressions, e.g. *Pate stehen.*

Other modes of expression have from the beginning existed side by side with some of the above, e.g. OHG (Hildebrandslied) *eddo ih imo ti banin werdan* 'or I (shall) become his murderer / oder ich (soll) ihm zum Mörder werden' or 'sein Mörder werden'. Similarly beside *seine Eltern wurden Bettler* one can say *seine Eltern wurden zu Bettlern.* Semantically there is no difference between the two, but the construction with the preposition may be more forceful and dramatic. We imagine the same will have been the case in times gone by.

VOCATIVE

In Primitive Germanic the vocative was, in certain declensions, a morphologically distinct case, but in German it fell together with the nominative before the beginning of written records. On the other hand, the vocative of adjectives was at one time formally indicated by the use of the weak termination (p. 41).

ACCUSATIVE

Accusative as the case of the direct object

The accusative is, *par excellence*, the case of the direct object; it is governed by a transitive verb. A number of verbs which today are only used absolutely or with a cognate accusative (see below) were formerly transitive; in these cases the transitive function has sometimes been taken over by prefixed forms, at other times a preposition is employed: OHG (Otfrid) *thie inan betôn wollent* 'those who wish to pray to him / die ihn anbeten wollen', MHG (Hartmann) *in klageten elliu diu lant / dâ er inne was erkant* 'all those countries, in which he was known, lamented for him / ihn beklagten all die Länder, in denen er bekannt war', NHG (Klopstock) *sing, unsterbliche Seele, der sündigen Menschen Erlösung*, which is reminiscent of our 'Arms and the man I sing'; contemporary German style would require *besinge*, as in *Waffen besing' ich und den Helden.*

Cognate accusative

In German, as in other languages, a number of intransitive verbs may take an object in the accusative when the object repeats more specifically the notion of the verb: *ein Lied singen*; one speaks here of a cognate accusative. Examples from German and English do not necessarily correspond idiomatically: *das Vaterunser beten* 'say the Lord's Prayer', *sein Leid klagen* 'complain, tell one's trouble'; these verbs were formerly transitive, see above. As an extension of the principle of the cognate accusative there are many examples where the object no longer stands in particularly close national relationship to the verb: *Gesundheit trinken, Gefahr laufen, Rede stehen.*

Double accusative

A few verbs may govern two accusatives: *ich werde dich Mores lehren* 'I'll teach you manners (that I will)'; similarly: *das kostet mich* (or *mir*) *viel Zeit*. Generally speaking, however, the language strives to avoid a repetition of the same case, cf. *er verband mich, er verband die Wunde*, but *er verband mir die Wunde.*

Syntactically distinct from the above are those examples where the second accusative functions as the predicate of the first: *sie nennen mich einen Narren.* This construction was more widespread in the older stages of the language: MHG (Wolfram) *wer sol mich ritter machen?* 'who shall make me a knight?'—the construction is still possible in English, but in German one must now say *zum Ritter machen* or, more idiomatically, *zum Ritter schlagen.* More recent examples: NHG (Luther) *ich habe dich einen Gott gesetzt über Pharao* = (Menge) 'ich mache dich für den Pharao zu einem Gott', (Holtei) *er fühlte sich den Liebling der Bevölkerung* 'he felt himself the favourite', today: *als Liebling.*

Elliptic accusative

Examples are common in conventional greetings, wishes, and the like: *guten Tag, gute Nacht, schönen Sonntag, angenehmes Wochenende, schönen Gruß zu Haus(e)* 'kind regards to those at (your) home', *herzlichen Gruß aus den Ferien* (greetings sent by a person on holiday), *guten Rutsch ins Neue Jahr, besten Dank*; similarly: *keinen Augenblick länger! keinen einzigen Schritt weiter!* They are mostly objects of verbs unexpressed, e.g. *ich wünsche (Ihnen) einen guten Tag.*

Adverbial accusative

Under this general heading we consider the traditional use of the accusative to form adverbial expressions of place, time, and quantity.

(*a*) *Accusative of place*

This accusative is commonest after verbs of motion; it was more used in the older language than it is today, as the modern renderings of the following examples show: OHG (Otfrid) *thô fuar er mit imo hôhe berga* 'dann fuhr er mit ihm über hohe Berge', MHG (Hartmann) *mit baren füezen streich er walt und bruoch* 'mit bloßen Füßen strich er durch Wald und Sumpf'. In reference to a distance covered, however, the accusative construction is still usual: *er geht seinen Weg, zieht seine Bahn, seine Straße,* as also in the older language: OHG (Otfrid) *floug er sunnûn pad, sterrôno strâȥa, wega wolkôno* 'he flew the path of the sun, the streets of the stars, the courses of the clouds'; older usage may, however, be no longer idiomatically possible: MHG (Helmbrecht) *swelcheȥ ende du kêrest* 'in welche Richtung immer du dich auch wendest'.

The accusative of place is commonly found in connexion with an adverb of direction: *sie stiegen den Berg hinan, das Schiff segelte die Küste entlang*; formerly also with *vorbei* and *vorüber*: (Gryphius) *meine Tür vorbeizuspazieren*, (Schiller) *die Lebenssatten gehst du vorüber*, where modern practice demands *an meiner Tür vorbei, an den Lebenssatten . . . vorüber*. It is also possible to say *das Schiff segelte an der Küste entlang*, but this implies rather 'hugged the coast'. Examples of this accusative occur in poetic diction: (Goethe) *da kam eine junge Schäferin / . . . die Wiese her*; *im flachen Bette / schleicht er* (the river) *das Wiesental hin*, but prosaically, e.g. *über die Wiese* (*her*), *durch das Wiesental* (*hin*).

(*b*) *Accusative of time*

The accusative regularly expresses duration of time: OHG (Otfrid) *wârun se allo worolti zi thir zeigônti* 'they have been pointing to thee throughout all ages', MHG (von Regensburg) *solte si ez drîe tage ane sehen* 'if she were to look at it for three days', NHG (Goethe) *wer nie die kummervollen Nächte an seinem Bette weinend saß*. The construction is, of course, still commonplace: *ich habe vorige Woche viel gearbeitet, die Eule schläft den ganzen Tag*. The idea of duration is often reinforced by the addition of an adverb: *den ganzen Tag über* or *hindurch*, much as English 'the whole day through'.

Less usually, the accusative expresses time at which: *er kommt den zweiten März*, but prepositional phrases are used as well: *er kommt am zweiten März*, and are generally speaking much commoner: *am Tag*(*e*), *in der Nacht, zu allen Zeiten und Unzeiten*.

(*c*) *Accusative of quantity*

Examples: *das Thermometer ist einen Grad gestiegen, sein Bruder ist einen Kopf höher*, though a construction with *um* is at least as common: *um einen Grad gestiegen, um einen Kopf höher*.

As far as usage with a comparative is concerned, the present accusative construction is a modern development replacing the genitive (p. 14).

Accusative with impersonal verbs

The accusative with impersonal verbs is a common feature of the older language: OHG *mih durstit* 'I thirst', *mih hungirit* 'I hunger', *mih langêt* 'I long for', *mih (gi)lustit* 'I desire'. In early NHG the dative sometimes replaces the accusative: *mir dürstet, mir hungert,* but the original construction finally prevailed, hence the modern *mich dürstet, hungert.* On the other hand, these impersonal verbs are now generally literary forms, ordinarily spoken German having *ich habe Durst, Hunger* or *ich bin durstig, hungrig.*

Accusative with adjectives

Examples: *einen Fuß breit, eine Elle lang, einen Daumen dick.* This now characteristic use of the accusative is not found before the NHG period, the earlier language employing the genitive: MHG *drîer jâre alt* 'drei Jahre alt', a construction which occurs sporadically in the modern period, too: (Luther) *eines Fußes breit,* (Hebel) *einer Elle lang,* (Grimm) *nur Daumens groß*; cf. *Daumesdick* 'Tom Thumb'. The use of the accusative here will have developed through association with the widely used adverbial accusative (p. 3).

The accusative is likewise found after such frequently used adjectives as *los, gewohnt, müde, satt, wert*: *den Schnupfen wird sie gar nicht los, er ist andere Umgangsformen gewohnt,* (Friedrich I) *ich bin es müde, über Sklaven zu herrschen, mein Vater hat den Kerl satt, du bist dein Geld wert.* With such adjectives, however, the genitive construction is still permissible, at least in literary style, while in a few phrases the genitive survives as the ordinarily used case: *er ist seiner Sache gewiß, es ist nicht der Rede wert,* cf. also *lebensmüde, -satt.* The present use of the accusative case is attributable to confusion between the genitive and accusative forms of the pronoun 'it' in later MHG, when the original genitive *es* fell together with the original accusative *ez* resulting in *es.* In practice, *es* was henceforth felt only as an accusative; thus in such a sentence as *ich bin es los,* where the pronoun was syntactically in the genitive, it now appeared to be in the accusative, hence analogically *ich bin den Schnupfen los,* etc. The transitional stage is strikingly illustrated in Luther (Matt. x. 10–11): *denn ein Arbeiter ist s e i n e r Speise wert . . . erkundiget euch, ob jemand darinnen sei, der e s wert ist.*

Accusative absolute

The now commonly used accusative absolute is a modern construction not older than the eighteenth century; it is associated with a prepositional phrase or a past participle: (Lessing) *so straff den Zügel in der Hand, kann man wohl eine Chronik zusammenklauben*, (Schiller) *Louise kommt zurück, einen Mantel umgeworfen*, cf. also such fixed expressions as *gesetzt den Fall.* We have here essentially an imitation of the French absolute construction. It was adopted in German as an accusative construction through association with native adverbial accusatives with which the absolute construction has some affinity. It remains to be noted that this originally literary feature of German style has now become part and parcel of colloquial speech as well, for example a sentence like *er kam herein, den Hut in der Hand* may be heard almost as often as the older construction *er kam herein mit dem Hut in der Hand.*

GENITIVE

Genitive with nouns

(*a*) *Genitive as the case of possession*

The genitive is the case which most typically denotes possession or a state of belonging to; it is first and foremost dependent on a noun: *das Geld des Mannes, der Ring der Frau*; *die Tür des Hauses, der Kragen des Mantels.* In this, its main function, the genitive faces competition from the dative (p. 21).

When dependent on a noun, the genitive has a number of other functions, some loosely associated with its main function, others syntactically more distinct. We do not propose to comment specially on such of these as are of theoretical rather than practical interest since parallel developments are present in English and many other languages, e.g. *die Völker der Erde, die Pflege der Zähne, der Held des Tages, ein Strahl der Hoffnung, der König der Könige.* As usual, idiomatic usage in any given two languages may not be identical: *ein Mann der Tat* 'a man of action', *ein Ding der Unmöglichkeit* 'an impossible thing'. In some instances the genitive has latterly passed out of use: (J. Paul) *aus Furcht der Strafe*, now *von der Strafe*, (Lessing) *Liebe des Vaterlandes*, now *zum Vaterland*, examples of a tendency in recent German to replace the synthetic genitive by an analytical construction.

(*b*) *Partitive genitive*

The partitive genitive is as commonplace in German as in English. In the modern language it may be governed by a noun or a pronoun or by an adjective in the comparative or superlative: *die Hälfte meines Königreiches, keine seiner Kaninchen, die schönere der beiden Frauen, die schönste aller Frauen.* In recent German this genitive is essentially the literary construction, the living language substituting a prepositional phrase (p. 19).

In the older language this genitive was also used after numerals, especially when qualified: MHG (Nibelungenlied) *starker rigele zwêne* 'two strong bolts'. When unqualified the noun is regularly in the genitive after numerals above twenty, but not usually otherwise: OHG (Hildebrandslied) *sumaro enti wintro sehstic* 'sixty summers and winters'. This usage seems to have developed from those numerals which contained a substantive: OHG *-zug*, *-zig* 'decade', or which came to be treated as such: OHG *hunt*, *dûsunt* 'hundred, thousand', and then spread sporadically to the lower numbers. But in the long run, the attributive construction became general. As a literary form, the genitive is still possible in the partitive sense proper: *fünf der Schüler*, also in the spoken language in the idiom *unsereiner.* Otherwise the genitive was largely lost by the beginning of the modern period, though occasional survivals are noticed: (Goethe) *langer Jahre zehn*, (Schiller) *dreißigtausend ehrlicher Soldaten.*

The genitive was formerly used after nouns denoting a measure or a quantity: MHG *ein pfunt vleisches, ein trunc wazzeres*, but now apposition is the invariable rule when the noun is unqualified: *ein Pfund Fleisch, ein Trunk Wasser.* The new construction belongs to the modern period when, in a large number of instances, the genitive no longer has a distinct case ending, e.g. in the plural and, with feminines, in the singular too. But where the noun was qualified, feeling for the correct case was naturally preserved and such genitives still occur today: *ein Glas roten Weins*, though apposition is also found, and is regular in the spoken language: *geben Sie mir ein Glas roten Wein.*

Substantivized adjectives of quantity were, in the early period, regularly construed with the genitive: OHG (Ezzos Gesang) *luzel liehtes* 'little light', MHG (Heinrich VI) *der gedanke vil* 'many thoughts'. Luther has still *viel Volks*, but in the present-day language the noun has no case inflexion: *genug Geld, genug Menschen.* Nowadays *viel* is generally treated as an ordinary adjective: *viel Geld, viele Menschen*; the expression *ein wenig* is invariable, but *wenig* now usually follows the adjectival declension:

mit wenigem Geld, wenige Leute. On the other hand, both *viel* and *wenig* are sometimes treated as indeclinable, and commonly so in the spoken language of some areas. In a few idioms, the genitive construction is preserved, notably: *viel Aufhebens* or *Federlesens* or *Wesens machen* and *ich bin Manns genug*; in literary style: *genug der Tränen.* Typically, the older construction has maintained itself better in poetry than in prose: (Heine) *es fallen vom Apfelbaume / der Blüten und Blätter viel.*

Genitive with adjectives

A genitive dependent on an adjective was an extremely common feature of the language until modern times when it lost much ground as part of the general decline in the use of the genitive case. It is scarcely productive now, but several examples survive in common use, though chiefly in formal style. A large number of compound adjectives having the genitive of the noun as the first element derive from this construction; many are part and parcel of the ordinary spoken language.

Examples: OHG (Hildebrandslied) *her was hêrôro man, ferahes frôtôro* 'he was the older man, the more experienced in life', (Otfrid) *wanana ist iȥ, frô mîn, thaȥ ih es wirdig bin?* 'whence is it, my lord, that I am worthy of it?', MHG (Hartmann) *doch was er unnâch alsô rîch / der geburt und des guotes / sô der êren und des muotes* 'but he was not nearly so rich in respect of birth and possessions as in respect of honour and disposition', (Wolfram) *sich zôch diu frouwe jâmers balt . . . in einen walt* 'full of grief the lady withdrew . . . to a wood', (Kürenberg) *des wære ich gemeit* 'I'd be happy about that', NHG (Luther) *ich aber, der ich dieser Dinge arm bin,* (Herder) *empfänglich des Eindrucks,* (Schiller) *des schönsten Anblicks wird mein Auge froh.* In contemporary language such genitives are mostly replaced by prepositional constructions: *reich, arm an, empfänglich für, froh über.* This analytical tendency begins early: MHG (Nibelungenlied) *er sach in bluotes rôten* 'he saw him red with blood' beside *swie rôt eȥ was von bluote* 'how red it [Siegfried's head] was with blood'. This new construction has not, however, become exclusive; *würdig* still regularly takes the genitive: *dessen würdig,* as do several others, e.g. *bar, bewußt, eingedenk, kundig, mächtig, teilhaftig, verlustig.*

In a few cases the old genitive has been (largely) replaced by the accusative (p. 5). In the case of *voll* various constructions are now found. The genitive is the oldest: (Otfrid) *fol bistu gotes ensti* 'thou art full of God's grace', and this is still possible in elevated style: *ein Krug voll duftenden Honigs*. But in more ordinary style juxtaposition of the two nouns is common: *ein Krug voll Honig*. Some colloquial styles prefer prepositions: *ein Krug voll von* or *mit Honig*. In certain connexions a now petrified case form *voller* may be used: *ein Aufsatz voller Fehler* (p. 40).

Genitive with verbs

(*a*) *Genitive as the case of the direct object*

Medieval German developed further the use of the genitive as the case of the direct object which it had inherited from Primitive Germanic. But with the general regression in the use of the genitive in the modern period this syntactical feature has disappeared as a productive construction though it is still present, chiefly in the literary language, in a number of survivals.

(*b*) *Genitive object has partitive character*

The object regularly occurred in the genitive where it had a partitive character, i.e. where only part of the object is affected by the verbal action: OHG (Otfrid) *thaȝ iagilîh thes âȝi* 'that each one might eat of it', *hiaȝ er sie bringan thero fisgo* 'he bade them bring (some, some of) the fish', MHG (Hartmann) *ich wil im mînes brôtes geben* 'I will give him of my bread', (Wolfram) *Îwanet . . . brach der liehten bluomen* 'Îwanet . . . plucked (some of) the bright flowers'. The construction is still common with Luther: *der Priester . . . soll des Bluts auf die Hörner des Altars tun*. Examples occur in the classical writers: (Goethe) *Freunde, deren man auf frequentierten Universitäten immer als Gäste zu finden pflegt*, (Schiller) *es schenkte der Böhme des perlenden Weins*, and occasionally later: (Grillparzer) *tragt nur zu des kostbaren Guts*. But today this construction, which has an exact counterpart in French (*il mange du pain* as distinct from *il mange le pain*) and to some extent in English, has quite passed out of living use. Circumlocutions are now necessary; Menge renders Luther (above): *der Priester . . . streiche etwas von dem Blut an die Hörner des Altars*.

Original partitive use may well explain the genitive found after such verbs as *brauchen, genießen, bedürfen*: OHG (Ludwigslied) *sô brûche her es lango* 'may he long enjoy it', MHG (Helmbrecht) *sô ist aber einer, / des al diu welt geniuzet* 'but then there is one from whom everyone derives advantage'. Such usage continued into modern times: (Goethe) *um Gut's zu tun, braucht's keiner Überlegung*, (Wieland) *ich genieße meines Reichtums*, though in present-day German these verbs now govern the accusative; *bedürfen*, on the other hand, still regularly takes the genitive, *was keines weiteren Beweises bedarf*.

(*c*) *Genitive object after negative verb*

The genitive was frequently the case of the object after a negative verb. Properly speaking, two entirely different constructions are included under this heading.

The first and older construction concerns the use of the genitive after the negative simplex *ni*: OHG (Samaritan Woman) *noh tû ni habis kiscirres* 'furthermore thou hast not a vessel (with which to draw water)'. Similar practice is quite common in Gothic, from which we conclude that OHG here conserves a rare relic of ancient Germanic usage. It is noteworthy that a parallel construction is traditional in the Baltic and Slavonic languages. It rather looks as though the three linguistic families in contact have participated in a common typological innovation.

The second construction concerns the use of the genitive after the extended negative OHG (*ni*) . . . *niowiht* > MHG (*ne, en*) . . . *niht*. In this case the genitive is really dependent on the negative extension which literally meant 'nothing' (p. 207); it is thus, in fact, a partitive genitive pure and simple. Examples: MHG (Hartmann) *du enmaht es niht bringen* 'you cannot carry it out', *du enhâst des tôdes niht gesehen* 'you have not seen death' or perhaps 'you have seen nothing of death', though one cannot establish now if *niht* in this context retained anything of its primary sense of 'nothing'. After the medieval period this common construction rapidly declined. Nevertheless, it is occasionally found later, and indeed survived until well on into the modern period: (Luther) *wenn ich mit Menschen- und Engelzungen redete, und hätte der Liebe nicht*, (Klopstock) *allein sie wollten nicht kommen, wollten des Liebenden nicht*. This construction after the extended negative may be closely compared with the French genitive in analogous cases: *je n'ai pas d'argent*, another reminder of Franco-German parallelism in the development of the negative.

(*d*) *Verbs traditionally governing the genitive*

In the older language the genitive is regularly used after verbs of asking, expecting, waiting, wishing: OHG (Notker) *die . . . wândon des suonetagen* 'who . . . expected the day of judgement', (Otfrid) *sie eiscôtun thes kindes, sârio thes sinthes* 'they asked about the child, next about the way', MHG (Nibelungenlied) *dô erbiten sie der nahte* 'then they waited for the night', (Helmbrecht) *er frâgte in der mære* 'he asked him for the information', NHG (Luther) *ich sitze unter dem Schatten, des ich begehre*, (Goethe) *der heitere Garten, / wo ich und Marthe deiner warten*. Today the accusative or a prepositional construction has normally replaced the genitive with verbs of this type: *sie erwarteten das jüngste Gericht*; *sie fragten nach dem Kind, dann nach dem Weg*; all the same this genitive can still occasionally be used in high style: *viel Neuland wartet noch des Pfluges*. Only *harren*, itself archaic, is still preferably construed with the genitive, but only in conscious imitation of older style, though it has some currency even in the spoken language: *na, wir harren der Dinge, die da kommen sollen*.

A second group of verbs formerly taking the genitive includes verbs of thinking, perceiving, caring for: OHG (Otfrid) *ni will ih . . . sînes bluates scolo sîn, / noh ouh therero dâto plegan borathrâto* 'I will not . . . be guilty of his blood, nor be too much involved in these matters', MHG (Walther) *hüetet iuwer ougen* 'attend to what your eyes are doing', (Helmbrecht) *ein herre næme der spîse war* 'a gentleman would take notice of that food', NHG (Luther) *keiner schonet des anderen; ich denke der alten Zeit, der vorigen Jahre*, (Goethe) *wir achten nicht des Weges, den wir treten*. Of such verbs *gedenken* alone governs the genitive today. It is, of course, not an ordinary colloquial word: *in seiner Trauerrede gedachte der Minister der großen Leistungen des Verstorbenen*. Otherwise the construction is found only in one or two fixed phrases, notably *seines Amtes walten*.

A third group of verbs governing the genitive consists of those denoting lack or oversight: OHG (Otfrid) *thie heiminges tharbênt* 'those who are deprived of their homeland', MHG (Helmbrecht) *dîner predige / got mich schiere erledige* 'God save me quickly from your sermon', NHG (Luther) *sie sind allzumal Sünder und mangeln des Ruhmes, den sie an Gott haben sollten*, (Lessing) *eine Tragödie, die ihres Zweckes verfehlt*. Today the accusative is, as a rule, the case of the object of such verbs, but two of them, *entbehren* (where *ent-* has—quite exceptionally—developed from a negative prefix) and *ermangeln*, may still take the genitive in elevated style. Notice the fossilized genitive in the flower name *Vergißmeinnicht* 'vergiß mich nicht'. A related genitive of separation was formerly common: (Schiller) *er löste die Generalstaaten ihres Eides*, though competing with prepositional constructions which are as old as the records: (St. Gall Paternoster) *lôsi unsih fona ubile* 'erlöse uns von dem Übel', (Muspilli) *lôssan sih ar dero lêwo vazzôn* 'lösen sich aus der Gräber Last'; Schiller's *des Eides* would today be *von ihrem Eid(e)*. Two verbs of separation, *berauben* and *überheben*, still govern the genitive: *sie wurde ihrer ganzen Barschaft beraubt*, *der Mühe ist er endlich überhoben*. Here, too, belong verbs with the privative prefix *ent-*: *er wurde seines Amtes enthoben*, though some of these may take *von* as well: *er wurde seiner* or *von seinen Pflichten entbunden*; in these cases the construction with *von* represents the more spontaneous, living usage.

Finally, the genitive is often found, in the older language, after verbs which are principally used absolutely, i.e. which do not necessarily require an object: MHG (Helmbrecht) *ich freu mich sîner künfte* 'I look forward to meeting him', *des erschrac der wirt vil sêre* 'the master of the house was very much taken aback by that', NHG (Luther) *der im Himmel wohnet, lachet ihrer, und der Herr spottet ihrer*, (Schiller) *wir wollen nicht frohlocken seines Falles*. Generally speaking the present-day language prefers a preposition: *sich freuen, erschrecken, lachen über*. In a few cases the genitive may still be found in high style: *man lebt des Glaubens, der Hoffnung*, beside the usual *in dem Glauben, in der Hoffnung*. After *sterben* the genitive regularly occurs in the cliché: *sie sind Hungers gestorben*. This use of the genitive after verbs chiefly used absolutely may be regarded as a transition to predicative use proper. There is not, for instance, any appreciable syntactical difference between *du sollst des Todes sterben* (as above) and the purely predicative use of the genitive in *du bist des Todes* (p. 13).

Genitive with accusative

A number of verbs govern the accusative of the person and the genitive of the thing. This is a traditional construction and is still used with certain verbs: *er würdigte sie keines Blickes*, *er belehrte mich eines Besseren*, and notably after verbs of accusing and the like: *sie klagten ihn des Betrugs an, man hat ihn des Verbrechens überführt.* Older examples: OHG (Otfrid) *thes zîhu ih inan* 'dessen zeihe ich ihn', MHG (Rolandslied) *mînes leides wil ich dich manen* 'I will remind you of my sorrow'. The same construction is very common in connexion with reflexive verbs: (Ludwigslied) *er gibuoȥta sih thes* 'he atoned for that', MHG (Heinrich VI) *ich verzige mich ê der krône* 'I would rather renounce the crown', Early NHG (Ackermann aus Böhmen) *ir jeder rumpte sich seines guten willen* 'jeder von ihnen rühmte sich seines guten Willens'; it is still a living construction with several other verbs: *er bemächtigte sich des Reiches, man enthalte sich des Alkohols.* In some instances prepositional constructions have now established themselves. When, in such cases, the genitive still survives, it belongs to more elevated style, e.g. literary *er konnte sich des Vorfalls nicht mehr erinnern*, less formal *an den Vorfall.* Exceptionally, the genitive has ousted a competing prepositional phrase in the case of the often-used idiom *sich annehmen*, e.g. *ich nahm mich seiner an*, where the former analytical construction was *um ihn*, cf. Hans Sachs: *und nam mich umb die Christin an.*

Genitive with Dative

In older German, some verbs took the dative of the person and the genitive of the thing, and this construction survived into the modern period: MHG (Walther) *daȥ alle krâ gedîen / alse ich in des günne* 'may all crows prosper as I wish them to', NHG (Luther) *des helfe ihm und allen Christus*, (Klopstock) *die ihm des Segens danken.* In contemporary language an accusative or a prepositional phrase is usual: *wie ich es ihnen gönne*; *dabei helfe ihm und allen Christus, die ihm für den Segen danken.*

Predicative genitive

Since the genitive may have the syntactical value of an adjective, it can be found in the predicative position in several languages. This was also the case in older German. The predicative genitive may either denote quality: OHG (Hildebrandslied) *huelîhhes cnuosles du sîs* 'of what tribe you be', MHG (Walther) *diu werlt ist innan . . . swarzer varwe* 'the world, on the inside, is . . . of a black colour', NHG (Luther) *selig sind, die reines Herzens sind,* or else it may denote possession: OHG (Otfrid) *allez sînes fater was* 'all was his father's', MHG (Nibelungenlied) *ez ist sô hôher mâge der marcgrâvinne lîp* 'the margravine has such noble relatives', NHG (Luther) *so gebet dem Kaiser, was des Kaisers ist.* The classical writers could still freely use this construction: (Goethe) *die Rache ist nicht des irdischen Richters,* (Schiller) *der Mann ist nicht freien Standes,* but it is no longer productive today except, in literary style, after verbs of motion or rest, where it is still regular: *sie huschte leisen Schrittes vorbei, schweren Herzens saß er da,* cf. also *stehenden Fußes* 'stante pede'. The old construction is recognizable in quite a number of fossilized survivals, such as *guter Dinge, guter Laune* (colloquial also *in einer guten Laune*), *der Auffassung, einer Meinung, des Teufels sein.*

It will be noticed that the predicative genitive is still normal in English wherever the Anglo-Saxon genitive is possible, cf. *of what tribe,* but *his father's* (above).

Genitive of cause

This construction did not survive into the modern period, but it is significant in earlier German: OHG (Otfrid) *kûmîg bin ih jâro filu manegero* 'I am infirm because of my very many years', MHG (Neidhart) *ir gewaltes bin ich vor in mînem schopfe grâ* 'I am prematurely grey because of their roughness', cf. also *wes* 'wherefore' and *des* 'therefore', which are so common in MHG.

Although the genitive of cause has not survived as such, it is nevertheless present in the traditional use of the genitive after certain interjections: MHG (Walther) *owê der wîse, die wir mit den grillen sungen* 'alas for the tune we sang with the crickets', NHG (Heine) *o des Jammeranblicks.* Contemporary literary style demands the genitive, even though in the earlier language it seems to have been optional: MHG (Helmbrecht) *owê verlorniu sibeniu* which becomes in the modern translation *o weh der verlorenen Sieben.* Cf. 'Dative after interjections', p. 31.

Genitive of comparison

This construction is regular in the older period: MHG (Helmbrecht) *truoc nie dehein meier / einen roc, der zweier eier / wære bezzer dan der sîn* 'no farmer wore a coat that was two eggs (i.e. 'one jot') better than his'. This genitive is occasionally found in

NHG: (Bürger) *eines Hauptes höher*, but in the modern language it has otherwise been replaced by the accusative; see 'Accusative of quantity', p. 4.

Genitive as the case of the subject

Very occasionally a partitive genitive functions as the subject: (Klopstock) *seines Gesanges erschallet noch.* In the common MHG phrase *des enmac niht sîn* which one translates 'that may not be / das kann nicht sein', it is most likely that *des* was (correctly) regarded as dependent on *niht*.

Genitive as ablative

It may be noticed that in several examples quoted in the preceding paragraphs the German genitive corresponds to the Latin ablative, e.g. (Cicero) *donum regale dignum tuo templo* 'a royal gift worthy of thy temple / ein königliches Geschenk würdig deines Tempels', (Nepos) *neminem veste spoliavit* 'he robbed nobody of his clothing / er beraubte niemanden seiner Kleidung'. Comparative philology reveals that at an early stage in the evolution of the Indo-European languages, the genitive and ablative were, to a large extent, not distinguished morphologically. With the subsequent reduction in the number of cases in the various branches of the family, it is not surprising that the genitive often took over functions proper to the ablative. In Germanic the lost ablative was absorbed partly by the genitive, hence the frequent correspondence between the German genitive and the Latin ablative, and partly by the dative; see 'Dative as ablative', p. 31.

Adverbial genitive

German inherited from Primitive Germanic the extensive use of the genitive to form adverbial expressions of various kinds. We mention the more significant.

(*a*) *Genitive of place*

Examples: OHG (Charm) *daz in wolf noh wulpa za scedin werdan ne megi, se wara se geloufan waldes odo weges odo heido* 'that neither he-wolf nor she-wolf may harm them, wherever they run in the wood or along the path or over the heath'. This usage is, however, rather limited, competing from the earliest times either with the adverbial accusative: (Otfrid) *gang thesan weg* 'go this way', or else with prepositional constructions: (Charm) *man gieng after wege* 'a man went along a road'. All the same, relics of the genitive of place are still found in the modern language, though mainly in literary style: *woher des Weges, er geht seines Weges.* A number of petrified local genitives are now pure adverbs: *gerade(s)wegs, rechts, rechter Hand, allerorten*; in the case of *keineswegs* one no longer thinks spontaneously of the literal meaning at all. The *s*-suffix has become productive to form new adverbs: *allerseits, unterwegs.*

(*b*) *Genitive of time*

This genitive was very prominent in the earlier stages of the language: OHG (Notker) *des pîtendo, wârin mir mîne trâne brôt tages unde nahtes . . .* (*trâne*) *aȥ ih tagolîches* 'awaiting him, my tears were bread to me day and night . . . (tears) I ate daily', MHG (Walther) *eines tages als unser herre wart geborn* 'on a day when our Lord was born', i.e. on Christmas Day; it is common with Luther: *das Fleisch soll . . . desselben Tages gegessen werden.* This genitive competed with the accusative of time and with prepositional constructions: (Walther) *deich den sumer luft und in dem winter hitze hân* 'so that I have fresh air in the summer and warmth in the winter'. But in spite of such competition, several genitives have maintained themselves, some chiefly as literary forms, such as *des Sommers, des Winters, dieser Tage*, others in ordinary colloquial use as well: *mittlerweile, eines Weihnachts.* The distinctive *s*-suffix of the masculine and neuter early became productive; this happened in the pre-literary period in the case of the word *nahtes* (above) > NHG *nachts*, also (Otfrid) *thes nahtes* > NHG *des Nachts*; in MHG the morphologically correct forms *der naht*, later *der nehte* are also recorded in adverbial use. Other analogical *s*-forms include OHG *tagolîches* (above), NHG *damals*, etc., *mittwochs, öfters.*

(*c*) *Modal genitive*

A genitive describing the manner in which an action is carried out is termed a modal genitive. Examples: OHG *managero dingo* 'in manifold ways', MHG *aller dinge* 'certainly', NHG *allerdinge* (now obsolete), later *allerdings* (with analogical *s*), *unverrichteter Dinge, einigermaßen, unbekannterweise.* Less usually the genitive is unqualified: OHG *dankes* 'with thanks', MHG *fluges* 'in flight', whence NHG *flugs*.

It may be remarked that English also inherited the adverbial use of the genitive: OE *ōðres weges* 'by another way', *dæges and nihtes* 'day and night', ME *winteres and sumeres* 'winter and summer'. As OE *nihtes* shows, the *s*-ending was productive in English, too. Other examples: *once* < OE *ānes* = OHG, MHG *eines* > NHG *einst*; *always* beside older *alway*, originally an accusative; *needs* but older genitive *nede* fem. The genitive of time was particularly common in older English and, in a sense, still lives on today since expressions like *of a morning* have arisen through the replacement of the old synthetic case by the new analytical genitive.

Position of the genitive

According to medieval practice the genitive most commonly, though not exclusively, precedes the noun it qualifies: OHG (Monsee Matthew) *fona entum lantes* "from the uttermost parts of the earth" (Vulgate: *a finibus terrae*), but *in haerda hrewe* "in the heart of the earth", *in wales wambu* "in the whale's belly", *widar mannes sune* "against the Son of man", in spite of the Latin word-order: *in corde terrae, in ventre ceti, contra filium hominis*. Clearly this was living idiom. It is equally prominent in the succeeding period: MHG (Landrechtbuch) *daȥ hâst du . . . der edeln würze süeȥen smac, der bluomen liehte varwe, der boume fruht . . . geschaffen* 'those things Thou hast created . . . the sweet taste of the cultivated plants, the bright colour of the flowers, the fruit of the trees'. By the beginning of modern times, however, it had become more usual for the qualifying genitive to follow the noun: (Luther) *er zeigte mir einen lautern Strom des lebendigen Wassers, klar wie ein Kristall; der ging von dem Stuhl Gottes und des Lamms*. But Luther has also very many examples of the older word-order: *in des Walfisches Bauch, dieses Volkes Herz, seiner Füße Schemel, des großen Königs Stadt*, which Menge renders into contemporary German as *im Leibe des Riesenfisches, das Herz dieses Volkes, der Schemel seiner Füße, die Stadt des großen Königs*.

In the living language of today the older usage is confined mainly to personal names or their equivalents: *Fritzens Haus* which competes with *das Haus von Fritz*, etc.; see 'Decline of the genitive' below. Otherwise the genitive precedes the noun it qualifies only in traditional expressions: *des einen Freud', des andern Leid*, or in set phrases of literary origin: *in meines Herzens Unschuld*. In poetry the older word-order maintained itself better than in prose. It has always been commonly used and is today still perfectly possible in this medium: (Lersch) *es hat ein jeder Toter des Bruders Angesicht*, and not necessarily only in solemn contexts, but equally well for instance in simple narrative: (Agnes Miegel) *des schlafenden Wächters Hund am Tor / fuhr leise knurrend an ihr empor*. Since elements of poetic diction are permissible in any form of high style, this archaic word-order may also be met with outside of poetry. Thus Menge sometimes leaves Luther's words unchanged: *ich bin des Herrn Magd, in meines Vaters Haus sind viele Wohnungen*. Similarly: *des Königs neue Kleider, der Welt letztes Felsenriff*.

When in the living language the old word-order ceased to be productive, many traditional groups were re-evaluated and merged to form inseparable compounds: *des Königs Schloß* became *das Königsschloß*, Luther's *des Menschen Sohn* is now *der Menschensohn*. And Luther, for his part, has for example *Otterngezüchte* "generation of vipers" where earlier translations have a dependent genitive: (Monsee Matthew) *nâtrôno chnôsles* (the latter word is erroneously in the genitive, too), (Tatian) *barn nâtrôno*; the Vulgate has *progenies viperarum*.

In passing we note that English has been more conservative than German, at least where it has preserved the Anglo-Saxon genitive which must precede the noun as it commonly did in OE: (Beowulf) *folces cwēn* 'people's queen', (Charm) *fīra mōdor* 'mother of men'.

When a genitive is dependent on an adjective, it normally precedes it; see 'Genitive with adjectives', p. 8.

Decline of the genitive

In the foregoing, we have several times had occasion to mention that many a once familiar genitive construction has today become rare, if not obsolete entirely. Indeed, this decline in the use of the genitive is one of the most remarkable developments in the history of German syntax. It requires some further comment.

The decline of the genitive has been traced to the thirteenth century, but the formal starting-point must be placed back earlier still, in fact to the end of the OHG period. The reduction of vowels in inflexional endings, which began in Late OHG, led to the loss of a number of distinct genitive endings. The changes were not great, nothing like so drastic as those which brought about the destruction of the case system in OE. But both languages had this in common: morphological indifference weakened feeling for the genitive as a syntactical case and encouraged the use of unambiguous prepositions, hence Eng. *of*, Ger. *von*.

With negligible exceptions, the modern German dialects have lost the genitive as a living category, and this appears to have been the position since the fifteenth century. The genitive is likewise absent from non-dialect colloquial speech, except as described below. Here the genitive in its most characteristic functions has been commonly replaced by *von* with the dative; in the case of living things the old genitive may be replaced by the dative used in connexion with a possessive pronoun. Thus, whereas one tends to write (literary style): *das Geld des Mannes*, *der Ring der Frau* (as in 'Genitive as the case of possession', p. 6), one tends to speak (colloquial style): *das Geld vom Mann*, *der Ring von der Frau* or, in some areas, often *dem Mann sein Geld*, *der Frau ihr Ring*. An exception to the general rule is seen in the use of unqualified personal names. Here the genitive has widespread currency in the spoken language and precedes the noun (archaic word-order): *Fritzens Haus*. This is in addition to, or instead of, the other constructions: *das Haus von* (or *vom*) *Fritz*, (*dem*) *Fritz sein Haus*.

It goes without saying that there cannot, in practice, be any absolute line of demarcation between a written and a spoken construction. It is impossible to keep the two styles entirely apart. Very often colloquial forms must be admitted to novels and plays. In such contexts one may, therefore, expect to find the constructions which we have defined above as typical of the spoken language. And vice versa, through reading, there is an ever-increasing tendency to imitate a bookish style even in casual conversation. Hence one hears, especially in the conversation of educated persons, the genitive construction characterized above as literary. In these circumstances feeling for style inevitably plays a part. Many speakers have more than one style and can adjust the pattern of their speech to the occasion, i.e. to what they estimate to be the requirements of the person addressed. An attitude in such matters is, of course, bound to be more or less subjective. Some regard the excessive use of the genitive in conversation as an affectation, others find a constantly occurring *von* rather childish, while very many would outlaw the dative construction as substandard or outright vulgar It may, however, be emphasized that in the sphere of the colloquial, regional differences in German are important, hence feeling for things at this level is not everywhere the same, though the main tendencies, as outlined above, are clear enough.

We have seen how the literary forms *das Geld des Mannes, der Ring der Frau* tend to be modified in the spoken language. Referring back to the examples quoted on p. 6, we can now say that *die Tür des Hauses, der Kragen des Mantels* will, in the spoken language, tend to become *die Tür vom Haus, der Kragen vom Mantel.* On the other hand, such phrases as *die Völker der Erde, die Pflege der Zähne, der Held des Tages*, etc., are hardly likely to be altered in colloquial speech, for by their very nature these expressions belong to a level of style above the simple colloquial. Their proper, scarcely changeable form is accordingly the literary form. When spoken, such phrases are transferred direct from their elevated milieu unchanged into the spoken context; they are, in fact, literary quotations. A large and increasing number of such genitive constructions may be heard in the speech of all classes: *die Preise der Lebensmittel, die Freuden des Lebens, ein Artikel des täglichen Bedarfs, der Präsident der Bundesrepublik.* Indeed, such phrases will be used (with the appropriate phonetic adjustments) even in broad dialect.

It remains to be said that feeling for the essentially literary quality of the genitive construction is such that, in good style, only a creative writer dare disregard it: (Goethe) *es kann die Spur von meinen Erdetagen / nicht in Äonen untergehen. / Im Vorgefühl von solchem hohen Glück / genieß' ich jetzt den höchsten Augenblick.* We remember a German acquaintance saying that, as a schoolboy, he thought Goethe had got his grammar wrong here.

Future of the genitive

The striking decline in the use of the genitive in modern German has led some linguists to predict the impending demise of the case. If that were to happen, German would reach, roughly speaking, the position of modern Dutch where the genitive survives only in fossilized idioms and, to a limited extent, as a stylistic feature of literary language. We do not think, however, that such a demise is likely. It is true that the naturally spoken language, which makes only a limited use of the genitive, today exerts a great influence on the written word. On the other hand, the literary language, the chief guardian of the genitive, now exerts at least an equal influence on the colloquial, especially on the colloquial of the educated who set the fashion in these matters. In the conversation of these people the genitive construction is noticeably to the fore and spontaneous. As the construction may effect some economy of utterance and achieve a certain elegance, it fulfils a need which seems to guarantee its continued existence in the foreseeable future.

Note on the construction dem Mann sein Geld

It will be convenient to note here that this construction, which in local speech often replaces the genitive (see 'Decline of the genitive', p. 18), has been present in the language since early times: OHG (Notker) *mit tiu infûorest tu demo gewaltîgen sîn zorn* 'thereby didst thou provoke the ire of the mighty one'. It is possible that an occurrence in Otfrid: *thaȥ ih druhtine sînan sun souge* 'that I may suckle the Lord's son' reflects an early stage in the evolution of the construction; here the dative may have had the force of 'for the Lord'. The construction occurs sporadically at all times, in the most recent period in imitation of popular speech: (Rotkäppchen) *was war's so dunkel in dem Wolf seinem Leib!* (Brecht) *das mit dem Kippernikus seinem Drehen.* The medieval examples show, however, that there was originally no feeling that this dative construction was stylistically inferior. The German idiom, incidently, recalls the old-fashioned English *Meggie Rose her sampler.*

Pleonastic genitive

Possession may be expressed pleonastically. Instead of the dative in association with the possessive adjective, we may find the genitive. The construction was at one time widespread in the spoken language and not uncommon in literature: (Schiller) *sie . . . sähen des Teufels sein Angesicht / weit lieber als unsre gelben Kolleter,* (Mörike) *des Wassermanns sein Töchterlein / tanzt auf dem Eis im Vollmondschein,* but it has since become unusual.

Dependent genitive uninflected

It may happen in the earlier language that a genitive dependent upon another remains uninflected: MHG (Väterbuch) *unde bin niht wirdec mannes cleit* 'and am not worthy of a man's garment', (Nibelungenlied) *des ist vil manec tac / deich hort der Nibelunge niene gepflac* 'it is many a day since I ever had anything to do with the treasure of the Nibelungs' (*pflegen* with genitive).

DATIVE

Dative as the case of the indirect object

The dative is fundamentally the case of (chiefly personal) participation in the action. It is therefore very commonly the case of the indirect object. It regularly precedes the direct object: *er gab dem Hund einen Knochen.* This was ancient practice in all the Germanic languages. In present-day English, although we have now lost the dative case, the old construction is still recognizable in the word-order when one says *he gave the dog a bone*, whereas *he gave a bone to the dog* is a later development connected with the extended use of prepositions.

The above construction, which naturally holds a dominating position in the language, may modify other constructions. We have already referred to the tendency in German to avoid a repetition of the same case (see 'Double accusative', p. 2); other examples may now be considered. The verb *lehren* by tradition governs a double accusative, but not infrequently a dative of the person occurs: (Kleist) *die mir daher nur zweifeln lehren würde*, (Th. Mann) *indem er die Griffe übte, die man ihm lehrte.* One says today *ich beneide Sie um Ihr Glück*, but Tieck has *ich beneide Ihnen Ihr . . . Glück.* The dative sometimes intrudes into the accusative and infinitive construction: (Luther) *der Herr hieß ihm verkaufen sein Weib*, (Lenau) *sie ließ mir, kindlich, bunten Flitter schauen*, where modern (and traditional) usage prescribes *ihn, mich.*

Dative as the case of the direct object

A considerable number of verbs govern the dative: *es gefällt mir, schadet dir, gelingt ihm, mangelt ihr, genügt ihnen.* Generally speaking, the behaviour of such verbs in this respect has remained constant throughout their history. In a few instances, however, the dative has succumbed to competition from the accusative. Luther still has the traditional dative with *rufen*, e.g. *er rief allen seinen Knechten*, which today would be *alle seinen Knechte*. Goethe has the dative, too, in *Faust*, where the Erdgeist, of all people, says: *wer ruft mir?* This raises a laugh in the schools for in such a context *mir* is inevitably associated today with the vulgar confusion of *mich* and *mir*. The verb *aufbieten* used to govern the dative: (Wieland) *ich habe allen meinen Kräften aufgeboten*, but nowadays *alle meinen Kräfte*. The compound *liebkosen* arose out of MHG *einem ze liebe kôsen* 'to talk to please someone', cf. Wolfram *dem ichȥ ze liebe kôse*, and accordingly took the dative. Later, in the seventeenth century, the accusative came into use instead after the analogy of near synonyms like *lieben* and *trösten*. Interestingly enough, there is an example of both constructions in the same sentence: (Tieck) *zärtlich liebkoste er mich, wie einem lieben Kinde*; this must reflect the uncertainty which would frequently arise during the transition. The reflexive *sich fürchten* was once a dative construction: MHG (Wolfram) *niene fürhte dir* 'fürchte dich nie'; here the modern accusative has been usual since the sixteenth century. In a few other cases the accusative formerly competed with the traditional dative only to lose the struggle in the long run. OHG *helfan* regularly takes the dative, rarely the accusative: (Ludwigslied) *Hludwîg, kuning mîn, / hilph mînan liutin* 'Ludwig, my king, help my people', but in MHG the accusative is commoner: (Walther) *mich hilfet niht, swaȥ ich dar an geklopfe* 'it doesn't help me, however much I knock there'. Then the accusative declines again, though examples are quite common until the eighteenth century: (Goethe) *ein Lärm würde mich nichts helfen*. In the not so distant past *begegnen* and *schmeicheln* often occurred with the accusative: (Heine) *wie wir selber sie oft im Leben begegnet haben*, (Lessing) *er hat mich übrigens sehr geschmeichelt*.

Dative of interest

This term we use to denote a traditional construction in which the dative is not the necessary adjunct of the verb, as follows.

One may say for example *sie kocht das Wasser*, or *die Zeit vergeht schnell*, or *es ist ein Vergnügen*, or *das kann zum Vorteil ausfallen*. Each of these sentences with their varying constructions is complete in itself. But one may add to these a dative of interest and say for example *sie kocht mir das Wasser, die Zeit vergeht dir schnell, es ist ihm ein Vergnügen, das kann einem zum Vorteil ausfallen.* This usage is possible in English, but only to a limited extent. We can use the dative in English in the first construction: *she boils me the water*, but otherwise a preposition is necessary: *the time passes quickly for you.* The preposition is, of course, optional in the first example, i.e. *she boils the water for me.* The preposition is similarly possible as an alternative in every case in German: *sie kocht das Wasser für mich*, etc.

Somewhat similarly: *die Hände zittern mir, die Augen gehen ihr über*; further: *er sah mir in die Augen, schlag es dir aus dem Sinn, es geht ihm durch den Kopf.* Notice also *du schneidest dir ins eigene Fleisch*, i.e. figurative use, but concretely *du schneidest dich in den Finger.*

Literary stylists, especially poets, make a rather free use of this dative of interest, employing it where normal idiom requires a preposition: (Goethe) *der Verstand, dem du schon Verzicht getan*, i.e. *auf den*, (Kleist) *was wollen diese Amazonen uns*, i.e. *von uns*, (Grillparzer) *nie hab' ich dem Tode gezittert*, i.e. *vor dem Tode.*

Ethic dative

Whereas the dative of interest (above) directly involves the person in the action, the ethic dative refers to a person whose involvement is more detached. The construction has a pronounced emotional content and is found essentially in colloquial styles. Close English translation is seldom possible. Paraphrases are needed to convey the nuances implied and even paraphrases are, as often as not, only approximations: (Luther, Sendbrief von Dolmetschen) *wer es nicht haben will, der laß mirs stehen*, (Goethe) *nur greift mir zu und seid nicht blöde*; the sense of *mir* in these two sentences is something like 'as far as I am concerned' or 'as far as I care'. Modern conversational examples: *du bist mir ein feiner Kerl* 'you're a fine sort, I'm telling you', *komm uns nicht mit solchen Ausreden* 'don't come here with excuses like that, we know you'.

Dative with adjectives

The dative is very often dependent on an adjective. This use is traditional with a group of mostly common adjectives, characteristically root words, as many examples in the older language show: OHG (Otfrid) *was in thrâto herti thaȥ wetar in theru ferti* 'the weather on the voyage was exceedingly severe for them', *wanta in thaȥ was filu sêr* 'for that was very sad for them', MHG (Walther) *ich bin dir holt* 'I am devoted to you', *bin ich dir unmære?* 'am I repugnant to you?', (Nibelungenlied) *niemen was ir gram* 'no one was ill-disposed towards her'. Other adjectives are *gut, klar, lieb, leicht, neu, recht, teuer, wert, böse, sauer, schwer*. In practice the pronoun is the part of speech most likely to occur in this construction, but nouns are of course equally possible: *meiner Tochter ist das nicht neu, es war den Lehrlingen schwer*. It will be noticed that this usage is predicative only.

A number of adjectives, nearly all compound or derivative, may be used with a dative either attributively or predicatively, among them *ähnlich, angenehm, bequem, eigen, fern, gehorsam, genehm, gleich, gleichgültig, nahe, verwandt, zugehörig*, e.g. *die Entschuldigung ist mir genehm, eine mir genehme Entschuldigung*. To the foregoing adjectives must be added the many verbal derivatives, including several recent formations, ending in *-lich*, e.g. *behilflich, begreiflich, dienlich, erfreulich, erinnerlich, förderlich, hinderlich, möglich, nützlich, schädlich, unfaßlich, unwiderstehlich, verbindlich, verständlich, zuträglich*. Examples of sentences: *der Vater war dem Söhnchen bei der Abfassung eines Schulaufsatzes sehr behilflich, die der Polizei nützlichen Erhebungen am Tatort wurden fortgesetzt*. A smaller number of derivatives ending in *-bar* also belong here, e.g. *annehmbar, brauchbar, denkbar, erreichbar*.

A further, formally distinct group are those past participles which very often function as adjectives pure and simple, such as *angeboren, beschieden, bewußt, ergeben, geneigt, gewogen, überlegen, verhaßt, zugetan*. Examples of sentences: *das Schaf besitzt einen ihm angeborenen Herdeninstinkt*; *er genoß das wenig Glück, das ihm beschieden war*.

In conclusion, we note that any adjective qualified by *zu* may take a dependent dative. Contrast *diese Aufgabe ist schwierig für mich* with *diese Aufgabe ist mir zu schwierig* (less usually *zu schwierig für mich*). The dative in such cases is always personal. Sentences of this type have therefore of necessity that element of personal participation which finds its characteristic expression in the dative case.

Dative with nouns

Nouns used predicatively may take a dependent dative: *sie ist ihm eine treue Gattin*; *er war ihr ein guter Vater*. In other examples the dative is found in an impersonal construction: *es ist mir ein Bedürfnis*, *das ist Ihnen die Hauptsache.*

Reflexive dative

The reflexive dative has been found from the earliest times: OHG (Otfrid) *ih zwelifi . . . mir irwelita* 'ich zwölf . . . mir erwählte / I chose . . . twelve', archaic or dialectal 'I chose me . . . twelve', *thie jungôron . . . in muas thô holêton* 'die Jünger . . . holten sich gerade Lebensmittel'. In such cases the reflexive dative functions as an ordinary dative; one could of course also say *die Jünger holten ihm Lebensmittel*, etc.

The reflexive dative may occur, however, with verbs which do not otherwise govern this case at all. After such verbs the dative can stand, in the first instance optionally, without causing any tangible semantic change. This is long established practice and is still usual: OHG (Hildebrandslied) *ik mê de ôdre wêt* 'ich weiß mir (*or simply* ich weiß) die anderen', *du bist dir, altêr Hûn, ummet spâhêr* 'du bist dir (*or simply* du bist), alter Hunne, maßlos schlau'. Similarly MHG (Hartmann) *als du dir lîhte hâst gedâht* 'wie du (dir) vielleicht gedacht hast'. On the whole, this optional usage seems to have declined in the modern period, for some of the old examples are no longer idiomatically possible, while others are confined to more colloquial (or dialect) styles. Thus OHG (Otfrid) *er sah imo thaz iâmar* cannot be transposed word for word into the modern language; we must translate either 'er sah den Jammer' or, if we retain the pronoun which today must be reflexive (p. 167) 'er sah sich den Jammer an'. Classical writers may use *fühlen* with a reflexive dative: (Goethe) *er hat sich neue, noch unentwickelte Kräfte gefühlt*, but *sich* would be omitted in present-day style. It will be noticed that the originally optional dative has, occasionally, become compulsory, thus *sich ansehen* (above); also *sich ergehen*, an essentially literary idiom: *der König erging sich im Lustgarten seines Palasts.*

Dative as the case of possession

A dative construction of the type *dem Mann sein Geld* has been found sporadically at all periods and is, at the present time, a regular feature of much spoken German, as explained on p. 21.

Dative after verbs compounded with a preposition (preverb)

In view of its functions in Indo-European (case of the indirect object, etc.), the dative was, originally, never governed by a preposition. This most ancient state of affairs is faithfully reflected in Latin. The Germanic dative, however, in addition to continuing the functions of the Indo-European dative, largely took over the functions of the former ablative, locative, and instrumental also (pp. 31–33), in connexion with which the use of prepositions had developed. Accordingly, the Germanic—and German—dative is seen to be governed by various prepositions.

Compound verbs began to develop at an early period in the history of the Indo-European languages. They consisted of a verbal simplex preceded by a particle which could become an inseparable prefix. Such preverbs, as they may also be called, were in origin adverbial words which in other syntagmas evolved into prepositions, as explained on p. 175. In Germanic many preverbs remained separable, and thus they led as independent an existence as the prepositions or adverbs; in these circumstances mutual contamination was always a possibility. The separable preverb, for instance, often shows the functions of a preposition, so much so that it actually seems to be a misplaced preposition proper; this is why we speak of verbs compounded with a preposition. Fundamentally, such compounds defined the action more precisely than the simplexes. The mode of formation is amply attested in the various Indo-European languages; for example, Latin *absolvere* 'discharge, absolve' from *ab* 'from' and *solvere* 'loose, disentangle, solve'. The feature was at least as widespread in Germanic, and has remained productive in German down to the present day; a close semantic parallel to the Latin example above is *ablösen* from *ab* and *lösen*.

Where, in such cases, the preposition came to govern the dative, this practice continued when the preposition was compounded with a verb if the preposition, rather than the verbal simplex, determined the construction. For instance, in the sentence *ein Kellner löst den anderen ab* 'one waiter relieves the other', it is the verbal simplex which determines the accusative construction. But if one says *du gehst ihm ab* 'he misses you', really 'you go from him', then clearly the preposition decides the construction, hence the dative case. Further examples of the dative: *die Haare fallen mir aus, er wohnt der Sitzung bei, sie steht dir nicht nach, der Gewinn fällt dem Staat zu.* One finds likewise a dative dependent on the preposition when the complement is the direct object in the accusative, e.g. *ich riß ihm den Mantel ab* where the literal sense is evident from the English translation 'I tore the coat off him'; similarly: *das schlägt dem Faß den Boden aus, man mißt dem Sieg große Bedeutung bei, er schmiß es ihm nach, sie warf ihm einen Handkuß zu.* The above are the main prepositions now taking the dative exclusively. It will be remembered that *ab* is no longer a preposition in Standard German where it has been replaced by a relatively new word *von* (p. 179). On the other hand, *ab* has maintained itself unimpaired in verbal compounds for *von* has not been able to penetrate this sphere at all; there are no verbs of a type **vonlösen*, for instance.

Throughout the history of German, the prefix *ent-* has been known solely as an (unstressed) inseparable verbal prefix. It has its counterparts, at least in the earliest period, in all the other Germanic languages. In Gothic, however, the corresponding verbal prefix *and-* also occurs as an independent preposition. In German, then, as in the related languages except Gothic, this preposition had lost its independent existence before the commencement of the literary period. In German it had the sense of 'out of, from' and a preposition with a meaning like that naturally took the dative. The meaning and the construction have, with very many verbs, remained constant since the first records: OHG (Charm) *insprinc haptbandun, invar vigandun*, i.e. normalized Early OHG *intspring haftbandum, intfar vîandum* 'leap from the binding bonds, escape from the enemies' or, mechanically transposed into modern German, 'entspring Haftbanden, entfahr Feinden'. Present-day examples: *er entkam der Gefahr, es entglitt meiner Hand, die Tochter ist unseren Fittichen bereits entwachsen.* When used transitively, various constructions are met with. In the oldest type the accusative object is regularly accompanied by the dative: *die Polizei entzog ihm die Fahrerlaubnis.* In accordance with modern trends, prepositions may qualify the dative: *wir haben (aus) Ihrem Brief entnommen, daß die Angelegenheit geregelt ist,* similarly *wir haben daraus entnommen, daß* .... Verbs with the prefix *ent-* often carry meanings which have brought them within the sphere of influence of verbs of separation. Such verbs traditionally govern the genitive. Accordingly, a number of verbs with the prefix *ent-* are seen to govern this case: *ich enthalte mich des Weines.* See further, p. 12.

Verbs containing the inseparable prefixes *be-* and *er-* are normally transitive. The prefixes go back to OHG *bi-* and *ir-*, also *ar-*, in the oldest texts occasionally *ur-*. These are identical with the prepositions *bi,* often replaced by the (originally stressed and secondarily lengthened) adverbial form *bî* (> NHG *bei*), and *ur* 'out of, from'. Both these prepositions governed the dative (cf. *bei* above), but from the beginning verbs compounded with unstressed *bi-* and *ir-* regularly govern the accusative as do their descendants today. Feeling for the connexion with the independent prepositions must have been lost early and the verbal simplex alone came to determine the construction. The phonetic changes resulting from the unstressed use of the prefixes would naturally hasten the rupture with the prepositions proper. When this happened, the prefixes could develop functions far different from those of the prepositions from which they had sprung. Thus both of them came to be used to form transitive verbs from intransitives, hence *er bestieg* or *erstieg den Berg* which equal in essentials *er stieg auf den Berg.* One could hardly conceive such a development if the prefixes had actually remained in touch with the prepositions. This does not mean, however, that original functions are not sometimes preserved as well. The intransitive use of *bestehen* and *erstehen,* for instance, is clearly very ancient: *Blumen, die im Sturm bestehen,* i.e. 'remain standing', lit. 'stand by', or *daraus erstehen Schwierigkeiten,* i.e. 'arise', lit. 'stand out of', where *er-* is seen to retain the sense of the now lost preposition *ur* (see above). Broadly speaking, the same will be true in principle of verbs containing the inseparable *ver-*, OHG *fir-*, a prefix of rather complex origin.

In several cases prepositions which can be compounded with a verb take not only the dative but also the accusative, the basic difference being that the dative indicates rest at, the accusative motion towards (see p. 3). The most significant prepositions in this connexion are *an* and *auf*, and in the modern language *vor* also, because although it originally denoted only rest at, it has in the modern period taken over a function of *für* which formerly indicated motion towards (see p. 190). When compounded with verbs, such prepositions automatically continued to govern the appropriate case in so far, of course, as they and not the verbal simplex determined the construction, e.g. in the case of the preposition *an*: (rest at) *Mängel haften diesem Werk an*, (motion towards) *die Rakete fliegt den Mond an*. But a new factor has added complications: there has been a tendency for the dative to spread here at the expense of the accusative. Luther wrote *da kam mich Furcht und Schrecken an*, but Goethe has *mir kommt die . . . Lust wieder an*. With *auf* and *vor*, indeed, the dative has become the invariable rule: *der bedenkliche Passus fiel mir sofort auf*; *ich stelle mir vor, daß die Gegenpartei gewinnt*; in both these cases the dative has replaced an original accusative.

The marked tendency for the dative to oust the accusative is well exemplified in the case of compounds containing *ein*. In origin *ein* is the regular modern diphthongization of MHG *în*, itself a lengthened form of *in*, developing in a stressed position when compounded with a verb. By its very meaning it could only denote motion towards, and the early texts show it regularly governing the accusative: OHG (Tatian) *ir inganget thaȥ hûs* 'you (will) enter the house'. In a few idioms this construction lives on still, e.g. *eine Ehe, Verpflichtungen eingehen*, also *jemanden einschüchtern*, but otherwise only the dative is now possible: *was fällt Ihnen ein?*

The preposition *wider* was formerly used with the dative as well as the accusative: reflexes of this older usage are apparently preserved in some cases when the word appears in a compound verb, for instance, *ich habe ihr widersprochen*, but *ich habe sie widerlegt*.

Dative after verbs compounded with adverbs of place

We are here dealing with a feature which has developed in the modern period. The dative construction is most typical: *ich bin ihm zuvorgekommen, sie eilen den anderen voraus, ein Unglück steht mir bevor*.

In connexion with *vorbei* and *vorüber*, which came into use at the beginning of the modern period, the earliest construction is the adverbial accusative (p. 3). Subsequently, this accusative was often replaced by the dative: (Heine) *ich kam eben der Sorbonne vorbei, er huschte mir rasch vorüber*. Nowadays only *an der S. vorbei, an mir vorüber* would be possible.

Dative after interjections

OHG *wê* 'woe' governs the dative: (Muspilli) *wê demo in vinstrî scal sîno virinâ stûên* 'woe to him who in darkness shall atone for his crimes!' This usage has continued down to the present day: *Weh dem, der lügt*, though in face of competition from other cases (see 'Genitive of cause', p. 14). The present construction is, however, original. This is confirmed not only by analogous constructions in the other Old Germanic languages, but also by Latin where *vae*, etymologically identical with OHG *wê*, is followed by the dative: *vae victis* 'woe to the conquered!' Other interjections follow suit: MHG (Hartmann) *phî im und sînem künne* 'fie upon him and his kin!', (Walther) *wol ir* 'well for her!', NHG *heil dir im Siegeskranz*.

Dative as representative of lost cases

(*a*) *Dative as ablative*

The Indo-European ablative was lost in Germanic, its role being taken over partly by the genitive (see 'Genitive as ablative', p. 15), partly by the dative. In one of its well-established functions as the ablative of comparison, the lost case can be traced in Germanic in the dative of comparison found as a living construction in Gothic and Old Norse. This was also the situation in pre-historic West Germanic, as is evident from the evolution of the prepositions OHG *êr*, OE *ǣr* 'before (of time), ere' and OHG *sît*, OE *sīþ* 'since', words which in origin are comparative adverbs meaning 'earlier' and 'later' respectively. As prepositions they govern the dative, and it can be assumed that the dative here represents the former ablative of comparison. But whether a West Germanic dative of comparison survived into the literary period of German as a living construction is not clear, for, although there are many examples of a dative after a comparative in the early records, these occur solely in texts translated from Latin or in works which show dependence on Latin style. One must, therefore, reckon with the possibility that this dative may be an approximate literary calque on the Latin ablative rather than a genuine survival of the Germanic construction. Compare the Vulgate *numquid tu maior es patre nostro Jacob* "art thou greater than our father Jacob?" with Tatian *eno thû bistû mêra unsaremo fater Jacobe.* Other examples: (Otfrid) *furira Abrâme* 'greater than Abraham', (Notker) *wîȥȥero snêwe* 'whiter than snow'. At all events German has, since the beginning, also employed a conjunction; in the early period it was *danne* 'than': (Otfrid) *furira thû ni bist thanne unser fater Jacob ist* 'thou art not greater than our father Jacob is', (Samaritan Woman) *ne bistû . . . kelop mêr danne Jacob* 'thou art not . . . more famous than Jacob' (p. 228). Doubtless this was the more usual construction even at the beginning of the literary period.

(*b*) *Dative as locative*

The role of the dative as inheritor of the functions of the one-time locative is clearly visible in a few examples from the older language: OHG, MHG *heime* 'at home', OHG *allên halbôn* 'on all sides', MHG, NHG *allenthalben*, OHG *bêdên halbôn* 'on both sides', MHG *bêdenthalben*: (Walther) *eȥ regent bêdenthalben mîn* 'es regnet beiderseits von mir'.

As may be inferred from the comparative syntax of the Indo-European languages, the locative case very frequently took on a temporal function, and it is to be assumed that the locative was also used in this way at an early stage in the evolution of the Germanic languages. Since in German there are no morphological indications of the lost locative, its former existence may only be traced in the syntax. It is known that the Indo-European locative was absorbed by the Germanic dative, so that where in German the dative occurs in a temporal function—which is not a function proper to this case—one may consider that the dative has replaced the old locative, e.g. in Otfrid *iu manageru zît* 'for a long time already'. However, there is another candidate in the field. Not only the Indo-European locative, the Indo-European instrumental could also have a temporal function, and indubitable traces of such use are found in OHG in the case of a few adverbs and pronouns (see further p. 36). Since the OHG dative had otherwise absorbed the instrumental as well as the locative (see 'Dative as instrumental', below), it is not really possible to say which of the prehistoric cases a temporal dative involving a noun actually represents. Normally, the temporal dative in OHG is governed by a preposition: (Notker) *in sînen zîten* 'in his times', (Ezzos Gesang) *be ir zîten* 'at their times / zu ihren Zeiten', i.e. as in the later language exclusively.

The locative function is usually expressed in German by a preposition, e.g. *zu Berlin* 'in Berlin' (high style). Similarly with verbs compounded with a preposition: *es steht ihr nicht zu, solches zu verlangen* 'she has no right to make such a demand', where the dative *ihr* has taken over the function of the vanished locative.

(*c*) *Dative as instrumental*

Although considerable relics of an instrumental proper survive in the oldest German, the functions of this case had, in general, passed over to the dative before the opening of the literary period. Normally, a dative functioning as an instrumental requires the preposition *mit* 'with', but there are in the earliest records a fair number of examples of archaic use without a preposition: (Hildebrandslied) *her frâgên gistuont fôhêm uuortum* 'he began to ask with few words', (Otfrid) *fuarun sêragemo muate* '(they) went with a sorry heart'. As a further development of the sociative use of the former instrumental are the dative plural forms of nouns and adjectives which, petrifying, became pure adverbs: OHG *hwîlôm* 'sometime' lit. 'with times' from *hwîla* 'space of time, while' / 'Weile', MHG *wîlen(t)*, NHG *weiland* (cf. older English *whilom*), *unzîtin* 'at the wrong time' from *unzît* 'Unzeit', *emmiȥîgên* 'continuously' from *emmiȥîg* 'continuous' > NHG *emsig*.

Any construction with the preposition *mit* implies, naturally, a one-time instrumental. This is equally the case where *mit* is compounded with a verb, two examples of which survive in the modern language: *mitteilen, -spielen*, e.g. *der Experte teilt mir mit* 'the expert informs me', *die Experten haben ihm arg mitgespielt* 'the experts have dealt with him severely'. Since the datives here are syntactically instrumentals, the basic sense of the idioms *einem mitteilen, einem mitspielen* is, respectively, 'to share with somebody' and 'to play with somebody'.

(*d*) *Dative absolute*

A noun and a participle in the dative may, in OHG, form an adverbial clause comparable to the Latin ablative absolute.

There is no doubt that the Latin construction is essentially an instrumental in origin, as many examples still clearly show: *quassante capite . . . incedunt* '(with) shaking head(s) . . . they march along'. Since the German dative case is known to have absorbed the Indo-European instrumental, one might think that the German absolute construction will be genetically identical with the Latin. However, there is a problem here. It is remarkable that the OHG dative absolute never occurs except in translations from Latin or in writings stylistically dependent on Latin. The very same is true of OE, where the dative absolute is also common. In view of this, one may legitimately hesitate and wonder whether the OHG (and the OE) construction is not merely a calque on the Latin, the dative being substituted for the ablative as the next best thing. The dative absolute is not found in Old Norse, but it does occur in Gothic. Since the Gothic dative absolute renders a Greek genitive abolute, one must conclude that Gothic, at any rate, here continues a genuine Germanic construction lost in Norse. All the same, the occurrence of an ancient Germanic idiom in Gothic does not prove at all that it survived in OHG and OE. A similar crux has already been ventilated in connexion with the dative of comparison and, as we saw, a definite solution is scarcely possible for want of further evidence. The same element of uncertainty must remain in the present case, too.

But even if the OHG dative absolute does not owe everything to Latin, it must certainly owe a great deal, for there cannot be a doubt that the presence of the ablative absolute in Latin would greatly favour the choice of the corresponding dative construction in German. Examples: (Tatian) *twâla tuonti themo brûtigomen, naffezzitun allo inti sliefun* "while the bridegroom tarried, they all slumbered and slept", lit. 'the bridegroom making delay', exactly as in the Vulgate *moram autem faciente sponso, dormitaverunt omnes et dormierunt*, (Notker) *alsô zestobenemo nebele, sah ih ten himel* 'the mist thus having cleared, I saw the sky' translating *haud aliter dissolutis nebulis, hausi caelum.*

As mentioned above, OE also uses the dative absolute: (Gospel) *þīnre dura belocenre, bide* "when thou hast shut thy door, pray", lit. 'thy door (having been) shut', Vulgate *clauso ostio, ora.* Whereas in OHG the construction became extinct without leaving any descendant, this is not so in English. It is true that, due to the decay of the OE inflexional system, the dative forms as such were lost, but the construction persisted all the same even though the noun and participle no longer had distinguishing case-endings. Not unexpectedly, these uninflected forms came to be felt as nominatives, and so the OE dative absolute turned into the ME nominative absolute as can be seen whenever a pronoun replaces the noun: (Chaucer) *what couthe a stourdy housebonde more devyse, / to prove hir wyfhode and her stedfastnesse, / and he contynuying ever in stourdynesse.* The construction is, of course, fully alive today: *she preferring the quiet of the countryside, we decided to move into a cottage near St. Just.* A modern German translation might run: *da sie die ländliche Ruhe bevorzugte, beschlossen wir, ein Häuschen in der Nähe von St. Just zu beziehen.*

INSTRUMENTAL

In early OHG a few masculines and neuters preserve, in the singular, traces of an otherwise lost instrumental case.

The earliest examples show that the noun in the instrumental may or may not be preceded by a preposition: (Hildebrandslied) *nu scal mih suasat chind suertu hauwan, / breton mit sînu billiu* 'now shall my own child hew me with the sword, strike me down with his brand'. There is no doubt that the construction without the preposition is older and original. Indeed, it faithfully continues Indo-European usage, just as still commonly in Slavonic languages, e.g. Russian *meč* 'sword', *mečom* 'with the sword'. But the instrumental was even in preliterary German a much broken-down category, already largely confused with the dative (see 'Dative as instrumental', p. 33). In such circumstances the need for an unambiguous preposition to indicate the instrumental function was often imperative and so *mit* 'with' came to be extensively used, eventually spreading to forms which were still morphologically recognizable as instrumentals. This situation is clearly documented in Otfrid. Here the use of the instrumental without a preposition is rare: *ingiang er thô skioro goldo garo ziero* '(he) entered then quickly, delightfully ornate with gold', but in combination with a preposition the instrumental is frequently found: *mit swertu* 'with the sword', *mit stabu* 'with the staff', also with abstract nouns: *mit gotes scirmu* 'with God's protection', *mit sînes selbes tôdu* 'with his own death', *far mit fridu* 'go in peace'. It is noticeable that in every instance the instrumental is unqualified; very seldom is the instrumental employed when the noun is qualified, as in the Hildebrandslied (above), and never in Otfrid. With him the dative is the invariable rule whenever the noun is accompanied by a qualifying word, hence *mit drôstu* 'with comfort' (instrumental) but *mit themo drôste* 'with the comfort' (dative). Obviously, the morphologically distinct instrumental had by this time become very largely redundant. As a living case it will hardly have survived into the tenth century, though formal relics continue for some time.

The following neuter instrumental forms of pronouns occur in OHG and continue in use in MHG: *diu* 'this, that', *hwiu*, later *wiu* 'what'. They are regularly used in reference to an abstract concept and are governed by prepositions which otherwise take the dative: OHG (Tatian) *after thiu was itmâli tag Iudeôno* "after this there was a feast of the Jews", (Muspilli) *sô mac huckan za diu . . . der sih suntîgen weiʒ* 'so he who knows himself (to be) sinful . . . can ponder over it'. In a number of cases the preposition has coalesced with the pronoun to form a new part of speech: (Tatian) *mittiu daʒ waʒʒer giruorit wirdit* (*mittiu* < *mit thiu*) "when the water is troubled", (Otfrid) *ziu sculun Frankon, sô ih quad, zi thiu einen wesan ungimah?* (*ziu* < *zi hwiu*) 'wherefore should the Franks, as I said, alone be incapable of that?', MHG (Helmbrecht) *ich enweiʒ zwiu eʒ sal* 'I know not for what purpose it is'. Compare also OHG *diu* before comparatives: (Otfrid) *thiu halt* 'the more / desto mehr', since Notker replaced by the emphatic *desdiu* (i.e. *des diu*) > *desde* 'desto'. OHG *diu* is the exact equivalent of the OE instrumental *þȳ* which still survives as *the*, e.g. *the shorter the better* 'je kürzer desto besser'.

Comparative Indo-European syntax shows that starting from the notion 'with the (course of) time' the instrumental came to be used in a temporal sense. Petrified relics of this practice are identifiable in two OHG words, both of which remain in use today: preliterary OHG **hiu tagu* 'this day' > OHG *hiutu* 'heute', preliterary OHG **hiu jâru* 'this year' > OHG *hiuru* 'heuer'. From the analogy of these forms it is reasonable to interpret OHG *hînaht* 'tonight' > NHG (dial.) *heint*, 'tonight, today' as an original instrumental, too. It is certain that, even then, the OHG words were to the speakers of the language unanalysable simplexes, the demonstrative *hi-* 'this' having been long extinct as an independent word.

II · ADJECTIVES

In the morphology of present-day German it is convenient to distinguish a strong, weak, and mixed declension of adjectives. The last is a secondary development arising out of a mixture of strong and weak declensions. These two, however, are traditional and go back to Germanic times. The division into strong and weak adjectives is basic and was originally semantically important.

STRONG ADJECTIVES

Origins

OHG inherited from Germanic an inflexional system for adjectives corresponding to Latin *bonus*, *-a*, *-um*. This is termed the strong declension of adjectives. In the nom.sg. in German, however, all three endings (as exemplified by the Latin) were regularly dropped in the preliterary period, so that even in the earliest records the adjective appears uninflected in this case: *guot man*, *guot frouwa*, *guot kind*. Less usually, the adjective followed its noun: *man guot*, etc. The numeral *ein* 'one' can precede and may function as an indefinite article: *ein guot man*. The strong adjective is also used predicatively: *man ist guot*.

During the Germanic period the morphology of the strong adjective, as handed down from Indo-European, was very largely reshaped owing to the contaminating influence of the pronominal declension. The twofold origin of the endings of the Germanic strong adjective can easily be traced in OHG. In the nom.sg. and acc.neut.sg., the secondary terminations occur side by side with the traditional ones. In addition to the type *guot man*, as above, one commonly also meets the type *guotêr man*, *guotiu frouwa*, *guotaȥ kind*, where the endings are to be compared for example with those of the demonstrative pronoun *der*, *diu*, *daȥ*, 'that (one)'. Further, with following adjective: *man guotêr*.

Or with an article: *ein guotêr man,* and predicatively: *man ist guotêr.*

Attributive adjective, inflected and uninflected

Both inflected and uninflected forms of the strong adjective could be used without any semantic difference: (Otfrid) *ein armaȥ wîb* 'a poor woman', (Hildebrandslied) *sô friuntlaos man* 'such a friendless man', and this usage continued throughout the medieval period: MHG (Nibelungenlied) *ein ûȥerwelter degen* 'a notable warrior' beside *ein edel man* (> NHG *Edelmann*) 'a noble man', *varnde* or *varndeȥ guot* 'movable property'. Some regional variation is, however, discernible. In the south the inflected forms are characteristic, but progressively diminish as one proceeds north, a variation still reflected in the modern dialects. The NHG literary language follows, of course, southern practice. But in Early NHG there are many examples of the uninflected form: (Luther) *groß Macht und viel List / sein grausam Rüstung ist.* In particular the uninflected neut.sg. is common: (Luther) *ein getrieben, lauter Gold* "one beaten work of pure gold", *ein gegossen Kalb* "a molten calf", *ein christlich Herz.* There are examples in traditional folk-song: *es flog ein klein Waldvögelein,* and for metrical and stylistic reasons, in the classical poets and after: (Lessing) *ein jung und artig Weib,* (Goethe) *ein unnütz Leben,* (Schiller) *ein liebend Paar,* (Heine) *sein sterbend Haupt*; similarly in the proverb: *ein gut Gewissen ist ein sanftes Ruhekissen.* The uninflected form also retained, to be sure, some currency in the living language, for examples survive in general use to this day: *auf gut Glück, ein gut Teil, lieb Kind sein, trocken Brot essen.*

In the case of certain pronominal adjectives, the uninflected form is very widespread. It is still regular in exclamations such as *welch ein Glück!, welch ein Künstler!,* also in *solch ein Glück!, solch ein Künstler!,* though *ein solches Glück!,* etc., are possible as well. One says *manch einer* or *mancher* according to district. The adjective *all* is very often uninflected before the article or demonstrative: *all das Bier, all diejenigen langen Jahre.* Uninflected forms also occur before adjectives: *welch, solch wunderbares Wetter!,* (Heine) *manch schönes Kind,* now usually *manches schöne Kind,* (Goethe) *manch gülden Gewand.* Finally, *ganz* and *halb* are always uninflected before place-names without an article: *ganz Griechenland, halb Wien.*

Postpositive adjective

In the older language the adjective is sometimes placed after its noun; the adjective is then termed postpositive. In the earliest stage both inflected and uninflected forms occur (see preceding section), e.g. (Notker) *in einemo felde scônemo* 'in a fair field', (Otfrid) *forasago mâri* 'illustrious prophet'. Then the uninflected form was generalized and, furthermore, spread to all other cases, singular and plural. This is the normal situation in MHG, but the construction was now only poetic, commonest in folk-epic: (Nibelungenlied) *die stolzen jegere balt* 'the dashing hunters bold', (Kudrun) *durch dîne triuwe grôʒ* 'through your great faith', though not infrequently found elsewhere: (von Aist) *slâfest du, friedel ziere* 'are you sleeping, fair love?' The inflected form is the exception: (Walther) *dô kom ich gegangen / an einen anger langen* 'then I came walking on to a long meadow'; indeed, the ending here reads rather like poetic licence. The postpositive adjective survived, as a legacy from medieval diction, in the older folk-song: *es ist ein Reis entsprungen / aus einer Wurzel zart*, and was later taken up in archaizing poetic style: (Uhland) *bei einem Wirte wundermild, / da war ich jüngst zu Gaste*; similarly Goethe's *Röslein rot.*

As in English, two adjectives linked by the copula often follow their noun: (Schiller) *ein Mädchen schön und wunderbar*. But here the connexion with the noun tends to be loose so that the attribute acquires more the character of an apposition, as in *das Städtchen, still und ehrwürdig, lädt zum Verweilen ein.*

Predicative adjective

As stated in the first section above, the predicative adjective in OHG may be either inflected or uninflected. Examples of both are commonplace, e.g. in the same poem: (Hildebrandslied) *du bist dir, altêr Hûn, unmet spâhêr* 'you are, old Hun, infinitely cunning', but *chûd was her . . . chônnêm mannum* 'he was known . . . to bold men', or even cheek by jowl in the same line: (Otfrid) *er ist gizal ubaral / . . . wîsêr inti kuani* 'he is above all courageous . . . wise and bold'. Contrast (Otfrid) *ther puzz ist filu diofêr* 'the well is very deep' with (Samaritan Woman) *disiu buzza ist sô tiuf* 'this well is so deep'. Likewise after *werdan*, e.g. (Ludwigslied) *kind warth her faterlôs* 'as a child he became fatherless', as against (Otfrid) *ther blindêr ward giboranêr* 'who was born blind'. But the uninflected form becomes commoner and is extended to the plural. Otfrid, for instance, has both the old inflected form: *sie sint . . . wîsduames folle* 'they are . . . full of wisdom', and the new uninflected form: *thie zîti sint sô heilag* 'the festivals are so holy'. In the middle period the predicative adjective is usually uninflected, but inflected forms are not rare: (Nibelungenlied) *die dâ wunde lâgen* 'those who lay wounded', (Hartmann) *sîn jâmer wart so vester* 'his misery became so great'.

In general, the use of inflected forms did not survive into the modern period, though one or two relics have been identified. We say 'identified' because the ending where it occurs is not understood since predicative inflection is no more a living principle in the language. Thus the ending *-er* in *voller*, for example, as it may appear in a phrase like *ein Aufsatz voller Fehler*, is not at all transparent. From the standpoint of the speaker of the modern language, *voller* can be imagined to be a gen.pl. or, alternatively, a comparative. Wunderlich–Reis, ii, pp. 224–5, refer to a *bon mot* made at some gathering of teachers of German which wittily incorporates both these lay interpretations: *ich habe das Haus schon voller gesehen, ich habe es schon leerer gesehen, aber so voller Lehrer sah ich es noch nie*. Unhappily, these lay views are both wide of the mark. Only historical syntax can show that the ending is most likely the old inflected nom.masc.sg. of the predicative adjective. Especially in Bavaria, this distinctive *er*-ending survived the demise of the other inflected predicative forms and acquired a certain vogue, as a phonetic ornament so to speak; *voller* will be such a form.

WEAK ADJECTIVES

Origins

Whereas the strong adjective, in its oldest inflexions at least, goes back to an Indo-European adjectival declension, the weak adjective is a purely Germanic innovation. But the seeds from which it sprang were already sown in Indo-European times.

Various languages could use an *n*-suffix to form attributive nouns from adjectives, e.g. Latin *silus* 'pug-nosed', *silo*, stem *silon-* 'pug-nosed person', Greek *strabós* squinting', *strábōn* 'squinting person'. In Primitive Germanic the potentialities of this formation were so exploited that the suffix could be automatically employed with any adjective. The Latin and Greek derivatives are masculines, but Germanic created parallel derivations for all three genders. Details of these developments can, of course, only be surmised, as they took place in prehistoric times. It is clear, however, from the testimony of the oldest recorded Germanic languages that the new forms could have the character of nouns, as one would expect in view of their origin. At the same time the new forms constituted a regular system organically connected with the basic adjectival system from which they were derived. It is therefore very possible that such forms were not nouns only, but were also adjectives with a special function. That, at any rate, is the picture seen from the most archaic records, when the formations under discussion most characteristically appear as the weak declension of adjectives.

Basic difference between weak and strong adjectives

The most archaic source in this respect is the OE poem *Beowulf*, an epic in traditional language. The German material is, generally speaking, less archaic, but it is possible to reproduce the oldest stage schematically with OHG words and illustrate the special function of the weak adjective.

The nom.masc.sg. of the weak adjective in OHG ends in *-o*, e.g. *guoto*; the *n*-suffix appears only in the oblique cases, as acc. masc.sg. *guoton*, etc. The weak *guoto* contrasts with the strong *guot(êr)*, see above, the special function of the weak form being to mark out a definite or familiar object and so distinguish it from an indefinite or less familiar one. Thus, while *guot(êr) man* meant '(a) good man', i.e. any good man, *guoto man* referred to a definite good man, i.e. 'the good man'. The latter was also the form of the vocative which in the nature of the case is only used in reference to somebody or something definite.

It may be emphasized that the example *guoto man* is not actually found in the texts. In reality OHG has *der guoto man*, i.e. with the definite article. But this is a secondary development. The definite article has, indeed, basically the same function as the weak ending of the adjective (see p. 86). Presumably the definite article was first used with unqualified nouns, but spread by analogy to those qualified by an adjective. The adjective in these cases would naturally always be weak and so there arose the pattern of agreement still familiar today: definite article plus weak adjective. The strong form of the adjective, on the other hand, was left to indicate the indefinite form. Then, as the indefinite article *ein* came into use it only appeared before the strong form of the adjective, giving the opposite pattern of agreement: indefinite article plus strong adjective. But scarcely had this second pattern established itself, when it was analogically reformed according to the mixed declension then developing after the possessive pronoun.

Although it was, above, convenient to construct theoretically the phrase *guoto man* 'the good man' to illustrate the original function of the weak adjective, actual relics of this oldest syntactic stage are occasionally found in OHG in association with the name of the deity: (Muspilli) *ni ist in kihuctin himiliskin gote* 'is not in the thoughts of heavenly God', or as vocatives: (Otfrid) *liobo man* 'dear man', (Wessobrunn Prayer) *cot almahtîco* 'God almighty'. But all feeling for the original function of the weak ending was lost in OHG as a consequence of the rise of the definite article. The weak ending of the vocative adjective must have soon been felt to be irregular. In MHG it was commonly replaced, in the singular at least, by the strong form, i.e. by that form which was ordinarily employed when the adjective alone was used with a noun. The weak plural survived better and occurs sporadically as late as the nineteenth century: (Heine) *lieben Freunde!* Today only *liebe Freunde!* is possible.

Mixed declension

Usage in OHG after *ein* 'one, a' (and its compounds, as *dehein* or *nihein* > *kein*) and after the possessive pronouns varied considerably, strong and weak forms competing. In the modern language the position has been stabilized in such a way that the strong adjective is used after the uninflected forms *ein*, *kein*, *mein*, *unser*, etc., otherwise the weak form is taken. To all intents and purposes this mixed declension had come into existence by the beginning of the MHG period, though exceptions are not infrequent: (Nibelungenlied) *an sîme roteme helme* 'on his red helmet', *in einer kurzer stunt* 'in a short while'. And as late as the eighteenth century, the nom.acc.pl. is still occasionally strong: (Lessing) *seine übrige komische Stücke*, (Goethe) *für meine noch zu schwache Schultern*, (Schiller) *an keine andere Schranken.*

Anomalies and alternation between strong and weak adjectives

The rules of agreement have sometimes been broken. It happens that, exceptionally, occurrences of the strong form are noticed after the definite article: OHG (Tatian) *themo unsûbremo geiste* 'to the unclean spirit', (Otfrid) *thie ungiloubîge* 'the unbelieving', MHG (Nibelungenlied) *die kreftige man* 'the powerful men', (Wolfram) *diu iâmerbæriu magt* 'the pitiful maid', (Hartmann) *sus sprach er zuo der guoter* 'thus spake he to the lady' lit. 'good one'. Examples are found in NHG too: (Lessing) *in dem allerernstlichem Ernste*, and especially in the nom.acc.pl.: (Herder) *die menschliche Kräfte*, (Goethe) *die vergangne Zeiten.* Schiller is a rather frequent offender: *die äußerste Enden, durch die tausendfache Stufen.* How such aberrations are to be explained is a problem. It is true that, after the establishment of the articles, the endings of following adjectives lost their former syntactic importance which could easily have led to the disintegration of the system of strong and weak adjectives. But in fact this did not eventuate, though usage has fluctuated in certain cases. Perhaps the exceptions are simply lapses. It will be remembered, too, that original final *n* is lost in some dialects, notably in Swabian. Unconscious dialect influence may well explain Schiller's forms.

The strong adjective may also be found occasionally after *dieser*: (Wieland) *diese schwarze Tücher*, (Goethe) *alle diese liebenswürdige Grausamkeiten.* There seems to be some tradition here, to judge by the earlier stages of the language. Though modern Bibles have (2 Sam. xvi. 9) *dieser tote Hund*, and (Acts iii. 11) *dieser Lahme*, Luther's own text was *dieser todter Hund, dieser Lamer.* In MHG the strong form was not uncommon: (Hartmann) *dirre ungevüeger schal* 'this unpleasant noise', (Nibelungenlied) *diz starkeʒ übermüeten* 'this great arrogance'. On the other hand, the strong adjective is rare after *jener*: (Herder) *jene überspannte Tätigkeiten.*

The weak adjective now obligatory after *aller* is not original. In MHG the strong adjective was the rule: (Rolandslied) *uʒ allem irdischem künne* 'from all earthly stock', (Walther) *alle bœse herren* 'all bad masters'; the weak form was the exception: (Hartmann) *vor aller vremden hôchvart* 'before all alien pride'. In NHG the weak form was generalized, but traces of the strong declension did not finally disappear until the early nineteenth century. Luther has *alle Hohepriester*, Menge *alle Hohenpriester*. Late examples: (Lessing) *alle methodische Bücher*, (Goethe) *alle zarte sentimentale und pathetische Situationen*, (E. T. A. Hoffmann) *alle nachfolgende Violinspieler*. By analogy, the neologism *sämtlich* is also followed by the weak adjective: *sämtliche neuen Bücher*. The weak forms of adjectives are now the rule after the inflected forms of *manch*, *welch*, commonly also after *solch*, but strong forms are found in the older literature: (Lessing) *welche geringfügige Ursachen*.

After indefinite numeral adjectives like *andere*, *einige*, *mehrere*, *viele*, *wenige*, the strong form is prescribed in the nom.acc., but in the older language weak forms are not rare: (Lessing) *andere verwandten Empfindungen*. In contemporary style the genitive adjective is often weak: *vieler guten Vorsätze*.

When two adjectives stand together before a noun without an article or pronoun they may, theoretically, be regarded either as co-ordinates, in which case both follow the strong declension, or the first may be regarded as the determinant, in which case the second takes the weak ending in the gen.dat.sg. and gen. pl.: *langes wirres Haar*, but either *mit langem, wirrem Haare* (where the comma often occurs to emphasize the co-ordination) or *mit langem wirren Haare*.

An adjective not preceded by an article or pronoun, has lost the original strong inflexion in the masc.neut.gen.sg. Luther wrote: *selig sind, die reines Herzens sind*, but Menge modernizes: *reinen Herzens*. The first signs of this change go back to the fifteenth century, but it was not finally confirmed until the middle of the nineteenth, after great confusion in the classical era. Notice how phrases like *besten Falls*, *nötigen Falls*, now written *bestenfalls*, *nötigenfalls*, led to the analogical formations *allenfalls*, *jedenfalls*, although *aller* has otherwise no weak forms and *jeder*, strictly speaking, only when preceded by the indefinite article, though 'ungrammatical' *jeden* may now occur: (newspaper) *Männer jeden Alters*.

After a personal pronoun the adjective in the older period is indifferently weak or strong: (Otfrid) *wir wênegon weison* 'we wretched orphans', (Walther) *ich nôtic man* 'I poor man'. In NHG a compromise allocation of forms has become the rule, as follows. In the nom.sg. the adjective is strong: *ich armer Mann, du liebes Kind, Sie Ärmster!* In the dat.sg. and in the plural, however, the adjective is weak: *es geschah mir dummen Frau, wir erbärmlichen Waisen,* (G. Hauptmann) *o Ihr weißen, maurischen Städte! Ihr südlichen Hänge!* In MHG an attribute commonly stood before a genitive: (Nibelungenlied) *durch sîn eines sterben starp vil maneger muoter kint* 'because of his death alone the child of many a mother died'. This construction has long been obsolete; modern renderings of the above context are, e.g. Simrock: *durch dieses Einen Sterben,* De Boor, more idiomatically: *um des einen Sterben.*

Comparative and superlative

In OHG both the comparative and superlative adjective were regularly declined weak. One said either *der* or *ein lengiro weg* 'the *or* a longer way' and *der* or *ein weg ist lengiro* 'the *or* one way is longer'; (Tatian) *thû bezzisto Theophile* "most excellent Theophilus". This was, of course, in consonance with the principle that the weak form denotes the definite. In the nature of the case, the superlative always refers to definite things, the comparative usually does. In the latter, the naturally predominant weak form was generalized. The exclusive use of weak endings did not survive into MHG where the comparative and superlative were treated like the positive.

DEFECTIVE ADJECTIVES

A number of adjectives cannot be used attributively and therefore occur only in the uninflected form, e.g. the modern formations *eingedenk, teilhaftig, verlustig.* The old adjectives *kund* and *leid* are now similarly defective, but they were formerly used attributively as well: MHG (Copeybuch der . . . statt Wienn, from Lexer) *gar ein kunder man* 'a well known man' (cf. Eng. *uncouth* lit. 'unkund'), (Das alte Passional, from Lexer) *si sprach mit leidem muote* 'she spoke with a sorrowful heart'. Whereas the old words *hold* and *unhold* are normal adjectives, the newer coining *abhold,* known since the fifteenth century, is defective. One or two anglicisms belong to this category: *gentlemanlike, sexy.* Several adjectives are found solely in fixed phrases, e.g. *gewahr werden,* of West Germanic age, corresponding to OE *gewǣr weorþan,* now *become aware*; purely modern examples are *habhaft werden, abspenstig machen.*

On the other hand, there are two groups of adjectives which cannot be used except attributively and therefore occur only in the inflected forms. The first group includes adjectives having some spatial reference: *der, die, das äußere, innere, vordere, hintere, obere, untere, mittlere,* (regional) *drübere,* e.g. *die drübere* (= *andere*) *Straßenseite,* also *linke* and its opposite *rechte.* The second group consists of adjectives in *-ig* derived from adverbs, as *der, die, das dortige, hiesige, heutige, diesjährige,* (South German) *heurige,* (local, substandard) *hinige,* e.g. *die hinigen* (= *kaputten*) *Schuhe.*

Other examples of defective adjectives will be found in the section 'From substantive to adjective', pp. 48 f.

FROM ADJECTIVE TO SUBSTANTIVE

In the old Indo-European languages any adjective could be substantivized, the person or thing understood being apparent from the gender, e.g. Latin *bonus* 'good man', *bonum* 'good thing'. German, like very many other modern Indo-European languages, makes full use of this inherited faculty.

Substantivized adjectives referring to persons

When referring to persons the weak form of the adjective was used in medieval German: OHG (Charm) *tumbo saȥ in berke* 'the dumb one sat on the hill', *der heilego tumbo* 'the holy dumb one', (Muspilli) *der suanâri . . . der dâr suannan scal tôtên enti lepêntên* 'the judge . . . who shall judge dead and living', MHG (Helmbrecht) *râte iu wol ein tumbe* 'if a plain man advise you', *ûf stuont ein alter grîse* 'up stood an old grey-head' < *grîs* 'grey'. In NHG it became the rule that the substantivized adjective should inflect according to the same rules as the attributive adjective, i.e. both weak and strong/mixed. The old weak declension may, however, still occasionally be found in the classical period and after: (Klopstock) *erwachende Toten,* (Lessing) *ein ehrwürdiger Alte,* (Herder) *Weltweisen gab es nicht,* (Heine) *Bedienten leuchteten uns.*

The modern noun *Junge* is a relic of the weak declension of substantivized adjectives (MHG *der, ein junge*). Of like origin is the family name *Braune* < OHG *Brûno,* cf. *brûn* 'brown'. There are some very early examples of substantivization. The oldest, of West Germanic age, are *Eltern* < OHG *eltiron, altiron* 'older ones, elders' from *alt* 'old', and *Mensch* < OHG *mennisko, mannisko* 'human' from *man(n)* 'man'. A purely German development is *Fürst* < OHG *furisto* lit. 'foremost, first'. Two possibly seventh-century formations are *Herr* < OHG *hêrro, hêriro* rendering Latin 'senior', and *Jünger* < OHG *jungiro* 'junior'. Except in the last instance, where attraction into the common class of agent nouns in *-er* has taken place, these nouns preserve, in essentials, the weak inflexion of the substantivized adjectives from which they sprang, in practice identical with the weak declension of nouns. NHG *Greis* < MHG *grîse* (see example above) has passed over to a strong declension of nouns.

Through regular substantivization a few adjectives have come very close to substantives proper, e.g. *der* or *die Deutsche, Fremde, Liebste, Nächste*. The term *der Geistliche* must be regarded as a pure noun; it has no feminine. There are many more examples among the participles (pp. 160 f., 164).

Substantivized adjectives referring to things

In the oldest German an abstract concept was expressed by the substantivized strong neut.sg., e.g. OHG (Wessobrunn Prayer) *du mannun sô manac coot forgâpi* 'thou (who) gavest men so much good', *arc za piwîsanne* 'to shun evil', (Otfrid) *ni fand ih liebes wiht in thir* 'I did not find aught good in thee'. Doubtless, these were already felt more as nouns than as adjectives—they inflect like the former—and similarly in MHG: (Dietmar) *liep âne leit mac niht gesîn* 'joy without sorrow may not be'. Notice, too, MHG *valsches laz* lit. 'innocent of the false', and *valscheite laz* lit. 'innocent of falsity', both used idiomatically to mean 'true, faithful'. Most of these, and others, continue into the modern language in every case as true substantives, sometimes with semantic change, hence: NHG *das Gut, Übel, Leid, Recht, Licht, Heil*, in poetic style *das Falsch* (otherwise *Falschheit*). OHG *liob*, MHG *liep* lives on in the phrase *zu Liebe* and, in a personal sense, in *Lieb* (poetic), *Liebchen*. OHG, MHG *wâr* 'the true, truth' remains in NHG *wahrsagen*.

In later substantivizations, however, the adjective was inflected strong/mixed and weak according to the modern development referred to above, hence *das Schöne, Schönes*. In this way *das Gute* arose since *Gut* now meant '(landed) property'; *das Lichte* and *das Rechte* came into being as *Licht* and *Recht* were now exclusively nouns meaning 'light' and 'law' respectively. The abstract nouns cannot form a plural, but the others, of course, can: *Güter*,

Rechte, *Lichter*, etc. Such was the regular situation by the beginning of modern times: (Luther) *das Wenige*, *das ein Gerechter hat*, *ist besser denn das große Gut vieler Gottlosen*. There was, and still is, a small amount of inconsistency with the new forms. Goethe wrote *ein ideales Ganze* where today *ein ideales Ganzes* is the accepted norm. On the other hand, *ein angenehmes Äußere* is a familiar expression in the language of today, but all the same only *ihr Äußeres* is possible.

In the course of the eighteenth century, the old mode of formation was resuscitated to give such neologisms as *das All* (*Weltall*), further *das Grün*, *das Naß*, but which are, of course, different from the true abstracts *das Grüne*, *das Nasse*. After the analogy of *das Licht des Tages* was formed its opposite *das Dunkel der Nacht*. With the names of languages both formations are possible, though without their being necessarily interchangeable: *Deutsch* and *das Deutsche*. For instance, only the former can be used after the indefinite article: *ein gutes Deutsch*. But one can say *in Deutsch* or *im Deutschen*, likewise *im heutigen Deutsch* or *Deutschen*. Stylistically, the second is rather more elevated or slightly more technical.

In a limited number of instances substantivization has occurred simply through dropping the noun. In the following examples we give the missing noun in brackets; it will be noticed that it can in every case be easily supplied: OHG *diutiska* (*zunga*) survived in MHG *diutsche* (*zunge*) as the normal term for 'German (language)', though it was later replaced by the substantivized neuter (see previous paragraph). NHG *die Rechte* (*Hand*) goes back to MHG, where it occurs occasionally beside the still more usual *zesewe*, OHG *zesawa* 'do.', also with 'hand' understood; *die Linke* is attested as far back as OHG *lenka* and has competed successfully with synonymous OHG *winistra*, MHG *winstre* (*hant*). Common enough terms are *ein Dunkles* or *ein Helles* (*Bier*); idioms of florid business style are *Ihr Wertes* or *Ihr Geschätztes*. Similar formations are the widely known Austrian expressions *der Heurige* (*Wein*), in the plural *Heurige* (*Erdäpfel*).

FROM SUBSTANTIVE TO ADJECTIVE

There are isolated examples of nouns turning into adjectives. For the greater part they are defective, though a few have become quite like ordinary adjectives.

In a sentence such as *er ist Arbeiter*, the noun has, syntactically speaking, something in common with the predicative adjective in, for example, *er ist fleißig*. From such a slender starting-point as this, the occasional transformation of nouns into adjectives must have begun. Hence from OHG *fruma* in such syntagmas as *thaz ist fruma* 'that is (an) advantage' there emerged MHG *vrum*, *vrom* 'advantageous, useful, capable, pious' > NHG *fromm*. Another early example is MHG *vîant* 'hostile' > NHG *feind*, a word regularly used adjectivally with the dative. It only occurs as a predicate, but in the medieval language developed degrees of comparison now lost: (Nibelungenlied) *dône kunde im Kriemhilt nimmer vînder gewesen* lit. 'then K. could never be more hostile towards him', i.e. the measure of her enmity could increase no more. A corresponding use of *freund* is attested, though only rarely: (H. Sachs) *die nacht ist niemand freund*. MHG *schade* is both a noun 'harm' and an adjective 'harmful'. The latter is secondary and survives today, but is only found in predicative use: *es ist sehr schade, sie ist sich nicht zu schade*. On the same level and of the same age is the adjective *schuld*, as in *ich bin schuld daran*.

MHG *ernest* was a noun meaning (*inter alia*) 'seriousness'. From such an idiom as *mir ist ernest* a line of evolution via sentences of the type *diu sache ist mir ernest* lead to the adjectivization of the noun which was an accomplished fact by the beginning of the modern period. Eng. *earnest* offers a striking parallel. Originally a noun only, as still in the phrase *in earnest*, this word first took on the functions of an adjective during ME times. MHG *angest* 'fear' developed along comparable lines, though not so far: the idiom *mir ist angest* survives in the contemporary language and in the often-heard phrase *mir ist angst und bange*, the original noun is co-ordinated with the adverb *bange*. Luther and others occasionally form a now obsolete comparative *ängster*. An exclusively MHG example is *zorn* 'anger', then 'angry': (Walther) *deist dir zorn* 'that is a cause for your anger, for your being angry', (Nibelungenlied) *dône kunde Gîselhêre nimmer zorner gesîn* 'then G. could never be more angry'. Finally, the adjectives *lila* and *rosa*. They are defective in that they do not inflect, but they may be used attributively as well as predicatively: *er sieht alles durch die rosa Brille, ihr Kleid ist lila*. These are cut-down forms of *lilafarben* 'lilac-coloured', etc., and have been in use since the beginning of the last century. To these add recent *prima*, simply *Prima* 'top class' used adjectivally.

III · ADVERBS

THE use of adverbs in German poses no special problems for the English learner. Adverbs are invariable parts of speech and, apart from inevitable idiomatic divergencies here and there, they function in essentially the same way in both languages. It will, therefore, suffice to consider briefly the origin and development of the chief types of adverb encountered in German.

Oldest stratum

To the oldest stratum belong those adverbs which are not recognized as having been derived from any flexional system, e.g. OHG *ana* 'an', *durh* 'durch', *fora* 'vor', *in* 'in', *oba* 'oben', *umbi* 'um', *ûz* 'aus'. While retaining their adverbial qualities, these adverbs regularly develop into preverbs and prepositions (see 'Origin of primary prepositions' and 'Preverb and preposition', pp. 175 ff.).

Other very old adverbs are characterized by an *r*-suffix, conjectured to have had a locative function: OHG *hiar* 'hier, hie', *dâr* 'da, dort', *hwâr* 'wo', *nidar* 'unten (nieder)', *untar* 'unten'. In two cases an additional dental suffix modifies the meaning: OHG *tharôt, dorôt* 'dorthin' (> MHG *dort* 'do.'), *hwârot* 'wohin'. A nasal suffix is commoner and productive: OHG *obana* 'von oben her, oben', *untanân* 'unten', cf. also *nordenân* 'von Norden her'. The original business of this suffix was to indicate movement away from, but it early came to denote rest at, as in the modern forms *oben, unten*, also *innen*, whence by analogy in modern times *drüben, hüben*, (in local use) *dorten*.

Adverbs from case forms

Case forms of nouns and adjectives sometimes develop into adverbs. This was a feature of Indo-European speech which has continued to be productive down to the present day. Very often the adverb has the form of the gen.sg. (see 'Adverbial genitive',

p. 15). Sometimes it has the acc.sg. Very old examples of this are OHG *filu* 'much' (> NHG *viel*) from a Germanic adjective **felu-*, cognate with Greek *polý-*, and *io*, older *eo* < **êo* 'ever' (> NHG *je*) = Gothic *aiw* 'do.', acc. of *aiws* 'age, eternity'; old-fashioned Eng. (*for*) *aye* is the same word. Later formations on these lines are MHG *lützel* 'little', *wênec* 'do.' (> NHG *wenig*). The dat.pl. occasionally functions as an adverb: OHG *emmizîgên* 'continually' (*emmizîg* 'continual' > NHG *emsig* 'busy'), *hwîlum* (> MHG *wîlen* > NHG *weiland*) 'formerly, one-time' (*hwîla* 'time, while'), cf. archaic Eng. *whilom*; MHG *sicherlîchen* 'certainly', *vollelîchen* 'completely', *tiutischen* 'in German' (Helmbrecht: *sprich ein wort tiutischen*), from *sicherlîch*, *vollelîch*, *tiutisch*. See also the next section.

General development of adverbs from adjectives

In OHG, adverbs were most commonly formed from adjectives by adding to the root an inflexion *-o* (in origin the Indo-European ablative): *stark*, adv. *starko*, *skôni*, adv. *skôno*, whence MHG *stark*, adv. *starke*, *schœne*, adv. *schône*. But in the modern period the distinct adverbial form has been given up: *stark* and *schön* are both adjective and adverb.

OHG inherited from Germanic times the means of building compound adjectives by using a suffix *-lîh* identical with the noun *lîh* 'body'. Thus *lioblîh* > NHG *lieblich* originally meant something like 'having a nice body'. This suffix became exceptionally productive and eventually could be added to already existing adjectives without altering the sense: *wâr* 'true', *wârlîh* 'do.'; from this new adjective a corresponding adverb was regularly formed: *wârlîhho*. Then a further development set in. The whole ending *-lîhho* came to be regarded as one purely adverbial suffix which could be freely attached to the root of any adjective. There now arose pairs like *gitriuwi* (adj.) 'faithful', *gitriulîhho* (adv.), there being apparently no adjective **gitriulîh* at this stage. This development continued apace in MHG, but when, at the beginning of modern times, the uninflected adjective and adverb fell together, the former could always be used for the latter and any need for separate adverbial forms disappeared. Nevertheless, there are several relics of the older state of affairs in the present-day language: *wahr*, *wahrlich*, *sicher*, *sicherlich*, but usually there is a distinct semantic difference between the two forms: *frei*, *freilich*, *schwer*, *schwerlich*. Another common example is *reichlich*, generally used as an adverb.

The situation in this respect in OE was quite comparable to OHG, but the analogous possibilities were developed in reverse proportions. For whereas in modern German the uninflected adjective can always be an adverb and formation by suffix is rare, in English the latter is now virtually universal and the former very much restricted. The OHG adverbial suffix *-lîhho* is paralleled in OE *-līce* > NE *-ly*, hence *rich*, *richly*. OE had an adverbial ending *-a*, etymologically the same as OHG *-o*, but occurring rarely, the usual ending being *-e*, traceable to an Indo-European locative. In the subsequent evolution of the language both these terminations were regularly lost, so that in modern English as in modern German, such adverbs are indistinguishable from the corresponding adjectives. But only a few examples actually survive today: *hold tight*, *stand fast*, *it serves you right*.

Other modes of forming adverbs

Adverbs are sometimes contracted phrases: NHG *desgleichen*, *immer* (MHG *iemer*, OHG *io mêr* 'ever more'), *inzwischen* (OHG *in zwiskên*; see p. 181), *unterdessen*; archaic NHG *fürbaß* (MHG *fürebaz*, *füre* 'forwards', *baz* 'better'), *sintemal* (MHG *sint dem mâle* 'since the time'; cf. p. 238).

Adverbs may also be formed by shortening a word group: NHG *weg* for MHG *enwec* < OHG **in weg*, cf. Eng. *away* < OE *on weg*; North German colloquial *lang* for *entlang*, e.g. *ich gehe die Straße lang*. More frequently the shortening is accompanied by some (analogical) modification: *beiderseits* (cf. MHG *ze beider sît*), *gleichermaßen* (from *in gleichen Maßen*), *meistenteils* (from *den meisten Teil*).

IV · PRONOUNS

PERSONAL PRONOUNS

Introductory

It is at once apparent that the 1st and 2nd person pronoun contrast in certain ways with the 3rd person. The former are invariable, while the latter is modified for gender both in the singular and (in the medieval language) in the plural. The first two persons normally refer to animate objects, but the 3rd person is regularly used of inanimate things, too. It is syntactically significant that the 3rd person takes on a meaning only by virtue of its referring to a substantive already mentioned. This pronoun is therefore something of a demonstrative. Indeed, the boundary between it and the demonstrative proper is not always clear and the two are sometimes interchangeable: *wer hat dir die Geschichte erzählt? — Wolfi Schulz — glaubst du dem etwa?* or *glaubst du ihm etwa?* Both pronouns can take up a preceding noun: *ich kenne eine Frau, die* or *sie ist von ihrem Mann geschieden.* These things are traditional: MHG (Helmbrecht) *den dritten nenne ich iu noch, der was geheizen Erge* 'I'll name you the third one as well, he was called E.', NHG (Luther) *es stand ein Baum mitten im Lande, der war sehr hoch; und er wurde groß und mächtig,* (Grimm) *es war einmal ein armes Mädchen, dem waren Vater und Mutter gestorben.*

Somewhat in contrast to this 3rd person pronoun stands the invariable reflexive pronoun (p. 67).

3rd person pronoun

Although conventionally termed a personal pronoun, the 3rd person does, of course, refer to things as well as persons. In fact, the neuter *es* refers chiefly to things. During the modern period, on the other hand, the genitive of the 3rd person pronoun (*seiner, ihrer*) is normally used only of persons: *sie sind ihrer vier(e), man schämt sich seiner.* In reference to things the genitive of either *der* or *derselbe* is used: *wir danken für das angebotene Geld, bedürfen dessen* (*desselben*) *jedoch nicht*; an older example: (Luther) *du wirst deß Freude und Wonne haben* 'du wirst Freude und Wonne darüber empfinden' (Menge). The construction is mainly literary and not heard in ordinary colloquial. A novelist might write: *mein Freund meinte, ich sollte die Trauben nehmen, er habe deren* (*derselben*) *genug*, but the actually spoken words would more likely be *nimm die Trauben, ich habe genug davon.* Owing to the general decline of the genitive, the present construction is not particularly prominent; in addition, the pronoun *derselbe* is rather clumsy but, nevertheless, it is the only possible pronoun which can be used as a genitive of the object: *zwischen der Baulegung des Hauses und unserer Vollendung desselben lag ein langer Zeitraum.*

The genitive of the demonstrative frequently replaces the 3rd person possessive pronoun: *zwischen Erhalt des Materials und dessen Weiterleitung an den Kunden sind zwei ganze Wochen verstrichen.* This is normal practice where reference is to things; in official style, however, it is also usual when referring to persons: (welfare report) *das Kind und dessen Mutter*, contrasting with ordinary style: *das Kind und seine Mutter*. Since the demonstrative is never reflexive, it is regularly employed to avoid ambiguity: *sie zog zu ihrer Tante in deren Wohnung*. The pronoun *derselbe* may sometimes be appropriate; it could be used, for instance, in the first example in this paragraph: *zwischen Erhalt des Materials und Weiterleitung desselben an den Kunden* . . . .

An accusative or dative pronoun after a preposition regularly refers to a living creature; in reference to a thing a combination of an adverb of place with the preposition is, for the most part, to be preferred: *hier ist der Plan, wir können uns danach richten* (see p. 58). Certain prepositions, however, cannot combine with an adverb; in such cases, a pronoun must be used: *da er keinen Sack für die Kartoffeln mitgebracht hatte, mußte er ohne dieselben* (*sie, diese*) *zurückgehen* (here the colloquial language in particular would tend to omit the pronoun altogether); *im Zimmer stand ein Tisch, außer ihm war kein einziges Möbelstück zu sehen.* Although nom. acc. *es* is regularly used in reference to the contents of a clause (see next section), the dative, surprisingly enough, may not be so used; only the demonstrative is possible: *man warnte ihn vor der Reise, aber er maß dem keinerlei Bedeutung bei.*

In the older language the genitive pronoun could be used appositively with *ein* or *selb*: MHG (Hartmann) *daȥ tæte ich durch sîn eines haz* 'I would do that through hate of him alone', *man giht, er sî sîn selbes bote* 'it is said that he is his own messenger', (Wolfram) *bogen unde bölzelîn, die sneit er mit sîn selbes hant* 'bow and bolts, those he cut with his own hand'. The construction with *selb* is well known to Luther: *ich sage aber von Gewissen, nicht dein selbs, sondern des andern.* A relic only survives in the contemporary language, i.e as the genitive of the object: *die Verachtung seiner selbst* (where *selbst* is a modern development of *selbs*).

MHG *ez* 'it' had as its genitive a traditional form *es.* As a syntactical case this genitive has been lost today. Doubtless its demise was rapid from the moment it fell together phonetically with *ez*. It remains, however, in such phrases as *ich bin's gewohnt, ich bin's satt,* though the ordinary speaker is not aware of it; in his linguistic consciousness *'s* is an accusative. (Cf. 'Accusative with adjectives', p. 5.)

Extended use of es

The range of the neuter *es* is very elastic. As the subject of a construction with the verb 'to be' and a noun predicate, it can refer to all three genders, singular or plural. This function was already developed in the earliest recorded German: (Isidor) *hwer ist dhese man dher dhar scoldii chiboran werdan? chiwisso ist izs dher hôhisto* 'wer ist dieser Mann, der geboren werden sollte? Gewiß ist es der Höchste'. The construction is, of course, commonplace in the language of today: *da kommt jemand, es ist die Wäsche* 'the Laundry'; *dort sind drei Tiere zu sehen, Schafe sind es*; *sein Werdegang bietet keine Besonderheiten, es war der übliche Lebenslauf eines angesehenen Bürgers jener Zeit.* The pronoun appears as substitute for a nominal predicate, especially after the verb 'to be': *Sie sind reich, ich bin es nicht.* It may anticipate an infinitive: *es war manchmal schwer, die ganze Zeit im Unterricht aufzupassen.* It may refer to a whole clause, either as a subject: *es ist schon eine Weile her, seitdem ich dort war*, or as an object: *er kommt zu spät, ich weiß es.* As an object, *es* is used in many idioms without reference to an antecedent: *er hat es gut, schlecht*; *er macht es sich leicht, schwer*; *er nimmt es genau*; *er hat es auf das Geld abgesehen*; *er hat es sich mit ihr verdorben.* Like all the rest, this development is traditional: OHG (Otfrid) *oba er . . . wola thâhti, zi thisu er iz ni brâhti* 'if he meant well, he would not have let it come to this'.

The last group of examples shows that *es* has moved away from its pronominal function proper and that this shift is as old as OHG. Indeed, it is likely to be considerably older, for even before the literary period *es* had come to be employed purely as the formal subject of impersonal verbs (p. 169). In any case, the presence of the same innovation in OE disposes one to think in terms of a West Germanic origin.

From the earliest times German had used the adverb *thô*, *dô* as a sentence opener (p. 239). Then, in MHG, *ez* appears with the same function. This was no more than an extension of the already existing (and expanding) use of the pronoun as the formal subject of impersonal verbs. For long, however, it remained rather rare: (Nibelungenlied) *ez wuohs in Burgonden ein vil edel magedîn* 'there came to age in Burgundy a high-born maid', (Kudrun) *ez was ein wert vil breiter und hiez der Wülpensant* 'there was a very wide island and called the She-Wolf-Sand'; only at the beginning of the modern era did the new construction spring into prominence: (Luther) *es streit' für uns der rechte Mann*, (folk-song) *es ist ein Schnee gefallen*. Presumably, the rapid extension of this use of *es* was not unconnected with the disappearance of MHG *dô* which was lost at the end of the medieval period owing to confusion with *da* (p. 227). The construction has, of course, remained very general and is indispensable. Comparison with parallel sentences construed without *es* reveals semantic and stylistic differences: *es kommen neue Leute* is a neutrally couched statement, contrasting with *neue Leute kommen* where emphasis is on the subject; *es bläst der Wind* is poetic only, the ordinary language has *der Wind bläst*.

Possessive pronouns

The possessive pronouns of the 1st and 2nd person are based on the genitive of the personal pronoun. The 3rd person sg.masc. and neut. is formed in the same way from the reflexive stem, but for the 3rd person sg.fem. and the plural of all genders there was in OHG and generally in MHG no possessive pronoun. Its place was taken by the genitive case of the personal pronoun, as explained on p. 68.

In OHG the possessive, when used adjectivally, for the most part precedes its noun, but in a good number of instances it occurs postpositively. Comparative evidence suggests that the latter was originally the normal order, the former emphatic order.

But in West Germanic languages prepositive order became the norm regardless of emphasis, which was henceforth solely a matter of stress. The possessive may be used with the definite article but in general continues to follow the strong declension of adjectives; in addition, uninflected forms occur. Examples: (Otfrid) *ist sedal sînaȥ in himile gistâtaȥ* 'his throne is placed in heaven', *sô sliumo sô ih gihôrta thia stimmun thîna, / sô blîdta sih ingegin thir thaȥ mîn kind innan mir* 'as soon as I heard your voice, my child within me rejoiced because of you'. It is noticeable that archaic order is regularly preserved in the conservative vocative: (Ludwigslied) *Hludwîg, kuning mîn, hilph mînan liutin* 'Ludwig, my king, help my people'.

MHG continues these features to a certain extent. The definite article may still sometimes be found with the prepositive possessive: (Walther) *got müeȥe eȥ ze rehte scheiden / durch die sîne namen drî* 'may God justly decide it for the sake of his names three', but the weak declension (which began in Late OHG with Notker) is now more typical: (Neidhart) *dû muost ân die dînen wât* 'you must (go) without your dress'. Postpositive use has become rarer, though it remains common in the vocative: *frouwe mîn*, and often occurs in connexion with the article: *diu sêle mîn*; like the ordinary adjective (p. 39) it is generally uninflected in this position: (von Morungen) *daȥ dem herzen mîn so nâhen lac* 'which lay so near to my heart'.

Postpositive use, in NHG entirely petrified, lingers on in the older folk-song: *ich allein tu klagen / dem liebsten Buhlen mein*, and may be imitated in modern verse: (L. Hensel) *Vater, laß die Augen dein / über meinem Bette sein.* A solitary relic of archaic vocative order is preserved in *Vater unser* 'Our Father' (hence *das Vaterunser* 'paternoster'). The combination of definite article and possessive, now following the weak declension only, lives on in predicative use: *das Haus ist das meine*, cf. MHG (Nibelungenlied) *du muost der mîne wesen* 'you must be mine'; the extended form, e.g. *das Haus ist das meinige*, is now unusual, though often met with in older modern German. The ordinary construction today is *das Haus ist meines*; in high style we may find *das Haus ist mein*, a traditional form: MHG (Anon.) *dû bist mîn, ich bin dîn* 'you are mine, I am yours'. Compare further substantivizations of the type: *jedem das Seine, ewig die Deine.*

Notice the now obsolete appositive use of the possessive pronoun with *ein*: OHG (Otfrid) *ein thîn gisibba* 'a kinswoman of yours', MHG (Walther) *ein mîn wange* 'one of my cheeks'; similarly: (Helmbrecht) *ieclîch dîn geselle* 'each of your companions'.

Pronoun replaced by adverb

As is well known, a pronoun after a preposition usually refers to a person, whereas in reference to a thing the preposition is characteristically combined with the general adverb of place: *es liegt daran*. We notice at once that two stressings are possible: *darán* or *dáran*, the adverbial element, when stressed, retaining its full demonstrative value. Further, in interrogative and relative use: *wóran liegt es? ich sage dir, worán es liegt*. The adverb *hier* is also involved: *es liegt híeran*.

We are here dealing with a West Germanic innovation—Eng. *thereby*, *-in*, *-of*, *whereby*, *hereby*, etc., are still familiar—and the construction is accordingly found in the oldest texts: OHG (Otfrid) *thaȥ fulin brâhtun; nâmun sie thô iro wât, legitun tharûf . . . thaȥ er thâroba sâȥi* '(they) brought the colt; then they took their raiment, laid (it) upon it . . . so that he might sit on it'. It will be seen that OHG had two forms corresponding to NHG *dar-*, namely an accusative *dar-* (from *dara* 'thither') and a dative *dâr-* (from *do*. 'there'). The difference was preserved intact in thirteenth-century MHG: (Helmbrecht) *diu wâren al dar ûf genât* 'they were all sewn on to it', *den buosem er dâ mit beslôȥ* 'he fastened the front (of the jacket) with it'. But following the general lengthening of short vowels in open syllables in later MHG (*dar ûf* > *darûf*, whence *dârûf*, etc.), this old distinction was obliterated.

The present construction plays an important role in anticipating, sometimes optionally, a subordinate clause: *ich kann den Unfall nur dadurch erklären, daß der Strom einen Augenblick unterbrochen war*; *wir sind stolz* (*darauf*), *das Spiel gewonnen zu haben* or *daß wir das Spiel gewannen*; *er hindert uns* (*daran*), *unsere Aufgabe zu erfüllen*.

A number of intransitive and reflexive verbs are joined to a noun complement by a preposition: *er strebt nach Glück*, *er verpflichtet sich zu besseren Leistungen*. These may require a preposition when joined to an infinitive. But apart from one or two exceptions (pp. 153 ff.), the infinitive cannot take another preposition on top of *zu*. The preposition required is, therefore, combined with the demonstrative adverb *da* which functions as the pronominal representative of the infinitive: *der Mensch strebt danach, glücklich zu werden*; *er verpflichtet sich dazu, bessere Leistungen zu erzielen.* With some verbs the preposition is optional, e.g. in the last sentence where *dazu* may be omitted, and similarly *ich zweifle nicht (daran), daß sie kommen wird.* In earlier literature the preposition may be omitted where it is obligatory today: (Wieland) *ich verzweifle doch, es jemals so weit zu bringen*, now *verzweifle doch daran*, (Lessing) *Geschwätz, das nur abzielen kann, näheren Untersuchungen vorzubauen*, now *darauf abzielen.*

In the standard language of today adverb and preposition are always inseparably combined. But the spoken language, in particular the colloquial of the north, sometimes divides them: *da wird man nicht dick von, da kann ich nichts für.* This is an ancient trait, for such divisions are commonplace in medieval German: MHG (Walther) *dâ merket alle ein wunder an* 'daran nehmt alle ein Wunder wahr', (Gottfried) *hie vâhet man den bern mite* 'hiermit fängt man den Bären'. Occurrences are still frequent in Luther: *ist das euer jüngster Bruder, da ihr mir von sageten?* An interesting example is *der Ort, da du aufstehest* "the place whereon thou standest". This is what Luther wrote, but in editions printed today one finds instead *der Ort, darauf du stehest*, for the modern reader —unless exceptionally well informed on the syntactical possibilities —would needs interpret the original words as meaning 'the place whereon thou gettest up'. Subsequently, the separation of adverb and preposition was found too inelegant for literature, though instances occur even in the classical period: (Goethe) *verlorne Liebe, wo ist da Ersatz für?*

An extension of the present construction, in which the demonstrative adverb is stated in anticipation, has been attested for some time: (Chr. Weise) *da kommen wir nicht dazu*, (Goethe) *da ist er ein Meister drinne.* Such usage is a feature of much spoken German today: *da kann man nichts dafür.* Another, less prominent development, also rooted in oral language, is the suppression of the adverbial element altogether: (Goethe, Letters) *wenigstens bin ich mit zufrieden, ich weiß kein Wort von.* This construction, too, is still part of the everyday colloquial of certain districts.

Exceptions to replacement rule

It must now be recalled that the use of the adverb instead of the pronoun, as outlined in the previous section, is not universal. One could say to a small child: *da hast du einen Buntstift, du kannst mit ihm zeichnen*, and it may be felt that *mit ihm* rather than *damit* is the *mot juste* for this context. Such things can naturally appear in print and seem to be on the increase, though some occurrences may be criticized as clumsy or inept: (Master's Certificate, Bakers' Guild) *NN ist berechtigt, den Titel eines Meisters im Bäckergewerbe zu führen und Lehrlinge in ihm auszubilden.* In some cases the construction with the pronoun is to be preferred: *er behauptete, seine Philosophie sei die einzig wahre, nur durch sie könne man die Welt erfassen*, for *dadurch* in this position would tend to refer to the whole of the preceding clause rather than to its subject only. Examples from literature: (Fontane) *neben dem Zaun aber, in gleicher Linie mit ihm, stand eine grüngestrichene Bank*, (Ebner-Eschenbach) *in der Mitte stand ein Tisch und auf ihm eine Anzahl irdener Teller*; similarly: (Luther, Psalm XIX) *auch wird dein Knecht durch sie* (the Commandments) *erinnert*—(Menge) *auch dein Knecht läßt durch sie sich mahnen.*

Where in the oldest German the neuter refers to a whole clause or to some idea, the pronoun was not replaced by the adverb as in the later language: (Otfrid) *then wân zellu ih bi thaȥ* 'ich spreche meine Meinung darüber aus'. The instrumental is noticeably common: (Otfrid) *ward after thiu inscritan . . . ein halb jâr* 'danach war ein halbes Jahr vergangen' (see also p. 35). MHG to some extent inherited this practice: (Walther) *mîner sorgen ich vergaȥ, / schiere entslief ich umbe daȥ* 'meine Sorgen vergaß ich, darum schlief ich rasch ein'. But the construction soon declined and the position in Late MHG is not unlike that in the modern language. Petrified relics of the old use survive in *indem, nachdem, seitdem, vordem*, where, however, the dative *dem* has taken the place of the original instrumental *diu*.

In line with the preceding are pairs like *worüber* or *über was lacht ihr? worum* or *um was handelt es sich?* where the uncombined preposition is more usual in the spoken language. Since *wem* has long been restricted to persons, the neuter *was* is now also found after prepositions governing the dative: *worauf* or *auf was liegst du?* Further: (Schiller) *zu was Besserm sind wir geboren*, in which construction *was* is, as often, interchangeable with *etwas*.

Certain prepositions cannot combine with an adverb (p. 54).

Pronouns of address

The oldest German distinguishes solely between *dû* used in addressing one person only, and *ir* used in addressing more than one person: (Samaritan Woman) *hêrro, in thir wigit scîn, thaz thû maht forasago sîn . . . unser altmâga suohton hia genâda; / thoh ir sagant kicorana thia bita in Hierosolima* 'Sir, it is apparent from your words (lit. 'in you') that you must be a prophet . . . our forebears sought grace here; yet you (i.e. the Jews) say that prayer is heeded (only) in Jerusalem'.

This primordial distinction was then disturbed by the introduction of forms of address meant to show, in the first place, subservience to those in authority. The origin of this development has been traced to the imperial *nos* 'we' used by the later Roman emperors. A man who spoke of himself as *nos* was accordingly addressed as *vos* and this person of the pronoun came to be the general form of address to a superior. The medieval German emperors imitated this principle in their official (Latin) documents and eventually Ger. *ir* began to be used in the same way. But it was no longer necessarily an expression of subservience, it was re-evaluated—when is not known exactly—as the pronoun of conventional politeness. As such it seems to have been used by the chivalrous classes among themselves. The minnesinger has: (Walther) *'nemt, frouwe, disen kranz' / alsô sprach ich zeiner wol getânen maget* ' "lady, accept this garland" '—thus I spoke to a fair maiden'. Such usage is commonplace in the Nibelungenlied among those on familiar terms with each other, though alternating with *dû*. Kriemhild uses the plural to her mother: *waz saget ir mir von manne?* 'what are you saying to me about a husband?', but Ute replies using the singular: *soltu immer herzenlîche zer werlde werden vrô, / daz gesciht von mannes minne* 'if you are ever to be truly happy in this world, that will come from a husband's love'. It was the same at Xanten; this must represent the genuine usage of the aristocratic circles of the day.

By the lower orders, however, *ir* was used as a mark of respect for their superiors; they also used it when dealing with strangers of unknown rank. There are several examples in Helmbrecht, where the formal *ir* contrasts with the familiar *dû*: (the farmer's son returns home, having supposedly got on in the world) *sprach daz frîwîp und der kneht: 'bis willekomen, Helmbrecht?' / nein, si entâten, / eȝ wart in widerrâten; / si sprâchen: juncherre mîn, ir sult gote willekomen sîn* 'did the free woman and the farm-hand say: "be welcome, H."? No, they did not, they were told not to; they said: "Young Sir, you are heartily welcome" '. Then Helmbrecht tries to hide his identity until at length his father exlaims: *und bist dûȝ niht Helmbreht, mîn kint, / sît ir ein Bêheim oder ein Wint, / so vart hin zuo den Winden* 'and if you are not H., my son, if you are a Bohemian or a Slovene, then clear off to the Slovenes'.

After the end of the Middle Ages, the use of *ir* as a polite form between members of the same class seems to have become normal, so that the difference between *ihr* and *du* in Early NHG was comparable to that between French *vous* and *tu*. Indeed, we suppose that French precept was decisive from the beginning; it was the vogue of the age. This position is still reflected, unchanged, in Yiddish. English with *you* and *thou* passed through this stage, too, but then went a step further, eliminating the singular form in ordinary use altogether.

In the seventeenth century still more courteous forms of address were developed in German. These involved the 3rd person pronoun and arose as follows. One can, even today in some places, notice a tendency to avoid the pronoun of direct address in certain situations. Instead of the forthright *was Sagen Sie dazu, Herr Lehrer?* one may hear the more deferential *was sagt der Herr Lehrer dazu?* This principle led, from the beginning of the seventeenth century, to the use of *Er* and *Sie* (with the 3rd sg. of the verb, of course) referring back in the first place to *der Herr, die Frau,* as often noticed in the texts: (Lessing) *Herr Wachtmeister, braucht Er keine Frau Wachtmeisterin?*, (Uhland) *Frau Wirtin, hat Sie gut Bier und Wein? / Wo hat Sie ihr schönes Töchterlein?* The seventeenth century was the heyday of honorific flourishes and the position of the 3rd person pronoun was strengthened by the continual employment of such expressions as *Euer Gnade* 'Your Grace'. But more than this, plural phrases like *Euer Gnaden* 'Your Graces' came into fashion as hyper-polite modes of address. This development provoked a corresponding employment of the 3rd pl. *Sie* as the most respectful pronoun of all; one could now address a person as 'They'.

By the second half of the eighteenth century the plural *Sie* had established itself but had not yet replaced its competitors. The status of the various pronouns is preserved in the literature of the age. We may take Lessing's *Minna von Barnhelm*. Here the educated persons address each other as *Sie* (pl.), even when intimate, as Minna to Tellheim: *ich soll Ihnen verzeihen, daß ich noch Ihre Minna bin?* The *Wirt* is similarly addressed by his guests. The *Graf*, however, *in loco parentis* addresses Minna as *du*, though she replies with *Sie* (pl.), which must reflect the family situation among the upper classes. Inferiors also use *Sie* (pl.) but only to their superiors; to each other they use *Er* / *Sie* (sg.), unless very intimate, when the pronoun of familiarity *du* is employed. Superiors also use these terms in the same way when speaking to inferiors. Tellheim addresses his ill-mannered *Bedienter*, however, as *Ihr*.

Today the situation is more stabilized: *du* with its plural *ihr* are the pronouns of familiarity, *Sie* the polite pronoun, singular and plural. Generally speaking, the practice of *Duzen* implies intimacy or close comradeship. A man using *du* to his mates at work may still use *Sie* when talking to his neighbours at home and continue this way all his life. Young children are, of course, addressed with *du*, but eventually, after traversing an embarrassing phase of uncertainty somewhere in the middle teens, young people become old enough to be addressed as *Sie*. The girls tend to reach maturity in this respect a little before the boys. Some closed organizations, notably trade unions and left-wing political parties, employ the pronouns of familiarity officially in their internal business. Public notices and advertisements commonly use them, too, very often in the singular: *sichere Dein Fahrrad, werde Sozialfürsorgerin*, sometimes in the plural, too: *gebt Acht im Straßenverkehr, wählt C. D. U.*, but also *gib Acht . . . , wähle . . . .* Similarly: *denke dir eine beliebige Zahl, vermehre sie durch 5, multipliziere die Summe mit 3 . . . .*

As a result of pressure from *Sie* (pl.) the pronouns *Er* and *Sie* (sg.) ceased to be indicative of respect and virtually turned into the opposite, being used when speaking to inferiors. As such, the singular pronoun survived into the present century. Only a few decades ago it was possible, in some localities, to hear workmen or serving women so addressed. Recent social changes have doubtless given the *coup de grâce* to this construction or at least brought it to the verge of extinction. The much older polite *Ihr* fared better, especially in the south where it is still a vital entity, as explained in the next section.

Pronouns of address in the South

The situation in Bavaria and Austria is deserving of brief mention. The MHG Bavarian plural pronoun nom. *eȥ*, acc.dat. *enc*—comparison with other Germanic languages shows that this was originally the dual pronoun 'you two'—lives on in modern Bavarian as *es* or *ös*, *enk*, used instead of *ihr*, *euch*. These are purely dialect words but are very widespread and consequently, in this area, the pronoun *Ihr* could be reserved as a polite form, plural as well as singular. When 3rd person pronouns came into vogue, they could not shake the position of *Ihr* in the plural, though they could oust it from the singular. As a result, over much of the countryside today, *Sie* is the polite singular, *Ihr* the polite plural. Where dial. *es* (*ös*) has declined, *Ihr* may be found indifferently as the polite or familiar plural. In Vienna, the use of the dialect pronoun is considered vulgar, but curiously enough even educated Viennese use the nominative every time they form the 2nd pl. of a verb. Standard Ger. *habt ihr* in the Viennese *Umgangssprache* becomes *habts ihr*, i.e. with two pronouns, the no longer recognized dialect pronoun being reduced to *s* and *ihr* added for comprehension. The 2nd pl. of the verb thus appears to be *habts*, not *habt*. By analogy, Standard Ger. *ihr habt* becomes Viennese *ihr habts*; by the same token, the imper.pl. is *habts*!

We have already referred to the use of the polite and familiar pronouns in the medieval family circle. Such things persisted for a very long time. In some country districts of the south, at any rate, children may to this day use a polite pronoun when addressing parents or older relatives.

Omission of pronoun

In Indo-European the pronoun was not used as a subject of a verb unless emphasis was intended, the ending of the verb being sufficient to express the person. This original stage is duly reflected in Latin: *rego* 'I rule', *regis* 'thou rulest', and will have been typical of Common Germanic too, as is to be inferred from Gothic and from the archaic diction of the Old Norse Eddic poems. But German had already abandoned this position by the beginning of the recorded epoch, for the oldest OHG is seen to make regular use of a pronoun when no emphasis at all was intended. Neverthe-less, the pronoun was not as general as it became in the later language: (Muspilli) *wânit sih kinâda diu wênaga sêla: / ni ist in kihuctin himiliskin gote, / wanta hiar in werolti after ni werkôta* 'the wretched soul hopes for grace for itself, but (it) is not remembered by heavenly God, because here in the world (it) did not act accordingly'. More often, the pronoun is omitted in translations from Latin. How far this can be due to faulty translation technique is sometimes an open question, but it seems that the unambiguous verbal endings of OHG could, to some degree, tolerate the omission of the pronoun: (Tatian) *thû fundi huldi mit gote; sênonu inphâhis in reve inti gibiris sun inti ginemnis sînan namon . . .* (invenisti enim gratiam apud deum; ecce concipies in utero et paries filium et vocabis nomen eius . . .) "thou hast found favour with God; and behold, thou shalt conceive in thy womb, and bring forth a son, and shalt call his name . . .". The subject pronoun was not used in the hortative construction (p. 106).

By the MHG period the use of the pronoun had become regular; in any case the partial loss of the distinct verbal endings of OHG made it as indispensable as it is in the modern language. Only in respect of the 2nd person imperative does German, in common with other languages, continue age-old practice; the pronoun is never used except for emphasis: (Luther) *sprich du in meiner Sache und schaue du auf das Recht.*

Exceptionally, the subject pronoun may not be expressed in the modern language. The 1st sg. pronoun is commonly omitted in *bitte* (always omitted in *bitte bitte* 'don't mention it'), *danke*, *bedaure sehr*, in the military *melde gehorsamst*, and in the respectful greeting *hab(e) die Ehr(e)* which survives to some extent in Austria. The pronoun is always omitted in the expression *sage und schreibe* 'just imagine it' and in the Austrian *küß die Hand*, a greeting to ladies or an expression of thanks, but not heard so much these days. The modern conjunction *geschweige* is in origin the 1st sg.pres.indic. of *geschweigen* (= 'verschweigen') with suppression of the pronoun. As a literary mannerism, omission of the 1st sg. pronoun becomes fairly common in the period of *Sturm und Drang*; examples from Goethe: *habe nun, ach! Philosophie . . . durchaus studiert*; *bin's wohl zufrieden, wollt' es wäre von jeher geschehen*; *schicke dir hier den alten Götzen*, similarly Claudius: *bin Freund und komme nicht zu strafen.*

In the enclitic position the 2nd sg. pronoun is particularly closely linked to the verb. Indeed, the *t*-suffix of the 2nd sg. of the verb arose as a result of this intimate attachment: OHG *nimis du* > *nimistu*, whence MHG *nimestu* (an often attested orthography), then through false division *du nimest*. One can observe in the conversational language of today how much the enclitic pronoun, unless stressed for emphasis, becomes reduced phonetically, even to the point of inaudibility. This will have been so in former times, and explains the fairly frequent absence of the pronoun in this position in literature: (Goethe) *kannst dich nicht vom Fehl befrein, / wirst du andern gern verzeihn*, (Schiller) *denkst auch noch an mein Mädchen?* The proclitic pronoun may also occasionally be missing: (Goethe) *füllest wieder Busch und Tal / still mit Nebelglanz, / lösest endlich auch einmal / meine Seele ganz*. We notice that this pronoun may now and again be dropped in *Umgangssprache*, as in the often heard *hast recht*, *kannst es glauben*, while on the lower level of unrestrained popular speech such omissions are quite common: *kommst mir zu spät*, *machst schon wieder eine Schweinerei*.

As in English, it is not unusual for the 3rd sg.neut. pronoun to be dispensed with in popular speech, thus commonly: *wird gemacht* or *läßt sich machen* (for *es wird*, *es läßt*), similarly: *geht wieder nicht* (e.g. a car, a clock). In ordinary speaking this pronoun is sometimes omitted (or is inaudible) before *sind*, and of this there are examples in literature: (Schiller) *laß sie gehen! sind Tiefenbacher*. In archaizing style the 3rd sg.masc. pronoun may be omitted before verbs of saying, calling, etc.: (Schiller) *und sprach's und schiffte schnell sich ein*. The pronoun is frequently absent in impersonal constructions. As the formal subject in the impersonal passive construction, *es* is only used when standing first: *es wurde mir gesagt*, but *mir wurde gesagt*. As the subject of an impersonal verb it is often left off before *sich*, doubtless as the result of phonetic assimilation: (insurance notice) *sollte sich ergeben, daß eine Wertsteigerung eingetreten ist, so beantragen Sie bitte eine Nachversicherung*. For regular omission of *es* with impersonal verbs see pp. 169 ff.

The polite pl. *Sie* is occasionally not expressed. Notice *gestatten* used in (rather old-world) introductions: *gestatten, Hauptmann Meier*, whereas *gestatten Sie!* means 'allow me!' (to help you into your coat, for instance). The pronoun can be suppressed after verbs of excusing when the tone is perfunctory. People pushing their way through a bus often say *verzeihen!* or *entschuldigen!* the difference being regional.

As an occasional feature of high style, the unexpressed pronominal subject is to be identified in the oblique case in a preceding sentence: MHG (Kudrun) *eȥ möhte uns wol gelingen und bræhten dir die frouwen* 'we could well succeed and bring the ladies to you', NHG (Luther) *das Meer bedeckte sie, und sanken unter wie Blei*; *es kam eine Furcht über sie alle, und redeten mit einander und sprachen*, (Goethe) *die Augen täten ihm sinken, trank nie einen Tropfen mehr.* The unexpressed subject may likewise be implied from a preceding possessive pronoun: (Luther) *und alsobald fiel es von seinen Augen wie Schuppen, und ward wieder sehend*, (Goethe) *jeden Nachklang fühlt mein Herz / froh- und trüber Zeit, / wandle zwischen Freud' und Schmerz / in der Einsamkeit.*

Reflexive pronoun

High German has preserved from earliest times an exclusively reflexive 3rd person pronoun, i.e. a pronoun which can refer only to the subject of the sentence. This is *sich*, in form and originally in function also, an accusative (cf. *mich*, *dich*), paralleled in Gothic, Old Norse *sik* and cognate with Latin *se*; like these it is indifferent to number or gender. This pronoun is, however, not found in English, in Frisian or in the oldest Low German. Among the West Germanic languages High Ger. *sich* is therefore an isolated archaism. Nevertheless, it managed to stage something of a comeback, for it was later borrowed into Low German (including Dutch) to become a regular feature there.

The reflexive pronoun was used in older German essentially as it is in the language of today, except that it could not be used as a dative. One infers from Gothic and Old Norse that an OHG reflexive dat. **sir* (cf. *mir*, *dir*) disappeared before the literary period, and the non-reflexive pronoun came to be used in its place. Examples are: OHG (Notker) *wanda diser, ih meino* Neptunus, *prâhta mit imo sîna chenun* Stigem 'for this one, I mean Neptune, brought with him his spouse Styx', MHG (Hartmann) *er nam im manege schouwe* lit. 'he took for himself many a look'. Luther still commonly uses it: *andern hat er geholfen, und kann ihm selber nicht helfen.* After this time dative use of *sich* quickly increases to become the accepted norm, but the older construction may still be found in the literature of the eighteenth century: (Wieland, trans. of Macbeth) *wer hätte gedacht, daß der alte Mann so viel Blut in ihm gehabt* *hätte?* In the colloquial of Bavaria and Austria the non-reflexive pronoun is common to this day, though now declining: *hat sie viel Geld bei ihr? haben Sie die Karten bei Ihnen?*

(*a*) *Changes in the genitive and possessive pronoun*

OHG, MHG gen.sg. *sîn*, NHG *seiner* and the corresponding possessive (OHG, MHG *sîn*, NHG *sein*) belong to the reflexive stem and were in the first place used solely as reflexives, as analogous forms in Gothic and Old Norse confirm. In the earliest German, however, they are already seen to be doing service for the non-reflexive 3rd person pronoun as follows: the gen.sg. of *er* is *sîn*, the possessive *sîn* is used for masc. and neut. The one-time difference between the reflexive and non-reflexive possessive pronoun had thus ceased to exist. Developments took a different course in the fem.sg. and the plural of all genders. Here the non-reflexive was generalized, i.e. fem.sg. *ira*, pl. *iro* lit. 'of her, of them' > MHG *ir*. This arrangement has remained, with only minor changes: the invariable MHG *ir* was converted into an inflecting form by the beginning of the modern period after the analogy of *mein*, *dein*, etc., and the gen.sg. of the pronoun is now *ihrer* parallel to *seiner*. The beginnings of this conversion, however, go back to Classical MHG, as occasional early attestations prove: (Wolfram) *ir heilic verch und iriu bein* 'their holy flesh and their bones'.

(*b*) *Ambiguity*

The above development, which destroyed the reflexive principle as far as *sîn* and its modern descendants are concerned, led to ambiguity. As it stands, the sentence *er schämt sich seiner* means either he is ashamed of himself or of some other person. True, the matter need be left in no doubt if the former sense is meant, for this may be conveyed by adding *selbst* (or *selber*), i.e. *er schämt sich seiner selbst.* But there is no such simple way of expressing the second meaning unambiguously.

The sentence *er hat sein Geld* means either he has his own money or somebody else's. English, which if it ever knew the Germanic reflexive pronoun, lost it before the first literary records, is in practice in the same position as German as regards ambiguity: *he has his money*, where *his* is the genitive of *he*, i.e. a non-reflexive form syntactically comparable to OHG *ira*, etc. Certainly both languages can state the reflexive meaning by further qualifying the noun: *er hat sein eigenes Geld*, exactly like Eng. *he has his own money*. Indeed, one might say that *eigen* was on the way to taking over the functions of a reflexive. Thus OHG (Otfrid) *thô fuarun thie ginôȥa . . . zi eiginemo lante* 'then the companions journeyed to their own land'; and still today: *sie haben eigene Schier* may mean *sie haben die eigenen, ihre eigenen Schier*. Furthermore, modern German, at any rate, can often employ the non-reflexive *dessen, deren* (p. 54). Yet the salient fact remains that the clear-cut distinction between reflexive and non-reflexive possessive pronoun, present in Common Germanic, has been lost in West Germanic and only very imperfectly replaced. Only the Scandinavian languages today observe the simple, ancient distinction, e.g. Danish *han har sine penge* 'he has his (own) money', *han har hans penge* 'he has his (somebody else's) money'. They are faithful to Indo-European tradition, also seen in Lat. *suus* beside *eius*, etc.

Quite distinct from the above are the few cases of ambiguity which arise when it is not clear whether the (genuine, living) reflexive refers to the subject or the object: *er ließ den Mann zu sich kommen* accordingly means either 'he ordered the man to come to him' or 'he waited until the man recovered consciousness'. Such a sentence is perfectly normal; only the wider context can convey the actual meaning.

(*c*) *Reciprocal use*

The reflexive pronoun is often used reciprocally: *sie haben sich gefunden* (said of people sharing the same sentiments). This usage is traditional as far as *sich* in the accusative is concerned. It easily developed from such reflexives as *sich einigen, gesellen, treffen* where the pronoun refers to different persons. Since MHG reciprocal *sich* has been competing with *einander* (p. 70), and many expressions make use of either pronoun indifferently: *die beiden haben sich/einander lieb, sie tuscheln unter sich/einander*. But despite competition, the use of reciprocal *sich* has greatly increased in the modern period when its extension to the dative led to new possibilities: *sie geben, reichen sich die Hände*. We may notice other modern developments. Reciprocal *sich* is today often reinforced by the adverb *gegenseitig*, e.g. *sie beschimpfen sich* (*gegenseitig*). A few intransitive verbs are now frequently used with reciprocal *sich*, e.g. *sich streiten, zanken*, also *sich beratschlagen, verabreden*. One party can be made the subject and the second joined by *mit*, hence *er streitet, zankt sich mit ihm*, commonly, too, *er schreibt sich, trifft sich mit ihm*; further: *er versteht sich mit ihm.* The pronoun thus loses its reciprocal character and becomes reflexive again. Presumably, this development is an imitation of ordinary reflexive use as found in *sich mit jemandem versöhnen, vertragen*, etc.

(*d*) *Suppression of reflexive pronoun*

The reflexive pronoun is often suppressed before the present participle: *die Mutter opfert sich auf*, but *die aufopfernde Mutter*, hence *die aufopfernde Pflege*. Similarly: *ein hingebender Mensch, eine herablassende Geste*. Older examples, however, may no longer be usual: (Schiller) *die ganze mitfreuende Gesellschaft*, (Heine) *über meinen Leichnam niederbeugend*, modern style in these cases preferring *sich mitfreuende, sich niederbeugend*. The vagaries of linguistic evolution can make a classical occurrence sound much out of place today: Schiller's *die türmende Stadt* all too easily recalls the modern colloquialism *türmen* 'clear off'. The pronoun cannot be omitted if used reciprocally, as this would alter the sense: *die Hunde beißen sich* (i.e. *einander*), *die sich beißenden Hunde*.

The infinitives of a number of reflexive verbs are commonly used as nouns; these do not take the pronoun: *das Benehmen* beside *sich benehmen*; similarly: *das Entzücken, Erbarmen, Sträuben, Vergnügen, Verhalten*. But in the case of casually substantivized infinitives the use of the pronoun is optional, unless necessary for the sense: *'finden Sie, daß das (Sich-)Hinsetzen Ihnen auch Schwierigkeiten macht?' fragte der Arzt den Gehbehinderten*; *das Sichärgern hat wohl selten jemandem geholfen.*

(*e*) *einander*

The invariable pronoun *einander* arose in MHG: (Walther) *sie liuhtent beide ein ander an* 'they both shine upon each other', and goes back to the predicative use of OHG *ein andremu* (dat.), *ein anderen* (acc.) 'another'. It is synonymous with reciprocal *sich*, with which it is often idiomatically interchangeable (p. 69).

DEMONSTRATIVE PRONOUNS

The general demonstrative der

The general demonstrative pronoun is *der*, traditionally used both substantivally and as an adjective. In the former use, the modern language has certain strengthened forms: *dessen*, *deren*, *denen*, with a special gen.pl. *derer*, only found when the demonstrative stands before a relative pronoun: (Hebbel) *reißt alle Blumen ab, sogar die Knospen derer, die erst kommen*; but should a noun stand between demonstrative and relative, then *deren* occurs: (Kleist) *trockne die Tränen von deren Gesicht, die um mich weinen.* Occasional aberrations from the present accepted standard are found in older writings. For instance, Goethe uses a strengthened form attributively: *auf denen Papieren, die sie haben*, now *den* (or *denjenigen*).

When an adnominal genitive is dependent on a preceding noun, the latter must, in the contemporary language, be represented by a demonstrative pronoun: *sein Rücken ist schwarz gestreift wie der* (or *derjenige*) *eines Zebras*. But in older style this pronoun could be omitted, as still in English: (Heine) *sein Rücken ist schwarz gestreift wie eines Zebras*, (Luther) *zur selbigen Stunde gingen hervor Finger als einer Menschenhand.*

The neuter *das* is syntactically close to *es*. It can refer to a noun regardless of number or gender: *das ist mein Vater, meine Mutter, das sind meine Geschwister*; *die Liebe, das ist das Einzige.* It can also refer to the content of a whole clause: *er arbeitet gern im Garten — das ist bei ihm eine Art Ausgleichsübung*. In some examples *das* has so far surrendered its demonstrative force that it can become the formal subject of an impersonal verb: *das sieht nach Regen aus, das riecht hier nach Farbe* are semantically identical with *es sieht . . . , es riecht. . . .* Such use is, however, mainly confined to colloquial style, though it is not absent from literature: (Goethe) *das drängt und stößt, das rutscht und klappert*. Eng. *that* has not gone so far.

The functions of the demonstrative pronoun sometimes overlap with those of the 3rd person pronoun, and in certain syntagmas the personal and demonstrative pronouns may be interchangeable (pp. 53 f.). Since OHG times the demonstrative pronoun has been employed as a relative (pp. 243 f.).

The demonstrative pronoun is commonly used adjectivally: *Sie nehmen am besten die Straße* 'your best plan is to take this (*or* that) road'. We note that the pronoun is stressed (ˈ*die* ˈ*Straße*) and that the meaning is indifferently 'this' or 'that' depending on the context—if the sentence is envisaged as the answer to a direction inquiry, then the context will be the way the speaker points. Since everything hinges on pronunciation, this use of the demonstrative is much more usual in the spoken than in the written language which, of course, does not normally indicate stress. It is, however, possible to use spaced type: *wohnt er in d e m Haus?* With some clichés only the stressed form is possible; these need cause no alteration in print: *von der Sorte gibt's mehr, als Sie denken* 'there are more of that sort than you think'.

Historically speaking, the definite article is the unstressed form of the general demonstrative *der* (above), cf. pp. 86 f.

dieser, jener

In preliterary times a new demonstrative was created by the addition of a deictic particle **se* to the already existing general demonstrative, hence (with transference of the inflexions to the end) OHG *thesêr, desêr* 'this/dieser'. The new word had a more specific meaning than the general demonstrative and contrasted with OHG *(j)ener* 'that (yon)/jener'. In recent German, at any rate, *jener* is not much used in the spatial sense: 'that house (there)' as opposed to 'this house (here)' is *das Haus dort*. The old contrast, still seen in *diesseits, jenseits*, has generally given place to a new opposition *das hier, das dort*, i.e. the general demonstrative (or the article, according to stress) is specified by an unambiguous adverb. A very common combination, parallel to the foregoing, is *das da*, but this idiom is semantically less precise, since *da* is the general demonstrative adverb and can mean either 'here' or 'there' as the context requires. It is also subject to regional fluctuations; in the south the commoner meaning is 'here', in the north 'there'. Both *dieser* and *jener* are chiefly used as (attributive) adjectives, but substantival use has always been possible as well: OHG (Notker) *enêr hîez in unsera wîs Ôtacher, tiser hîez Thioterih* 'the former was called in our language O., the latter was called T. / jener hieß in unserer Sprache O., dieser hieß T.' The neuter pronoun *dies* has always been common, parallel to *das*, e.g. *dies sind meine Wünsche*.

Primitive Germanic had a separate root-word for 'this', which German inherited. It seems, however, to have declined very early, but traces of it have been detected in the words *heute, heuer* lit. 'this day, this year', also (dial.) *heint* 'tonight' lit. 'this night'; etymological details on p. 36. The same root appears in the adverb *hier*.

derjenige

There arose in the twelfth century the pronoun *der jene*, which owed its article to the influence of *der selbe* (see below). It survived until the early seventeenth century: (Opitz) *dem jenen, der ihren Ruhm erhöht.* In the fifteenth century the extended form *der jenige* appears. It was, like *der jene*, at first used with a relative clause, as it still may be today when it (optionally) replaces the general demonstrative: *derjenige* (or *der*), *der es beobachtete.* In modern use *derjenige* also represents a preceding noun in connexion with a preposition, again as an alternative to the general demonstrative: *nicht diesen Garten meinte er, sondern den(jenigen) mit dem großen Rasen.* It is also found with an adnominal genitive dependent on a preceding noun (see example, p. 71). We are dealing with a purely literary formation, and even in the written style it is, by comparison with the general demonstrative, somewhat stilted.

derselbe

The pronoun of identity *derselbe* goes back to OHG *der selbo* which replaced an earlier *der samo* (cf. Eng. *the same*) known from occasional occurrences in the oldest glosses. Eng. *selfsame* incorporates both vocables. Apart from a limited substantival use of the neut.sg. (*dasselbe gilt für alle, es kommt auf dasselbe heraus*) the word is today, in its original function as the pronoun of identity, only used adjectivally: *dieselbe Schule, dasselbe Kind, er ist immer derselbe*, syntactically equivalent to *er ist immer der alte.* As a substantive *derselbe* is today essentially a demonstrative pronoun.

Semantically it is no great step from the pronoun of identity to the demonstrative. It is sometimes scarcely possible to distinguish between them: (Chamisso) *es* (the cross) *war dasselbe, das er sonst getragen.* From early times OHG *der selbo* is seen to have the demonstrative sense as well: (Otfrid) *zi iru sprah thô ubarlût / ther selbo druhtines drût* 'then spoke clearly to her that confidant of the Lord', (Notker) *tero selbûn erdo, also luzzelero wider demo himile, ist echert ter fîerdo teil besezen fone uns chundên menniskôn* 'of this earth, so small in comparison with heaven, only the fourth part is occupied by human beings known to us'. A good MHG example is Hartmann (Armer Heinrich, 29) *er las daz selbe mære* 'he read this tale', for in this case one manuscript actually shows the variant reading *er las ditz mære*. Examples continue into Early NHG: (Luther) *dies Gerücht erscholl in dasselbe ganze Land* "the fame hereof went abroad into all that land".

After this time the adjectival use of *derselbe* in the demonstrative sense ceases, but as a demonstrative substantive it has continued in the language down to the present time. As has been shown (pp. 53 f.) the (general) demonstrative and the personal pronoun not infrequently have the same function and meaning and are then interchangeable. Naturally enough, *derselbe* became involved in the same exchanges. It is as a substitute for the personal pronoun that, in Early NHG, the demonstrative *derselbe* reaches its greatest prominence: (Luther) *die Himmel erzählen die Ehre Gottes . . . er hat der Sonne eine Hütte in denselben gemacht; und dieselbe geht heraus als ein Bräutigam*; often with an extended form *derselbige*, now obsolete: *aus derselbigen einem wuchs ein klein Horn* "out of one of them came forth a little horn". In this same function the pronoun survives, to a restricted extent, in the contemporary language.

It will not be out of place to illustrate here the interchangeability of the above-mentioned pronouns. We take the examples in John i. 2–4. The Vulgate, in agreement with the Greek original, has *hoc . . . per ipsum . . . sine ipso . . . in ipso.* The (notoriously literal) Dutch Bible duly follows with *dit . . . door hetzelve . . . zonder hetzelve . . . in hetzelve.* But the Authorised Version has this sequence: *the same . . . by him . . . without him . . . in him.* German texts realize the possibilities differently. Luther offers, apparently, his own stylistic interpretation: *dasselbe war im Anfang bei Gott. Alle Dinge sind durch dasselbe gemacht, und ohne dasselbe ist nichts gemacht . . . in ihm war das Leben*, while the translator of Tatian, six centuries before, put *thaȥ was in anaginne mit gote. Alliu thuruh thaȥ wurdun gitân inti ûȥȥan sîn ni was wiht gitânes . . .* (*thaȥ*) *was in imo lîb.* Menge's contemporary version runs: *dieses war im Anfang bei Gott. Alle Dinge sind durch dieses geworden, und ohne dieses ist nichts geworden . . . . In ihm war Leben.*

We observe, in conclusion, that the adverb analogous to *derselbe*, namely *daselbst*, was equally prominent in Early NHG: (Luther) *es war aber daselbst Jakobs Brunnen.* It subsequently fell into disuse (Menge has *dort war aber der Jakobsbrunnen*) except in a few contexts: *geboren 1863 in Köln, gestorben 1935 daselbst.*

solch (derartig)

NHG, MHG *solch*, OHG *solîh* (a compound of *sô* 'so' and *-lîh* '-lich'), a parallel formation to Eng. *such*, OE *swilc*, functions as a pronominal adjective. The German and English words have the same basic role, but their idiomatic application may be rather different, e.g. *er erwartete von ihr den ersten Brief, und dieser Brief kam nicht, denn sie erwartete einen solchen von ihm*; *er brachte ihr ein Geschenk, ein solches, daß sie vor Freude errötete.* Replacement by other demonstratives is sometimes possible: *mein Vater trug sich nie mit anderen Gedanken als mit solchen* (or *denen*) *der Sorge.* The demonstrative *derartig* is synonymous (though not always interchangeable) with *solch*, as: *man erteilte ihm solche* (or *derartige*) *Rügen, daß er sich ganz zerknirscht fühlte.*

When occurring attributively, *solch* in the singular is most often used with *ein* which either precedes or follows: *an solch einem Tag, an einem solchen Tag*, the latter being perhaps commoner. If *ein* is not used, the phrase has a more formal and purely literary character: *an solchem Tage.* Formerly, *solch* was used as a predicate, but in this function is now replaced by *so* (or adverbial *derartig*): OHG (Williram) *die solîh sîn, daȥ* 'who are such that / die soderartig sind, daß'. Later, *so* began to appear in the attributive position as well. Accordingly *so ein Tag* became synonymous with *solch ein Tag, ein solcher Tag*, and of the three this is undoubtedly the most usual expression in colloquial German today. Less usually, *so* can occur directly before the noun: *es gibt so Leute.* The idiom *so (et)was* has quite pushed *solch etwas* or *etwas solches* into the background. In actual speech the words *so ein* are frequently contracted to *so'n*, whence the substandard pl. *so'ne* 'solche', e.g. in the cliché *das sind so'ne Sachen* (more refined *solche Sachen, so Sachen*) 'things are like that'.

INTERROGATIVE PRONOUNS

wer, †weder

From the morphological point of view the interrogative *wer* is very defective, as comparison with the structurally similar demonstrative *der* at once shows. There is only a two-gender system, animate and inanimate, the masc. *wer* having absorbed the feminine; there are no plural forms whatsoever. This reduction is already characteristic of the oldest German; it does, in fact, reflect a West Germanic innovation, Gothic, for instance, preserving a fuller declension, though here, too, there is no trace of plural forms.

The neuter *was* has the same wide range of reference as *das*, e.g. *was ist er — Maurer? was ist er — böse? was sind Ihre Wünsche?* What appears to be a genitive occurs attributively in one or two literary clichés: *wes Geistes Kind, wes Standes (und Geschlechts) ist er?* Behaghel, i, p. 365, explains the form *wes* in this peculiar construction as representing *welches*. The dative *wem* may only be used of persons: *zu wem wollen Sie übersiedeln?* Where reference is to things, the adverb of place is generally substituted for the pronoun: *wozu ist das gut?* or else, chiefly as a substandard construction, invariable *was* may be found: *zu was ist das gut?*

An inflected form *waser*, hitherto unexplained, occurs in an attributive use of the pronoun found in early modern literature. We take a scriptural example. Although a Luther Bible, printed today, has (Mark xi. 28) *aus was für Macht tust du das?* ("by what authority"), this is an anachronism; the reformer's own words were *aus waser Macht*. The construction was never prominent and soon declined; after the middle of the seventeenth century the grammarian Schottel noted '*waser* . . . nicht gar oft gebraucht'. On *was für*, see the next section.

The Old Germanic languages inherited a dual interrogative 'which' (of two), hence OHG *hwedar*, inflecting as a strong adjective. Examples: (Monsee Matthew) *hwedar ist za wâre mêra, gold odo kirihha, diu daȥ golth wîhit?* 'which is in truth greater, gold or the Church that hallows the gold?', (Muspilli) *sorgên mac diu sêla unzi diu suona argêt, / za wederemo herie si gihalôt werde* 'well may the soul be in anguish until the decision is reached as to which of the two hosts it shall be brought'. We recall that the corresponding OE *hwæþer* survived long enough to find a place in the Authorized Version (Matt. xxvii. 21) "whether of the twain", and compare Tatian *wedar thero zweio*. The pronoun is still usual in MHG: (Walther) *dâ sach ich bluomen strîten wider den klê / weder ir lenger wære* 'there I saw flowers wrangling with the clover as to which of them was longer'. In the modern period, however, it is found only in Upper German, especially Swiss: (Tschudi) *bisz er vernemmen möchte, wäderer künig das feld behalten hatte.* It disappears from literature in the early seventeenth century.

Though now extinct in its original function, this pronoun is of course contained in the conjunctions *weder* (p. 219), *entweder* (p. 217).

welch, was für

The adjectival interrogative *welch*, corresponding to the substantival *wer*, has been in use since the earliest times. It may also occur as a substantive: *welchen von den beiden Brüdern meinst du?* As with other pronouns, the neut.sg. can be used regardless of gender or number: *welches ist der kürzeste Weg? welches sind die Triebkräfte? der alte Rabe wußte sofort, welches die Flinte und welches nur der Stab sei.*

In the first place, however, *welch* meant 'what kind of', as is seen from the etymology: OHG *welîh*, older *hwelîh, hwalîh*, i.e. a compound formed from the interrogative stem plus *lîh* 'body'. The primary sense is still kept in the medieval language: MHG (Helmbrecht) *nû sich, herre vater, welch / knaben sint an der schar* 'now, father, see what kind of fellows are in the gang'. In the modern period the word occurs in this sense typically in exclamations, though only as an essentially literary idiom: *welch ein Mensch! welch (ein) großer Wissenschaftler! mit welcher (welch einer) Begeisterung gab sie sich der Arbeit hin!* More familiar style has instead the neologism *was für*, e.g. *was für ein Mensch!*

The two elements of this neologism, *was* and *für*, were originally independent, the preposition regularly governing the accusative noun: (Eyb) *was Christus mit seinen jungern für speysz genossen hat*, from which example one may also notice that the basic sense of *für* in this construction is 'by way of'. The order of the elements could formerly be reversed: (H. Sachs) *es sey für kranckheit, was es wöll*, and *welch* could be used instead of *was*: (Lessing) *Sie mögen auch für einen Weg . . . nehmen, welchen Sie wollen.* The essential step in the further evolution of the modern construction was taken when the two elements were brought together: besides the older *was ist das für eine Sache, ein Ding?* it became possible to have *was für eine Sache, ein Ding ist das?* Since the nom. and acc. were so often the same, as in the fem. and neut. just given, a new syntactical interpretation of the two elements in juxtaposition took place. Henceforth *was für* was felt to constitute a single entity, of an adjectival nature qualifying, but not governing, the noun following, as may be demonstrated when the noun is masc. sg. *was für ein Mann ist das?* Whence analogically *was ist das für ein Mann?* and then in substantival use *was für einer?* By a final development prepositional phrases of the type *von was für einem Mann, wegen was für Leute(n), mit was für (einer) Begeisterung* become commonplace, thus completing the replacement of *welch* 'what kind of' in the ordinary language.

It remains to remark that the construction with the elements juxtaposed—*was für ein Mann ist das?*—is preferred in higher style, the construction with separated elements—*was ist das für ein Mann?*—being more a feature of popular speech.

INDEFINITE PRONOUNS AND ADVERBS

wer, wo, welch

In the Old Indo-European languages the interrogative pronoun and adverb became indefinite if they lost their accent. This very same practice appears in the German of today, but chiefly as a characteristic of oral usage: *hast du wen getroffen? hast du ihn wo gesehen?* Especially common is the neuter: *hast du ihm was gesagt?* Literary occurrences are rare: (Heine) *werd' ich wo in einer Wüste / eingescharrt von fremder Hand?* They are even rarer in the medieval language, so that modern usage will, after all, hardly be a direct continuation of venerable tradition but rather the product of recent shortening of the MHG compound forms *ete(s)wer, -wâ, -waȥ*, forms going back to the earliest German. See p. 79.

The adjectival *welch* also occurs as an indefinite pronoun, the substantive in question being understood: *hast du Eier? — ja, ich habe welche — was für welche?*

'some, any'

We next distinguish between two classes of indefinite pronouns, those meaning 'some' and those meaning 'any'. The earliest German still made use of the old pronoun *sum* 'some', both singular and plural: (Ludwigslied) *suman thuruhskluog her, suman thuruhstah her* 'one he pierced, another one he stabbed', *sume sâr verlorane wurdun sum erkorane* 'some were soon lost, some chosen'. But the word disappeared shortly afterwards and its place was taken by *ette(s)wer*, *-waȥ*, and *-welîh* > *-lîh*: (Notker) *Selmon heiȥet etelîh perg* in Palestina 'S. is the name of a certain mountain in P.'.

In the oldest texts 'any' is expressed by (presumably unstressed) *wer* (cf. p. 78): (Tatian) *oba wer mir ambahte, mir folge* 'if anyone will serve me, let him follow me'. This usage soon declines, the place of the traditional simplex being taken by the compounds *ioman* 'anyone', *iowiht* 'anything': (Otfrid) *ist iaman hiar in lante, es iawiht thoh firstante?* 'is there anyone in this land (who) may indeed understand anything about it?' A similar function was held by *einîg*, a parallel formation to OE *ǣnig* > Modern Eng. *any*: (Monsee Matthew) *âno einîga blûcnissa* 'without any timidity', and by *dehein*: (Notker) *er ist hôhor, danne deheiniu* corpora celestia 'he is higher than any celestial bodies'. Later, owing to frequent use in negative clauses, *dehein* and its abbreviated form *kein* themselves acquired a negative meaning: MHG (Walther) *deheinen rât konde ich gegeben* 'no counsel could I give', *der keineȥ lebet âne haȥ* 'none of them lives without enmity'. The original meaning lived on, however, into the modern period, especially after comparatives: (Luther) *besser denn kein Gold* 'better than any gold', even (Goethe) *mehr als kein anderer*.

The semantic distinction between the OHG compounds *ette(s)wer*, etc., on the one hand and *ioman*, etc., on the other, was preserved in classical MHG, but afterwards the shades of meaning became blurred; *etewer* and *ieman*, *etewaȥ* and *ieht* were in the end inextricably confused. In the modern period *etewer* and *ieht* were dropped as redundant, the others held the field, hence NHG *jemand*, *etwas*. These have now, indeed, the definite force of 'someone, something', indefinite force being now expressed by *irgend*, i.e. *irgend jemand*, etc. (See below.)

The pronouns *etlich* and *einig* were also fated to compete but at a later date. The medieval distinction is still preserved in Luther: *der Teufel wird etliche von euch ins Gefängnis werfen* ('some of you'), *kein Handwerksmann einiges Handwerks* ('of any trade'). But in the eighteenth century *einig* began to take on the meaning of *etlich* and at the same time to replace it, while a new term *irgend welch* 'any' moved into the gap. Today *etlich* has largely disappeared from ordinary use; it is, however, very much alive in Austria. Here the local development has been that *irgend welch* has replaced *einig*, but the latter has not replaced *etlich*. All the same, Austrian cannot escape the levelling influence of average German. Consequently, *einig* occurs in Austria as well, but many feel it still as a bookish word and often avoid it in ordinary conversation; they say: *wir haben etliche Freunde dort, es ist etliches übrig geblieben* (= Standard Ger. *einige*, etc.).

The MHG adverb of place *ete(s)wâ* 'somewhere' lives on in NHG *etwa*, now used to express a possibility: *haben Sie etwa gedacht?* or to indicate an approximation: *in etwa* (= *ungefähr*) *drei Stunden*. The corresponding adverb of place from the 'any' series is OHG *iowergin*, MHG *iergen*, NHG (with excrescent dental) *irgend* and (with analogical *-s*) *irgends*. This latter modern form has since disappeared, but the parallel negative *nirgends* is an everyday word synonymous with *nirgendwo*. The adverb *irgend* lost its local meaning in Early NHG and was henceforward simply an indicator of indefiniteness as such: *tun Sie es bitte, wenn Sie irgend können*. It came close to *etwa* and in older modern German can occur in contexts where *etwa* is now required: (Gottsched) *irgend zwanzig* 'about twenty'. Today *irgend* is chiefly found qualifying indefinite pronouns and adverbs. With the former the old sense 'any' is usual: *irgendwer*, *irgend welcher*, *irgendeiner* all meaning 'any one'. With adverbs the sense 'some' is the rule: *irgendwann* 'some time', *irgendwie* 'somehow', *irgendwo* 'somewhere' (*zu irgendeiner Zeit* 'any time', *in irgendeiner Weise* 'anyhow', *an irgendeinem Ort* 'anywhere'). It will be understood that we are here speaking of the basic meanings of 'any' and 'some'. The idiomatic use of the English pronouns is governed by rules with no parallel in German, e.g. 'I've lost it somewhere' (basic sense), but the interrogative form may be 'can I have lost it anywhere?' German must keep to the one form: *ich habe es irgendwo verloren, kann ich es irgendwo verloren haben?*

je, immer

There were two common adverbs meaning 'always' in OHG: *io* and *iomêr* (*mêr* 'more, further, from now on'); both continued as MHG *ie*, *iemer*. Although synonymous, these adverbs were distinguished: the simplex referred to the past, while the compound, as its literal meaning would suggest, referred to the present and the future: MHG (Helmbrecht) *wirde ich geriten, / ich triuwe in hovelîchen siten / iemer alsô wol genesen, / sam die ze hove ie sint gewesen* 'if I am mounted, I believe I shall always get on in courtly ways as well as those who have always been at court'. And similarly the MHG negatives *nie*, *niemer*, OHG *nio*, *niomêr*. At the beginning of the modern period, however, this traditional difference was lost: *nimmer* could henceforth refer to past time, e.g. (Luther) *es war eine Prophetin, die kam nimmer vom Tempel*, while *nie* could refer to the future, e.g. (Aventin) *das es sider nie hat aufkumen mügen* 'that it (the Roman Empire) could never afterwards recover'. The now inevitable competition between the two adverbs ended with the establishment of *nie* as the ordinarily used negative and this word has, in everyday German, replaced *nimmer*. The latter is, however, often found in high style: (Goethe) *fließe, fließe, lieber Fluß!/nimmer werd' ich froh*, (Schiller) *nimmer, nimmer stand ich still*. Furthermore, *nimmer* can often be heard in the dialects and substandard speech of the south, whereas in more standard spoken forms it is confined to an occasional cliché as *nie und nimmer*, *auf Nimmerwiedersehen*.

The positive adverbs meaning 'always' have been subjected to still greater changes. Today *immer* is used for past time also, *je* in its original sense survives only in *seit eh und je*, *von jeher*. The decline of MHG *ie* in this sense was already heralded in the middle period, since it was in addition regularly used both in the sense 'ever': (Helmbrecht) *owê daȥ ie gebûre / solhe hûben solde tragen* 'alas that a peasant should ever wear such a cap', and also in a distributive sense: (Helmbrecht) *ie zwischen zweien frouwen stuont . . . ein ritter* 'a knight stood between every two ladies'. It is in these meanings that *je* is a truly living adverb today, hence, for example, *das größte Unglück, das mir je zugestoßen ist*; *er gab ihnen je zwei Schillinge*. A reciprocal meaning also lives on in *je länger, je lieber* (and substantivized: *das Jelängerjelieber* 'honeysuckle'). This construction could still be used in the classical period: (Lessing) *je mehr ihr lernt, je mehr vergeßt ihr*, but nowadays *je . . . desto* or *umso* are found.

In Early NHG, *je* often appears with the meaning 'certainly': (Luther, 1546 ed.) *es were vns je besser den Egyptern dienen, denn in der wüsten sterben*. But this usage is quite incomprehensible to the ordinary reader of today, and a modern edition must perforce make some alteration. In the present case (Exod. xiv. 12) it has been done, smartly, by substituting *ja*, i.e. *es wäre uns ja besser, den Ägyptern dienen, denn in der Wüste sterben*. The loss of the temporal meaning seen in this last example is, in principle, much older than Early NHG. The compound *jedoch* 'however' goes back to twelfth-century *iedoch* attested in Williram, while OHG *ioman* 'anyone', *iowiht* 'anything' and several other similarly formed pronouns and adverbs show that *io* very early developed secondary non-temporal senses. Furthermore, since OHG *iowiht*, for example, has an exact counterpart in OE *āwiht*, Modern Eng. *aught*, it becomes clear that the semantic shift is ancient. OHG *io* has been etymologized as the acc.sg. of a lost noun meaning 'eternity' (see p. 51).

In the modern language *immer* may also have a non-temporal sense. Indeed, it has a very important function in this respect, for it regularly supports generalizing relatives, usually together with *auch*: *was* (*auch*) *immer du tust, überlege dir die Folgen*; *wohin* (*auch*) *immer Sie gehen, seien Sie stets auf der Hut*. These forms are the cumbersome modern equivalents of MHG *swer*, etc. (p. 246). Non-temporal *immer* also occurs after *so* in sentences like *ich spare so viel ich immer kann*, though in this position it faces serious competition from *nur*. It may be noticed that non-temporal *immer* corresponds to English non-temporal *ever*. In older modern German such use of *immer* was considerably more widespread: (Julius v. Braunschweig) *wie gehet das immer zu?* nowadays *wie geht das nur zu?*, (Schiller) *die zärtliche Sorgfalt . . . , als nur immer die stärkste persönliche Sympathie hätte hervorbringen können*, now *wie nur* and omission of *immer*.

jeder, jedweder, jeglich; all, beide

Earlier OHG used two pairs of pronouns having the meaning 'each, every', both based upon *hwedar* 'which' (of two) or *hwelîh* 'which' (of more than two). Historically speaking, the older pair is *gahwedar* 'each' (of two) and *gahwelîh* 'every': (Tatian) *zwêne sculdîgon . . . thô forgab her giwederemo* 'two debtors . . . then he forgave each', *giwelîh dê dâr trinkit* 'every one who drinks'. The latter is typically preceded by the gen.pl.: (Monsee Matthew) *allero rîhho gahwelîh* 'every kingdom', in which position the shortened forms *gilîh* and *welîh* are also found: (Muspilli) *chunno kilîhaz* 'every nation', *allero manno welîh* 'every man'.

It has been noted in the previous section that OHG *io* played a part in the formation of indefinite pronouns even before the beginning of written records. At the selfsame time this adverb also combined with the pronouns *gahwedar*, *gahwelîh*, so that in the earliest German texts a second pair *iogahwedar* and *iogahwelîh* > *iogilîh* occur as synonyms of the simpler forms. During the course of the OHG period the longer words replaced the shorter, so that they alone appear in MHG: *ieweder* > *ieder*, also *ietweder* (explained as a development of an unrecorded intermediary stage OHG **iogweder* where the unusual combination *gw* became *dw* and then *tw*), and *ieglîch*. The usages are still as in OHG, but *ieder* and *ietweder* can, in later MHG, also have the meaning 'every' and so begin to compete with *ieglîch*. In the modern language *jeder* has become the ordinary term, the variant *jedweder* and the old competitor *jeglich* living on as occasional literary alternatives. The optional, redundant *ein* in *ein jeder*, *ein jeglicher* is not found until Early NHG.

In the modern language, *jeder* is often construed with a (following) gen.pl.: *jeder seiner Gründe*, i.e. not unlike OHG *gahwelîh* (above). As a consequence of its acquiring the meaning 'every', *jeder* approached the sense of *alle* (pl.) and in earlier modern German analogous plural forms of *jeder* appear, commonly together with *alle*: (Lessing) *alle und jede Dichter*, but also independently: (Goethe) *jede Gründe*, where nowadays only *alle Dichter*, *alle Gründe* are possible. Conversely, *all* could formerly occur in the singular where in contemporary usage only *jeder* is acceptable: (Luther) *alle lebendige Seele starb in dem Meer*, (Schiller) *der Satz, durch welchen alles Ding Bestand und Form empfangen*. We recognize a relic in the saying *aller Anfang ist schwer*. All this is, of course, clearly distinct from the ordinary employment of the singular of *all* today, as in *alles Geld* = *all das Geld*, i.e. *das ganze Geld*. This usage too was, incidentally, at one time more widespread: (Luther) *und er kam in alle Gegend um den Jordan*, but (Menge) *er durchzog also die ganze Gegend am Jordan*.

In its original dual sense *jeder* touched upon the territory of *beide*. An early result of this contact was the appearance of a neut. sg. *beidez* having the same wide range of reference as other neut. sg. pronouns: MHG (Minnesinger, D.W.) *fröude und trûren wonte in beidez bî* 'joy and sorrow both dwelt with them'. The construction remains part and parcel of the language: *die neue Auflage des Buches enthält keinen Holzschnitt, auch keine Lithographie, beides die Hauptillustrationsverfahren der alten Auflage.* The process of attraction went further and led to the creation of an attributive singular which continued into the eighteenth century: (Lessing) *auf beide Weise* 'in both ways'. A relic survives in *beiderseits,* Early NHG *beiderseit*, MHG *ze beider sît* (p. 52).

The construction 'both . . . and' was, at one time, as common in German as it still is in English. The pronoun originally varied for gender according to the strong declension, but in MHG the masc.–fem. *beide* may appear instead of the neut. *beidiu*: (Helmbrecht) *dem kneht gap man âne fluoch / beide hemede unde bruoch* 'they gave the farm-hand without demur both smock and breeches', where traditional rules of concord require the neuter (p. 200). The form *beide* is usual with Luther: *beide oben im Himmel und unten auf Erden.* Shortly afterwards the neut.sg. was generalized and the construction survived until the turn of the eighteenth century when it finally yielded to *sowohl . . . als* (*auch*): (Pestalozzi) *es mangelte mir ein Eindringen beides in das ganze Detail und den ganzen Umfang meines Tuns.*

Since the earliest times *beide* may be accompanied by the general demonstrative *die* (stressed), as still today ˈ*die beiden* 'those two'. Unstressed, the demonstrative, of course, becomes the definite article, which is employed optionally: *beide* (*Bücher*) or *die beiden* (*Bücher*). The weak ending of the pronoun here is, however, a development of the modern period; traditionally, *beide* was always strong: MHG (Nibelungenlied) *Gîselher unt Dancwart, die bêde eȥ ringe wac* 'it little worried those two, G. and D.' Similarly: (Helmbrecht) *für die werc beide* 'for both those (*or* the) jobs'; this latter still occurs in the modern language as a poetic licence: (Storm) *schließe mir die Augen beide / mit den lieben Händen zu!*

man, einer, sie

The indefinite pronoun *man*, in origin none other than the substantive *Mann*, appears in the earliest texts: (Hildebrandslied) *mit gêru scal man geba infâhan* 'with the sword shall one receive a gift', (Muspilli) *dâr wirdit diu suona, dia man dâr io sagêta* 'there will take place the judgement which was always spoken about'. It is noteworthy that the comparable use of French *on* (i.e. *homme*) is attributed to German influence dating back to the period of Franconian ascendency in the early Middle Ages. The English use of *one* in this connexion is an imitation of the French, the numeral having been suggested by the entirely unrelated *on*.

Recollection of the substantival origin of the pronoun seems to have remained for a long time, as one infers from late examples showing *man* taken up by the personal pronoun *er*: Early NHG (Fischart) *wann man ein Ding recht lernt und kann, so mag er sich wohl rühmen deß*. Contemporary usage requires a repetition of the indefinite pronoun, hence in modernizing: *so mag man sich dessen wohl rühmen*. The use of the possessive *sein* points, of course, in the same direction: *man muß seine Schäfchen ins Trockene bringen*. The oblique cases are supplied by the numeral *ein*: (Lessing) *so was erinnert einen manchmal woran man nicht erinnert sein will*. Likewise dat. *einem* (see also p. 199). In consequence of the use of these oblique forms, an indefinite nom. *einer* was made, as in the hackneyed quotation: *wenn einer eine Reise tut, so kann er was erzählen*, where *einer* replaces Claudius's original *jemand*, or in the curious idiom *da sieh mal einer an!* 'now look at that! what a surprise!' This form is quite often heard in colloquial speech as an alternative to the more usual *man*, e.g. *wie kann einer das wissen?* Generally speaking, it may be characterized as slightly substandard. It comes close to, but remains distinct from *einer* (= *irgendeiner*) 'anyone', e.g. *ist in diesem Raum einer* (or *irgendeiner*), *der mir sagen könnte . . . ?*

The English construction with *one* cannot be described as a genuinely popular construction: *it makes one think* belongs to a more elevated plane than the homely *it makes you think*. But Ger. *es gibt einem zu denken* embraces both levels; one may also say *es gibt dir zu denken* (popular style only).

It is often possible to translate Ger. *man* by Eng. 'they': *in Kopenhagen spricht man dänisch* ('they speak'). Such use of the 3rd pl. as an indefinite pronoun is not unknown in colloquial German: *wo ist dein Fahrrad?— sie haben es gestohlen* ('it's been stolen'). As in English, such usage is certainly old, though in German the construction is now stylistically rather inferior: (Luther) *daselbst haben sie Abraham begraben und Sara, sein Weib* "there they buried Abraham and Sarah, his wife", but (Menge) *dort ist Abraham und seine Frau Sara begraben*.

V · ARTICLES

Origins

It is believed that the use of articles was unkown to Primitive Germanic, but evolved subsequently in the derivative languages. Gothic makes limited use of a definite article, but the surviving Gothic text (Bible fragments, *c.* A.D. 350) is a rather slavish rendering of a Greek original; the occurrence of the article in Gothic is admittedly due to Greek influence. The earliest Norse (runic inscriptions, third to ninth century) makes no use of articles at all. On the other hand, the early West Germanic languages (known since the seventh century) show a considerable development in the use of the definite article and also possess the indefinite article, though they use it sparingly. The question may be asked: how did these articles arise?

We begin with the definite article. The primary reason for the rise of a definite article, in any language, lies in a desire to mark out a definite or familiar object and so distinguish it from an indefinite or less familiar one: *the man* (definite, not any man). The article has thus primarily an individualizing function. In close association with this development goes a tendency to use the article to qualify the name of any familiar object, even where there is only one: *the sun.* At this stage only nouns denoting concrete objects are involved; abstract nouns, on the other hand, are not yet affected. The natural way of giving linguistic expression to the desire to draw attention to the definite or familiar is to qualify the noun in question with a demonstrative pronoun, i.e. with a word meaning 'this' or 'that' or both. But in this new function, the demonstrative force of the word automatically diminishes, eventually disappearing altogether; when this happens the article is born.

Precisely this took place in prehistoric German. The demonstrative (we give the modern forms for convenience) was *der*, *die*, *das*, and this came to be employed as the definite article. Remarkably enough, the modern language preserves the original function of this demonstrative as well, which helps us to see how things actually happened. One may say, for example, ˈ*der* ˈ*Mann* (with stress on both words) meaning 'this man' or 'that man' according to context (cf. pp. 71 f.), but *der* ˈ*Mann* 'the man' where the original demonstrative now bears no stress, having become an article pure and simple. Analogous developments are found in other languages; suffice it to recall that the French article *le* goes back to the Latin demonstrative *illum*.

We pass on to the indefinite article. If the evidence of other European languages be any guide, we may assume that the indefinite article in German arose as a consequence of the emergence of the definite article. When, in a given language, the definite article has come into use, an indefinite object is automatically characterized by the absence of the article. Some languages, for instance Welsh and Irish, find this a workable arrangement and are content to manage with the definite article only; the same was true of Ancient Greek. Other languages, however, may feel the need for a parallel article which will mark out an indefinite object from others of the same category, and so a second article comes into being: *a man* (indefinite, any one man). As with the definite article, the underlying principle is again one of individualization.

Two articles evolved in Vulgar Latin in this way and these were inherited by Old French. In this latter language the use of the definite article is to all intents and purposes as in Modern French, but the occurrence of the indefinite article is much more limited, so that in many cases where *un* or *une* are found today, the old language has no article at all, in essentials the same situation as in early German or early English. An explanation is not far to seek. At the period in question the definite article, which is the primary article, had already consolidated its position, whereas the indefinite article, which is secondary, was still in the process of establishing itself. Finally, we remark that the choice of a word for use as the indefinite article was fairly obvious—the numeral 'one', hence Ger. *ein*. As an article, the word is unstressed and hence various reduced forms are often heard in the spoken language. Phonetic attrition has here gone further in English than in German, for OE *ān* (numeral and article) has given two distinct modern forms: the numeral *one* and the article *a*(*n*).

In the foregoing we have endeavoured to show in outline how a language can create for itself that part of speech which we call the article. But a further question is pertinent: why did the articles found in early German and English arise when they did, i.e. at some time before the first texts but after the end of the Primitive Germanic stage? It seems that any attempt to answer this question must take into account contemporary developments elsewhere. At all events it is certain that, about the same time, a parallel evolution of articles was taking place in Vulgar Latin and the Romance tongues emerging from it. This was at a period when Latinity was exerting enormous influence on barbarian Europe. It may therefore be thought likely that the articles found in German and English are not of spontaneous Germanic growth, but are ultimately calques on Vulgar Latin. Narrowing the chronological limits, we think in terms of Latin influence on West Germanic exerted when the languages were in particularly intimate contact at the time of the Migrations of the Peoples and the Merovingian kings. Then, having developed the use of the articles, West Germanic passed on this typological innovation to the Scandinavians; records from the tenth century onwards amply illustrate the spread of this part of speech in Old Norse.

Definite article

The functions of the definite article in OHG and OE are, in general, as in the modern languages, though there are a number of differences, as will be pointed out below. But what most noticeably distinguishes the old from the modern period is the very great number of survivals, in the former, of the pre-article stage. Contrast these two lines from the OHG Ludwigslied with the modern German rendering: *sang was gisungan, wîg was bigunnan, / bluot skein in wangôn; spilôdun ther Vrankôn* 'der Sang war gesungen, der Kampf hatte begonnen, das Blut leuchtete in den Wangen; dort kämpften die Franken'. The original contains five nouns, but not one is qualified by the article, whereas the present-day version requires an article before each of them. Nearly all the nouns occurring in the Ludwigslied (composed in 881 or 882) are used without an article, but there are some exceptions. Since, however, *der*, *diu*, *daȥ* may also be a demonstrative, it is not always possible to interpret each occurrence with certainty. For instance, *ther* in the half-line *ther kuning reit kuono* may have been stressed, then the meaning would be 'that king rode boldly', similarly *thiu* may have had demonstrative value in *giskerit ist thiu hierwist* giving the meaning 'allotted is this life on earth'. On the other hand, there is no doubt that, in certain cases, all demonstrative force has been lost and that we are therefore dealing with pure articles, e.g. *sô wê hin hio thes lîbes* 'so woe to their lives for ever', lit. 'to them . . . of the life', or *kuning was ervirrit, thaʒ rîhhi al girrit* 'the king was absent, the realm all confused'. This last example is instructive for it shows the old construction (*kuning* without the article) beside the new (*rîhhi* with the article) in one and the same line. Such inconsistencies are not unusual at this period of transition. Consider this passage from Muspilli (about 830): *sô daʒ Eliases pluot in erda kitriufit, / sô inprinnant die perga, poum ni kistentit / ênîhc in erdu, ahâ artruknênt, / muor varswilhit sih, swilizôt lougiu der himil, / mâno vallit, prinnit mittilagart, / stên ni kistentit; verit denne stûatago in lant, / verit mit diu vuiru viriho wîsôn.* Some of the nouns take the definite article, but more, which today require the article, do not have it, as the modern German translation illustrates: 'wenn des Elias Blut auf die Erde träufelt, dann flammen die Berge auf, kein Baum bleibt stehen auf der Erde, die Flüsse versiegen, das Meer verzehrt sich, versengt ist der Himmel von der Flamme, der Mond fällt, der Erdkreis brennt, kein Stein bleibt stehen; dann fährt das Strafgericht ins Land, fährt mit dem Feuer, die Menschen heimzusuchen'.

Allowing for the fact that the poetic texts tend to be conservative in their diction, we find that the use of the article becomes more general as the OHG period progresses. The same tendency continues into MHG, by which time the use of the article is, in most respects, almost as frequent as it is in the language of today (but see 'Archaic use after prepositions', pp. 192 f.).

Turning for a moment to our own language, we observe an analogous evolution in the use of the definite article. In OE there are many relics of the pre-article stage, particularly in traditional poetic style: (Beowulf) *sweord wæs swātig, secg weorce gefeh* 'the sword was bloody, the man in the work rejoiced'. The article becomes usual in the ME period, but poetry sometimes preserves the older usage: (Sunset on Calvary) *nou goth sonne under tre* 'now the sun goes down behind the tree'.

Indefinite article

As we have seen (p. 87), the indefinite article would arise as a consequence of the emergence of the definite article. In the first part of the OHG period, the indefinite article is still not used freely, the indefinite noun being thus usually unqualified: (Otfrid) *thô quam boto fona gote, engil ir himile* 'then came a messenger from God, an angel from heaven'. But in the same work there are a number of instances where the indefinite article does occur: *in dagon eines kuninges . . . was ein êwarto* 'in the days of a certain king . . . was a priest'. In later OHG such use of the indefinite article becomes general, but the older style is still found, occasionally, even in MHG: (Dietmar) *sô gesach si valken fliegen* 'then she espied a falcon flying'.

Usage in English closely parallels that in German: OE (Chronicle) *Severus . . . geworhte weall* 'Severus . . . built a wall', where the indefinite article has been required since ME.

In view of its origin as the numeral 'one', the indefinite article is not naturally adapted to function in the plural. Nevertheless, German occasionally constructs plural forms to agree with a plural noun: OHG (Otfrid) *las ih . . . in einen buahhon* 'I read in a book' (*buah* pl. in archaic style), *fora einen ôstaron* 'before Easter' (cf. p. 201), MHG (Nibelungenlied) *daz was in einen zîten dô vrou Helche erstarp* 'that was at a time when Lady H. died', where *zîten* is an example of an abstract noun used in the plural (p. 201), NHG *eine zwölf Monate.* Exceptional developments like this are found in other languages; there is one survival in Modern English: *a few.*

Generalizing use of the articles

We have already described the individualizing use of the article, whether definite or indefinite, as the primary stage in the evolution of this part of speech (see 'Origins' above). Once the use of the articles in an individualizing function has been established, it is not a big step to their employment in a generalizing function as well, for in both cases there is that slight element of emphasis which can be expressed by an article. This further development took place in German also. In some cases it is the definite article which has become usual: *der Mensch ist sterblich, der Affe ist ein Säugetier*; in other cases the indefinite is used: *sogar ein Kind begreift das*, while in not a few contexts the articles are virtually synonymous, so that either may be employed: *soll die* (*eine*) *Frau dem* (*einem*) *Manne untertan sein?*

The generalizing use of the definite article is first attested in MHG: (Freidank) *swer lobet des snecken springen / und des gouches singen, / der kam nie dâ der lêbart spranc / noch dâ diu nahtegale sanc* 'he who praises the snail's jumping and the cuckoo's singing has never been where the leopard sprang nor where the nightingale sang'. The generalizing use of the indefinite article, however, is relatively recent; absence of article is still the rule in MHG: (Walther) *schœner troum enwart nie mê* 'there never was a lovelier dream'. As for OHG, the generalizing use of the articles was apparently undeveloped: (Otfrid) *sô muater kindelîne duat* 'as a a mother does for her child / wie die (eine) Mutter dem (einem) Kinde tut'.

Other languages have likewise developed the generalizing use of the articles. But the results may be different in detail. Compare the English translation of the first two German sentences in this section: *man is mortal, a monkey is a mammal.* German uses the definite article in both, but in English we require, in the latter, the indefinite article, while in the former we are still at the pre-article stage.

Survivals from the pre-article stage in later German

In an appreciable number of cases nouns are still used without an article. This older state of affairs survives, e.g. in proverbial sayings and, particularly, in a large number of stereotype pairs: *Gebranntes Kind scheut das Feuer, Morgenstunde hat Gold im Munde* (where *im Munde* is a corruption of a now obsolete *in mund* 'in hand'), *Mann und Frau, Vater und Sohn, Haus und Hof, Himmel und Erde, Grund und Boden*; likewise *Alt und Jung*. Many pairs are found only in connexion with a certain preposition: *über Berg und Tal, mit Kind und Kegel, unter Dach und Fach, hinter Schloß und Riegel, bei Tag und Nacht*; cf. p. 92. Most likely such pairs are all traditional; many are actually met with in the older records: MHG *lant und liute* 'Land und Leute', (Walther) *lîp und sêle lac dâ tôt* 'laity and clergy lay there dead', cf. 'mit Leib und Seele'.

The use of the definite article has, to some extent, spread to proper names also (see p. 94), but since such names are by nature definite, they are in most cases typically used without the article. In certain contexts, where appellatives approach the status of proper names, these too take no article, e.g. in legal parlance: *Kläger, Verklagter,* or in business correspondence: *Schreiber dieser Zeilen, Überbringer der Dokumente.* Somewhat close to these are the names of professions and the like; when in the predicative position they are used without an article: *er ist Maurer, Witwer; sie ist Stenotypistin, Junggesellin*; similarly when qualified: *er, sie ist Mitglied des Elternbeirats.* Here also: *er ist Vater, sie ist Mutter* (*zweier Kinder*). This pattern of usage is certainly traditional: MHG (Hartmann) *dienstman was er ze Ouwe* 'he was a *dienstman* (holder of a fief) at Aue'.

A notable archaism occurs in folk-song: *Feinsliebchen, das schaute zum Fenster hinaus*, and is imitated by later poets: (Goethe) *Knabe sprach . . . Röslein wehrte sich und stach*, (Schiller) *Meister muß sich immer plagen*, (Lenau) *Schwager ritt auf seiner Bahn.*

Archaic use after prepositions

Prepositional phrases have often maintained their traditional construction in spite of changes in the syntax of the language. So it comes about that in present-day German the pre-article stage is still found in many such phrases.

The article is not found after *zu* in a large number of old expressions. In some the preposition retains the otherwise obsolete sense of rest at a place, for example: *zu Tisch*(*e*) 'at table', *zu Haus*(*e*) 'at home', *zu Bett*(*e*) 'in bed', *zu Fuß*(*e*) 'on foot', *zu Pferd*(*e*) 'on horseback', *zu Wasser und zu Land*(*e*) 'by land and sea', *zu Anfang, Ende* 'at the beginning, end', *zu Zeiten* 'at times'. In other examples the preposition has the modern sense: *zu Tisch*(*e*), *zu Bett*(*e*), *zu Markt*(*e*) 'to table, bed, market', *zu Boden* 'to the ground', and a few more which, however, only occur in invariable locutions, chiefly with a figurative sense like *zu Kreuz*(*e*) *kriechen* 'humble oneself', *zu Wort*(*e*) *kommen* 'have one's say', *zu Kopf*(*e*) *steigen* 'go to one's head', *zu Grund*(*e*) (often *zugrunde*) *gehen* 'perish', *zu Grab*(*e*) *tragen* 'bear to the grave'—a common literary cliché. The article is likewise not used after various other prepositions in a restricted number of cases, for example: *bei Tisch*(*e*) 'at table', *bei Zeiten* (also *beizeiten*) 'betimes, in time', *auf Erden* 'on earth', *an Bord* 'on board', *über Bord* 'overboard', *sich über Wasser halten* 'keep one's head above water', *über Tag* 'during the daytime', *über Nacht* 'overnight', *von Kind an* 'from childhood (on)', *vor Anker liegen* 'lie at anchor', *in See stechen* 'put to sea', *nach Haus*(*e*) 'home(wards)' which has, in the standard language at any rate, replaced *zu Haus(e)* in this sense, cf. the old saying *es wird ihm zu Hause und zu Hofe kommen* 'it will come home to him'. Similar petrified groups are also, for example, the adverbs *beiseite* 'aside', *heutzutage* 'nowadays' (cf. Eng. *today*) or the prepositions *anstelle*, *anstatt* 'instead of'. The persistence of such prepositional phrases will have encouraged, here and there, recent analogical formations: *mit Rad fahren* 'go by bike', *auf Dienst gehen* 'go to work'.

It should, however, be noticed that not all the above traditional phrases are used exclusively; modern alternatives are possible for some of them. Beside *zu Bett(e)* we find *im* or *ins Bett*, more recent constructions employing the definite article. Instead of *zu Kopf(e) steigen* one may say *in den Kopf steigen*, the phrase *zu Markt(e)* is less usual today than *auf den Markt*, while the clearly archaic phrase *auf Erden* (where *Erden* is the old inflected dative) only occurs in appropriately solemn contexts, otherwise *auf der Erde* is used.

In the MHG period the number of archaic expressions of this type was, understandably, much greater. We quote some instances from Walther von der Vogelweide and supply a Modern German translation: *ze himile* 'im Himmel', *ze helle* 'in der Hölle', *ze siechhûs* 'im Krankenhaus', *ze wunsche* 'zum Wunsche', i.e. 'vollkommen', *wünsche mîn ze selde, niht ze walde* 'wünsche mich (zu dir) an den Hof, nicht in den Wald', *dier im ze muoter hât erkorn* 'die er sich zur Mutter gewählt hat', *von himel* 'vom Himmel', *von simonîe* 'von der Simonie', *in sunnen* 'in der Sonne', *under kranze* 'unter dem Kranz(e)'. The reader will notice that evolution in English has run roughly parallel to the German. In several cases the two languages have preserved identical archaisms: *zu Markt(e)* 'to market'. Sometimes English has innovated: *zu Boden* 'to the ground', sometimes German: *in der Hölle* 'in hell', but the over-all tendencies in both languages have been the same. We need not go back far in our own literature to meet prepositional phrases construed without the article in a way which would be impossible today: (Little Geste of Robin Hood) *Robin was a proud outlaw, / the while he walked on ground*, or *Robin dwelt in greene wood / twenty year and two.*

Article and preposition as inseparable unit

In spite of a large number of archaisms, it remains a fact that most nouns governed by prepositions do require an article in

Modern German: *an dem* or *am Fluß*, *auf das* or *aufs Land.* It is noteworthy, moreover, that in very many cases, particularly in idiomatic phrases, the article has coalesced with the preposition and can no longer be separated from it, for example: *am Anfang* 'in the beginning', *am Tag(e)* 'by day', *am Leben* 'alive', *am Main* 'on the Main', *ans Herz legen* 'make one's special concern', *ans Werk gehen* 'set about a job'; *aufs Haar stimmen* 'agree precisely', *aufs Korn nehmen* 'take aim'; *beim Himmel* 'by heaven', *beim Wort nehmen* 'take at one's word'; *fürs Auge* 'for the eye', i.e. 'to look at, admire', *fürs Leben* 'for life'; *im Krieg(e)* 'in (the) war', *im Frieden* 'in peace', *im Ernst* 'seriously', *im Voraus* 'in advance', *ins Fäustchen lachen* 'laugh up one's sleeve', *ins Gedächtnis zurückrufen* 'recollect', *ins Ohr flüstern* 'whisper into one's ear', *ins Wort fallen* 'interrupt'; *übers Herz bringen* 'find it in oneself', *übers Jahr* 'a year hence'; *zum König machen* 'make king', *zur Gattin wählen* 'choose as one's wife', *das ist zum Lachen* 'that is laughable', also in tavern names and suchlike: (*Gasthaus*) *zur Scharfen Ecke*, (*Apotheke*) *zum Weißen Schwan.* These inseparable forms are a development of the modern period.

Definite article with proper names

Though proper names are most commonly used without an article, there are some exceptions, among them the following.

The use of the article developed where the name was qualified by an adjective: *der treue Johannes*, *die kluge Else.* This is an old trait: MHG (Walther) *denke an den milten Salatîn* 'think of (the) generous Saladin'. Similarly: *der allmächtige Gott*, but in the oldest period there was no article: OHG *almahtîgo got.*

At the beginning of the modern period the article began, to a limited extent, to be used with proper names to denote case relationship. Later, this practice became fashionable with names from classical antiquity, but has since been discarded except for the genitive: *der Kriegszug des Xerxes*, *die Gedichte der Sappho.* In the eighteenth century such names, when masculine, often took analogical *-s* in the genitive: *die Ilias des Homers*, but nowadays only the uninflected name is regular: *des Homer.* Other names have followed suit; Goethe wrote *die Leiden des jungen Werthers*, but modern style prescribes *des jungen Werther.* The construction is normal today when the name is accompanied by a title: *die*

Dissertation des Herrn Sternemann, des Fräulein Uhlisch, or when there is more than one name: *die Gesichte der Simone Marchard.*

The article may occur descriptively. It is so used in colloquial style: *ist der Wichmann da?* implying that Wichmann is well known. In the case of women, at least, the article is used in formal style, too: *die Romane der Seghers*; such usage is also regular in legal style: *die Hermann wurde für schuldig erklärt* 'the woman H'. The article is further regularly employed in connexion with the names of works of art or literature: *der Laokoon, die Emilia Galotti, eine Aufführung des Faust.* Similarly with the names of ships (all fem.): *die Bismarck*; cf. the English use of 'she' in this respect. Types of motor-cars are masc.: *der Wartburg*, types of aeroplanes are fem.: *die Fokker*, perhaps suggested by *der Wagen, die Maschine* 'plane'. The names of stars can take the article, but in texts where such names occur frequently this practice is not followed consistently, except in the gen. and dat. where it is required to indicate the case: *die Bahn des Mars, die Rakete nähert sich der Venus.*

Originally descriptive use has become general with river names, which are nowadays only masc. or fem.: *der Rhein, Inn, die Donau, Saale.* This use of the article occurs in MHG (Nibelungenlied) *ze Wormȥe bî dem Rîne* 'at Worms by the Rhine', *dâ daȥ Inn mit fluȥȥe in die Tuonouwe gât* 'where the Inn flows into the Danube', but the older, pre-article stage is also represented in the same work: *sie fuoren über Rîn* 'they crossed the Rhine', *ein stat bî Tuonouwe* 'a town by the Danube', cf. OHG (Notker) *ennônt Tuonouwo* 'from beyond the Danube', (Hamelburg) *ubar Sala* 'over the Saale'. Similar things have happened in English: OE (Chronicle) *nēah þīere īe þe mon hǣt Temes* 'near that river which one calls (the) Thames'. This style remained general until about three hundred years ago. Unlike German, English has kept the traditional construction in place-names: *Henley-on-Thames*, contrast *Halle an der Saale.*

Other geographical names take the article if they are masc. or fem.: *der Irak, die Türkei*; exceptionally also *das Elsaß*, otherwise neuters have no article: *Lothringen, Tirol, Italien.* A few compound names, the last element of which is (or was) felt as an appellative, are still regularly used with the definite article: *der Odenwald, der Oderbruch* lit. 'Oder Marsh', *die Altmark, die Rheinpfalz* (also *die Pfalz*), *das Breisgau, das Allgäu, die Niederlande.* The names of all towns, on the other hand, are now treated as neuters; this is clearly seen when the name is qualified and needs an article: *das alte Frankfurt, das Wien meiner Träume*. Similarly: *das kleine Dänemark, das gespaltene Deutschland*. Notice: *des Odenwalds*, but *des Irak, des gespaltenen Deutschland, die beiden Deutschland*.

Treatment of nouns denoting substances, abstract nouns, etc.

Except as a regionalism in Southern German (see below), the indefinite article is not now used with nouns denoting substances. These may, however, take the definite article in its generalizing function, so that such nouns can appear indifferently with or without the article: *muß (das) Geld die Welt regieren?* 'must money rule the world?' But should such a noun be the grammatical object, the article can only have an individualizing function, as in English: *er nimmt das Geld* 'he takes the money' contrasting with *er nimmt Geld* 'he takes money'. In the dative case, however, the article is always necessary: *ich ziehe Wein dem Bier vor* 'I prefer wine to beer', *ich ziehe den Wein dem Bier vor* 'I prefer the wine to the beer'. The article is also compulsory in the genitive; here it is not possible to distinguish generalizing and individualizing functions: *die Kaufkraft des Geldes* 'the purchasing power of (the) money'. In connexion with brands and qualities of various substances, both articles may be employed: *die verschiedenen Weine* 'the different wines', *hier braut man (ein) schlechtes Bier* 'here they brew bad beer'.

Abstract nouns are somewhat similarly treated. They can take the generalizing definite article. It may be optional in the nominative and accusative: *(die) Not kennt kein Gebot; er liebt (die) Ruhe*, but it is necessary as an indicator of case in the genitive and dative: *sie bedarf der Pflege, wir sind dem Erfolg näher gekommen*. In a number of set phrases no article is used, most often in agreement with English practice: *Hilfe leisten* 'render aid', *Anstalten machen* 'take steps'.

Articles in Southern German

Southern German colloquial makes freer use of the articles than Standard German. At the level of dialect speech in the south, indeed, nearly every noun takes an article at all times. 'Das Substantiv ist nicht gern nackt' as a witty book on Bavarian German puts it. In fact, such excessive use of the articles reminds one of developments in French. On the level of educated colloquial one notices this trait in the regular use of the definite article before proper names: *der Erich*, *die Edith*, *der*, *die Huber*. More striking still to the outsider is the unexpected use of the indefinite article: *um ordentlich zu arbeiten, muß man eine Ruhe haben* (instead of simply *Ruhe*); such usage makes possible local idioms unknown (and unappreciated) elsewhere: *ich habe einen Schlaf*, i.e. *ich bin schläfrig*. Or with nouns denoting concrete objects, especially in reference to quantity: *wir haben ein gutes Fleisch zu Mittag* '(a piece of) nice meat', *der Bauer hat ein Heu dort liegen* '(some) hay', *ein Butterbrot* 'a slice of bread and butter'. But, in fact, such things continue ancient practice: MHG (Walther) *swære als ein blî* 'heavy as a lump of lead', (Hartmann) *er tranc eines wazzers* 'he took a drink of water', (Helmbrecht) *er truoc ein hâr* 'he had (a head of) hair', though none of these is idiomatically possible today.

Articles with pronouns

In a few cases articles have come to be used with certain pronouns. In Late MHG, for instance, beside *jener* 'that (one)', appears *der jene*, extended in NHG to *derjenige*; in addition to *beide* 'both' there is now the alternative *die beiden*. Similarly with the indefinite pronoun: as well as the traditional MHG *jeder* or *jeglîcher* 'each (one)', we find *ein jeder* and *ein jeglîcher*. Further, beside MHG *solher* 'such (a one)' occur the neologisms *ein solher* and *solch ein*. Such usage, which is still current, is obviously redundant since the pronouns are by nature either definite or indefinite, as the case may be. Semantically there is nothing to choose between the various alternatives. The present situation has resulted from the working of analogy: what was good for the nouns has been made to apply to pronouns as well.

Idiomatic usage

We have already had more than one occasion to note that, as far as the use of the articles is concerned, English and German are in broad agreement on essentials, but often go their separate ways in matters of detail. This can be due to the fact that the boundaries between spheres of usage are sometimes unclearly defined or, indeed, scarcely definable at all. For instance, we can translate the sentence *sie richtet jeden Tag das Mittagessen* literally: 'she gets the dinner ready every day'. In both languages, however, we can replace the definite article by the indefinite, or indeed omit it altogether. It is very hard to define any tangible semantic difference between these three possibilities, though some might detect a stylistic one, which may not be the same for both languages. At times, in the inexhaustible material which the living languages provide, we can detect the working of analogy, at other times we may suspect it. And since articles are such an all-pervading feature, the complexity of idiomatic usage is well-nigh endless. In English we may say either *I've caught a cold* or, omitting the article, *I've caught cold* (= idiomatically *ich habe mich erkältet* or *verkühlt*); we can also say *I have a cold*, but this time we cannot leave out the article, precisely as in German: *ich habe eine Erkältung* (*Verkühlung*). Yet if we use the term *Schnupfen* 'cold in the nose', there are three possibilities: *ich habe Schnupfen*, *ich habe den Schnupfen*, *ich habe einen Schnupfen*, but in English only 'I have a cold'. An OHG charm begins *man giang after wege*. Are we to translate 'a man was walking along a road' or 'along the road'? In English we may hesitate, but in German there is no problem; the spontaneous translation is 'ein Mann ging den Weg entlang'.

Both articles combined

There are a number of medieval instances of the combined use of both articles to form an idiom no longer used—or understood—today. Two types may be distinguished; in each case the meaning of the definite article prevails. The combination can qualify a noun determined by a relative clause: (Nibelungenlied) *er truoc in sîme sinne ein minneclîche meit, / und ouch in ein diu frouwe, die er noch nie gesach* 'he had in his thoughts a lovely maid, and the woman, whom he had not yet seen, also (had) him (in her thoughts)'. More often, the combined articles appear before a superlative, which need not be determined by a relative clause: (Hartmann) *ezn dorft' nie wîbe leider / ze dirre werlde geschehen, / wand si muose tôten sehen / ein den liebsten man* 'a woman could not have had a greater misfortune in this world, for she was fated to see her dearest husband dead'.

The idiom is the result of a fusion or mixing of the normal constructions: *ein diu frouwe, die* is from *ein frouwe, die* plus *diu frouwe, die*; *ein den liebsten man* is from *ein der liebsten manne* 'one of the dearest men' mixed with *den liebsten man*.

VI · VERBS

General typology

THE German verbs fall into two great classes, strong and weak. The first is of Indo-European age. Its earliest forms are best preserved in Greek. For instance, Greek *leípein* 'to leave', perfect 1st sg. *léloipa*, aorist 1st sg. *élipon*, show an original pattern of root vowel change (ablaut) which also lies behind OHG *rîtan* 'to ride', past 1st sg. *reit*, 1st pl. *ritum*, or OE *rīdan*, *rād*, *ridon* (the Germanic past tense being a conflation of the Indo-European perfect and aorist). The other ancient Indo-European languages make ample use of ablaut for purposes of word formation, but had largely abandoned it in the formation of tenses. In Primitive Germanic, however, ablaut was highly developed as a regular mode of tense differentiation, for in the Germanic languages all the strong verbs are primary verbs.

Weak verbs are most often secondary, i.e. derived from some other part of speech during Germanic times or later. Thus the verb OHG *fiskôn* 'to fish' is a derivative of *fisk* 'fish', similarly OE *fiscian* from *fisc*. The past tense of a weak verb is formed with a dental suffix: OHG *fiskôta* > 'fischte', OE *fiscode* > 'fished'. It is possible that this dental element is a relic of the verb OHG *tuon* > 'tun', OE *dōn* > 'do', so that *I fished* may have originally meant 'I fish did'. Properly speaking, only weak verbs are productive. This has been the case, not only during the whole historical period, but since early Germanic times. The strong verbs thus constitute a petrified, archaic stratum. There has been a tendency, inevitable under the circumstances, for originally strong verbs to become weak; only rarely has the power of attraction of the strong class been sufficient to absorb an originally weak verb.

By comparison with Latin, Greek, Sanskrit, and other ancient Indo-European languages, the tense system of the Germanic verb is extremely simple. It contains, in fact, only two inflected tenses: present and past (or preterite), e.g. *ich reite, ich ritt* / *I ride, I rode*. All other tenses are periphrastic, e.g. *ich werde reiten* / *I shall ride*, *ich habe geritten* / *I have ridden*. These latter are secondary developments (pp. 111, 114), only the two inflected tenses have come down from Indo-European times. How is the drastic reduction in the number of inherited tenses to be accounted for?

It is certain that those dialects of ancient Indo-European speech, which eventually emerged as Germanic, were very thoroughly modified in the process by the speech habits of other, non-Indo-European peoples. Extraneous influence on Primitive Germanic explains such non-Indo-European features as initial stress and the whole complex of consonant shifts characteristic of the Germanic family of languages. Such influence must have likewise led to the simplification of the tense system. We believe we can identify those responsible.

It is a remarkable fact that the Finno-Ugrian languages also have a two-tense system: present and past. The more cultured languages of this family, such as Finnish, have developed a series of periphrastic tenses much as the modern Germanic languages, but more conservative languages, such as Ostyak, mainly non-literary and less affected by modernizing trends, are still innocent of any tenses other than past and present. In antiquity, the Finno-Ugrian languages occupied a vast area in northern Europe from the Urals to Scandinavia. This was the language family with which Germanic was in early contact. The two-tense system of Primitive Germanic finds its natural explanation as a typological calque on Finno-Ugrian.

Aspects

The comparative philology of the Indo-European verb strongly suggests that, in Primitive Indo-European, different verbal forms distinguished not only tenses, but also aspects. In other words, the Indo-European verb had the means of expressing how an action took place in addition to when it took place. The aspects were perfective and imperfective. In the first, the action was conceived as already completed or to be completed, in the second the action was conceived as existing without any reference to its completion.

In the Slavonic family of languages the principle of aspect was so greatly extended that it came to dominate the whole verbal system and virtually every verb had the two aspects. This remains to the present day an outstanding characteristic of Slavonic speech.

In these languages the perfective aspect is very often formed from the imperfective by the addition of a preverb, e.g. Russian *pisat'* (imperf.) 'to write', *napisat'* (perf.), where *na-* literally means 'on' (etymologically cognate with Eng. *on*, Ger. *an*). Sometimes there is a lexical difference between the aspects: *znat'* (imperf.) 'to know / kennen', *uznat'* (perf.) 'to recognize / erkennen'. It will be noticed that the German preverb *er-* (< OHG *ir-*, see p. 195) is, to this extent, functionally comparable to the Russian *u-*.

Other preverbs in German can also express this perfective aspect. Contrast the pairs *heben—anheben*, *lachen—auflachen*, *schlafen—einschlafen* or *entschlafen*. But of all preverbs, the one which has departed furthest from its original prepositional (adverbial) function is *ge-*, OHG *gi-*, older *ga-*, most likely cognate with Latin *cum*, *con-*, *co-* 'with'. Its primary sense 'together' is still to be seen in *gerinnen* 'coagulate' lit. 'run together' (cf. *zusammengehen* 'curdle') and in *gefrieren* 'freeze (up), turn to ice'. But its commonest function was to make an imperfective verb perfective: OHG *sizzen* 'sit / sitzen', *gisizzen* 'seat one's self / sich setzen', *swîgan* 'be silent / schweigen', *giswîgan* 'fall silent / verstummen'. Thus there existed a certain parallelism between the simplexes, which were for the most part imperfective, and the perfective compounds formed with *gi-*. This was a feature which OHG inherited from Germanic. But a fully coherent system was never evolved. In the first place, there were a small number of common simplexes which were in themselves perfective, as OHG *bringan*, *findan*, *queman* 'come', *treffan*, *werdan*; these did not form compounds with *gi-*. Conversely, there were verbs compounded with *gi-* without the corresponding simplexes: OHG *gilouben* 'believe / glauben', *ginesan* 'remain alive / (genesen)'. It occasionally happened that the perfective meaning of the compound was blurred through the influence of non-verbal forms. Beside OHG *denken*, *gidenken* there was only one type of noun: *gidank*, *gidâht* 'thought', which could carry no implication of aspect. Both verbs remained in use, but the difference between them ceased to be aspective and became purely lexical, cf. NHG *denken*, *gedenken*. Occasionally the simplex and the compound evolved very different meanings. In such cases, feeling for the original relationship was not merely disturbed but quite destroyed, as with OHG *biotan* 'offer / bieten', *gibiotan* 'command / gebieten'. Furthermore, the perfective preverb had to a large extent been generalized before past participles, an understandable development since the past participle implies a completed action. Thus OHG *gisagêt* functions as the past participle of both *sagên* and *gisagên*. An expression like (Hildebrandslied) *wuntane bauga* 'twisted rings / gewundene Ringe' is an archaism. The perfective simplexes quoted above, however, retain the original past participle without *gi-*, e.g. (Otfrid) *ih habên iʒ funtan* 'I have found it / ich habe es gefunden'. But the past participles of other perfective simplexes were involved in the generalization of *gi-*. The verbs *fallan*, *sterban* are usually perfective, all the same they invariably form the past part. *gifallan*, *gistorban*. The former, indeed, had an alternative infinitive *gifallan*, hence the two NHG verbs *fallen* and *gefallen* (see p. 103).

Such disturbing factors must have been getting out of hand before the beginning of the literary period. One obvious result was a growing uncertainty in the use of the forms as can easily be exemplified from OHG texts. Beside (Muspilli) *daʒ hôrtih rahhôn dia weroltrehtwîson* 'that I heard the knowledgeable people relate' one finds (Hildebrandslied) *ik gihôrta ðat seggen* 'I heard that said', or (Muspilli) *der himiles kiwaltit* 'he who rules heaven' but (Hildebrandslied) *waltant got* 'ruling God'. Or take these lines from the Petruslied: *daʒ er mac ginerian / ze imo dingenten man . . . dar in mach er skerian / den er wili nerian* 'that he can save the man whose hopes are on him . . . therein he can admit whoever he wishes to save'. It is apparent that OHG *gistantan*, *-stên* had the regular perfective sense 'come to stand' if only because this meaning is implicit in the modern *gestehen* 'confess' lit. 'come to stand' (before the court to make a statement). But the form occurs in Muspilli in anything but perfective use: *mâno vallit*, *prinnit mittilagart*, / *stên ni kistentit* 'the moon will fall, the earth burn, no stone remain standing'. The presence or absence of *gi-* was, in fact, being partly determined by considerations which had nothing to do with aspect. The more ample evidence of MHG (p. 103) conveys some idea of what these considerations were.

We return for a moment to the Slavonic aspects. It was noted that, in Slavonic, preverbs regularly turn the imperfective simplex into a perfective compound. The same principle obtains in the Baltic languages. We conclude that the striking typological correspondence in this respect between these families and Germanic presupposes a period of close contact in prehistoric times.

The preverb ge- *in MHG and NHG*

Uncertainty in the use of the preverb *gi-* in OHG implies that feeling for its original function as a perfective element was being lost. The MHG evidence more than confirms this postulate. A few pairs of verbs are still always differentiated according to the old principle of aspect variation, thus *sitzen—gesitzen, swîgen—geswîgen* continue to be used in MHG as they were in OHG. But, to a very considerable extent, the use or otherwise of *ge-* depended upon new factors which had their origin in the previous period.

To begin with, the redundant use of *ge-* is noticeably common in negative sentences: (Walther) *nie kristenman gesach sô jæmerlîchiu jâr* 'never did a Christian see such wretched years'. The preverb could be used, also quite meaninglessly, with an infinitive dependent on an auxiliary: (Dietmar) *liep âne leit mac niht gesîn* 'love without sorrow cannot be', (Nibelungenlied) *Hagene . . . in nie gerouwen lie* 'Hagen . . . never let him rest'. By the same token, *ge-* may appear before an infinitive depending on other verbs: (Nibelungenlied) *von bezzerm pirsgewæte gehôrte ich nie gesagen* 'I never heard tell of better hunting garb'. Apart from such noticeable tendencies, the optional use of *ge-* appears to have become very free. In poetry, at any rate, it could be used or not solely according to the requirements of the metre. Almost all verbs could be so treated, exceptions being those few which still maintained the distinctions of aspect, and the auxiliaries, though *lâzen* (*lân*) 'let / lassen' may take *ge-*, and *sîn* 'be / sein' may have it in the infinitive (example above).

In one important sphere, however, the presence of *ge-* is directly attributable to its perfective force, namely in subordinate clauses whenever this aspect is implied. Modern German or English requires the pluperfect tense in such cases, e.g. (Helmbrecht) *dô si dô mit freuden gâzen, / . . . er frâgte in der mære, / wie der hovewîse wære* 'when they had eaten with enjoyment . . . he asked him what life at court was like / nachdem sie mit Vergnügen gespeist hatten . . . fragte er ihn, wie das Hofleben sei'.

The use of *ge-*, redundantly or otherwise, as described above, died out in the latter half of the fifteenth century. Thus MHG *sitzen, sagen* continue in NHG, but *gesitzen, gesagen* have not survived. Nevertheless, NHG does contain several pairs such as *denken—gedenken, bieten—gebieten, stehen—gestehen, fallen—*

gefallen 'please' from the basic sense 'fall to one's share'. In such cases there is a definite lexical difference between the words in each pair; in the last three the speaker is not even conscious of the fact that the words originally belong together. In other cases, the simplex has died out, leaving the compound as an isolated lexical item, cf. OHG *winnan* 'struggle', *giwinnan* 'obtain by struggle', MHG *winnen, gewinnen,* but NHG only *gewinnen,* further OHG *beran* 'carry', *giberan* 'give birth', lit. 'carry for a certain time, finish carrying', MHG *bern, gebern,* NHG only *gebären.* (Eng. *win* in the sense 'gewinnen' and *bear* in the sense 'gebären' go back to OE *gewinnan, geberan.*)

In the modern language *ge-* has spread to the past participles of all simplexes, but it is not added if the verb does not have initial stress, as in the case of the many verbs ending in *-ieren.* In MHG, however, such verbs did take *ge-*: (Wolfram) *dô kom geleischieret . . . ein ritter* 'there came a knight riding at full speed' (*leschieren* lit. 'ride with loose reins'). In this respect Modern Dutch is more conservative: *georganiseerd, gestudeerd* 'organisiert, studiert'. The old participles of the perfective simplexes mostly survived until modern times. Luther still has *bracht, kommen, troffen.* The form *kommen* was not replaced by *gekommen* until the eighteenth century. Traces of the old forms are still found, e.g. in *willkommen,* also *rechtschaffen* and *worden* beside *geworden* (see also p. 158).

A note on English tenses

It is obviously true that any English learner of German will tend to consider the foreign language in terms of his own. In so doing, he observes many similarities between the two languages. But similarities can be more apparent than real, and this seems to be particularly so in the case of the verb. We therefore recall the basic premise of all foreign-language learning that the foreign material must, in the last analysis, be explained in terms of itself alone. Thus an attempt to understand a piece of German through an unqualified literal translation into English may be misleading. One must, for instance, resolutely resist the temptation to equate absolutely *ich gab* with 'I gave', and *ich habe gegeben* with 'I have given'. In reality, such a purely mechanical equation of preterite with preterite and perfect with perfect conceals a number of fundamental differences, as may be seen from the relevant discussion (p. 121 ff.).

It will not be out of place to add a note on English tenses. The modern English tense system is very unlike the tense system of OE. The latter was typically Germanic. But during the ME period the so-called continuous or progressive tenses spring into prominence and develop apace. These tenses were, to begin with, no more than foreigners' bad English. The foreigners in this case were Celts, for the tenses in question are calques on Celtic, cf. Welsh *yr wyf yn myned* '(I) go', lit. '(I) am in going', cf. older English 'a-going', where 'going' is a verbal noun answering to *myned*. The construction would spread either from the Celtic fringes (adstratum) or, more likely, from groups of Celtic survivors within the English-speaking area proper (substratum). In time, these exotic constructions came to register shades of meaning different from the inherited Germanic tenses and in this way gained a recognized place in the standard language. See further, p. 161.

The new tenses have greatly enriched the English verb, making it capable of expressing nuances of time and aspect far beyond anything conceivable in the typical Germanic system. To take the simplest of cases. The phrases 'he goes to church' and 'he is going to church' are not, of course, interchangeable, each having its own defined use or uses. But both can be given in German only as *er geht in die* (or *zur*) *Kirche*—the choice of preposition being essentially a regional matter. In other words, one German verbal form covers idiomatically all the nuances conveyed by the two English forms. The German need not necessarily be ambiguous, though it can be. Generally the wider context makes things perfectly plain, as in any language. But it is important to note that the English verb, thanks in particular to its special tenses, is much more sensitive than the German verb which has remained within the traditional Germanic setting.

INDICATIVE

The indicative is the mood which makes a statement about a fact: *dort steht das Haus, dort stand das Haus*; see further under 'Tenses of the indicative and their uses', below. In proverbial style, as in other languages, the indicative may express a timeless assumption: OHG (Notker) *târ der ist ein funt ubelero fendingo, târ nist neheinêr guot, unde dâr der ist ein hûs folleʒ ubelero liuto, târ ist neheinêr chustîg* 'where there is a pound of bad pennies, none of them is good, and where there is a house full of evil people, none of them is savoury'. Similarly, in the modern language: *wer sich mit Hunden ins Bett legt, steht mit Flöhen auf.*

In the earliest German the 1st pl.pres.indic. formed the so-called hortative: (Otfrid) *faramês sô thie ginôʒa ouh andara strâʒa* 'let us, like those companions, also take another road'. This construction gave way in later OHG to the present subjunctive (p. 131).

The indicative may occur instead of the usual (potential) preterite subjunctive as follows: (Münchhausen) *überlebte die Bestie den Stoß, so war ich in Stücken zerrissen,* (serial story) *schon die nächste Welle konnte die wertvolle Kiste über Bord befördern.* In such cases the indicative serves to emphasize the infallible certainty of the action. In the present tense, of course, the indicative mood alone is possible: *überlebt die Bestie den Stoß, so bin ich . . . .*

Since MHG times, and especially in the modern period, the indicative has been replacing the subjunctive in most types of subordinate clause (see under 'Subjunctive', below, *passim*).

TENSES OF THE INDICATIVE AND THEIR USES

Present tense

The present tense has the same basic functions as the English present, but some features require comment; in particular the German present tense very commonly expresses the future, see the next section.

We notice first the use of the present to denote an action which began in the past and has continued up to the present: OHG (Ludwigslied) *sô lango beidôn wir thîn* 'so long have we been waiting for you', MHG (Nibelungenlied) *dem sint die wege von kinde her zen Hiunen wol bekant* 'the ways to the Huns have been known to him since childhood', NHG *ich sitze hier bereits drei Stunden* 'I have been sitting here three hours already'. Cf. 'Other uses of perfect', p. 125.

The present tense regularly expresses an instruction: *der*

zweite Durchschlag bleibt im Institut 'the second carbon-copy will remain in the institute'; it may sometimes express a command: *du gehst raus!* 'out with you!'

The present historic, used instead of a past tense to give variety or vividness to the style, is remarkably rare in medieval German. Among the isolated examples are: OHG (Ludwigslied) *gode lob sagêda, her sihit thes her gerêda* 'to God (he) gave praise, he sees what he desired', MHG (Berthold) *er tet daʒ unde sprach . . . und er gêt dar und tuot den kasten ûf* 'and he did that and spoke . . . and he goes to the box and opens it'. But there are a fair number of examples in Late MHG and the construction becomes commonplace in the modern period. The present historic is very prominent in the spoken language, more so than in English, e.g. (from a verbatim report about a stolen car) *ich wollte meine Freunde nach Hause bringen, und wir gehen zur Tür, da sehe ich, daß der Wagen weg ist,* (reminiscence about a broom which had broken the week before) *ich habe keine fünf Minuten mit dem Besen gefegt, und der Kopf ist schon wieder herunter*—English idiom would require 'came off'.

Present as indicator of future time

In OHG, as in all Old Germanic languages, future time is most commonly expressed by the present tense: OHG (Ludwigslied) *hêrro, sô duon ih . . . al thaʒ thû gibiudist* 'Lord, so shall I do . . . all that thou commandest', (Samaritan Woman) *ther trinkit thiz waʒʒer, be themo thurstit inan mêr* 'he who drinks this water will thirst again'. Such usage remained a common feature of German, and medieval occurrences are often still idiomatically appropriate: MHG (Nibelungenlied) *des tuon ich dir ze râte* 'I shall relieve you of it', (Simrock) 'dessen überheb' ich dich', (Hartmann) *ich mache iuch mir alsô holt, / daʒ ir mich harte gerne nert* 'I shall make you so well disposed towards me that you will most gladly cure me / ich mache euch mir so wohlgesinnt, daß ihr mich sehr gerne heilt.' In the medieval as in the modern language, the present tense is usual when an adverbial expression or a conditional clause makes it evident that the future is meant: OHG (Otfrid) *thultênt sie in êwon* 'they will suffer eternally / sie leiden ewiglich', MHG (Hartmann) *bin ich heilbar, sô genise ich* 'if I am curable, I shall recover / bin ich heilbar, dann genese ich'. Or the future may be otherwise implied by the general context: (recent thesis) *die*

Frage nach der Herkunft der Partikeln kann in dieser Arbeit nicht weiter verfolgt werden; sie ist Gegenstand einer speziellen Untersuchung des Partikelproblems, die bisher noch nicht vorliegt. Accordingly, the present is often used to indicate compliance with a request and the like: *na schön, wir sagen es ihm* 'all right then, we'll tell him', *bleiben Sie bitte sitzen, ich hole den Lehrer* 'please remain seated, I'll fetch the teacher'.

The present tense of perfective verbs regularly has a future meaning: *ich treffe dich am Eingang und überreiche dir das Geld* 'I'll meet you . . . ', *du findest den Schlüssel unter dem Fußabstreifer, damit schließt du die Tür auf* 'you'll find . . . '. Such usage is, of course, fundamental, and recalls the practice in Slavonic languages where the present tense of perfective verbs mostly has this meaning. Similar trends, inherited from prehistoric times, were present in the oldest German. At this time the characteristic perfective preverb *gi-*, older *ga-*, was still fully alive, although its original functions were often obscured or lost (p. 101). It is, nevertheless, tempting to see in certain occurrences of this preverb a reflex of the one-time future meaning of the present tense of a perfective verb: OHG (Monsee Matthew) *dea ninevetiscun man arrîsant in tom tage mit desemo chunne enti ganidarrênt* (viri Ninivitae surgent in iudicio cum generatione ista et condemnabunt eam) 'die Leute von Ninive werden auftreten am jüngsten Gericht mit diesem Geschlecht und werden es verdammen' (Luther).

Arising from the use of the present tense for future time, an unmistakable modal shade appears in sentences of the type (personal advertisement column) *wer heiratet herzensgute, alleinstehende Enddreißigerin? wer erteilt einem Schüler der 7. Klasse Englischunterricht?* Here the sense is 'who wishes to marry?', etc.

OE commonly used the present tense to denote future time, but the practice was largely abandoned in ME. An isolated relic survives in the expression *I tell you what.* Otherwise the simple present is today chiefly confined to statements in which some programme is envisaged: *we leave for Dublin in the morning.* This semantic nuance will be of relatively recent origin, the simple present here differing from the continuous present which cannot bear any implication of a programme or the like, as may be seen from the following two sentences: *when do you come out? when are you coming out?* Needless to say, the German verb is, of itself, unable to convey this shade of meaning.

Periphrastic future tenses

(*a*) *Modals as future auxiliaries*

The future may, of course, be expressed periphrastically, and *werden* has been the standard auxiliary since the beginning of the modern period. In the earlier language, on the other hand, certain modal verbs, notably *sollen* and *wollen*, were the more typical indicators of future time. The former seems to have been the one preferred: OHG (Otfrid) *er scal sînen drûton thrâto gimuntôn* 'he will well protect his friends', MHG (Nibelungenlied) *si sihet iuch gerne . . . ir sult ir willekomen sîn* 'she will be glad to see you . . . she will make you welcome', lit. 'ihr werdet ihr willkommen sein'. It is, however, rarely possible to be certain that the auxiliary has quite given up its modal meaning and become purely an indicator of future time. An example will illustrate the difficulty. Tatian has *nio in altare, ûʒar sîn namo scal sîn Iohannes* (nequaquam, sed vocabitur Iohannes) "not so, but he shall be called John". Even though the Latin original has the future, one feels that *scal* probably expressed more than just futurity. Luther, at any rate, is explicit: *mitnichten, sondern er soll Johannes heißen*, where *soll heißen* certainly meant 'is to be called', Luther's future auxiliary being *werden*, as in the contemporary language. Today, *sollen* is essentially a modal auxiliary. As an indicator of future time it was replaced at the beginning of modern times by *werden*, except in certain Low German dialects; here it maintained its position as the future auxiliary and may influence standard speech in these parts, as illustrated below. Not surprisingly, then, it is the regular auxiliary in Dutch: *hij zal komen* 'er wird kommen'.

The second auxiliary *wollen* is not so prominent in the records as the first, but examples occur from early times: OHG (Otfrid) *then alten Satanasan wilit er gifâhan* 'he will capture that old Satan'—in the poem this line follows *er scal sînon drûton thrâto gimuntôn* (see preceding paragraph), apparently as a stylistic variation, MHG (Nibelungenlied) *ir welt iuch alle vliesen, welt* (variant *sult*) *ir die recken bestân* 'you will all perish if you oppose the warriors'. In the standard language of today, *wollen* is essentially a modal auxiliary, but it is still used to form the future in the dialects in some parts of north Germany and this use colours the standard speech of such areas, as illustrated below. Apart from this, *wollen* must always be used in the future infinitive construction (p. 112).

Although both *sollen* and *wollen* are, properly speaking, today modal auxiliaries, it is, nevertheless, true that in certain contexts, a modal element is scarcely present, so that they may still be sometimes regarded as part of the future periphrasis: *die Misere will kein Ende nehmen, was soll aus der Menschheit werden?* to all intents and purposes semantically the same as *die Misere nimmt kein Ende, was wird aus der Menschheit werden?* Regional differences can be important. For instance, one may hear in Schleswig: *ich soll noch Kohlen holen* where there is no implication of duty, the sentence being simply the local equivalent of the usual *ich werde noch Kohlen holen.* The teacher in a Berlin school announces: *wir wollen jetzt eine Arbeit schreiben* 'we'll have a test now', but it never occurs to any pupil to mutter *wir wollen nicht*, for in this context *wollen* is purely a future auxiliary without any modal shading. In Vienna, however, the teacher says: *wir werden jetzt eine Arbeit schreiben.* If he were to use *wollen*, the class might well protest that it didn't want to!

Mention of *sollen* and *wollen* naturally recalls the English cognates *shall* and *will.* These, however, have now largely lost their original modal connotations and become mainly future auxiliaries. In the older language, both were used to form the future without the present restriction of *shall* to the 1st person and *will* to the 2nd and 3rd. This is a recent arrangement, introduced by grammarians, but about which nobody is entirely happy. The spoken language, in particular, freely ignores it and often takes refuge in the contraction *'ll* (actually from *will*), a convenient device as it is neutral. The situation is further complicated by regional differences, as in German; one notices, for instance, an excessive use of *shall* in some parts, such as Lancashire.

Another case of contamination is found in Yiddish. The future paradigm runs as follows: sg. 1 *vel*, 2 *vest*, 3 *vet*, pl. 1, 3 *veln*, 2 *vet*, where *vel*, *veln* correspond to Ger. *will*, *wollen*, but *vest*, *vet* to Ger. *wirst*, *wird*, and *werdet.* This argues for a considerable use of *wollen* at least in some of those dialects of High German from which Yiddish evolved and makes it likely that this auxiliary was, in fact, more widely used in Germany than the indigenous records can tell us.

The use of modal auxiliaries to form the future tense is a widespread phenomenon, and appears to rest upon philosophical speculation. The future is a time apart; unlike the present and past it has no real existence. An action taking place in the future may be regarded as the result of a decision (*sollen*) or of a desire (*wollen*). Future actions can also be ascribed to duty or fate. This outlook gave rise to a future periphrasis which formed the starting-point for the development of the (now synthetic) future tenses of the modern West Romance languages, e.g. French *je donnerai* presupposes Vulgar Latin *ego donare habeo* lit. 'I have to give'. Perhaps such a view lies behind the occasional use of *müssen* to denote future time. Consider these MHG lines: (Nibelungenlied) *er sprach: ir guoten ritter, daȥ wil ich iu sagen, / ir sult vil rîchiu kleider dâ ze hove tragen, / want uns dâ sehen müeȥen vil minneclîchiu wîp* 'he spoke: you goodly knights, this I will tell you, you shall wear very fine clothes there at court, for very lovely women will see us there', (Simrock) 'denn uns wird da schauen manch minnigliches Weib'. It is, however, also possible that this use of *müssen* developed out of the sense 'may' commonly attested in the medieval language: OHG (Otfrid) *giwerdo uns geban, druhtin, . . . wir unsih muaȥin blîden mit heilegon thînen* 'deign to give us, Lord, . . . (that) we may rejoice with Thy saints'.

(*b*) werden *as future auxiliary*

German has made limited use of a periphrasis consisting of the verb *werden* and the present participle in order to express an ingressive or inchoative aspect: OHG (Otfrid) *thô ward mund sînêr sâr sprehhantêr* 'then his mouth at once began to speak', lit. 'became speaking', MHG (Berthold) *die sint . . . ouch sam des êrsten tages, dô sie got an sehende wurden* 'they are still . . . as on the first day when they began to look at God', NHG (Luther) *da ward das ganze Heer laufend, und schrieen, und flohen* "and all the host ran, and cried, and fled", lit. 'started to run'.

Since *werden* was, at an early date, used as the future of *sein*—as still today: *er wird Arzt* 'he is going to be a doctor'—the above construction could easily take on a future meaning: OHG (Tatian) *thie . . . mîn scamênti wirdit* (qui . . . confusus me fuerit) "whoever . . . shall be ashamed of me", MHG (Nibelungenlied) *iâ wirt ir dienende vil manic wætlîcher man* 'many a fine man will indeed serve her'. At the same time the infinitive may be found instead of the participle: OHG (Notker) *gehôre unsih, sô wirde ih anaharên* 'hear us, when I shall call upon (thee)' paraphrasing 'exaudi nos in die, qua invocaverimus te', MHG

(Psalm LXXXVIII/LXXXIX) *wer wirt in den luften gelîchen dem herren* (quoniam quis in nubibus aequabitur Domino) "for who in the heaven can be compared unto the Lord" lit. 'will compare . . . to the Lord'. Here the infinitive appears to be secondary. It can be imagined that the (unaccented) ending of the participle *-ende* became *-enne*, *-ene*, then with loss of final *e* giving a form identical with the regular infinitive. Such a development is known to have taken place in virtually all the spoken dialects.

At all events, the two constructions mentioned above were interchangeable, as may be seen in the different mss. of the Schwabenspiegel: (*a*) *sô wirt dir got wegende mit der rehten wâge*, (*b*) *sô wirt dir got mit der rehten wâge wegen* 'so God will weigh you with the true balance'. Both constructions continued until the end of the medieval period. Neither could be called common, though towards the end of the period the construction with the infinitive is seen to be making headway at the expense of the other, possibly supported by the parallel construction with modal auxiliaries (see previous section). By the beginning of the modern era *werden* with the infinitive was well established as a common periphrasis for forming the future. It was preferred by Luther, and afterwards the (predominantly Central German) grammarians played a considerable part in winning acceptance for *werden* which then became, with one exception, the regular future auxiliary in the standard language. The exception concerns the future infinitive; here *werden* cannot be used, *wollen* alone is possible: one says *es wird regnen* 'it will rain', but *es scheint regnen zu wollen* 'it seems it will rain'.

The establishment of *werden* as a future auxiliary meant a considerable decline in the use of the simple present. We may contrast a passage from the OHG Tatian with Luther's version; the Latin original is construed with the future tense: *ther ist mihhil inti thes hôisten sun ist ginemnit, inti gibit imo truhtin sedal Davides sînes fater, inti rîhhisôt in hûse Iacobes zi êwidu, inti sînes rîhhes nist enti* (hic erit magnus et filius altissimi vocabitur, et dabit illi dominus sedem David patris eius, et regnabit in domo Iacob in aeternum, et regni eius non erit finis) 'der wird groß und ein Sohn des Höchsten genannt werden, und Gott der Herr wird ihm den Stuhl seines Vaters David geben, und er wird ein König sein über das Haus Jakob ewiglich, und seines Königreichs wird kein Ende sein'.

German acquired in *werden* a future auxiliary which, by its nature, is free from the modal associations generally inherent in *sollen* or *wollen*. It may, however, convey modal nuances of its own. Since no future action can be postulated with the same certainty as a present or past action, any future tense can easily imply modality. The ordinary German for 'he'll come soon' is *er kommt bald* (see p. 107), whereas *er wird bald kommen* tends to include an element of promise or assurance. Compare: *sie will den Weg finden und sie wird ihn finden* 'she wants to find the way and she's going to find it'. Hence the future commonly expresses a supposition, especially in connexion with such adverbs as *vielleicht* or *wohl*, e.g. *er wird vielleicht jetzt in München sein*.

The auxiliary *werden* can be used in energetic commands: *du wirst Ruhe geben!* This construction is clearly parallel to the imperative use of *suln* in MHG: (Helmbrecht) *ir sult iuch balde heben ûz* 'get out at once!'

It may be supposed that the development of a future tense in German was encouraged by the existence of a future tense in Latin and French, German writers and translators feeling the need for a corresponding means of expression in their own language. At any rate, we may note that the future with *werden* is in some ways rather a bookish construction. There may, therefore, be a difference between literary and spoken styles, and inevitably discrepancies arise. Some would prefer, in a given context, the simple present, others the periphrasis with *werden*, others again the periphrasis with *wollen*, etc. Furthermore, in some areas, notably in the South, *werden* is used in the spoken language only when a modal nuance is implied; otherwise the present is here the regular tense for future time just as it was in the oldest German.

Preterite

In view of their common origin, the German preterite had essentially the same functions as the English preterite, which contrasted with those of the perfect. The original distinctions are, however, much better observed in Modern English than in Modern German, where the role of the preterite is, in certain circumstances, taken over by the perfect; see 'Relationship between preterite and perfect', pp. 121–3.

As the preterite may traditionally express any form of past time (next section), this tense is often found where strict logic would prescribe the pluperfect (see pp. 125 f.).

The preterite occasionally conveys a modal nuance: (waiter) *pommes frites bekamen Sie, nicht wahr?* 'it was chips you were having, wasn't it?'

We note here that, whereas English conventionally uses the present tense in news headlines: *Dog Bites Thief*, German has the logically correct preterite: *Hund biß Dieb.*

Development of periphrastic past tenses

Primitive Germanic had only one past tense, the preterite, formally a conflation of the Indo-European perfect and aorist (p. 99), and the German preterite is, of course, the same tense. Before the beginning of the literary period of German, however, two new past tenses were evolving: a perfect and a pluperfect. These were periphrastic tenses formed with the verbs 'to have' and 'to be'. They became a permanent feature of the language, hence the types familiar today: *ich habe, hatte gekauft, ich bin, war gelaufen.* The future perfect belongs to the same system, but the now current forms *ich werde gekauft haben, ich werde gelaufen sein* will scarcely have come into use before the beginning of modern times.

Today the two types of periphrasis, that based on 'to have' and that based on 'to be', are so closely linked that they are felt to be simply alternative forms of the same construction. Indeed they are interchangeable in so far as the auxiliary *sein* is replaced in some regions by *haben*, as Swiss German *ich habe gelaufen*, and to some extent vice versa, hence South German *ich bin gesessen.* In reality, however, the two types are of very different origin; they arose independently, only coming together later to form the past periphrastic system as we now know it.

(*a*) *Periphrastic tenses with the verb 'to have'*

Periphrastic tenses formed with the verb 'to have' occur in all the Old West Germanic languages, but not in Gothic, which operates with the traditional preterite only. The periphrastic West Germanic tenses have an exact parallel in the Romance languages where tenses formed with the verb 'to have' partly replace the synthetic past tenses of Classical Latin, e.g. French *j'ai acheté*, Italian *ho comprato.* Such periphrastic tenses had become general in

Vulgar Latin and occasional occurrences in literature indicate that the genesis of the construction goes back to the first century B.C. at least. Since these tenses are unknown in Gothic (*c.* A.D. 350), one is inclined to regard their emergence in West Germanic as taking place later, i.e. not very long before the appearance of the first written records in the seventh and eighth centuries. At any rate, their evolution may be considered as subsequent to developments in spoken Latin and the embryonic Romance languages, which suggests that they are not the outcome of native Germanic processes, but rather a typological borrowing from Romance.

The creation of the periphrasis, linguistically speaking, is quite transparent. Such a sentence as *habeo casam comparatam* or *comparatam casam* lit. 'I have (i.e. possess) house bought *or* bought house', where 'bought' is a past participle agreeing with 'house', forms the starting-point. It will usually be the case that the person who speaks the sentence has himself done the buying, and therefore the stage can be reached when 'bought' ceases to be felt as a participle qualifying the object and becomes instead part of a verbal periphrasis 'I have bought'. When this happens, the passive quality of the participle gives way to an active conception, since the participle now helps to express the action of the subject. As a further consequence of this development, the inflexional ending of the participle loses its grammatical significance. As implied by its origin, the construction was at first confined to transitive verbs. Later it spread by analogy to intransitive verbs if these were imperfective.

These various stages can all be traced in German. A sentence in Tatian, formally speaking, reflects the earliest phase: *phîgboum habêta sum giflanzôtan in sînemo wîngarten* (arborem fici habebat quidam plantatam in vinea sua) "a certain man had a fig tree planted in his vineyard". True, this example should only be quoted with the reservation that it can hardly have been idiomatic German at the time (*c.* A.D. 830). It is too obviously a word-for-word rendering of the Latin sentence, which for that matter, is an equally servile calque on the Greek. But there is no doubt that German could imitate this Latin construction as such idiomatically, as a more advanced example from Otfrid shows: *sie eigun mir ginomanan lioban druhtîn mînan* 'they have taken my dear Lord from me' (in OHG *eigan* competed with *habên* as the auxiliary in this periphrasis). But the inflexional ending, having become functionless, soon falls into disuse: (Otfrid) *thaz eigut ir gihôrit* 'you have heard that'. By the turn of the eleventh century the construction had been extended to the imperfective intransitive verbs: (Notker) *nu habênt sie dir ubelo gedanchôt* 'they have now thanked you badly', *wir eigen gesundôt* 'we have sinned'.

(*b*) *Periphrastic tenses with the verb 'to be'*

The periphrastic system with the verb 'to have', outlined above, did not spread to those intransitive verbs which were perfective, as these were already involved in another periphrasis. These verbs had a past participle with an active meaning and periphrastic forms employing the verb 'to be', syntactically equivalent to those using 'to have', had been in existence for some time. This periphrasis is not only found in all the Old West Germanic languages, it also occurs in Gothic. A similar construction existed in Vulgar Latin, whence the compound past tenses of the Romance languages, e.g. French *je suis venu*, Ital. *sono venuto*. What original connexion, if any, there may have been between Germanic and Romance in this matter, is not ascertainable, but it is to be supposed that trends in Germanic were at least supported by developments in the other languages mentioned, with which it was in such close contact.

In the oldest form of the periphrasis with the verb 'to be'—this is the only stage attested in Gothic—the participle is an adjective agreeing with the subject: OHG (Tatian) *after thiu thô wârun argangana ahtu taga* (et postquam consummati sunt dies octo) "and when eight days were accomplished". Then the nature of the participle changes. It ceases to denote the state, and refers instead to the action which led to the state, in this way uniting with the auxiliary verb to form a periphrastic tense. Its inflexional ending becomes unnecessary and disappears, the usual position in OHG: (Otfrid) *druhtîn was irstantan* 'the Lord had arisen'.

Distribution of the auxiliaries 'to have' and 'to be'

As the result of the developments reviewed in the preceding section, German had acquired by the beginning of the literary period two semantically equivalent, but formally differentiated periphrastic systems to denote past time: (1) transitive verbs and imperfective intransitive verbs conjugated with 'to have', (2) perfective intransitive verbs conjugated with 'to be'. In essentials this basic distinction has been maintained down to the present day. On the other hand, considerable modifications in the original distribution of the auxiliaries have occurred, due principally to the loss of feeling for aspect and to changes in the categories of transitive and intransitive verbs, i.e. some formerly transitive verbs have become intransitive and vice versa.

(*a*) *Aspective differences*

In the case of intransitive verbs the aspective differences are generally well preserved: *er hat gehungert* 'he went hungry', *er ist verhungert* 'he died of hunger'; *ich habe gefroren* 'I was freezing', *ich bin durchgefroren* 'I'm frozen (through)', *das Wasser ist gefroren* 'the water has frozen', *der Teich war zugefroren* 'the pond was frozen over'; *die Bäume haben geblüht* 'the trees blossomed', *die Bäume sind aufgeblüht* or *erblüht* 'the trees have burst into blossom', *die Bäume sind verblüht* 'the trees have finished blossoming'; quite exceptionally, all such verbs compounded with *aus* in the sense of 'to the end' take *haben*, hence *die Bäume haben ausgeblüht* = *sind verblüht*.

(*b*) *The verbs* liegen, sitzen, stehen

In the medieval language the verbs *liegen*, *sitzen*, *stehen* were both imperfective and perfective. As perfectives they commonly took *ge-*, and meant respectively 'lie down, sit down, stand up / sich legen, sich setzen, aufstehen'. When perfective, they were regularly conjugated with the verb 'to be', when imperfective with the verb 'to have': MHG (Hartmann) *dô er was gesezzen* 'when he had sat down', (Wolfram) *ich hân für wâr / hie gesezzen manec jâr* 'forsooth, I have sat here many a year'.

By the modern period, feeling for aspective distinctions was being lost, and *ge-* was regularly dropped. But whereas in the North *haben* established itself as the sole auxiliary, in the South it was *sein* which was generalized, hence N. *ich habe gelegen*, S. *ich bin gelegen*. The standard language has chosen the former, but southern writers often use their naturally spoken *sein*. In a number of cases the historically correct use of *sein* is everywhere preserved, for instance in association with the adjectival use of *gelegen*, e.g.

Bonn ist am Rhein gelegen 'Bonn is situated on the Rhine', further *unterlegen*, e.g. *unsere Truppen sind dem Gegner unterlegen* 'our troops are inferior to the enemy', older sense 'have succumbed to the enemy'; this older sense is still the normal one in some contexts, e.g. *er ist mit einer Stimme unterlegen* 'he lost by one vote'. The compounds *aufsitzen* 'mount (a horse)', *absitzen* 'dismount' are always conjugated with *sein*, thus *der Jockey ist aufgesessen* 'the jockey has mounted his horse'—but *aufsitzen* when meaning 'sit up' takes *haben* like the simplex: *sie hat die ganze Nacht aufgesessen*, though in the South of course: *sie ist die ganze Nacht aufgesessen*. The compounds *aufstehen, entstehen* are perfective: *ich bin spät aufgestanden*. The compound (*auf*)*erstehen* is likewise perfective, though *erstehen* can also be used transitively when it must take *haben* in any form of German: *er hat ein Haus erstanden* 'he purchased a house'. The literary language can, we are told, actually distinguish aspective use in the case of *stillstehen*, thus perfective: *es ist hier stillgestanden* 'it came to a standstill here / es kam hier zu einem Stillstand', imperfective: *ihre Zunge hat keinen Augenblick stillgestanden*. But it is doubtful if such differences are really felt spontaneously anywhere today. The only real difference will be simply the north–south contrast between *haben* and *sein*.

(*c*) *Verbs of motion*

The verbs of motion have undergone a special development. These verbs can be regarded either as perfective or imperfective, the former when the motion is conceived as beginning or ending, the latter when the motion is considered simply as taking its course. Hence the periphrasis both with 'to have' and 'to be' has been known from the earliest times and examples are still commonplace: *sie haben gestern abend getanzt, sie sind aus dem Saal hinausgetanzt*; *wir haben oft gesegelt, wir sind über den See gesegelt*; *ich habe viel gewandert* (but southern *ich bin . . .*), *ich bin nach Oberammergau gewandert*.

But such basic differences are by no means always observed in the modern language, owing to the spread of *sein* at the expense of *haben*. Since verbs of motion imply some change of position, the notion of change often came to dominate and led to the choice of the perfective *sein* in place of an older *haben*. Luther could write: *haben wir nicht in einerlei Fußstapfen gegangen?* Today only *sind wir . . . ?* is possible regardless of the original distinctions of aspect. Luther wrote further: *ich habe mit Euch gefahren, wie ein Vater mit seinem Kinde.* In the idiom of a later date, *fahren* was here replaced by *verfahren,* i.e. *ich habe mit Euch verfahren,* but in the current language this must become *ich bin mit Euch verfahren.* Needless to say, *fahren* itself, unless transitive, nowadays invariably takes *sein.* By virtue of the same trend the imperfective verb *folgen,* which in the older language was always conjugated with *haben,* now takes *sein* when used in its literal sense: *sie ist ihrem Manne nach Amerika gefolgt.* But in figurative use, where there is no idea of motion, the old construction remains: *das Kind hat brav gefolgt,* i.e. 'obeyed'.

In many cases a verb which does not of itself specifically express movement will be conjugated with *sein* if motion is implied by the general context: *er ist weggeeilt* 'he hurried away', but *er hat damit geeilt* 'he hurried with it'. Other examples: *er ist durch den Wald geirrt, er ist davongesaust, er ist die Treppe hinuntergepoltert, er ist ausgerissen,* (casual style) *er ist abgehauen* or *getürmt* 'cleared off', (substandard) *er ist nach Amerika gemacht* 'he went off to America'.

Occasionally, confusion of subjects has led to a modification in the meaning of a verb. *Das Wasser läuft aus dem Wasserhahn* is reshaped as *der Wasserhahn läuft,* but in this new association *laufen* may no longer be treated as a verb of motion and can take *haben,* hence *der Wasserhahn* (or simply *Hahn*) *hat die ganze Zeit gelaufen.* But development has not been uniform. Very many areas did not change the auxiliary, therefore *der Wasserhahn ist die ganze Zeit gelaufen* is at least as common as the former.

(*d*) *Interchange of transitive and intransitive*

The verbs *rennen* and *sprengen* are in origin causative verbs, lit. 'make to run' and 'make to jump'. When not actually expressed, the object 'horse' was understood and the auxiliary naturally 'to have'. In the course of time, however, the two verbs came to be felt as intransitives and 'to be' appears instead of 'to have', at first in competition with it, but finally as the only valid auxiliary. In certain idioms another causative *setzen* 'set' lit. 'make to sit', can be used intransitively and may then be conjugated with *sein* or *haben,* thus *wir sind* or *haben über den Fluß gesetzt*; but *haben* is doubtless commoner.

A number of verbs used both transitively and intransitively now sometimes take *sein*, especially in composition: *das hat (ihn) getroffen*, but *er ist in Weimar eingetroffen*; *ich hatte (den Gehsteig) vor der Haustür gekehrt*, but *er war im Kölner Hof eingekehrt*. Formerly *haben* was used: (Lessing) *hat meine traurige Ahnung eingetroffen*, (Mörike) *da habt ihr auf dem Schloß eingekehrt*. Where both auxiliaries are possible, the use of *haben* underlines the action, the use of *sein* the resultant state: *der Falke hat auf die Taube gestoßen*, *das Schiff ist auf ein Felsenriff gestoßen*. Regional differences may occur: *er hat* (southern *ist*) *auf einen spitzen Stein getreten*.

Intransitive verbs can be made transitive by adding inseparable prefixes. In such cases, *haben* has become the regular auxiliary, thus *die Tiere sind um ihn herumgesprungen*, but *die Tiere haben ihn umsprungen*—the sentences are synonymous, the latter stylistically more elevated. Similarly: *ich bin alle Stadien durchgelaufen* or (better style) *ich habe alle Stadien durchlaufen*. Compare further: *ich bin durch Frankreich (durch)gereist*, but *ich habe Frankreich durchreist*—the first sentence implying simply transit, the second a more thorough visit. Older style permitted the use of *sein*: (Kleist) *durchlaufen bin ich die furchtbare Laufbahn*, *von dort aus bin ich Frankreich in zwei Richtungen durchreist*.

(*e*) *Auxiliary with the verb 'to be'*

It is a curious fact that such a decidedly imperfective verb as *sein* should be conjugated only with *sein*. In this respect, High German stands alone among the other Germanic languages, all of which use the auxiliary 'to have' (except where High German influence has made itself felt, e.g. on Modern Dutch). In Central German, *sein* was sometimes conjugated with *haben* in the older language, whence Luther occasionally has forms like *er hat gewest* (= *gewesen*). The periphrasis with *sein* is doubtless of Upper German origin, presumably arising at a time when feeling for aspect was waning and in a milieu where *sein* was extending its range at the expense of *haben*.

(*f*) *Developments in English and Romance*

In OE the auxiliaries 'to have' and 'to be' were distributed essentially as in older German. Subsequently, 'to have' spread at the expense of 'to be' and is now the only productive auxiliary, though the other is still well known from old-fashioned contexts:

I have come, but Biblical *I am come to set a man at variance against his father.*

In the Romance languages developments analogous to those in English and German have taken place. Spanish and Portuguese have generalized the type represented by 'to have', French and Italian use both, though with a tendency for 'to have' to replace 'to be', cf. Old French *est couruz* 'has run', Modern French *a couru.* As in German, a number of French verbs can take either auxiliary according to the sense: *il a demeuré* 'he has lived / er hat gewohnt', *il est demeuré* 'he has stayed / er ist geblieben', where the former fixes attention on the action, the latter on the state.

Relationship between preterite and perfect

Throughout the whole history of German, the preterite has had to compete with the perfect. In view of its origin, the latter basically denotes a past action seen in its relation to the present (p. 114), cf. Otfrid: *wolaga elilenti! . . . ih habên iȝ funtan in mir; ni fand ih liebes wiht in thir* lit. 'oh, exile! . . . I have found it in myself; I did not find aught good in thee'. Here Otfrid, now safely returned to his home, reflects on the hardships of sojourn in a foreign land. His first sentence may be translated more idiomatically 'I have experienced it myself'; in the second sentence, the preterite may be kept in translation as in the original, i.e. 'I did not find' (as above), but the perfect would be equally possible: 'I have not found'. In other words, there is in certain cases no sharp distinction between preterite and perfect. What is here true of English was naturally true of German also.

(*a*) *Perfect replacing preterite*

The preterite–perfect relationship in German eventually developed in such a way that the latter began to encroach upon the proper domain of the former, that is to say, the perfect came to be used when the action was in no way considered in its relation to the present. This development originated in living speech, which in those days meant essentially dialect speech. Indeed, in the spoken language, the perfect seems early to have driven the preterite out of use. In OHG the latter had been a normal conversational tense, as is evident from the two bilingual tenth-century *Gesprächsbüchlein*, e.g. *ih hogazta simplun fona mir selpemo* (ego cogitavi semper de me ipsum) 'I thought always of myself', *quesasti min erre ze metina?*—normal OHG *gisâhi du mînan hêrron zi mettînu?*—(uidisti seniorem meum ad matutinas?) 'did you see my lord at matins?' But during the twelfth century, at the latest, the perfect must have largely usurped the place of this conversational preterite. This is clear from MHG epic, where the perfect regularly occurs as the spoken form, while the preterite is seen as the typical narrative tense: (Nibelungenlied) *der künec si gruozte schône; er sprach: sît willekomen, / wer iuch her habe gesendet, des'n hân ich niht vernomen* 'the king greeted them kindly; he spoke: be welcome, I have not heard who sent you here'.

By the fourteenth century, however, the perfect is noticed to occur as a narrative tense as well. It makes its appearance in texts which show marked dialect forms, thus confirming that its origin is to be sought in dialect, i.e. in spoken German: (Beheim) *und vile schare sint zuo ime gesammenet, alsô daz her ûf steic in ein schiffelîn und saz*, but contrast Luther with the historically correct preterite: *und es versammelte sich viel Volks zu ihm, also, daß er in das Schiff trat und saß.* Though the reformer scrupulously observed the original distinctions between preterite and perfect in his Bible translation, showing indeed a preference for the former where a choice was possible, the same is by no means true of some of his less meticulous writing: *bisher hat man uns also gepredigt, daß wir die Heiligen sollen anrufen, daß sie unsere Fürbitter seien gegen Gott; da sind wir zu unsrer lieben Frau gelaufen und haben sie zur Mittlerin gemacht.* These sentences have the directness of living speech, but since such constructions are not found in the Bible, one must conclude that a sense of literary propriety was barring their entry into high style. This is essentially the position today as well: the perfect has by now largely replaced the preterite in the ordinarily spoken language notably in the South (see 'Preterite and perfect in the spoken language today', pp. 123 f.), but the preterite is to be preferred in literary style, thus (colloquial) *ich habe den Fall gestern geprüft*, (formal, written) *ich prüfte den Fall gestern.*

The above general formulation is not to imply that a 'spoken' perfect cannot be written in good style. It must be used, of course, to reproduce natural conversation. Schiller (a southerner) makes great use of it, not only in his private correspondence, but also in his literary work, especially in the realistic passages in prose: (Räuber) *schon die vorige Woche hab' ich meinem Vater um Vergebung geschrieben, hab' ihm nicht den kleinsten Umstand verschwiegen.* But it is not entirely absent from the lofty diction of his verse either: (Jungfrau von Orleans) *ich selbst, als mich in später Dämmrung einst / der Weg an diesem Baum vorüberführte, / hab' ein gespenstisch Weib hier sitzen sehn.*

The perfect may have a definite stylistic function, especially in works written in the South and particularly in Austria or Switzerland. Here the use of the colloquial perfect imparts a certain informality to the style without being felt too lax; it is often found side by side with the usual preterite: (M. Giustiniani) *wie aus einem Brief ihrer Schwester zu entnehmen ist, hat Marie zu jener Zeit einige Wochen bei Kasimir gewohnt. Da er unter dem Verdacht stand, an dem Attentat gegen Alexander II mitgewirkt zu haben, hat er aus Rußland fliehen müssen, ist in Genf revolutionärer Publizist gewesen, später in Paris Student der Medizin und schließlich Arzt.* A northern writer would most likely have used the preterite throughout, i.e. *wohnte, mußte, war.* Apart from such regional preferences, the perfect may often be found in artless writing of all kinds anywhere in the German-speaking world: (from a reader's letter to a Berlin newspaper) *auch Hitler hat unter dem Deckmantel des Patriotismus eine rein chauvinistische Politik betrieben.* Here the influence of the spoken style is apparent in the use of the perfect.

Since it is possible to interchange a spoken perfect and a written preterite, it follows that these tenses must have exactly the same meaning. It follows further that it may be misleading to equate automatically, e.g. *ich habe geprüft* with 'I have checked' and *ich prüfte* with 'I checked', because the different tenses in English express different shades of meaning. But neither of the German tenses has the power to express anything more than simply past time as such. In contemporary German then, older distinctions, still observed in English, have been lost, and the choice of preterite or perfect has become solely a matter of style. It may therefore be just as appropriate to render a German perfect by an English preterite and a German preterite by an English perfect. Only the wider context will determine which English tense is idiomatically appropriate.

(*b*) *Preterite and perfect in the spoken language today*

In the dialects of the southern half of the country and also in more standard forms of speech affected by these, the preterite has been replaced by the perfect entirely. Even such familiar forms as *ich hatte, ich war* are missing; instead we hear *ich habe gehabt, ich bin gewesen.*

In the colloquial of the northern half of the country, however, the preterite survived to some extent, but has everywhere lost ground to the perfect. The forms *hatte, war* are well preserved. The preterite is common in the case of the other auxiliaries and certain other frequently occurring verbs, but usually interchangeable with the perfect so that from one and the same speaker both forms may be heard: *ich konnte, habe gekonnt*; *ich sagte, habe gesagt*; *fand, habe gefunden*; *ich ging, bin gegangen.* But, even in the north, the great majority of verbs are not now heard at all in the preterite in ordinary conversational use: (comic paper) *schon der Vater war Straßenbahner, und wir Geschwister sind alle linientreu geblieben. Bloß mit Otto ging es abwärts, der ist zur U-Bahn abgewandert.*

So far in this chapter the spoken language has been considered as something apart from literary language. But, as we have also seen in connexion with the use of the genitive (p. 19), there is no absolute dividing line between a spoken and a literary construction and, particularly at the present time, both styles affect each other profoundly. As a consequence of the influence of the printed word, many speakers from all parts of the country, especially the more educated, incline to make fairly extensive use of the preterite in their ordinary conversation, particularly if recounting a sequence of events. This tendency represents either a revival of the tradition partly preserved in North German, or a return to it, as the case may be. But there is, of course, no question of a restoration of the original semantic differences between the preterite and the perfect; these have vanished beyond recall.

(*c*) *Preterite replacing perfect*

We have seen that, as a result of the spread of the perfect at the expense of the preterite, the nuances of meaning originally distinguishing the two tenses were lost. There is therefore no semantic reason why a preterite should not occur instead of a perfect. And it does occur, for stylistic purposes. It is found in poetry where the exigencies of the metre have often allowed the succint preterite to take the place of the cumbersome perfect periphrasis: (Goethe) *und wenn der Mensch in seiner Qual verstummt, / gab mir ein Gott zu sagen, wie ich leide*, where the sense of *gab* is clearly 'has given'. The short forms of the preterite may not be so necessary in prose, but they may be found helpful for sentence rhythm. Such use is common today both in careful style and in humdrum journalese: *ob sein Werk auch von diesem Gegenstand handelte, wissen wir nicht, weil uns keine einzige Abschrift erhalten blieb*, i.e. *geblieben ist*; *wir dürfen nicht eher ruhen, bis auch der letzte Verbrecher seiner gerechten Strafe zugeführt wurde*, i.e. *worden ist*.

(*d*) *Other uses of perfect*

The perfect may denote an action which began in the past and is still continuing: MHG (Wolfram) *ich hân für wâr / hie gesezzen manec jâr* 'forsooth, I have sat here many a year', NHG (Bock) *ich hab' schon auf den Ruf des Herrn gewartet*. This construction has a parallel in English, but in German such an action is usually denoted by the present: *fürwahr, schon manches Jahr sitze ich hier, ich warte schon lange auf den Ruf des Herrn* (cf. p. 106).

In the same way as the present tense can stand for the future (p. 107), so the perfect tense can stand for the future perfect: *noch eine Viertelstunde und er hat es geschafft* 'another quarter of an hour and he'll have done it'.

Future perfect

The future perfect developed as part of the past periphrastic system: MHG (Nibelungenlied) *der valke den du ziuhest, daz ist ein edel man; / in welle got behüeten, du muost in sciere vloren hân* 'the falcon you will rear, that is a noble man; unless God wishes to protect him, you will soon have lost him', Simrock 'sonst ist es bald um ihn getan'. But since the beginning of modern times the periphrasis with *werden* has naturally been the rule: *noch ehe der nächste Wechsel fällig ist, werden wir unser Bargeld ausgegeben haben*.

Like the simple future, the future perfect commonly expresses a supposition: *sie wird wohl in der Stadt zu Mittag gegessen haben*.

Pluperfect

Although the pluperfect arose as part of the past periphrasis since the simple preterite, inherited from Germanic times, was ambiguous, a strictly logical distinction between the two tenses has not always been observed. In the current language the pluperfect and preterite (in speaking especially also the perfect) are often interchangeable, notably in subordinate clauses: *als ich angekommen war* or *als ich ankam, erblickte ich meinen Vater.* In many instances an increasing preference for the pluperfect may be noticed: (recent thesis) *die Albaner in Süditalien sind zu Skanderbegs Zeiten dorthin ausgewandert, wie wir oben erwähnt hatten*, i.e. 'as we (have) mentioned above'. In older German, however, the preterite is normally found in such constructions: OHG (Hildebrandslied) *wuntane bauga . . . sô imo se der chuning gap* 'twisted rings as the king had given him them', MHG (Gottfried) *aber seite er ieglîchem dô, als er den boten ê seite* 'then he again said to each one as he had said before to the messengers'. Often the perfective aspect (with *ge-*) is used in such cases, see p. 103. Cf. also pp. 139 f.

In the southern half of Germany, where the preterite has been replaced in colloquial use by the perfect (see pp. 123 f.), the traditional pluperfect has naturally gone as well, since it contains the auxiliary preterites *hatte* and *war.* These forms were driven out by the corresponding perfects *habe gehabt* and *bin gewesen*, so that there arose a new, double periphrasis *ich habe gefragt gehabt, ich bin gegangen gewesen*, which are the ordinary southern conversational equivalents of the standard *ich hatte gefragt, ich war gegangen.*

In north Germany the old pluperfect is formally intact, but it is less stable semantically, for it may be used instead of the expected preterite or perfect, not only in subordinate clauses but commonly also in main clauses. It is very frequently heard in some spoken styles: *was war das gewesen?* 'what was that?' (aliter *was war das? was ist das gewesen?*), *wer war noch zugestiegen?* (routine call of bus conductors, travelling ticket collectors) approx. 'who else has got on?' (aliter *wer ist noch zugestiegen?*). This usage often occurs in popular journalism: (Soraya) *als die Zustände in Persien kritisch wurden, begann der Schah, sich den Rückzug zu sichern. Eines Tages war er zu mir gekommen und hatte gesagt. . . .* This pluperfect seems to be spreading and may appear in more formal style: (obituary) *für seine Verdienste in Lehre und Forschung war der Verstorbene 1957 von der Regierung . . . geehrt worden*, i.e. instead of *wurde der Verstorbene . . . geehrt.* That some may dispute the propriety of the construction does not alter the fact that it quite often occurs.

Finite verb suppressed

The suppression of a finite verb may be noticed in proverbs: *Ende gut, Alles gut*, and in a few clichés: *wer da? was tun? so weit Schulz* 'that is what S. has to say'. Compare also MHG *sam mir got* 'as (truly as) God (helps) me'.

A feature of certain literary styles is the optional suppression of the auxiliaries *haben* and *sein* in subordinate clauses. Instances are frequent in poetry: (Schiller) *die Drangsal' alle soll ich offenbaren, / die ich gesehen und meistens selbst erfahren?* Examples are also numerous in some forms of narrative prose: (Heine) *mein Herr Hauswirt verstand nämlich die Kunst, den Teetopf, woraus schon getrunken worden, wieder mit ganz vorzüglich heißem Wasser zu füllen, und der Tee, der mir so gut geschmeckt, und wovon ich so viel geprahlt, war nichts anderes als der jedesmalige Aufguß von demselben Tee, den meine Hausgenossin, Lady Woolen, aus Livorno kommen ließ.* Though not quite so common as formerly, such omissions are still permissible: (adventure book) *vier Tage tobt jetzt neuerdings der Blizzard, ein Orkan von ungewöhnlicher Heftigkeit, wie er keinesfalls im antarktischen Sommer zu erwarten gewesen*, (children's magazine) *der König war lange Witwer gewesen, und da er seine erste Frau so sehr geliebt, wollte er sich nicht ein zweites Mal verheiraten.* Examples go back to Late MHG. Much rarer is the suppression of *sein* as the main verb: (Lessing) *so muß die Tragödie, wenn sie unser Mitleid in Tugend verwandeln soll, uns von beiden Extremis des Mitleids zu reinigen vermögend sein; welches auch von der Furcht zu verstehen*, (Heine) *die Damen, die zufällig gegenwärtig, wurden von mir zum Tee eingeladen.* This usage is now outmoded except in poetic diction: (Storm) *auf daß es einst mir möge sagen, / wie grün der Wald, den ich durchschritt.* The construction has been attested since Late OHG.

SUBJUNCTIVE

Tenses and basic uses

There are two tenses of the subjunctive: present and past (or preterite), both inherited from Germanic. This subjunctive is formally a continuation of the Indo-European optative; in its functions, however, it represents not only the Indo-European optative, but also the otherwise lost Indo-European subjunctive.

Theoretically, two basic uses of the subjunctive in German may be distinguished: volitive and potential. The former expresses a wish or request, the latter a possibility or supposition. A supposition, in its turn, may imply doubt or uncertainty, or it may express an opinion or a conception. The conception can accord with indubitable fact, but still a subjunctive may be used: OHG (Otfrid) *thiz was sus gibâri, theiz geistlîchaz wâri* 'it was of such a nature that it had symbolic significance', MHG (Walther) *diu krône ist elter danne der künec Philippes sî* 'the crown is older than king Philip is'. As regards tense, it is seen that in general the difference is modal and no longer temporal, the preterite subjunctive being simply further removed from reality than the present. In subordinate clauses the tense of the verb follows, as a rule, that of the main clause, so that here even the modal difference has gone, as in the examples above. Then, in the modern period, great changes supervene: the subjunctive, whether present or preterite, is often no more than a formal indicator of indirect statement and more or less interchangeable with the indicative.

Decline of the subjunctive

In OHG the indicative and subjunctive were morphologically distinct throughout. Then, in MHG, as a result of the general reduction of final endings, the indicative and subjunctive fell together in the majority of instances. Only in the preterite of the strong verbs, where the ablaut variations in the stem syllables remained, were the two moods still quite distinct. Such a high degree of formal identity between the indicative and subjunctive could not but weaken feeling for the semantic differences between the two. In the nature of the case, the subjunctive was the loser, and has since been a declining category. The ordinarily spoken language of today makes only limited use of subjunctive forms, except for the preterites of certain auxiliaries (*hätte, wäre, würde, möchte*, etc.), a reflexion in the last analysis of developments in the modern dialects where the subjunctive is also variously restricted, in some areas dispensed with altogether. The literary language has been more conservative, but great changes have not been lacking there either.

Common Germanic observed a sequence of tenses of the same sort as occurs in Latin, and this is preserved in medieval German as follows: a main verb in the present is followed by the present subjunctive in the subordinate clause, while a main verb in a past tense is followed by the preterite subjunctive. In the modern period this sequence of tenses has broken down, the present subjunctive to a considerable extent usurping the place of the preterite, as may be seen *passim* in the sections below. The traditional scheme of things has been further disturbed by the spread of the indicative, mostly the present indicative, which often replaces the older subjunctive in subordinate clauses. In the spoken language the indicative is as good as universal in those positions where the subjunctive had lost its modal significance. We have already mentioned the morphological confusion between indicative and subjunctive which undermined the position of the latter. One could, in addition, point to a syntactical reason for the spread of the indicative. In the case of perfective verbs, the present tense normally expresses the future (p. 108); in other words it refers to an event not yet materialized. This will be the logical explanation of the often occurring sentence type *ich glaube, daß er kommt.* The construction could easily spread by analogy, especially as the ground was already prepared by phonetic decay.

English inherited the same constructions here as German. As far as the use of the subjunctive is concerned, even more sweeping developments have taken place, for in English the subjunctive has by now very largely disappeared. On the other hand, the original sequence of tenses is better preserved than in German, as may be noted from the various examples below.

Subjunctive in main clauses

In the present tense, a volitive subjunctive in a main clause closely approaches the meaning of an imperative: (notice in a tramcar) *wer aussteigen will, melde sich bitte rechtzeitig,* to be compared with another version: *wer aussteigen will, bitte Klingel läuten,* i.e. with infinitive in an imperative function (p. 155). This use of the subjunctive is now largely confined to the 3rd sg. since the other present subjunctive forms have, in most verbs, fallen together with the indicative. In OHG, Otfrid could write (subjunctive) *bimîde ih hiar thaȥ wîȥi thuruh sîna giburt* 'may I here escape the punishment through his birth' distinct from (indicative) *bimîdu ih . . .* which would mean 'if I escape . . . '. But OHG *bimîde* subsequently coalesced with *bimîdu* giving MHG *bemîde*, cf. NHG *vermeide*, so that the two constructions were no longer formally differentiated. The originally indicative construction prevailed, while the originally subjunctive one declined and was generally replaced by a paraphrase, hence Otfrid's sentence would be translated today 'möge ich hier durch seine Geburt der Strafe entgehen'. However, the subjunctive can still occur where it is different in form from the indicative: (Schiller) *ich sei, gewährt mir die Bitte, / in eurem Bunde der dritte*. It did, indeed, survive to some extent even when homophonous with the indicative, e.g. Luther (Gen. i. 14) *es werden Lichter an der Feste des Himmels* parallel with (15) *und seien Lichter*, which Menge renders *es sollen Lichter . . . werden / sein*, Eng. *let there be lights* in both cases. The same construction lies behind the present-day polite imperative, e.g. *kommen Sie herein* 'come in' means lit. 'may they come in'; it is directly apparent in the 3rd sg. imperative: (Lessing) *warte Sie doch, mein schönes Kind* 'but wait, my fair child' (on the pronouns, see p. 62). The often-heard *sind Sie so gut* 'be so kind' in place of *seien Sie so gut* perhaps reflects a confusion of indicative and subjunctive forms widespread in dialect; see further, p. 258.

In the periphrastic construction referred to above, the modal auxiliary was in the earliest phase *muoȥan*: OHG (Notker) *sô muoȥe ih* psalmum *singen in êwa* (sic dicam) 'so may I recite the psalm for evermore', MHG (Walther) *mit sælden müeȥe ich hiute ûf stên* 'may I arise today with blessing', NHG (Luther) *so müsse ich säen* 'so may I sow'. Then, as *müssen* assumed the meaning of 'must' exclusively, *mögen* took its place in the periphrasis, hence *möge ich . . . der Strafe entgehen* (as above). Occasionally *sollen* has been used in a similar function: *da soll uns Gott davor* (*bewahren*) 'may God save us from it'.

In Indo-European, prohibitions were expressed, not by the imperative, but by the injunctive, a mood which later merged with the subjunctive. Germanic must have continued this tradition to a considerable extent, for in Gothic prohibitions are still usually found in the subjunctive and there are also examples in early OHG: (Tatian) *ni slahês, ni huorôs, ni tuês thiuba, ni quedês luggi giwiȥnessi* (non occides, non adulterabis, non furtum facies, non falsum testimonium dices) "thou shalt do no murder, thou shalt not commit adultery, thou shalt not steal, thou shalt not bear false witness". However, the same text generally uses the imperative:

niowiht ni nemet ir in wege, in heidanero weg ni gêt ir (nihil tuleritis in via, in via gentium ne abieritis) "take nothing for your journey, go not into the way of the Gentiles".

In the older language the 2nd pl. subj. *sît* from *wesan / sîn* 'to be' was used besides the true imperative *weset*. The first (isolated) occurrence is noticed in Tatian: *sît gifago iuwara lîbnara* "be content with your wages". By MHG, however, *sît* had superseded *weset* and become the regular imperative: (Walther) *sît willekomen, hêr gast* 'be welcome, noble guest!', hence NHG *seid*. OHG imper. sg. *wis* continued in MHG either unchanged or altered to *bis*, but in Early NHG a singular *sei* was extracted from *seid*, and this neologism promptly drove out the traditional imperative: Late MHG (Beheim) *bis mite hellinde dîme widersachen* "agree with thine adversary" = Early NHG (Luther) *sei willfertig deinem Widersacher*.

The 1st pl. pres. subj. early took over the role of the so-called hortative (p. 106). Contrast (Petruslied, hortative) *pittemês den gotes trût* 'let us pray to the friend of God' with (Notker, subjunctive) *prechên, châden sie, iro gebende, unde werfên aba uns iro joch* 'let us break, quoth they, their bands, and cast away their yoke from us!'. The construction is then usual in MHG, though in most verbs the formal distinction between subjunctive and indicative had by now been lost: (Nibelungenlied) *nu binden ûf die helme* 'now let us fasten on our helmets!', but generally with the personal pronoun: (Walther) *gên wir zuo des meien hôchgezîte* 'let us go to the May festival!'—both side by side in (Anon.) *springe wir den reigen / nu, frouwe mîn, / fröun uns gegen dem meigen* 'let us tread a dance now, my lady, let us rejoice at the coming of May!'. The construction is still current: *machen wir einen Ausflug! — nein, bleiben wir lieber zu Hause!* It has often been replaced since the fourteenth century by *laßt uns*+infinitive, of northern provenience, which became the usual construction in Early NHG: (Luther) *lasset uns zerreißen ihre Bande, und von uns werfen ihre Seile!* It is an essentially literary idiom, now much declined, but still with high stylistic value. Hence Menge retains Luther's diction and Böhm renders Walther's sentence (above) as *laßt uns zu dem Freudenfest des Mai gehen!* We may notice that, in English, this last construction has replaced the older subjunctive in average use entirely, though occasional occurrences of the traditional construction are noticed in poetry: (Scott) *part we in friendship from your land!* In conclusion, we note that MHG *suln* with the infinitive could have a hortative function: (Walther) *dâ suln wir si brechen beide* 'da laßt uns beide sie pflücken!' In the modern language, *wollen* may be similarly used: *ob ein Unglück passiert ist? Wir wollen gehen und schauen, daß wir irgend etwas erfahren!*

Though doubtless an integral feature of the language, a volitive preterite subjunctive is but rarely attested in a main clause in the oldest period: OHG (Notker) *wolti got habêtîn wir deheina* 'would God we had none!', but it is recorded commonly enough in MHG, when it is most usually preceded by an interjection: (Walther) *owê, gesæhe ich si under kranze* 'oh, could I but see her under a garland!' In the contemporary language an expletive adverb (*doch, nur*) is often associated with this subjunctive: (Böhm) *ach, erblickte ich sie doch unterm Kranz!* Periphrastic constructions also occur: MHG (Walther) *möhte ich verslâfen des winters zît* 'könnte ich nur den Winter verschlafen!' (Böhm).

No certain example of a potential present subjunctive in a main clause appears in German, but its existence in Gothic, e.g. *hwa sijai þata?* 'what may this be?' lit. 'what be this?' indicates that German did not continue a construction which had been present in Common Germanic times. On the other hand, a potential pres. subj. was highly developed in subordinate clauses, and this remained a feature of the language until comparatively recently, see below. Potential use of the pret. subj. is fundamental in conditional sentences (p. 139).

Subjunctive in subordinate clauses

In the following, reference is made to the more significant types of subordinate clause containing a subjunctive verb.

The oldest construction used to express purpose was, perhaps, *zi diu daz* with the subjunctive: (Physiologus) *sôser . . . de iagere stinkit, vertîligot er daz spor mit sînemo zagele ze diu daz sien ne vinden* 'if he [the lion] scents the hunters, he obliterates his spoor with his tail so that they cannot find him'. However, *daz* alone occurs and becomes general: OHG (Tatian) *inti santa inan in sîn thorf, thaz er fuotriti swîn* 'and sent him into his village that he might feed swine', MHG (Kudrun) *dô gâhte er deste vaster, daz er diu mære ervunde* 'then he hastened all the more that he might learn the tidings'. This construction continued into the modern period: (Luther) *es sammle sich das Wasser unter dem Himmel an besondere Örter, daß man das Trockene sehe.* Since the twelfth century, however, *damit* (p. 225) had been developing as a final conjunction; it largely supplanted *daß* and successfully competed with *auf daß* which had also arisen as a final conjunction: (Luther) *das ist aber alles geschehen, auf daß erfüllet würde* . . . . This conjunction is still found in high style, but is generally replaced by *damit*, hence Menge: *damit das Wort erfüllt würde.* For a time, the subjunctive remained the regular mood after *damit*: (Luther) *sammelt die übrigen Brocken, damit nichts umkomme*, similarly (Schiller) *Pathos muß da sein, damit das Vernunftwesen seine Unabhängigkeit . . . sich handelnd darstellen könne.*

In alignment with developments in other types of subordinate clause, the indicative is next seen to usurp the place of the original subjunctive. Today, the indicative has become customary when the main verb is in the present: *er ruft, damit jemand kommt.* Menge, modernizing Luther's Genesis verse above, writes *damit das Trockene sichtbar wird.* The subjunctive is, however, often continued when the main verb is in the preterite, e.g. with the traditional sequence of tenses: *er rief, damit jemand käme*, the same construction as Menge *damit das Wort erfüllt würde* (above). This is now primarily a literary construction (characterized also by the essentially literary preterite *rief*, cf. p. 123). In the spoken language, which generally prefers the perfect to the preterite, the present indicative is regularly used in the subordinate clause without regard to the traditional sequence of tenses: *er hat gerufen, damit jemand kommt.* The preterite can, of course, quite often occur in the spoken language too, especially in the speech of the more educated. If such a conversational preterite is used in the main clause, the construction in the subordinate clause can remain unaffected, hence *er rief, damit jemand kommt.*

Such use of the present indicative in the living language, in marked contrast to the literary preterite subjunctive, led to uncertainty in handling the latter, and a compromise construction came into being: *er rief, damit jemand komme*, i.e. having the present tense of the subordinate verb to accord with spoken usage, but retaining the subjunctive mood in consonance with literary convention. This type is now very widespread: (newspaper) *die Kompagnie überquerte den Fluß bei Nacht, damit der Feind sie nicht sehe.*

It remains to be said that *daß* final survives in poetry: (Novalis) *wenn alle untreu werden, / so bleib' ich dir noch treu, / daß Dankbarkeit auf Erden / nicht ausgestorben sei.* It survives also in the everyday speech of the Centre and South, though naturally construed with the indicative: *mach zu, daß niemand 'reinkommt* = *damit niemand 'reinkommt.*

In the older language, subordinate clauses dependent on verbs of begging, commanding, hoping, praying, wishing, and the like, regularly have a subjunctive verb with the traditional sequence of tenses: MHG (Helmbrecht) *swer iu ditze mære lese, / bitet, daz im got genædic wese / im und dem tihtære* 'pray that God may have mercy on him who chances to read you this story, and on the author too', (Wolfram) *den gebôt si allen an den lîp, / daz si immer ritters würden lût* 'she commanded them all, on pain of death, that they should never mention anything about a knight'. In ordinary literary style today, however, the subjunctive is usually replaced by the indicative when the main verb is in the present: *wir wollen, daß er es tut*, but the construction with the subjunctive remains when the main verb is in the past: *wir wollten, daß er es täte.* Examples of the use of the indicative go back to the end of medieval times, and instances occur in the classical period: (Lessing, in a private letter) *es verlangt ja niemand von dir, daß du einen Sarg trägst*, though the subjunctive is still the rule: (Lessing) *was wollen Sie denn, daß aus mir werde?* But it looks as though the indicative had long been established as the actually spoken form. Today it is normal in ordinary speaking regardless of the tense of the main verb: *wir wollten* or *haben gewollt, daß er es tut.* When today a writer puts a subjunctive in the present tense (as in the above example from Lessing), then it is only because of the modern literary convention that any indirect statement may be formally indicated by the subjunctive (see p. 136). Needless to add, such a subjunctive is entirely innocent of any volitive nuance.

A wish or request may appear in a relative clause; the verb is then in the subjunctive: (wish) *wir sind unserem König, den Gott erhalte, von Herzen dankbar*, (request) *eine Bedingung, die hier ausdrücklich hervorgehoben sei, ist die folgende.* In other cases, the meaning of the relative clause comes close to that of a final clause: (Luther) *ich will ihm eine Gehilfin machen, die um ihn sei*, (Schiller) *schickt einen sichern Boten ihm entgegen, / der auf geheimem Weg ihn zu mir führe.* But this construction is now obsolete. The final meaning of the lost subjunctive can best be represented today by the use of auxiliaries, i.e. *führen kann* or *soll*. Or the indicative is used and the nuance remains unexpressed: (Menge) *ich will ihm eine Hilfe schaffen, die ihm zur Seite steht.*

In the medieval language the subjunctive was used in subordinate clauses which stated a comparison: MHG (Walther) *sô diu bluomen ûȥ dem grase dringent, / same si lachen gegen der spilden sunnen* 'when the flowers spring up through the grass, as though they are smiling at the sparkling sun'. Present-day German needs the conjunctions *als ob*, *als wenn*, or it may use the hypothetical pret. subj., as in Böhm's translation of the MHG example just quoted 'wenn die Blumen aus dem Grase sprießen, als lachten sie der leuchtenden Sonne entgegen' (cf. p. 140).

Until fairly recently a potential pres. subj. occurred in relative clauses. We recall that the potential sense may be weakened to the point where the subjunctive denotes no more than something thought of: MHG (Helmbrecht) *eȥ ist nindert nâhen bî / ein wirt, der mich behalte* 'there is no innkeeper anywhere near by who could (might) put me up', NHG (Gryphius) *nichts ist, das ewig sei*, (Uhland) *nimmer findet er den Heiligen, / der an ihm das Wunder tu'*. As in the case of the volitive subjunctive (above), the potential subjunctive in relative clauses is nowadays replaced either by the indicative or by the auxiliaries *können* or *sollen* with the infinitive. The difference between the indicative (which stated a fact) and the potential subjunctive is well illustrated by the following example from Luther: *ich will den Tempel, der mit Händen gemacht ist, abbrechen und in dreien Tagen einen andern bauen, der nicht mit Händen gemacht sei.* But Menge, in this century, was unable to recapture the distinction Luther knew: *ich werde diesen Tempel, der von Menschenhänden errichtet ist, abbrechen und in drei Tagen einen andern bauen, der nicht von Menschenhänden errichtet ist.*

In the older language, the subjunctive occurs in a *daß*-clause functioning as the subject of the main verb: (Luther) *es ist nicht gut, daß der Mensch allein sei*, (Schiller) *Zeit ist es, daß die schwere Prüfung ende.* The more recent language ignores this nuance, hence (Menge) *es ist nicht gut für den Menschen, daß er allein ist.*

The subjunctive was also regularly used in a *daß*-clause functioning as the object of the main verb; it expressed a supposition: OHG (Muspilli) *doh wânit des vilo . . . gotmanno, / daȥ Elias in demo wîge arwartit werde* 'but many priests believe that E. will be wounded in the fight', MHG (Nibelungenlied) *mich dunket, daʒ diu mære iu niht rehte sîn geseit* 'I think that the tidings have not been told you correctly', NHG (Grimmelshausen) *ich hoffe, daß ich nicht verbunden sei, schwedische Dienste anzunehmen.* In the contemporary language, however, the semantic value of this subjunctive has been lost. The mood itself may still be used as a literary convention or may be replaced by the indicative, as explained in the next section.

Subjunctive versus indicative in indirect statement

As we have seen, a supposition is traditionally expressed by the subjunctive. Accordingly, in the nature of the case, the subjunctive regularly occurs in *daß*-clauses after such verbs as *dünken, glauben, meinen.* After verbs of saying, however, use of the subjunctive in *daß*-clauses was general, regardless of whether reference was to a supposition or to a fact: OHG (Otfrid) *si quad, si wâri sîn thiu* 'she [Mary] said she was his handmaid', MHG (Walther) *kristen, juden, heiden jehent, / daʒ diz ir erbe sî* 'Christians, Jews, Saracens assert that this is their inheritance'. The same practice is also regular when the conjunction is omitted: OHG (Samaritan Woman) *siu quat, sus libiti, commen ni hebiti* 'she said, as (true as) she lived, she had no husband'. On the other hand, after such verbs as *hören, sehen, verstehen,* the verb in the *daß*-clause was in the indicative since reference was to a fact: OHG (Tatian) *thô er gihôrta, thaʒ Archelaus rîchisôta in Iudeon . . . forhta imo thara faren* "but when he heard that A. did reign in Judaea . . . he was afraid to go thither", MHG (Wolfram) *der schifman hôrte . . . daʒ in minne twanc* 'the boatman heard that love compelled him', NHG (Luther) *da er aber hörte, daß Archelaus im jüdischen Lande König war . . . fürchtete er sich, dahin zu kommen.*

Subsequently, there developed a tendency in the written language to employ the subjunctive as an indicator of indirect statement generally. In this way it came to replace the logically correct indicative: (Goethe) *durch Schiller erfahre ich von Zeit zu Zeit, daß es Ihnen wohl gehe,* and as a literary convention this subjunctive holds a firm position today. In modernizing the Matthew passage above, Menge introduces the subjunctive as now stylistically appropriate in such a context: *als er aber vernahm, daß Archelaus . . . König über Judäa sei, trug er Bedenken, dorthin zu gehen*; the pret. subj. *wäre* would also be possible; on the use of the pres. subj., see p. 138.

It follows that such employment of the subjunctive necessarily led to the loss of the original semantic difference between indicative and subjunctive in this construction. Today a sentence like *er sagt, daß er krank sei* does not differ in meaning from *er sagt, daß er krank ist*. It is a fiction to interpret the use of the subjunctive as implying that the statement is to be treated as a supposition rather than a proved fact, as is often stated. If an older generation saw a difference, this is definitely no longer the case. The subjunctive here cannot now express a supposition or any sort of modality; it is simply a convention found in the written language: (magazine) *nach seiner Besichtigung des weltbekannten Museums sagte der hohe Gast, daß hier ein überaus wertvoller Beitrag zur Geschichte der Menschheit geleistet worden sei*. It is not, however, an exclusive convention; the indicative is also possible, as is shown below.

In sentences where *daß* is omitted, the subordinate clause is particularly in need of a subjunctive to draw attention to its subordinate character and in such cases the subjunctive is normal: (newspaper) *solchen pessimistischen Darlegungen zufolge müßte man glauben, es gebe keinen Ausweg*. As a further development, this subjunctive (especially the 3rd sg. pres.) regularly occurs in main clauses in reporting style: (newspaper) *die Grippewelle dieses Jahres hat auch Frankreich erreicht. Dies sei jedoch kein Grund zur Beunruhigung, äußerte ein Stellvertreter des Ministers für Gesundheitswesen. Die Krankheit beginne zwar häufig mit recht hohem Fieber, nehme dann jedoch einen verhältnismäßig leichten Verlauf und klinge meistens in fünf bis sieben Tagen ab*. Similarly H. Mann: *er . . . ward grob. Eine Geliebte, die ihn an seiner Karriere hindern wollte, könne er überhaupt nicht brauchen. So habe er sich die Sache nicht vorgestellt*.

The use of the subjunctive as an indicator of indirect speech is naturally proper to written style; it is not a regular constituent of average conversational language. All the same, forms like *sei*, *seien*, and *habe* may frequently be heard from ordinary speakers, doubtless owing to the influence of the press and news broadcasting.

While the above-mentioned, purely literary, tendency was establishing itself, the spoken language was moving in a different direction. In fact, a development was taking place parallel to that already noticed in other subordinate clauses: the indicative was becoming the more usual mood in this type of subordinate clause, too. Inevitably such a trend in the living language is reflected in writing: (Lessing) *ich stelle mir vor, daß eine Einwilligung des Himmels darin liegt.* Indeed, it is nowadays common to find the indicative even when dependent on a (literary) preterite: (newspaper) *sie erkannten, daß er es allein verstand.* The subjunctive *verstünde* is possible, but to many would sound pedantic. Similarly (school book) *in seinen theoretischen Arbeiten zeigte Boyle, daß die Chemie die volle Aufmerksamkeit der Wissenschaftler verdiente und daß noch viele Fragen unbeantwortet waren.* Another author might have used the distinctive pres. subj. *verdiene* and could also have put *seien* or *wären.* It seems likely that the writer in question instinctively used the down-to-earth indicatives as more to the taste of his juvenile readers.

From the eighteenth century onwards, the conflicting tendencies led to mounting confusion. Even the use of the subjunctive as indicator of indirect statement met with internal difficulties since the subjunctive was often formally identical with the indicative. Finally, a measure of agreement was reached. In good style, the pres. subj. was to be used for the 3rd sg. since this form is always distinct from the indicative (hence Menge's *sei*, p. 136), but for the plural (except for *seien*) the pret. subj. should be taken since the pres. subj. was here identical with the indicative. Thus, for example, in classical style: *ich glaubte, er habe gesagt*, but *ich glaubte, sie hätten gesagt.* In the case of the 1st and 2nd sg. the pres. subj. was to be used whenever the forms were distinct, otherwise the matter was left open. Such prescriptions were based on a use of the subjunctive which was in any case already to some extent artificial; it conflicted so often with the reality of the living language that it was never strictly adhered to. The difficulties are still not resolved. On the one side are the literary usages, some of which have acquired an aesthetic value; on the other side are the forms of the evolving spoken language which constantly challenge the purely literary conventions. Since the tendency today is for the written and spoken languages to draw nearer together, it is to be expected that more recognized norms will eventually be reached. But, in the meantime, considerable variation both in tense and mood will be found, e.g. contrary to the classical rules exemplified above: (Winnie the Poo) *Pu . . . glaubte, Kaninchen hätte von seiner Familie gesprochen*, (serial story) *erschrocken riefen die beiden Unbekannten: 'Wir glaubten, der Chef hat heute Ausgang.'*

Subjunctive in dependent interrogative clauses

The evolution of the *daß*-clauses, outlined above, is paralleled in the dependent interrogative clauses. In the earlier language, the indicative in such clauses stated a matter of fact, the subjunctive a supposition. Examples of the indicative: OHG (Otfrid) *hugi, wio ih thâr fora quad* 'remember what (lit. 'how') I said before', MHG (Helmbrecht) *hie wil ich sagen waʒ mir geschach* 'here I will tell what happened to me', NHG (Luther) *der Vater . . . zeiget ihm alles, was er tut.* Examples of the subjunctive: OHG (Muspilli) *diu sêla . . . ni weiʒ wiu puaʒe* 'the soul knows not wherewith it may atone', MHG (Nibelungenlied) *wil der mære vrâgen, waʒ si haben getân* '(I) will inquire what they have done', NHG (Luther) *sehet einen Menschen . . . ob er nicht Christus sei?* Later the subjunctive appears as a formal marker of indirect statement: (Goethe) *du siehst, wie ungeschickt ich in diesem Augenblick sei.* But the living language, which in the meantime had generalized the indicative, also makes its presence felt: (Schiller) *da fragt niemand, was einer glaubt.* Today the indicative is much more usual in writing than it was in the classical period. Goethe's *sei* (above) is too stilted now; *bin* would be normal today.

Subjunctive in conditional sentences

The potential use of the preterite subjunctive is found in both clauses of a conditional sentence if the condition is an unfulfilled supposition or is contrary to known facts. This construction has existed unchanged since the earliest records: OHG (Tatian) *ni wâri dese von gote, ni mohti tuon thes iowiht* 'wäre dieser nicht von Gott, er könnte nichts tun' (Luther) / 'wenn dieser Mann nicht von Gott her wäre, so vermöchte er nichts zu tun' (Menge). The condition need not, of course, be expressed in so many words: MHG (Walther) *gerne sliefe ich iemer dâ / wan ein unsæligiu krâ / diu begonde schrîen* 'gern hätte ich ewig dort geschlafen, aber eine verwünschte Krähe fing an zu krächzen' (Böhm).

It will be noticed that, in the last example above, the MHG pret. *sliefe* refers to past time, where NHG needs the pluperf. *hätte geschlafen.* This is regular medieval practice, the use of the pluperfect being a modern refinement. Speaking of the gifts brought by the magi for the infant Jesus, Otfrid comments: *sie mohtun bringan mêra* 'they could have brought more / sie hätten mehr bringen können'. The poet of the Nibelungen, having described the panic when Siegfried released a bear and the efforts to recapture it, goes on to add that Siegfried's companions 'would have been glad, if all had been over': *und wære iz wol verendet, si heten frœlîchen tac* 'sie wären froh gewesen, wenn alles vorbei gewesen wäre'.

Miscellaneous use of preterite subjunctive

Clauses introduced by *als ob* arose from conditional clauses (*ob* = 'if') and are therefore regularly construed with the pret. subj.: *er tut, als ob er Geld hätte* = *er tut, als hätte er Geld*, cf. p. 240. The indicative is, however, also possible: *er tut, als ob er Geld hat.*

The subjunctive in sentences containing *beinahe* and similar words, e.g. *ich wäre beinahe ertrunken* 'I nearly got drowned' is a modern development resulting from a confusion of two conceptions: (*a*) *ich war nahe daran zu ertrinken* 'I was near to drowning', and (*b*) *ich wäre ertrunken* 'I would have drowned (if somebody hadn't saved me)'.

By a curious transference the pret. subj. is regularly used where there is no question of any condition: *ja, das wäre meine Geschichte* 'yes, that's my story', *das hätten wir nun geschafft* 'we've got that done now'. In these cases *wäre, hätten* are quite interchangeable with *ist, haben*, so that pret. subj. and pres. indic. are semantically identical. Sentences with the pret. subj., however, always refer to something just completed. A pret. subj. with the meaning of the pres. indec. may not uncommonly be heard in answers to enquiries: *jawohl, hier wäre noch Platz* 'yes, there's still room here', for the subjunctive conveys a suggestion of politeness not implicit in the pedestrian *hier ist noch Platz*. This usage, at any rate, seems to be related to the use of the pret. subj. to imply a certain reserve or reluctance: *ich hätte noch eine Frage* 'I have another question (if you don't mind)'.

The pret. subj. occurs in subordinate clauses when the main clause contains a negation: MHG (Berthold) *ich enger des niht, daz ich ein künec wære* 'I do not desire that I should be a king', NHG (Lessing) *der seltsamste kann so seltsam nicht sein, daß er nicht natürlich scheinen könnte*. But the pres. subj., as a relic of the old sequence of tenses, may also be found: (Goethe) *du findest keinen, der seines Nachbarn sich zu schämen brauche*. Today the indicative is usual, in accordance with the general inclination towards this mood in the contemporary language.

Finally, the pret. subj. is used in subordinate clauses introduced by *als daß* linked to an adjective with *zu* in the main clause: (newspaper) *der Schaden ist zu groß, als daß an eine baldige Instandsetzung zu denken wäre*. This is essentially a literary construction, the spoken language preferring a subordinate clause with *um zu*+infin. (see pp. 153 f.).

Pret. subj. of werden *with infinitive*

In the contemporary language the pret. subj. is extensively replaced by a periphrasis consisting of the pret. subj. of *werden*+ the infinitive of the verb in question. Thus *wenn ich es nur verstehen würde* may be preferred to the older, now formal-sounding construction *wenn ich es nur verstünde*; likewise (and especially) when the pret. subj. has fallen together with the pret. indic.: *wenn wir in einem solchen Boot segeln würden* beside the more formal *segelten*. This periphrasis may be regarded as normal in the spoken language. Only in the case of the auxiliaries *hätte, wäre, müßte*, etc., has the pret. subj. maintained itself in ordinarily spoken style, though even here the periphrasis is often used as well: *würde haben*, etc.; also *brauchte* frequently equals *würde brauchen*. Since, in German, preterite and pluperfect are not always logically distinguished, the periphrasis may occur instead of the pluperfect: (serial story) *sie lachten und amüsierten sich, als ob sie sich ein Leben lang kennen würden*, a loose alternative to *gekannt hätten*.

The present construction developed rapidly at the beginning of the modern period, but the prototype was already well established much earlier. Doubtless as a reaction against homonymity brought about when the pret. subj. of so many verbs, i.e. nearly all the weak ones, fell together with the pret. indic., there arose in MHG periphrastic forms consisting of the pret. subj. of *sollen* or *wollen*, the usual future auxiliaries at the time: (Wolfram) *heten wir einen houbetman, wir solden vînde wênic sparn* 'had we a captain, we should little spare the foe', (Hartmann) *hulfeȥ eht, ich woldeȥ klagen* 'if it would help at all, I would bewail it'. One notices that English evolved the same type of periphrasis, hence *should* and *would* in the translations of the examples just given. In fact, English has gone further than German in this respect, but the older state of affairs is still familiar from the Bible: *if thou hadst been here, my brother had not died*, cf. contemporary German (Menge) *wärest du hier gewesen, so wäre mein Bruder nicht gestorben.*

Subjunctive replaced by modal auxiliary with infinitive

As already noticed (pp. 134 f.), the weakening to vanishing point of the original volitive or potential nature of the subjunctive in certain constructions has led to its being replaced (or replaceable) in the modern language by a periphrasis consisting of a modal auxiliary with the infinitive of the verb concerned. This development is commonly observed after verbs of saying, ordering, etc., e.g. (Luther) *und ward zu ihnen gesagt, daß sie ruheten noch eine kleine Zeit* / (Menge) *und es wurde ihnen gesagt, sie möchten* (oder *müßten*) *sich noch eine kurze Zeit gedulden* "and it was said unto them, that they should rest yet for a little season", (Luther) *es ward zu ihnen gesagt, daß sie nicht beleidigten das Gras . . . , sondern allein die Menschen* / (Menge) *es wurde ihnen geboten, sie sollten dem Gras. . . keinen Schaden zufügen, sondern allein den Menschen* "it was commanded them that they should not hurt the grass . . . but only these men".

IMPERATIVE

The imperative traditionally expresses a command or entreaty: *komm her! sei so gut!*

Since the beginning of the literary records, the imperative has also expressed a prohibition: *geh nicht!* In the earliest German, however, there are examples of an older construction using the subjunctive (see p. 130).

Commands and prohibitions may be expressed in various other ways (see pp. 107, 113, 129, 155, 165).

In the spoken language the imperative (or equivalent construction) may be replaced by a clause beginning with *daß*, the main clause being omitted: *daß ihr nicht drein redet* 'don't interfere', *daß du sofort Ruhe gibst, daß Sie das bitte nicht verlieren.*

PASSIVE

German inherited a periphrastic passive consisting of a combination of the verb 'to be' or the verb 'to become' with the past participle. Since the past participle of transitive verbs has a passive meaning, combinations like *es ist getan*, *es wird getan* are, in the nature of the case, automatically passive verbal forms. They are, in fact, counterparts of the active verbal forms which arose when the participle has an active meaning, i.e. when the verb is intransitive, as *es ist gekommen* (p. 116). Gothic, alone among Germanic languages, preserves the Indo-European inflected passive, though only in the present tense. Without a doubt the genesis, at least, of the periphrastic passive belongs to the period of Common Germanic.

Evolution of the passive periphrasis

In the oldest OHG, *wesan / sîn* is the regular auxiliary for the present: (Tatian) *mîn tohter ubilo fon themo tiuvale giweigit ist* (filia mea male a demonio vexatur) "my daughter is grievously vexed with a devil". In reference to future time, however, the auxiliary is normally *werdan*, which was also being used as the future of the verb substantive (cf. p. 111): (Muspilli) *sorgên mac diu sêla, unzi diu suona argêt, / za wederemo herie si gihalôt werde* '(well) may the soul be in anguish until the judgement is given, to which of the two armies it will be brought'. In the preterite both auxiliaries are commonly found: (Tatian) *ther heilant was gileitit in wuostinna fon themo geiste* (Iesus ductus est in deserto (*sic*) a spiritu) "Jesus was led up of the spirit into the wilderness", (Muspilli) *daz frôno chrûci, / dâr der hêligo Christ ana arhangan ward* 'the glorious cross, on which the holy Christ was hanged'.

It is evident that expressions of the type *es ist getan*, lit. 'it is done', can easily assume the meaning 'it has been done'. There are examples in Otfrid, as *wanta ist gibet thînaz fon druhtîne gihôrtaz* 'for thy prayer has been heard by the Lord'. This usage became general towards the close of the OHG period: (Notker) *taz mag man wola sehen an dero* sphaera, *diu* in cella Sancti Galli noviter *gemachôt ist* 'one can see it well on the globe which has recently been made in the monastery of St. Gall'. From this time on, *wesan / sîn* was the regular auxiliary for the perfect (and pluperfect) and structurally parallel to the perfect periphrasis of the active voice (type *es ist gekommen*), the analogy of which doubtless played a part in inducing the above changes in the passive. The new construction then remained usual throughout the Middle Ages and lasted into modern times: MHG (Nibelungenlied) *mir ist selten gescenket bezzer wîn* 'never have I been served better wine',

(Hartmann) *im was der rehte wunsch gegeben / von werltlîcher êre* 'the perfection of earthly honour had been given to him', NHG (Luther) *sie sind . . . oft vertrieben und weggeführt in fremde Land.*

As a result of the development outlined above, the auxiliary *wesan / sîn* could no longer be used for the present, except in the imperative where semantic confusion was scarcely possible, hence still today *sei mir gegrüßt.* Otherwise its place is taken by *werdan,* which had hitherto formed the future periphrasis. The change was easy since with other verbs one tense regularly expressed both present and future; in fact, after this change, things could be said to have become more regular than they were before. In Late OHG, *werdan* was confirmed as the usual auxiliary both for present and preterite. Examples: (Notker) Aristoteles *lêret . . . daz* iro partes *mit* puncto *underskidôt werdên* 'Aristotle teaches . . . that its parts are divided by a dot', Gothi *wurten dannân vertriben fone* Narsete patricio 'the Goths were driven thence by Narses the Patrician'. But the verb 'to be' was for long still used in the infinitive passive and is the commoner construction in MHG: (Helmbrecht) *hêt ich wîn, / der müeste hiute getrunken sîn* 'had I wine, it would have been drunk today'.

A further development, which was to complete the modern pattern of forms, began in MHG, though it did not become general until well on in modern times. Starting from the established use of *werden* as the auxiliary for the present and preterite, new analogical forms were constructed for the perfect and pluperfect: *bin . . . worden, was . . . worden.* A distinctive future periphrasis was similarly evolved: *wirde . . . werden.* Medieval instances are, however, still rare; the first is (Wolfram) *nu was ez ouch über des jâres zil, / daz Gahmuret geprîset vil / was worden* 'now it was also more than a year since G. had been much praised'.

With this new refinement, the use of *sein* and a past participle came to be felt to represent a state only and not an action: *sie ist von allen guten Geistern verlassen* 'she has taken leave of her senses', contrasting with *sie ist von ihrem Manne verlassen worden* 'she has been deserted by her husband'. Other examples are *der Laden ist längst geschlossen,* but *eben ist der Laden geschlossen worden,* and *das muß verstanden sein,* but *daß das gar nicht möglich ist, muß verstanden werden.* The sentence *das Kind ist am 23. Februar geboren* contrasts with, say, *das Kind wird voraussichtlich gegen Ende Februar geboren,* but notice that it is synonymous with *das Kind wurde am 23. Februar geboren.* This latter (more formal) alternative recalls modern English usage where only a past tense is now possible. But this was not always so, cf. Authorized Version *unto you is born this day . . . a Saviour*. Luther has the same tense: *euch ist heute der Heiland geboren*, still idiomatically correct in German. The few verbs which can only denote a state, and not an action, are naturally always found with *sein*, e.g. *in diesem Gefäß ist Wasser enthalten, sie waren von einem Wahn besessen.*

A similar distinction between a state and an action was not impossible in the earlier language before the further development of the periphrastic forms, though it was obviously more limited: MHG (Hartmann) *dô der herre Heinrich alsus geniete sich . . . werltlîcher wünne — er was für al sîn künne / geprîset und gêret — sîn hôchmuot wart verkêret* 'when the Lord Henry was thus in possession . . . of worldly happiness—he was (in a state of being) praised and honoured beyond all his kind—his joy was (lit. 'became') changed'.

Apart from those using *sein* (as above), the great majority of transitive verbs can form a passive with *werden*. In the case of intransitive verbs, however, only the impersonal passive (see below) is possible, e.g. *es wird gewartet.* A number of transitive verbs are similarly treated when, in certain idioms, the verb and its object form a close unit, as *Argwohn schöpfen.* This idiom is syntactically different from, say *Wasser schöpfen*, in that *Argwohn* cannot become the subject of the verb; only the impersonal passive is found: *es wurde Argwohn geschöpft.* Other examples are *Atem schöpfen, Blut verlieren, Reue empfinden, Urlaub nehmen.*

Exceptionally, a few transitive verbs quite lack a passive voice. Of the common verbs for 'receive, obtain, get', *empfangen* and *erhalten* regularly form a passive (with *werden*), but *kriegen* and *bekommen* cannot be used passively at all. Nor can the verb *haben* make a passive, though a past participle has been used: (Th. Mann) *die gehabten Eindrücke.* Reflexive verbs (p. 116) have no passive. Should a passive concept be involved, another verb must be used: *ich weigere mich hineinzugehen* 'I refuse to enter', but *der Eintritt wird mir verweigert* 'I am refused entrance'.

Impersonal passive

Impersonal passives are found in the oldest German. The rise of the construction is obscure, but it must have owed something to the various other impersonal constructions already in existence (p. 169). It will be noticed that the impersonal passive spread by analogy to the intransitive verbs which cannot otherwise form a passive since their past participles have an active meaning. When a verb in the active voice takes a genitive or dative, this case remains in the passive construction. Although the impersonal passive as a syntactical feature was fully developed in preliterary times, it became commoner during the course of the OHG period, at the end of which it may be said to have reached its present range. Examples: OHG (Otfrid) *thes êr iu ward giwahanit* 'you were told before about that', MHG (Walther) *des wirt noch gelachet* 'people still laugh about it', (Helmbrecht) *ez wart geloufen / alle mit einem houfen* 'they all went running in a crowd', *ez wart in widerrâten* 'they were advised against it', NHG *hier wird gewalzt* 'steamroller at work', *ihm kann nicht geholfen werden.* On the use of *es*, see pp. 169–71.

Passive in English and other languages

Like German, English also inherited from Common Germanic the use of the verb 'to be' (*wesan / bēon*) and the verb 'to become' (*weorðan*) as passive-forming auxiliaries. Both are common in OE: (Matthew) *þe hǣlend se þe ahongen wæs* (Iesum qui crucifixus est) "Jesus which was crucified", (Phoenix) *þonne weorðeð his / hūs onhǣted þurh hādor swegl* 'then its house is (will be) warmed by cloudless heaven'. But the latter became rare in ME and had disappeared entirely by the end of the fourteenth century, leaving *be* as the sole auxiliary used in the passive construction.

Periphrastic passive tenses are found in other languages, as Latin. But the periphrastic present here developed into a narrative perfect, hence *amatus sum* means not 'I am (being) loved', but 'I was / have been loved', and the ancient synthetic present *amor* was not replaced, as was generally the case in Germanic. The modern Romance languages, however, have reshaped the inherited passive and use periphrastic forms only. The meanings of the tenses in Romance and Germanic correspond, e.g. French *je suis aimé* 'I am (being) loved / ich werde geliebt'.

INFINITIVE

Introductory

The German infinitive has been identified as the descendant of an Indo-European verbal noun which, in Germanic times, became associated with the present tense. In OHG the infinitive was inflected: nom.acc. *neman* 'take', gen. *nemannes*, dat. *nemanne*, and inflected forms continued for some time in MHG: nom.acc. *nemen*, gen. *nemen(n)es*, dat. *nemen(n)e*. The dative was the most commonly occurring case, being regularly used in connexion with the preposition OHG *za*, *zi*, MHG *ze*, also *zuo* (p. 193). During the course of the middle period, however, the dative ending tended more and more to be discarded, and though it sometimes occurs in the modern period (see below), it is not typical of it, hence NHG *zu nehmen*.

The genitive of the infinitive is used in the same way as the genitive of nouns: MHG (Nibelungenlied) *der helt in werfennes pflac* (*pflegen*+gen.) 'the hero threw it [the stone]', *nû was ouch ezzens zîte* 'and now it was time to dine', cf. NHG *Essenszeit*.

Examples of the dative are given in the next section. Here it will suffice to mention that in MHG the dative ending *-enne* sometimes appears as *-ende*. This ending may still occur in Early NHG: (Closener) *der satte xxv cardinale die lute zu toufende uñ zu begrabende* 'he appointed twenty-five cardinals to baptize and bury the people'. This feature is significant for the rise of the so-called passive participle in modern German (p. 152).

Simple and prepositional infinitives in competition

In its oldest main function, the infinitive appears as the complement of the noun, adjective, or verb, whereby it characterizes the action as the purpose or consequence of the governing word. The meaning conveyed by the infinitive could be emphasized by the addition of the preposition OHG *za*, etc., and by the time of the earliest records this—the prepositional infinitive as opposed to the simple infinitive—is seen to have become by far the commoner construction. In the subsequent period it has further extended its range at the expense of the simple infinitive.

In the oldest German, the prepositional had almost replaced the simple infinitive as the complement of a noun or an adjective:

OHG (Wessobrunn Prayer) *forgip mir . . . craft, tiuflun za widarstantanne* 'give me . . . strength to withstand devils', (Tatian) *thes ni bim wirdîg giscuohu zi traganne* (cuius non sum dignus calcimenta portare) "whose shoes I am not worthy to bear". Only rarely is the simple infinitive found in such cases: (Tatian) *ni bim wirdîg ginemnit wesan thîn sun* (non sum dignus vocari filius tuus) "I am not worthy to be called thy son".

As the complement of verbs, the simple infinitive resisted the encroachment of the prepositional form much better, though it has nevertheless lost much ground. Compare OHG (Hildebrandslied) *her frâgên gistuont* 'he began to ask', (Ezzos Gesang) *tô begonda rîcheson der tôt* 'then death began to reign', but NHG *begann zu fragen*, etc. A number of other verbs now taking the prepositional infinitive are still usually found in MHG with the simple infinitive, e.g. *trouwen, vurhten*: (Nibelungenlied) *ich trouwe an im erdwingen / beidiu liut unde lant* 'ich traue mir zu, ihm Land und Leute abzuzwingen', *daz (kint) vorhte si verliesen* 'sie fürchtete, das Kind zu verlieren'. Similarly MHG *pflegen*, commonly used expletively: (Nibelungenlied) *wie güetlîche vrâgen diu marcgrâvinne pflac* 'how solicitously the margrave's wife inquired'. We may notice that Yiddish here preserves the simple infinitive (in a past tense peculiar to this language): *ikh fleg shteyn* 'I used to stand', where in NHG only the prepositional infinitive is possible: *ich pflege, pflegte zu stehen.*

In the modern language, the simple infinitive is best preserved when its connexion with the finite verb is particularly intimate. This is naturally the case after modal auxiliaries which require an infinitive to complete the sense. Here the simple infinitive remains the general rule: *ich darf sagen, ich kann sagen*, etc., but notice *ich vermag zu sagen*, regular since Early NHG: (Luther) *Gott vermag dem Abraham aus diesen Steinen Kinder zu erwecken.* The simple infinitive may still sometimes be found after a few other verbs. It is regular to say, for instance: *ich lernte ihn kennen*, but *ich lernte, auf mich selbst zu schauen.* It is correct to say *er lehrte mich rechnen*, but both *er lehrte mich bescheiden sein* and *bescheiden zu sein* are possible and equally common. Alternative constructions are often of long standing: (Luther) *welcher lehrete den Balak ein Ärgernis aufrichten vor den Kindern Israel, zu essen Götzenopfter und Hurerei treiben.* In the South, the verb *brauchen* takes the simple infinitive: (Vienna) *ich brauche nicht hingehen*, but the North has the prepositional: (Berlin) *ich brauche nicht hinzugehen*. The latter may be regarded as standard usage, though the former is more traditional, for here *brauchen* has replaced *dürfen* used in this sense until the eighteenth century.

In the older language, the simple infinitive was the usual construction after verbs of motion: MHG (Nibelungenlied) *wâr umbe bîtet Hagene . . . daz er niht gâhet strîten* 'why does Hagen tarry that he does not hasten to fight?', *ouch îlten in dô dienen die Guntheres man* 'and then Gunther's men hurried to serve them'. This construction is still found to a certain extent after the verb *gehen*, e.g. *sie geht einholen, essen, schlafen, spazieren*. Some of these idioms have become productive, hence *spazieren fahren, sich schlafen legen*, the latter going back to MHG. The same construction often occurs after *kommen*, e.g. *ich werde dir helfen kommen*, though the prepositional infinitive is a possible alternative: *ich werde kommen, dir zu helfen*. As the order of words here clearly shows, the connexion of the infinitive with the finite verb becomes less close when *zu* is added. This use of *zu* appears early: (Luther) *ich bin nicht kommen aufzulösen, sondern zu erfüllen*; it has today a definite stylistic value, so that Menge does not alter Luther's text at this point (apart from modernizing to *gekommen*). Otherwise, purpose is now ordinarily expressed by *um zu*+infin. (p. 153), thus one can also have *ich werde kommen, um dir zu helfen*.

The infinitive is very commonly used beside an object which is the complement of the finite verb. In this construction, too, the simple infinitive was formerly more widespread than it is today: MHG (Walther) *mich mant singen ir vil werder gruoz* 'her kindly greeting exhorts me to sing'. Today *mahnen* requires *zu*, e.g. *er mahnt uns, die Rechnung sogleich zu bezahlen*. The construction with the simple infinitive is still regular after *hören, sehen*, and *lassen*, e.g. *ich höre, sehe, lasse ihn kommen*. It is also regular after *heißen* 'command, order': (Goethe) *heiß mich nicht reden, heiß mich schweigen!* The use of *heißen* in this sense today is, however, confined to archaizing style; current German is *befehlen*, etc., +*zu*. The simple infinitive is further found after *fühlen*, at least in short sentences: *sie fühlte ihr Herz klopfen*, though the same concept is also ordinarily expressed by *sie fühlte, daß* or *wie ihr Herz klopfte*.

The familiar English construction with the verb *make* once had a common counterpart in German: MHG (Gottfried) *daz mahte sîne sinne in zwîvele wanken* 'that made his thoughts waver in doubt', NHG (Luther) *die Männer, die . . . wider ihn murren machten die ganze Gemeine.* Storm could still write *der Ton ihrer Stimme machte ihn fast zusammenschrecken*, where contemporary style requires *ließ ihn fast zusammenschrecken.* But there are survivals in certain idioms still in living use: *jemanden glauben machen* and (without the accusative) *von sich reden machen.* In the oldest period, *finden* occurs with the present participle: (Otfrid) *er . . . fand sia drûrênta* 'he found her [the Virgin] in pensive mood' (*drûrênta* formally = NHG *trauernd*), but in MHG, when examples become more plentiful, the infinitive is found as well: (Nibelungenlied) *hey waz man guoter spîse in der aschen ligen vant* 'oh, what excellent food was found lying in the ashes!' Luther uses now the one construction, now the other: *des Morgens . . . fand er den Stecken Aarons . . . grünen, und die Blüte aufgegangen, und Mandeln tragen* beside *ihr werdet finden das Kind in Windeln gewickelt, und in einer Krippe liegend.* Both are still possible, though the participle is probably commoner. Today the infinitive is usual with *liegen, sitzen, stehen*, and common also with *hängen*, otherwise the participial construction is the one most likely to be met with. Certain other idioms contain the simple infinitive on the above pattern, e.g. *er schickt die Frau arbeiten, sie legt das Kind schlafen* (cf. *sich schlafen legen*, above).

Since about 1500, *haben* occurs with an infinitive and accusative object, though only a few verbs are involved, notably *liegen, sitzen, stehen*, also *hängen.* Beside standard *sie haben einen Schrank in der Ecke stehen*, a prepositional *zu stehen* is normal in the spoken German of some places. As this form is used by all classes of society, it will, as like as not, eventually enter the literary language. We have noticed that an elementary-school teacher in Berlin added *zu* as a 'correction' to a child's essay.

On the whole, the prepositional infinitive alone is possible with the majority of verbs today, e.g. *anweisen, bewegen, ersuchen, nötigen, überreden, verleiten*, thus *er hat sie verleitet, die Unwahrheit zu sagen*, etc.

The object may be in the dative case: MHG (Nibelungenlied) *ir wart erloubet küssen den wætlîchen man* 'she was permitted to kiss the handsome man', NHG (Luther) *gib mir trinken.* But the prepositional infinitive has since completely replaced the simple infinitive, hence nowadays, for example, *gib mir zu trinken.* A sole exception is allowable in the case of *helfen* and then only when the subject performs the same action as the person in the dative: *ich helfe dir den Korb tragen*; otherwise the preposition is prescribed: *ich helfe dir, dich aus der Affäre zu ziehen.*

The construction involving the accusative and simple infinitive cannot usually be put into the passive; an exception is *gelassen werden*, e.g. *die Sache wurde fallen gelassen.* In the case of the prepositional infinitive the passive construction is both regular and common: *er wurde angewiesen, die Truppen zurückzuziehen*; with the dative: *ihm wurde befohlen, die Truppen zurückzuziehen.*

The extension of the prepositional at the expense of the simple infinitive in German has a close parallel in the history of English. Examples typical of OE are: (Orosius) (*hē*) *ongan rīcsian* 'he began to reign' just like OHG *begonda rîcheson* above, (Homily) *dryhten, hwæt hǣtst þū mē dōn* 'Lord, what dost thou command me to do?', cf. Ger. (archaizing style) 'Herr, was heißest du mich tun?' The simple infinitive was, in some positions, still holding its own in Elisabethan times: (Winter's Tale) *I list not prophesy*, (Othello) *you were wont be civil.* The contemporary language retains the older construction *I help him carry the basket* as an alternative to the newer *I help him to carry the basket.*

Accusative and infinitive

An accusative and an infinitive may unite to form a single syntactical entity; this is the accusative and infinitive construction well known from Latin. Since the construction is found in OE and Old Norse, it may have been Common Germanic also. But if it was, it has left little trace in German. Perhaps its occurrence after *wissen* in German is traditional, as in MHG (Wolfdietrich) *dâ weste si einen juncbrunnen stân* 'she knew that a spring was there' lit. 'there she knew a spring to stand'. But otherwise the presence of the construction in German must be attributed to Latin influence. This is quite patent in Notker: *wer zwîvelôt* Romanos *iu wesen allero rîcho hêrren* 'who doubts that the Romans were once the rulers of all kingdoms?' The construction again becomes noticeable in the writings of the humanist period and occurs frequently until the beginning of the eighteenth century when it rapidly wanes: (Luther) *ich achte es billig sein*, (Gryphius) *ich schau in Engelland nur wilde Tiere wohnen.* The simple infinitive in this construction was sometimes reinforced by *zu*, hence Luther's sentence above (2 Peter i. 13) was subsequently amended to *ich achte es billig zu sein*, though in modern editions the infinitive seems to be omitted altogether: *ich achte es billig*.

Infinitive replacing present participle

Although the simple infinitive has to a large extent been ousted from its traditional constructions, it has managed to gain a little ground at the expense of the present participle. The starting-point for this movement was the progressive weakening of the termination of the present participle which began in some dialects as far back as the end of OHG times. As a result, the present participle became identical in form with the infinitive: *-ende* > *-enne* > *-ene* > *-en*, which could not fail to lead to a degree of confusion between these two parts of the verb. Consequently, in expressions like *liegen bleiben* 'remain lying', the infinitive *liegen* has replaced an older present participle, cf. MHG (Lamprecht) *iʒ mûʒ da ligende blîben* 'it must remain lying there'.

We have already referred to syntactic confusion between infinitive and present participle in connexion with the rise of *werden* as a future auxiliary, p. 111.

Infinitive with passive meaning, passive participle

As a rule the infinitive has active meaning, but can usually form a passive consisting of the auxiliaries *sein* or *werden* and the past participle (p. 142). Occasionally, however, in association with certain verbs, the active infinitive can take on a passive meaning. Compare the sentences: *er ließ seine Werkleute die Mauer bauen* 'he had his workmen build the wall' and *er ließ die Mauer von seinen Werkleuten bauen* 'he had the wall built by his workmen', or *ich hörte es jemand sagen* 'I heard somebody say it' and *ich hörte es von jemand sagen* 'I heard it said by somebody'. The words *ich hörte es sagen*, spoken in isolation, are therefore ambiguous, meaning either 'I heard it (e.g. a child) say' or 'I heard it said'. Such use of the infinitive with passive meaning is traditional, e.g. (Hildebrandslied) *ik gihôrta ðat seggen* which—in its context—can only mean 'I heard it said'.

The prepositional infinitive assumes a passive meaning when used with the verb 'to be': OHG (Isidor) *nist zi chilaubanne, dasz* ... 'it is not to be believed that ... / es ist nicht zu glauben, daß . . . '. Elliptic phrases occur: commonly *was tun?* for *was ist zu tun?* The passive sense is found with one or two other verbs: *es steht zu befürchten, daß . . . , es bleibt zu erwägen, ob . . . .*

This usage led to a peculiar formation which may be called the passive participle. In such a sentence as (Lessing) *der Rat ist nicht übel und zu befolgen,* both predicative adjective and prepositional infinitive are, syntactically speaking, on the same plane. It is now not a big step to the use of the infinitive attributively, since after the analogy of *der nicht üble Rat,* one can construe *der zu befolgende Rat.* However, the form *befolgende* instead of the expected **befolgene* requires elucidation. The present construction has been attested since the beginning of the seventeenth century. It arose, therefore, at a time when the ending of the prepositional infinitive could still be *-ende* (p. 146) and this form was apparently generalized in the new construction. That this so happened was doubtless due to the influence of the present participle. The novel use of an infinitive in the attributive position, where it was naturally subject to adjectival inflexion, would suggest affinity with the participle which, of course, regularly had the desinence *-ende* also. Finally associations, semantic as well as phonetic, with Latin gerundives—such as *addendus*—may have played a part, for the present construction was created in the officialese of the chanceries. All in all, the original character of the infinitive was inevitably obscured when it came to stand before a noun. Following the precept of Latin, the new form is sometimes known as the gerundive; we have preferred the term 'passive participle'.

By the eighteenth century, the construction was being employed in literature, but it has remained a bookish idiom, never entering the ordinarily spoken language. In everyday colloquial speech the concept *der zu befolgende Rat* might be rendered *der Rat, der zu befolgen ist* or by some other paraphrase, say, *der Rat, den man zu befolgen hat,* much as we would have to say in English 'the piece of advice to be followed', etc.

The construction um zu, *etc.*

In the modern period, the prepositional infinitive may be combined with certain other prepositions. The most prominent of these combinations is *um zu* which has now largely replaced *zu* in the final sense: OHG (Tatian) *samasô zi thiobe giengut ir . . .*

mih zi fâhanne (tamquam ad latronem existis . . . comprehendere me) = Luther *ihr seid ausgegangen als zu einem Mörder . . . mich zu fangen*, but Menge modernizes: *wie gegen einen Räuber seid ihr . . . ausgezogen, um mich gefangen zu nehmen*. The older construction, however, may still be found in high style (p. 149). By the same token, *um zu* may often replace final *daß* (p. 132): OHG (Tatian) *sîne jungôron giengun in burg, thaz sie muos couftîn* (discipuli enim eius abierant in civitatem, ut cibos emerent) = Luther *seine Jünger waren in die Stadt gegangen, daß sie Speise kauften*, but Menge *seine Jünger waren nämlich in die Stadt weggegangen, um Lebensmittel zu kaufen*. The construction is also used after adjectives preceded by *zu* or followed by *genug*, e.g. *er war zu schwach, um eine solche Arbeit zu verrichten* (= *als daß er eine solche Arbeit verrichten könnte*, cf. pp. 140 f.); *ich war nicht erfahren genug, um seine Machenschaften zu durchschauen*. In more recent usage, the construction has taken on a new semantic turn when it expresses an unintended result: *ich half ihm wieder, um nur noch einmal enttäuscht zu werden* 'only to be disappointed a second time'.

The construction *um zu* originated as follows. A sentence such as *er schickt mich um Brot* could be extended by adding a prepositional infinitive as a complement to the noun, without at first affecting the grammatical structure of the original sentence: *er schickt mich um Brot zu holen*. Such things are actually attested, e.g. Early NHG (Ackermann) *bit got umb vernunft dir zu verleihen*. After a time, the noun which had been in the accusative by virtue of its being governed by *um*, came to be treated as the object of the infinitive, while *um* itself was, as a consequence, brought into association with the infinitive. Through such syntactic displacement a new construction came into being: *er schickt mich, um Brot zu holen*. From now on, the object dependent on the infinitive was no longer essential, hence sentences of the type *er schickt mich um einzukaufen* became possible.

Instead of *um zu*, a substandard *für zu* is found locally: *er schickt mich, für Brot zu holen*. The idiom may be a calque on French, e.g. *pour me prendre*, since it is confined to the frontier districts of the West. It is parallel to Eng. *for to take me* (in Matt. xxvi. 55, above).

The other constructions with the prepositional infinitive are *anstatt zu* and *ohne zu*, the former known since the middle of the seventeenth century, the latter since the beginning of the eighteenth.

They presumably arose after the analogy of *um zu*. But whereas *um zu* (and *für zu*) can refer to the object in the same way as the traditional infinitives do, e.g. *er schickt mich, um Brot zu holen*, this is not the case with *anstatt zu* and *ohne zu*. These can only refer to the subject of the sentence: *anstatt selbst das Brot zu holen, schickt er mich*; *er schwor einen Meineid, ohne mit der Wimper zu zucken*.

Infinitive as imperative, etc.

The simple infinitive very frequently has the force of an imperative. This is notably the case in affective situations: *immer zusammen sein! sich nie trennen!* Hence it is common when talking to small children: *Händchen geben! nicht weinen!* It is further familiar from official style, instructions and the like: (traffic notice) *langsam fahren! Vorfahrt behalten!* (airline advertisement) *Minuten fliegen, Stunden sparen!* (suggestion on a packet of cereals) *eine feine Sache ist auch: gepufften Weizen einfach aufrösten*. Such things may occasionally be spoken: (call of station staff on giving signal for departure of train) *zurückbleiben!* It is not easy to account for this infinitive, though it is also a commonplace in other European languages, such as French and Italian. In German, the construction is known only from the modern period, but there are French and Italian examples going back to the Middle Ages.

The prepositional infinitive also occurs with the same function. The context may be literary: (Goethe) *im Namen des Kaisers ihr Wort nicht zu halten!* It is, however, chiefly found in official style: (label on bottle) *zur besseren Verteilung des Fruchtfleisches vor Gebrauch zu schütteln*. Examples such as the latter are clearly elliptical. One may contrast the usual wording *vor Gebrauch schütteln*.

A comparable use of the infinitive in exclamations and questions, still a well-known feature of the contemporary language, appears to be connected with the foregoing. Examples from classical writers: (Goethe) *was, fortlaufen! Er hatte keine Hand voll Leute mehr!* (Schiller) *ein Schwert in den Rat zu nehmen!* — (Goethe) *ich dich ehren?* (Schiller) *wozu noch weiter sich bemühen?*

Infinitives as nouns

From the earliest times infinitives have been used as (neuter) nouns. This is a development common to many languages in view of the hybrid nature of the infinitive. It has at once verbal and substantival character and sometimes the former is overshadowed or even eclipsed by the latter. Compare, for example, Ger. *Irren ist menschlich* with Lat. *errare humanum est* and these again with Eng. *to err* (or *erring*) *is human*. An infinitive can be regarded as fully substantivized when it occurs with an attribute: OHG (Otfrid) *thaȥ drinkan deilet untar iu* 'share the drink among yourselves', *in thes tihtônnes reinî* 'in the purity of the poetry', MHG (Nibelungenlied) *durch sîn eines sterben* 'through his death alone'.

In the modern language, any infinitive can be readily used as a noun, and such usage has become a very prominent feature of the present-day language on all stylistic levels: *man erlebt ein Aufblühen der bildenden Künste*, *ich bin dieses ewige Herumwarten herzlich satt*, (I. Keun) *da war also mein Gehen ein Stehenbleiben zwischen einem Weitergehenwollen und einem Zurückgehenwollen.* As a consequence of very frequent use, however, a large number of substantivized infinitives have, wholly or in part, lost their verbal character. One speaks of *das Geschehen der Zeit*, where the verbal connexions of the infinitive are quite apparent, but they are less so in the compound *Zeitgeschehen*, in fact this word may be found as the idiomatic equivalent of 'current affairs'. Verbal affinities are obvious in *unser Hiersein* 'our being here', but not at all so in *unser Dasein* 'our existence'. The following are everyday examples of substantivized infinitives which have become isolated from the corresponding verbs; in certain instances the isolation is increased by semantic developments, sometimes to the extent that the infinitives now denote concrete objects: *Abkommen*, *Andenken*, *Aufsehen*, *Begehren*, *Behagen*, *Leiden*, *Schreiben*, *Verbrechen*, *Verfahren*, *Verhalten*, *Vermögen*, *Versprechen*, *Vertrauen*, *Vorhaben.* In a few examples the original character of the formation has apparently prevented its use as a plural, e.g. *Bemühen*, *Bestreben*, *Vergnügen*; here the plurals are *Bemühungen*, etc. In the case of *Wesen*, which arose in the MHG period, the corresponding infinitive has long been extinct (MHG *wesen* = *sîn* 'to be'). Other formations going back to MHG are *Leben* 'life' and *Essen* 'food; meal', both of which are today nouns pure and simple. But it may be noted that, even in such cases, a spontaneous substantivization of the infinitive is still possible: *übermässiges Essen* 'excessive eating'.

tun *with infinitive*

A periphrasis with the verb 'to do', of the sort which has become so prominent in English, has been in use in German since the Middle Ages at least: MHG (Walther) *nû biten wir die muoter / und ouch der muoter barn, / . . . daʒ si uns tuon bewarn* 'now we beseech the mother and also the mother's child . . . that they do protect us'. The construction becomes quite common at the beginning of modern times in some sources. Hans Sachs makes great play of it; Luther, on the other hand, eschews it, and the construction is not now in ordinary literary use. But it does survive vigorously in the spoken language of certain areas: *was tun sie spielen? — sie tun Karten spielen* 'what are they playing?—they are playing cards' or 'what do they play?—they play cards'. It will be noticed that the construction has quite lost any emphatic character, as has Eng. *do* in questions and negative statements. But since the construction enables the infinitive to be put at the head of the sentence and so achieve an emphasis by virtue of the word order, it does have a certain justification in the language. It is precisely in this idiom that the construction is most widely used: *schmerzen tut es schon* 'it does indeed hurt'.

This periphrastic use of *tun* is quite common in the South, but it occurs at the other end of the country too, *denn 'tuten' tut der Mecklenburger auch.* The periphrasis occurs in folk-song: *die Feder tut regieren / die ganze weite Welt* and is not entirely unknown in modern literature: (Goethe) *und tu' nicht mehr in Worten kramen.* The regular MHG preterite has often been imitated in archaizing poetic diction: (Uhland) *aus der Tiefe tät ihn mahnen / ein wunderbarer Gesang.*

The infinitive with *tun* in this construction is to be analysed as a substantivization, i.e. *er tut Karten spielen* would properly be *er tut Kartenspielen* (see previous section).

Infinitive instead of past participle

When compound past tenses are used with a simple infinitive, the expected past participle is replaced by the infinitive in a number of instances, above all and most consistently in the case of the modal auxiliaries and *lassen*. Thus *er hat gekonnt*, but *er hat schreiben können*; further *er hat kommen müssen, er hätte gehen sollen, er hatte die Maschine laufen lassen.* Here the infinitive is today the invariable rule, though exceptions are not unknown in earlier writings: (Goethe) *man hatte das Köfferchen stehen gelassen.* The infinitive is still common after *hören* and *sehen*, e.g. *ich habe ihn kommen hören / sehen*, but *gehört / gesehen* are also correct. The infinitive occurs, too, in literary use, with *heißen*, e.g. *er hat mich schreiben heißen*—the living language would have *er hat mich gebeten (aufgefordert) zu schreiben.* The infinitive may also be found, especially in older style, after *helfen*, e.g. *ich habe ihr den Raum sauber machen helfen*, but the now current idiom is *ich habe ihr geholfen, den Raum sauber zu machen.* The combination *kennen lernen* was formerly unchanged: *ich habe ihn kennen lernen*, but now only *kennen gelernt.* Until relatively recently *machen* in the sense of *lassen* (pp. 149 f.) was similarly used: (Goethe) *er hat mich weidlich schwitzen machen*, as were sundry other verbs, among them *anfangen, brauchen, pflegen, wissen*, which at that time, of course, took the simple infinitive (p. 148).

The present construction was, however, sometimes retained when the verb in question began to be followed by the prepositional infinitive: (Hebel) *sie hätten nichts damit anzufangen wissen*, but today only *gewußt* is admissible. We have already referred (pp. 148 f.) to a peculiarity of *brauchen* which occurs both with and without *zu*, hence the double construction: *wir haben uns nicht schämen brauchen* or *wir haben uns nicht zu schämen gebraucht.* Th. Mann combined these two possibilities when he wrote *wir haben uns nicht zu schämen brauchen.*

The construction has been current since the thirteenth century; early instances are: (Gottfried) *durch welchen list hâst du daȥ schif sus lâȥen gân* 'by what art hast thou caused the ship to sail thus?' (Kudrun) *ich hân daȥ hœren jehen* 'I have heard that said'. The construction must owe its origin to a confusion between the past participle and infinitive. Such confusion could often arise in MHG since these parts of the verb were sometimes identical in form, notably in the case of the auxiliary *lâȥen* 'lassen' or 'gelassen', i.e. before the spread of the prefix *ge-* to all past participles (pp. 101 f.), and by analogy often also *heizen* 'heißen', *jehen* 'behaupten' when used as auxiliaries. But also in cases where *ge-* had become attached to the past participle, confusion with the infinitive was still a possibility since the infinitive in MHG frequently took *ge-* in certain syntactical situations (p. 103). As likely as not, the verb *lâȥen* provided the starting-point for the development of the construction.

It remains to be said that, in some spoken German, the past participle of the modal auxiliaries is always replaced by the infinitive, e.g. instead of (Berlin) *ich habe gemußt, ich habe nicht gekonnt*, one hears (Vienna) *ich habe müssen, ich habe nicht können*, clearly an offshoot of the construction just described.

PARTICIPLES

Present participle

It is naturally not possible to determine the extent to which the present participle was used in preliterary German, but it is certain that it became more frequent when the language began to be written. From the first beginnings of the literary tradition, both translators and more independent authors make very free use of the German present participle to copy its Latin counterpart.

There are the countless avowed interlinear renderings: (Benedictine Rule) *sie kewisso farmanênti farhoctôn mih* (ipsi autem contemnentes spreverunt me) 'they, however, being contemptuous, spurned me', (Ambrosian hymn) *wîho magadi . . . tragante heitariu liotfaȥ, / mihileru frôônte mendî* (sanctae virgines . . . gestantes claras lampadas, / magno laetantes gaudio) 'holy virgins . . . bearing bright lamps, rejoicing with great joy'. But similar literal renderings are almost as common in texts which make some pretence at translating properly: (Tatian) *arstantenti Maria in thên tagon gieng in gibirgu* (exurgens Maria autem in diebus illis abiit in montana) "Mary arose in those days and went into the hill country", *her thaȥ bouhnenti in thuruhwonêta stum* (ipse erat innuens illis et permansit mutus) "he beckoned to them and remained speechless". In original German: (Notker) *diêmuôte wesendo und mih selben luzzellîchondo, erhuge ih dîn* 'being humble and abasing myself, I meditate upon thee'. In this way Latin usage was frequently naturalized in German and the ground prepared for the liberal employment of the participle in subsequent periods as well. Later on, the influence of French models was to encourage this trend, but the use of the present participle has always remained essentially a feature of the written language. Where it occurs in modern *Umgangssprache* it is of literary origin, most spoken dialects having long since given it up (p. 112).

Two syntactic uses may be distinguished in the OHG material above: (1) participle purely in apposition, (2) participle governing an object. The evidence of OE and Old Norse suggests that the latter is not native Germanic, and its occurrence in German therefore entirely due to Latin prototypes. Both constructions are commonplace today: (1) *an bestellten Feldern vorbeifahrend, gelangten wir zum Bauernhof*; *sie verließ das väterliche Haus, nicht ahnend, daß sie es nie wieder betreten sollte*, (2) *die Stirne in tiefe Falten legend, durchlas der Lehrer den mißglückten Aufsatz.*

Present participles function to a great extent as adjectives. They are, of course, commonly used attributively with nouns: *kochendes Wasser, eine weinende Frau, wildlachende Sieger*. In many cases the participle loses in varying degrees its verbal character; it may be used figuratively and have become part of a cliché and so appears more or less as an ordinary adjective: *der springende Punkt, die hervorragende Lehrerin, eine glänzende Leistung, eine stehende Redewendung, ein vermögender Mann, ein leuchtendes Beispiel, einleuchtende Worte*. Today all negative present participles are adjectives pure and simple: *ungenügend, unpassend, unwissend.* The last, however, was used by Kleist in a verbal function: *unwissend, wohin sie sich wenden sollte*; today only *nicht wissend* is syntactically possible. The above usage has become an important ingredient in modern style, but it was well developed in the Middle Ages: MHG (Hartmann) *sîn swebendeȥ herze daȥ verswanc, / sîn swimmendiu fröude ertranc* lit. 'his hovering heart ceased to fly, his swimming joy was drowned'. Doubtless the roots go further back, cf. MHG *varnde(ȥ) guot* 'movable property', a traditional legal term.

A present participle can be substantivized; again the verbal character may be diminished or have disappeared altogether: *der* or *die Brüllende, ein Bedeutendes, Badende, Zuwiderhandelnde, Theologiestudierende*. In the case of *der* or *die Vorsitzende* there is no corresponding participle proper, the term being calqued on French *président*. Examples occur from earliest times: OHG (Otfrid) *wanta himilrîchi theist lebêntêro rîchi* 'for heaven that is the kingdom of the living'. Indeed, such things were happening in preliterary times. A small number of present participles were substantivized with their (original) consonantal inflexion, of which three survive: *Feind, Freund, Heiland* < OHG *fîant, friunt, heilant*, cf. *fîan* 'hate', **frîôn* 'love', *heilen* 'save', the last apparently a sort of calque on Lat. *salvator* 'saviour', as also OE *hǣlend*.

sein *with present participle*

German formerly used a periphrasis consisting of the verb 'to be' and the present participle. It is not clear whether this is an inherited construction or an imitation of Latin, cf. OHG (Tatian): *was thaȥ folc beitônti Zachariam* (erat plebs expectans Zachariam) "the people waited for Zacharias". The idiom never becomes prominent, though there are a good number of examples in Otfrid who, however, uses it as a rhyming device: *nû birun wir mornênte / mit sêru hiar in lante* 'now we are mourning with grief here in the country'; like the simple present, it may have a future connotation: *kuning nist in worolti, / ni sî imo thionônti* 'there is no king in the world who will not serve him'. Later instances are: MHG (Hartmann) *daȥ er im bitende wese / der sêle heiles* 'so that he may pray for the salvation of (his) soul', NHG (Luther) *es waren aber Juden zu Jerusalem wohnend*, (Schiller) *ich bin alle Tage seine Antwort erwartend*. When, in the current language, the present participle (formally speaking) occurs in this way, it always has the character of a pure adjective: *es war befriedigend* 'satisfactory' or lit. 'satisfying'. Although the exact nuance expressed by the above construction can scarcely be determined now, it may be supposed, by reason of its verbosity, to have imparted a degree of emphasis to the verbal action, out of which some feeling for durative aspect arose.

The same construction is attested in medieval English: OE (Charm) *bēo þu grōwende on godes fæþme* 'be thou growing in God's embrace', ME (Homily) *þa wreche sunfulle, þe þer were wuniende* 'the wretched sinners who were living there'. We notice, however, that this construction is not structurally identical with that of the modern continuous or progressive tenses, e.g. *be thou growing*. Whereas OE *grōwende* is a regular Germanic present participle, the modern *growing* is a verbal noun as its ending *-ing* indicates. As explained on p. 105, this latter is an imitation of a Celtic idiom, though its remarkable vogue may well have been encouraged by the fact that, from the earliest times, English had used a periphrasis with the present participle. The spread, in the course of the ME period, of the originally substantival termination *-ing* to the present participle proper, resulting in the loss of the regular ending (OE *grōwende cild*, Modern Eng. *growing child*), is a secondary development.

Modern German makes a similar use of the verb 'to be' in other periphrastic constructions, though only to a limited extent, e.g. *die Preise sind im Steigen* 'prices are rising', (in local use) *er ist am Essen* 'he is eating'.

Past participle

Two Indo-European verbal nouns, one with a characteristic dental (*t*) suffix, the other with a nasal (*n*), were adapted in Germanic as past participles proper. The former was generalized for weak, the latter for strong verbs. The difference between the two types is therefore morphological, not syntactical.

The past participle of a transitive verb has a passive meaning: *das gelobte Land, ein gebrochenes Herz*. But there are a few exceptions, though in these cases the original participles have become pure adjectives. A very old example is *trunken* (now only poetic or figurative: *vor Freude trunken*) paralleled in English and the other Germanic languages. As early as OHG, *trunkan* had lost its position in the verbal paradigm, having been replaced by *gitrunkan* with perfective prefix (p. 102). Another example is *gelernt*, e.g. *ein gelernter Tischler*, syntactically the same as Eng. *my learned friend*, and by analogy *ein studierter Mann*. One speaks of *ein verdienter Wissenschaftler*; active meaning also occurs in compounds like *ehr-, pflichtvergessen*. Further *ein geschworener Feind* exactly as Eng. *sworn enemy*. Other examples are now extinct, e.g. OHG *giwizzan*, MHG *gewizzen* 'knowing, clever' from OHG *wizzan* 'know', MHG *ungezzen*, formally 'ungegessen' but meaning 'fasting', as still in Early NHG: (Luther) *der König . . . blieb ungegessen*, with a comparable contemporary *ungetrunken*.

The past participle of an intransitive verb has an active meaning: *ein gefallener Baum, ein entlaufener Sträfling, eingeschlafene Füße*. It will be noticed that the verbs in question are perfective (pp. 101 f.). Imperfective verbs, on the other hand, did not acquire a past participle until the development of the periphrastic past tenses and the periphrastic passive. To this day, they can only be used within these constructions: *ich habe gelebt, ich bin gelaufen, es wird geschlafen*.

Past participles, like present participles, function to a great extent as adjectives. We have seen above how participles could be isolated from the verbal paradigm and turn into pure adjectives. There are, indeed, a great many instances of this trend. Consider *erhaben* lit. 'raised', or *gediegen* lit. 'well or fully grown', originally belonging to the verbs *erheben* and *gedeihen*; their past participles today are the newly formed *erhoben, gediehen*. In not a few cases the verb in question has vanished from the language, but the one-time past participle continues its own life. Thus *gedunsen* is all that remains of MHG *dinsen* 'swell', *verschollen* alone preserves a reminiscence of the obsolete verb *verschallen* 'die away, fade out'. There are, in fact, a considerable number of isolated past participles with the prefix *ver-* employable only as adjectives: *verdattert, verdorrt, verdutzt, verhärmt*, etc. All negative past participles are pure adjectives; this has been the case since the earliest stage of the language: OHG *ungilêrit* 'ungelehrt', *ungiskeidan* (formally 'ungeschieden') 'ungetrennt'. Several such participles are now more isolated by reason of their having acquired a new, figurative sense: *ungehalten, ungereimt, unumwunden*. A few have, in the standard language at any rate, no counterpart of any sort in the positive: *unbescholten, unentwegt, unverhofft*.

Such things as these have always been happening. The adjectives *alt* and *kalt* have been etymologized as original past participles meaning 'having grown up' and 'having got cool' respectively; the doublets *feist* (southern) and *fett* (northern) are an original past participle 'having been fed'. They were already adjectives in Common Germanic times. Like developments inevitably occur in any language given analogous circumstances. There is no lack of examples in English. Compare *ill-gotten* with past part. (*have*) *got*, though American English still keeps the older (*have*) *gotten*. Modern Eng. *forlorn* corresponds to Ger. *verloren*, the rest of the verb having dropped out of the language during the ME period. Eng. *numb* is a survival of the past participle of OE *niman* 'take' and means literally 'taken (with cold, etc.)'.

Not only such isolated past participles have become true adjectives in German. An exceptionally large number of examples are ambivalent and a considerable semantic shift as between pure participle and pure adjective may be involved. It could be said that the language has a positive predilection for converting past participles into adjectives. Consider the following pairs: *es wird gewogen | sie ist ihm gewogen, der Mann hat aufgeschlossen | der Mann ist aufgeschlossen, man hat das Kind ausgelassen | das Kind ist sehr ausgelassen, er hat sie geschickt | sie ist recht geschickt*—in the last example the meaning of the adjective harks back to a medieval use of *schicken* in the sense 'arrange'.

The past participle may be used in apposition, but unlike the present participle it cannot take an object, since the past participle of a transitive verb has a passive meaning. The construction is essentially a literary one: *wegen ihres Mißerfolges bei der Prüfung deprimiert, warf sie sich geistige Minderwertigkeit vor*; *ich habe ihn im Laboratorium erblickt, schweigsam über seine Apparate gebeugt.*

A past participle can be substantivized; again the verbal character may be diminished or have disappeared altogether: *der* or *die Bekannte, Gefangene, Gelehrte, Geliebte, Verstorbene, die Verwandten, Eingemachtes, Gefrorenes, mein Erübrigtes.* The term *der* or *die Abgeordnete* is effectively isolated, there being no corresponding participle in use, while in the case of *der Beamte* feeling for the participial antecedents of this chancery word is quite lost; moreover it forms the feminine *Beamtin.* Nevertheless, the typically adjectival double inflexion is preserved, i.e. weak: *der Beamte,* strong/mixed: *ein Beamter,* pl. *Beamte.* Needless to say, the substantivization of the past participle is traditional: OHG (Tatian) *sênu arstorbanêr was gitragan* (ecce defunctus efferebatur) "behold, there was a dead man carried out".

Past participle after kommen

Quite unique is the use of the past participle after *kommen.* The OHG records give no clue to the possible age of the construction, but it is well attested in MHG: (Helmbrecht) *ûf eine burc kam er geriten* 'to a castle he came riding', (Wolfram) *dort kom geschûftet her | drî ritter* 'there three knights came galloping up'. The construction has remained standard ever since: (Schiller) *die Sonne kommt mit Prangen | am Himmel aufgegangen.*

The presumption is that the unexpected past participle has taken the place of an earlier infinitive with the prefix *ge-*, OHG *gi-* (p. 101). One imagines (fortuitously unrecorded) Late OHG sentences of the type *sie kwâmun gifaran* 'they came riding', where the infinitive with *gi-* is, of course, identical in form with the past participle. It is to be supposed that other ambivalent forms, for example, *giloufan* 'laufen' or 'gelaufen' or *gigangan* 'gehen' or 'gegangen' often occurred in this connexion. It has been plausibly suggested that the latter verb was the likely point of departure. In this case, the infinitive *(gi)gangan* was being replaced towards the end of the OHG period by the short forms *gân*, *gên* > NHG *gehen*. But in the present idiom, so the argument runs, the old infinitive remained, which meant that it eventually came to be regarded as a past participle. And so a new construction arose which, thanks to its frequency, led to the corresponding use of the past participle of all other verbs.

We mention, in conclusion, that in Early NHG an infinitive instead of the regular participle is occasionally attested: (Spee) *da kam ein sanftes Windlein sausen*, and even with the *ge-* prefix: *Regen klar gar lieblich kommt gefließen*. Examples such as these could be echoes of the earlier tradition postulated above.

Past participle as imperative

This striking development is first encountered in MHG: (Helmbrecht) *wâfen / geschrirn über den vater dîn!* (*geschrirn* = NHG 'geschrieen') 'call weapons over your father!' i.e. 'a curse on your father!' The phrase *wâfen geschrirn!* is short for *wâfen sîn geschrirn!* 'weapons be called!' In the same way NHG *stillgestanden!* arose from *es wird stillgestanden!* with omission of the unemphatic auxiliary. For a time the construction was a favourite with the poets: (Schiller) *drum frisch, Kameraden, den Rappen gezäumt, / die Brust im Gefechte gelüftet!* It remains in everyday use, both in light and serious vein: *hereinspaziert, Burschi!* 'just walk in, laddie!', *aufgepaßt!* 'pay attention!'

Other absolute use of past participle

Elliptical expressions, closely related to those in the preceding section, are the common clichés *wohl gemerkt* and *offen gestanden*; one imagines that *es sei* has been suppressed.

Sometimes the participle stands for the verbal concept pure and simple: *gesagt, getan*, (Lessing) *ist das geschimpft, oder gelobt?* (Chamisso) *gesprochen ist gesprochen, das Königswort besteht*. The absolute participle may be interchangeable with the infinitive: *das nenne ich geritten* or *Reiten*, (Lessing) *warum nicht lieber eine neue Klasse gemacht, als sich mit éiner beholfen?* contemporary style: *machen, (zu) behelfen.*

A small number of participles are regularly used absolutely: *einbegriffen* or more usually *inbegriffen, eingerechnet, eingeschlossen* and the opposites *abgerechnet, abgezogen*, e.g. *der Pensionspreis belief sich auf DM* 50, *Bedienung inbegriffen.* Another very common example is *ausgenommen*, e.g. *sonntags ausgenommen.* These expressions derive from official style and doutless reflect to some extent foreign influence. Thus *ausgenommen* may be compared to French *excepté*—and to Eng. *excepted.* Some participles express a condition: *angenommen, vorausgesetzt, zugegeben*, often *angenommen, daß*, etc. Foreign precedent has presumably again played a part, for instance *gesetzt, daß* recalls French *supposé que*. English may use either the present or the past participle: 'supposing', 'assuming', but 'granted', 'provided'.

REFLEXIVE VERBS

Archaic Indo-European languages, such as Ancient Greek, make considerable use of the so-called middle voice. This voice is used when the action of the verb takes place within the sphere of the subject and the consequences of the action refer back to the subject. Parallel to Greek active *lyō* 'I unbind' is the middle *lyomai* 'I unbind for myself, in my own interest'. It is not difficult to understand that subjective concepts like 'remember' or 'enjoy' came to be expressed by a verb in the middle voice, as Greek *mētiomai, hēdomai.*

The ancient Indo-European languages also used reflexive verbs. The special reflexive pronoun found in this connexion was felt as embodying both the subject and the object. As a result, reflexive verbs came particularly close in meaning to middle verbs and often replaced them. This is what happened historically in Germanic, where reflexives have assumed the role of the lost middle voice. Only in Gothic, the oldest of the Germanic languages, are there still a few formal traces of the Indo-European middle.

Among reflexive verbs, those expressing subjective concepts are well to the fore. These are among the reflexives par excellence, verbs which exist solely in the reflexive form, e.g. *sich erinnern, vergnügen* (compare Greek *mētiomai, hēdomai*, above), *entrüsten, schämen.* As inherited elements, reflexive verbs have naturally been in existence in German since the beginning. They have always been prominent and there is no sign of any impending change; on the contrary, the use of the reflexive is, if anything, more marked than ever before. The above mentioned verbs are all to be found in medieval German, but others are more recent. The verb *sich verlieben* and some more of the same type are absent from older writings. This is not to imply that there have been no losses. Take MHG (Helmbrecht) *ich wil mich niht durch wîp verligen* 'I won't miss my chances because of a woman'; it would hardly do to claim *sich verliegen* as a recognized part of the present-day lexicon.

Some reflexive verbs have a non-reflexive counterpart from which they are distinguished semantically: *sich befinden, verlassen, versprechen, zutragen*. Compare also *sich gedulden*, but Early NHG only *gedulden* 'tolerate / dulden', and *sich ereignen*, a modern creation developing irregularly out of MHG *eröugen* 'show'. Another group of reflexive verbs may be compared with the corresponding non-reflexive transitive verbs: *sich ändern, drehen, klären, öffnen, wenden, zeigen*. Notice the function of the reflexives *sich legen, setzen, stellen*, contrasting with *liegen, sitzen, stehen*. A perfective once did duty here, compare at any rate OHG *gi-sizzen* (p. 101), MHG *gesitzen* (p. 103) 'seat one's self'. The verb *baden* has been employed both transitively and intransitively since MHG; used intransitively today it means either 'bathe' or 'take a bath', used reflexively it has only the latter meaning. In reference to ablutions *ich habe gebadet* and *ich habe mich gebadet* are, in practice, used indiscriminately. NHG *sich stürzen* is semantically different from the older intransitive *stürzen* in that it denotes an intentional action.

Reflexive verbs are close to intransitive verbs. This circumstance has led to some movement from one category to the other with a certain amount of overlapping. The matter can be conveniently illustrated from the contemporary language in cases where reflexive and intransitive forms exist side by side. The meaning of each pair will be basically the same, but we note, incidentally, a strong tendency to semantic or at least idiomatic differentiation. Thus *eilen* and *sich eilen* are identical in meaning, yet not always interchangeable: *ich eile hinaus*, but *eile dich!* (also *beeile dich!*). The reflexive *sich flüchten* is proper to a few specialized contexts, the ordinary term is *flüchten*. Further, *sich irren* 'err', but *irren* commonly 'wander (aimlessly)', though sometimes 'err' too. The everyday verb *sich ausruhen* has developed via a now obsolete *sich ruhen* from the intransitive verb *ruhen*; when not semantically distinct, the two are, in general, contextually so: *eine ruhende Venus* is a technical expression pertaining to art, *eine sich ausruhende Venus* is merely facetious.

A reflexive object may, of course, be in the accusative or dative, e.g. *er hindert sich und andere, er hilft sich und anderen*. The same applies in the case of reflexive verbs. In practice, the accusative occurs more frequently, though the dative is also common, as in *sich etwas aneignen, anmaßen, ausbitten, einbilden, erlauben, vorstellen*. In the course of time, changes have sometimes taken place, e.g. *sich fürchten, trösten* originally had the dative: OHG (Otfrid) *ni forihti thir, biscof* 'fear not, bishop!', (Ludwigslied) *trôstet hiu, gesellion* 'take comfort, comrades!'

It is presumed that the reflexive construction was, in the first place, only used when the subject was a person. Gothic would appear to have remained close to this stage, since in that language a non-personal subject is rarely found in a reflexive context. But the oldest German had already decisively broken with such a tradition, non-personal subjects being commonplace: (Otfrid) *ioh, in thia meina, sô spialtun sih thie steine; / thiu grebir sih indâtun, ioh giangun ûȥ thie dôtun* 'and, in truth, then were the stones cleft; the graves opened, and the dead walked out'. The same is true of the later medieval as of the modern language. Especially noteworthy is the large number of impersonal reflexives current today, e.g. *es findet sich, gehört sich, schickt sich, tut sich, versteht sich*. Often such expressions approach the passive sense; we translate *es versteht sich* by 'it is understood', and in not a few instances a reflexive construction is synonymous with a passive: *eine Lösung hat sich gefunden — eine Lösung ist gefunden worden*. However, when the subject cannot be envisaged as itself causing the action, only the reflexive construction is possible: *der Saal füllt sich, leert sich*.

Reflexive constructions with a purely passive meaning are occasionally met with: (Luther) *die Geduld und Furcht Gottes lernt sich*, (Goethe) *diese Familie vergleicht sich jener sehr gut*. The reflexive passive is familiar today, though only in association with an adverb (as in the above quotation from Goethe): *das Buch liest sich leicht*. The construction is believed to be an old calque on French, e.g. *le livre se lit facilement*. Impersonal use, a special development of the original construction, is common in the present-day language: *hier sitzt's sich sehr bequem.* An early instance is (Chr. Weise) *es gehorchet sich übel.*

See also 'Reflexive pronoun', p. 67.

IMPERSONAL VERBS

The oldest group of impersonal verbs is made up of those which denote natural phenomena, e.g. *es donnert*, *hagelt*, *regnet*, *schneit*. This is part of the Indo-European inheritance. Then, by analogy, arose such expressions as *es dunkelt*, *tagt*, *friert*, *taut*, *ebbt*, *flutet*. The formal subject *es* (OHG *iȥ*) has generally been expressed since the beginning of the written records: (Tatian) *iȥ âbandêt* "it is toward evening". This is, however, a secondary development of West Germanic, for both Gothic and Old Norse keep to older, Indo-European practice and use such impersonal verbs without a subject: Old Norse *rignir* 'it rains', Lat. *pluit* 'do.'. German long preserved a reminiscence of this archaic state of affairs whenever the impersonal verb occurred in the infinitive: OHG (Otfrid) *ther io ni liaȥ . . . regonôn* 'who did not allow it to rain' and still in Early NHG (Luther) *über sieben Tage will ich regnen lassen*, but now only with the formal subject: (Menge) . . . *will ich es . . . regnen lassen.* As part of this impersonal system, a construction consisting of *werden* with a predicate has existed since the earliest records: OHG (Tatian) *thô iȥ âband ward* 'als es Abend wurde'. Why the impersonal subject developed is not known. We notice, however, a parallel trend in the neighbouring French, for old *ploet* becomes modern *il pleut*, where *il* is neuter. Other Romance languages here remain conservative: Ital. *piove*, Span. *llueve*. We see that we are dealing with a French–West Germanic innovation.

Much later on, in the MHG period, another set of impersonal verbs arose, the so-called occasional impersonals. These originally took a definite subject and still commonly do so, thus *die Glocke läutet* besides *es läutet*. Other modern examples are *es braust*, *brennt*, *dröhnt*, *duftet*, *gießt*, *klingelt*, *klingt*, *klopft*, *pocht*, *raucht*, *riecht*, *schmeckt*, *spukt*, *zieht*. Among MHG occurrences are: (Hartmann) *dâ sluoc er an, daȥ eȥ erhal, / und daȥ eȥ in die burc erschal* 'he struck upon it so that it rang out and echoed into the castle', (Helmbrecht) *den wîben eȥ durch diu ôren klanc* 'it sounded in the women's ears'.

There is a further group of impersonal verbs, which is, however, syntactically different from the preceding in that *es* may be omitted —and more commonly is omitted—except when it opens the sentence: *es dürstet mich* but *mich dürstet* (this in practice the more frequently occurring word order), less usually *mich dürstet es*; similarly *dürstet euch?* commoner than *dürstet es euch?* Historically speaking, the formal subject is here of later origin than in the examples in the previous paragraphs and has only partially established itself. It is still unknown in OHG, while in MHG it appears sporadically, though only at the beginning of a sentence: (Walther) *eȥ troumte . . . ze Babilône . . . dem künge* 'the king in Babylon dreamed'. See further on these verbs in the next section.

As the above examples show, the verb in question takes either an accusative or dative of the person. Other verbs are: (with accusative) *mich hungert*, *friert*, *fröstelt*, *schläfert*—see further on these verbs in the next section—similarly *mich reut*, *schmerzt*, in high style *mich dünkt* ('methinks'), (with dative) *mir graut*, *graust*, *gruselt*, *schwindelt*. Uncertainty as to case has occasionally led to recognized alternatives: *mich* or *mir ekelt*, *schaudert*. Although the formal subject may sometimes be found with these verbs when in non-initial position (see above), this is no longer usual today. Accordingly the presence of *es* in older writings sounds unfamiliar to modern ears. It has turned out unfortunate that Gretchen had to say *Heinrich! Mir graut's vor dir*.

Subsequently, on the analogy of such formations as the above, other verbs were attracted into the impersonal system. By this time, naturally, the formal subject had become a very prominent feature of impersonal constructions generally. This may explain why, in the case of the newly formed impersonal verbs, *es* is never left out, thus *es juckt mich* or *mich juckt es* (both common), similarly *es kitzelt mich*, *leidet mich*, *lockt mich*, *reizt mich*, *treibt mich*, *zieht mich*, all pedestrian idioms, e.g. *es litt ihn nicht mehr in der Fremde*, *mit aller Macht zog es ihn in die Heimat*. It will be remembered, of course, that beside these more recently created impersonal forms, the original personal ones continue as before: *jemand zieht mich*, *jemand kann mich gut leiden*, etc. This group is seen to have much in common with the 'occasional impersonals' above.

A small number of verbs denoting need or lack now regularly take *es* in all positions: *es bedarf*, *braucht*, and (with personal case, if required) *es fehlt mir*, *mangelt mir*, e.g. *nur bedarf es eines*

Hinweises, an Geld soll es (mir) nicht fehlen. The obligatory use of *es* was established by the beginning of the modern period: (Luther) *da es an Wein gebrach.* In the earlier language, however, the formal subject was not required: MHG (Hartmann) *im enwart über noch gebrast* 'he had neither excess nor lack'. Some of these verbs may be used personally, see next section.

A large number of impersonal idioms are known mostly from modern times; the formal subject is always indispensable: *es läuft mir kalt über den Rücken, es hält mich nicht länger, es kommt darauf an, es eilt damit, es geht (mir) gut, schlecht.* The last example also occurs in medieval writings: MHG (Hartmann) *eȥ gât dir ûf dîne hût* 'es geht dir ans Leder'. The now ubiquitous *es gibt* is later than Luther who wrote (Psalm xiv) *es ist kein Gott,* but Menge *es gibt keinen Gott.* Somewhat similar is the much less frequently used *es setzt*: (Schiller) *auf der Stange prangt ein Hut;/ wenn man ihn nicht grüßen tut, / kommt der Geßler gleich in Wut, / und dann setzt es Blut.* This expression is only used of unpleasant things, cf. the cliché *es setzt Prügel* or *Schläge* (= *es gibt Prügel,* etc.). In the spoken language of some places *es hat* may be heard as well as *es gibt,* e.g. *hier im Teich hat's viele Fische.*

The impersonal passive has been treated on pp. 145 f. Here it will suffice to add that, in this construction, the formal subject only occurs when it is needed to open the sentence: *es wird getanzt, hier wird getanzt,* MHG (Nibelungenlied) *eȥ enkunde baȥ gedienet nimmer heleden sîn* 'warriors could not have been better served', *von heleden kunde nimmer wirs gejaget sîn* 'warriors could not have hunted worse'. Comparative evidence suggests that the use of the formal subject is not much older than MHG.

From impersonal to personal construction

We have in the previous section noted many examples of the impersonal construction arising from personal verbs. The opposite development is also well attested, though it has not been so frequent.

Beside *mich dürstet, mich hungert* there have occurred since OHG times alternative idioms in which the accusative case of the (original) impersonal construction appears as the subject: *ich dürste, ich hungere.* The transition from accusative to nominative was effected via sentences like (OHG) *daȥ kind hungarit* where *daȥ kind*, although accusative in the original impersonal construction, could easily be felt as the subject of a personal one. The latter, however, only became really common in the modern period. Both constructions may be found in recent literature, though the living language now has *ich bin durstig* or *habe Durst*, etc. Similarly *mich friert, fröstelt* co-exist with *ich friere, ich fröstele* and these personal forms are the more usually spoken terms nowadays. From *mich schläfert* a subject developed, but only to form a transitive verb: *ich schläfere jemanden ein*; the impersonal verb is solely literary, with an archaic flavour, the living language having *ich bin schläfrig*.

The impersonal *mir träumt*, now confined to poetic and other high style, was first challenged in the eighteenth century by the newly created personal *ich träume*, the ordinary construction today. About the same time, *ich ahne* came into being to compete with *mir ahnt*, earlier (MHG) *mich anet*, and the personal verb has meantime become much commoner, especially so in persons other than the 1st sg. The possibly related, though still etymologically obscure, *mir schwant*, known since the sixteenth century, has not been involved in the change from impersonal to personal construction. In elevated style *mich verlangt* may still occasionally be met with, but beside this the now usual personal form *ich verlange* has been in existence since the sixteenth century. A still older example is MHG *ich erbarme mich* beside original *mich erbarmt*, which survived into the modern period, to be then eclipsed by the personal construction.

In several cases transition from an impersonal to a personal construction can be attributed, in the last analysis, to a phonetic change, as follows. When, in later MHG, *ȥ* fell together with *s*, the older nom. *eȥ* 'it' became indistinguishable from gen. *es* 'of it', both being now *es*. The nominative obviously proved the stronger and soon the genitive, no longer properly understood, dropped out of use. This, in turn, led to the syntactical change mentioned. The MHG impersonal construction *mich verdriuȥet es* (acc. of person, gen. of thing) would now be interpreted 'it vexes me', the original genitive of the thing being felt as the subject of a personal verb, hence today *etwas verdrießt mich*. In practice, naturally, the MHG impersonal idiom often occurred without actually using the pronoun *es*, e.g. *mich verdriuȥet des dinges*, and such examples kept some feeling for the old construction alive. It survived into the classical period: (Goethe) *es verdreußt ihn des Gaffens* (where *es* is merely the formal subject obligatory in initial position). By the same token MHG *mich wundert eines dinges* was converted into the present-day personal *etwas wundert mich*, though again the older impersonal construction continued for a long time: (Wieland) *gleichwohl wundert ihn des schwarzen Ritters*. Similarly MHG *mich jâmert es*, now personal *etwas jammert mich*, but still in the last century: (Mörike) *den Hauptmann jammerte des Mannes*; furthermore (semantically differentiated) MHG *ich jâmere*, NHG *ich jammere*. MHG (Hartmann) *des genüeget mich von dir* corresponds idiomatically to NHG *das genügt mir von dir* (with further change of accusative of person to dative).

The verb *gelingen* and its opposite *mißlingen* are now used either with an infinitive: *es ist mir nicht gelungen, ihn davon zu überzeugen* = *ihn davon zu überzeugen ist mir nicht gelungen*, or with a noun: *der Versuch mißlang (mir) vollkommen*. These, however, are modern usages, the traditional construction being an impersonal one: MHG (Helmbrecht) *wande selten im gelinget, der wider sînen orden ringet* 'for he who attempts to alter his station in life never succeeds', in modern German 'denn es gelingt einem nie, sich gegen seinen Stand aufzulehnen'. Here *gelingen* is no longer a true impersonal, the formal *es* merely anticipates the real subject, i.e. the whole of the second clause; with which compare the first two examples in this paragraph. Notice also beside the older impersonal *es fehlt an Menschen* or *an Menschen fehlt es* the equivalent, newer personal *es fehlen Menschen* or *Menschen fehlen*. On the other hand, in the case of the parallel examples with *mangeln*, e.g. *es mangelt ihm an Mut* beside (rarer) *der Mut mangelt ihm*, it is the personal construction which is primary, formerly with the genitive: (Luther) *sie sind allzumal Sünder und mangeln des Ruhms*.

To conclude, we note that in German as in many other languages, the basic impersonal construction relating to natural phenomena is frequently modified especially in figurative contexts: (Luther) *er wird regnen lassen über die Gottlosen Blitz, Feuer und Schwefel*; also various often-heard clichés: *die Lawine donnert*, *blitzendes Gold*.

VII · PREPOSITIONS

Introductory

In German, as in English and other languages, a preposition indicates the relationship between a noun and the word governing it, which may be a verb, another noun, or an adjective: *ich frage nach dem Grund, das Haus von Fritz, arm an Mineralien.* Of these, the use after verbs is primary. In OHG, indeed, prepositions rarely occur after nouns or adjectives, pure case forms being employed instead. But this traditional system was greatly modified in the latter half of the Middle Ages as a consequence of the extended use of prepositions, as explained on p. 19.

From the standpoint of the speaker of the modern languages, the preposition is felt to be the connecting link between the noun and the word governing it. Hence one speaks of prepositions as governing nouns. In the case of German, though not of English, one can be more specific and say that a preposition governs a certain case of the noun. The syntactical situation is, however, basically the same in both languages, even though English has lost the case system. We may here notice that case endings in words governed by a preposition are superfluous in so far as the preposition is semantically unambiguous. Usage demands that a given preposition governs such-and-such a grammatical case. There are historic reasons for this, of course, but from the point of view of comprehension the distinct case endings found in German are, broadly speaking, quite unnecessary. Standard grammar prescribes that we say, for instance, *das habe ich von der Frau.* Yet, if we were to say *das habe ich von die Frau,* we should nevertheless be understood perfectly. One might be inclined to label such a solecism 'pidgin' German. Of course, it might be!—but, as a matter of fact, such things are regularly heard in genuine native use. The present example is normal in the substandard colloquial of Berlin, where it reflects the usage in the dialects until fairly recently current in the rural environs of the city, and is typical of the North German dialects generally. In these dialects developments have been, partly at any rate, as in English, i.e. case distinctions have become redundant after an explicit preposition and have accordingly been abolished.

We may recall here, however, that some German prepositions are not, of themselves, semantically explicit. As is well known, *auf* and *in* mean respectively 'on' and 'in' when governing the dative, but 'onto' and 'into' when governing the accusative. Yet, in practice, in the great majority of actual occurrences in the language, the general situation makes it quite clear which sense is meant, so that the case distinctions are mostly superfluous here, too. Only in a few contexts are the case distinctions still significant, e.g. *er läuft in dem Park(e)* 'he runs in the park' and *er läuft in den Park* 'he runs into the park'. Here German still needs the formal case distinction in order to avoid ambiguity, whereas English, having lost the comparable case endings, must use different prepositions. As a general rule, however, the German prepositions are semantically unambiguous, and their extensive use has certainly hastened the decay of morphological endings which has been so conspicuous a feature of the language, especially in its dialect forms, since the beginning of the modern period.

Origin of the primary prepositions

It has been said above that, from the standpoint of the modern speaker, the preposition is felt to govern the noun. This was not, however, originally so, as may be deduced from the fact that the prepositions (at least the oldest of them, the primary prepositions) were originally adverbs of place. Thus, by their nature, they were primarily associated with verbs, not with nouns. Subsequently a twofold development of these adverbs is seen to have taken place. A tendency to put the adverb immediately before the verb, in this way to define it more precisely, was the first step towards the formation of compound verbs. At the same time, adverbs placed next to the noun governed by the verb served to emphasize the former; eventually they came to be associated with the noun rather than with the verb and so the new category of prepositions arose.

This evolution can be traced in Latin. In the sentence *Capuam veni* 'I came to Capua', the verb regularly governs the accusative in accordance with ancient Indo-European practice, the case expressing motion towards. Into such a sentence it was naturally possible to introduce the adverb *ad*, which in Italic indicated motion towards; this reinforced the concept already stated baldly in *Capuam veni.* If used in particularly intimate connexion with the verb, the sentence ran *Capuam adveni*; if used to emphasize the noun *ad Capuam veni.* In the former position, the adverb became an (inseparable) preverb; in the latter position, it became closely linked with the noun and so turned into a preposition 'governing' the accusative. Furthermore, it is likely that *ad* could be used redundantly in our sentence as well: *ad Capuam adveni*; at any rate, the construction is amply attested, e.g. *se ad philosophiam adplicare* 'to apply oneself to philosophy'. In the present case, these secondary developments were accompanied by a decline in the use of *ad* as an independent adverb. As such it must have largely disappeared before the beginning of the literary period, though a reminiscence of its original function is preserved in an early writer, Ennius: *adque adque* 'and onwards and onwards'.

Similar things happened in Germanic. To continue with the same example, we note that the etymological equivalent of Latin *ad* was Germanic *at*, its OHG form being regularly *aʒ*. In High German the word died out about the middle of the ninth century, but the surviving examples indicate that it was well developed both as a preverb and as a preposition. Since in Germanic the word *at* indicated not only motion towards, but also rest at, it could appropriately govern the dative as well as the accusative. We give examples of the preverb and the preposition: (Tatian) *ich bim Gabriel, thie aʒstantu fora gote* (ego sum Gabriel, sum adsto ante deum) "I am G., that stand in the presence of God", (Muspilli) *dâr scal er vora demo rîhhi aʒ rahhu stantan* 'there he shall stand to account before the ruler'. There are no certain examples of the adverbial use in OHG, perhaps fortuitously, since the evidence of other Old Germanic languages shows that the word retained, to a considerable extent, its independent adverbial functions.

Among primary prepositions in common use today are *an*, *bei*, *durch*, *hinter*, *in*, *über*, *um*, *unter*, *zu*; all were originally adverbs of place, some definitely of Indo-European age, all at least Common Germanic. The process of forming prepositions from adverbs continued after the end of the Common Germanic period. Thus, as comparative evidence indicates, such prepositions as *auf*, *aus*, *nach*, or *von* did not develop until the prehistoric period of German as a separate language.

Preverb and preposition

In Germanic, the dividing line between preverb, preposition, and original adverb generally remained fairly fluid, more so than in Latin. This is still the position in German today. Consider the use of *bei* as an adverb, a preverb, and a preposition, as exemplified in these sentences: *er steht bei* 'he stands by', *er steht ihm bei* 'he stands by him' i.e. 'he supports him', *er steht bei ihm* 'he stands by him' i.e. 'he stands near him'. The semantic difference between the preverbal and the prepositional construction is typical; the former has usually the figurative sense, the latter tends to be more literal. Other examples: *ich rede ihm zu* 'I urge him (to do something)', *ich rede zu ihm* 'I talk to him'; *das übersteigt meine Kräfte* 'that exceeds my strength', but *ich steige über die Mauer* 'I climb over the wall'. German has kept alive an ancient syntactical device which enables it to register semantic and stylistic differences. English also inherited this facility, and there are some examples in the modern language, e.g. *the house overlooks the sea*, *he looks over her shoulder*, but in English today such differences are normally expressed by contrasting a verb borrowed from French or Latin with the native word, cf. *exceed*, *urge*, *support*, above.

We have already seen (p. 176) that Latin made use of a construction in which the original adverb appeared both as a preverb and as a preposition in one and the same clause. One could regard this as a construction which, by the redundant use of *ad*, aimed to emphasize the idea of motion inherent in the word. The same tendency was certainly present in Germanic and has continued in German down to the present time, e.g. *wir knüpfen an den Faden der letzten Stunde an*. The construction now takes its most typical form when the preverb is further compounded with the adverbs of direction *hin-* or *her-*, e.g. *ich kann nicht an seine Leistungen herankommen*. Other examples: *er springt aus dem Fenster hinaus* (*heraus*), *er läuft in den Laden hinein* (*herein*), *er hängt von dem Baum hinab* (*herab*). In connexion with the last two examples we add the note that *ein* (as in *hinein*) is in origin the stressed form of *in*, and that *von* has replaced *ab* as a preposition (cf. p. 179).

The prepositions mit, ohne, sonder

The preposition *mit* is not only Common Germanic (Gothic *miþ*, Old Norse *með*, OE *mid*), but also of Indo-European age (Greek *metá*). The word may be used adverbially and as a preverb, so that in function it closely resembles the adverbs of place. Its opposite *ohne* (MHG *âne*, OHG *âno*) is likewise Common Germanic (Gothic *inu*, Old Norse *án*) and also of Indo-European ancestry (Greek *áneu*), but this preposition differs radically from *mit* in that it is never found as a preverb, nor can it be used with *da* as *damit*, etc. (p. 54). It appears, therefore, to be without original adverbial affinities. The etymology of the word is not entirely clear. But it was suggested long ago that it could contain a grade of the Indo-European negative particle seen in *un-*, e.g. *unschwer*. We would accept this interpretation of the preposition *ohne* as an originally negative particle, also because, by implication, it accounts for the syntactical behaviour.

The preposition *mit* governs the dative as the continuer of the Indo-European instrumental. The preposition *ohne*, now used exclusively with the accusative, was in the old and middle periods often construed with the genitive. In Early NHG, *ohne* not infrequently takes the dative, owing to the attraction of *mit*; such usage survives sporadically into the classical era, and has bequeathed a relic to the living language in *ohnedem*. Observe that the dative is used after *mit oder ohne*, e.g. *mit oder ohne den Ergänzungen*. MHG *âne* developed an adverbial function when it could be associated, predicatively, with a preceding genitive. For a time this construction was a commonplace: (Walther) *ir fürsten, die des küneges gerne wæren âne* 'you princes, who would gladly be rid of the king'. The idiom then became extinct in Early NHG, but has left a trace in the often used *zweifelsohne*.

It will be convenient to discuss here a preposition which arose very much later than the above; this is *sonder*. The OHG adverb *suntar* sometimes had the meaning 'apart' (cf. Eng. *asunder*), in which sense the word in MHG developed into a preposition synonymous with *âne* and, like it, governing the accusative: (Walther) *rôse âne dorn, ein tûbe sunder gallen* 'rose without thorn, a dove without gall'. Occasionally the words are used together: (Dietmar) *sunder âne mîne schulde* lit. 'without my guilt'; perhaps this combination implied emphasis in the first instance. In the modern language the preposition *sonder* is rare, and mostly poetic: (Chamisso) *das Riesenfräulein . . . / erging sich sonder Wartung*. In Dutch, interestingly enough, *zonder* has become the exclusive word for 'without'. It will be noticed that *sonder* is, by definition, a primary preposition; a late developer in fact.

The prepositions auf, aus, außer, von

We have remarked above (p. 176) that adverbs of place were continuing to develop into prepositions during the prehistoric period of German as a separate language. In such cases the development can be traced in some detail.

We here take four examples. The first, *auf* < OHG *ûf* and cognate with Eng. *up*, had established itself firmly as a preposition before the beginning of the literary records. It had apparently made headway at the expense of the very old preposition OHG *ana* > NHG *an* (p. 176). An even more successful newcomer is seen in OHG *ûȥ* > NHG *aus*, etymologically identical with Eng. *out*; together with *ûȥar*, it had completely ousted the traditional preposition *ur* before the end of the ninth century. The word *ûȥar* > NHG *außer* arose as follows. In prehistoric German, the adverb *ûȥ* 'out' could appear before the preposition *ur*+dat. 'from' (see below)—actual examples of such usage are found in Gothic and Norse—much as one can say *aus von* in Modern German. By the time of the earliest written records in German, however, the two words had coalesced to give a new preposition *ûȥar* 'from, out of, outside'. Although naturally governing the dative in the first place, examples with the genitive appear in NHG, one of which remains in current use: *außer Landes* 'abroad'. The accusative, too, is attested, as still in the idioms *außer allen Zweifel setzen*, *außer den Schutz des Gesetzes stellen*. Otherwise only the traditional dative is now usual: *wir essen regelmäßig außer dem Hause* or simply *außer Haus*, and indeed the preposition in its primary meaning is today mostly heard in such fixed phrases; other examples: *außer Atem*, *Betrieb*, *Dienst*. Apart from occurrences such as the above, the preposition in the contemporary language means only 'except': *alle waren dort außer mir*. In its primary sense, *außer* has largely succumbed, first to *aus*, and then to *außerhalb*. The preposition *von* basically 'from' was already common in the earliest German: OHG *fona*, older *fana*. This word is a neologism unknown outside the German dialects, perhaps derived from Germanic **af* 'from' with the adverbial suffix *-ana* to reinforce the idea of separation from. By the opening of the historical period it had largely supplanted *ab*(*a*), the regular OHG form of the Germanic simplex **af*, (pp. 169 f.).

In every instance the new prepositions continue to govern the same cases as the traditional prepositions whose places they have taken, apart from the recent aberrations noted for *außer*.

Evolution of secondary prepositions

We saw above that the primary prepositions occurring in German were all originally adverbs of place, most of them inherited from the Common Germanic period, but a few developing in the prehistoric period of German as a separate language. There exists as well, however, a large number of secondary prepositions, that is to say, prepositions which have sprung from parts of speech other than adverbs of place. Of these, the great majority have only come into existence during the course of the literary period, but a handful arose some time before the beginning of the written records. A few occur only in German and must therefore have arisen after German had developed into a separate language, while some have parallels in other West Germanic languages, which argues for an earlier origin.

(*a*) *Preliterary period*

We mention here certain prepositions whose origin is to be placed in the preliterary period. Two of these are in origin comparative adverbs: OHG *êr* 'before (of time), ere' and *sîd* 'since'. Morphologically they belong to the abbreviated type (like NHG *baß* beside the full form *besser*) and their literal meanings are 'earlier' and 'later' respectively. Being comparatives, they would be regularly followed by the dative, which in Germanic had replaced the Indo-European ablative (p. 31). Due perhaps to their exceptional morphology, as well as to the general decline of the dative construction after comparatives, the words had come to be felt as prepositions before the beginning of the written monuments. The former survived throughout the medieval period: OHG (Tatian) *quâmi êr zîti* (venisti ante tempus) "art thou come . . . before the time?", MHG (Crane, from Lexer) *êr mînen tagen* 'before my days', and has left an isolated relic in NHG *ehedem* (OHG *êr* > MHG *ê*(*r*) > with emphatic reduplication NHG *ehe*). The latter is still an everyday preposition: *seit dem Krieg*.

A third preposition is *neben*, which goes back via MHG (*e*)*neben* to the OHG phrase *in eban* lit. 'in equal (to)', cf. OE *on efn* 'do.'. In view of its origin, this preposition was naturally used with the dative; subsequently it came to be construed with the accusative as well (see p. 188). The form *nebst* (with dative only) is secondary and no older than the seventeenth century. It arose from *nebest* < *nebenst* < *nebens* (with analogical, originally adverbial *-s*), variants of *neben* which came into being at the beginning of modern times. A fourth example is *samt* going back to OHG *samant*, in the first place an adverb 'together' which, like its correspondence OE *samod*, had developed into a preposition 'together with' and as such competed with *mit*; it took the dative, as would be expected. This preposition is attested at all periods, but has now rather declined. In particular, older instances are often no longer idiomatically possible, e.g. (Dietmar) *owê du füerest mîn fröude sament dir* 'ach, du nähmst meine Freude mit dir hinweg!' MHG *mit same(n)t* > NHG *mitsamt*, now at any rate only pleonastic, first appears in the thirteenth century.

On the evolution of *nach*, see p. 194.

In conclusion, and as a curiosity, we refer to the widely used North German dialect word *mang* 'among'; it occurs in Berlinese: *ik war ooch dort mang de Leute*. This word is also recorded in Central MHG (*in*) *manc*+dat., lit. 'in a crowd', closely akin to our *among* < OE *on gemong*, *-mang*, a phrase similarly used in the other Old West Germanic languages.

(*b*) *Literary period*

By far the greater number of secondary prepositions have come into being during the historical period of the language. We mention some of the more prominent.

The word *zwischen* is not recorded in its present sense before MHG; in OHG its function was commonly performed by *untar* which also meant 'among': (Tatian) *untar iu inti untar uns mihhil untarmerhi gifestinôt ist* (inter vos et nos chaos magnum firmatum est) 'between you and us is a great gulf fixed'. Formally, *zwischen* is from OHG *zwiskên*, dative of the plural distributive numeral *zwiske* 'two each', which occurs in the common phrase *untar zwiskên* 'between each other'. From such a combination as this the second word eventually took on the character of a preposition which properly belonged to the first, but as it referred to two only, it had the specific meaning 'between'; *untar* continued in use, but with the meaning 'among'. The new preposition automatically governed the same cases as *untar*. It is noteworthy that English developed a similar use of the distributive numeral: *betwixt*, with the related formation *between*. Both words go back to the earliest times. Perhaps the German construction was present in embryo long before it was acutally recorded. Many languages fail to distinguish 'among' and 'between', using the same word for both, as Latin *inter*. The West Germanic languages, however, seem to have felt a need for differentiation and some form of the numeral 'two' was a fairly obvious choice. Perhaps OHG (Hildebrandslied) *untar heriun tuêm* lit. 'among armies two' really meant nothing more than 'between the armies'; an approximate OE parallel would be *bi sǣm twēonum* 'between the seas'.

In Late OHG *halb* lit. 'side' appears as a preposition or, more technically since it follows its noun, as a postposition. A word with such a basic meaning naturally governed the genitive which, as was then usual, preceded (p. 17): (Notker) *ube got unser halb ist, wer ist danne wider uns* 'if God is on our side, who then is against us?'. It occurs sporadically down to the classical period, but is now extinct though it has left relics in *deshalb*, *weshalb*. In MHG a synonymous *halben* (formally dat.pl.) is often recorded; it lived on into the classical period, but has now disappeared apart from the little-used survivals *meinethalben* < MHG *mînen(t)halben*, *deinethalben*, etc. In the fifteenth century *halber*, presumably another case form, became prominent and is still productive: *äußerer Umstände halber*. The adverbial accusatives *inner-*, *ûȥer-*, *ober-*, *niderhalp* became prepositions in MHG and, as they are in origin nouns, they govern the genitive: *inner-*, *außer-*, *oberhalb* are still everyday words, but *niderhalp* has been replaced by a newer formation *unterhalb*. Associated with this series of prepositions are the MHG formations *dis-*, *jenhalp* 'this, that side of'; they survived into the sixteenth century. Synonymous MHG *dis-*, *jensît*, containing the more viable word *sît* 'Seite', passed regularly into Early NHG as *dies-*, *jenseit* (so Luther), but were then gradually superseded by forms with secondary (adverbial) *-s*, whence contemporary NHG *dies-*, *jenseits*.

Other new prepositions originated in a combination of an already existing preposition with a noun, e.g. since the thirteenth century *von . . . wegen*; here *von* governs *wegen* (dat.pl.), which in its turn governs a preceding genitive. A relic of this construction is the often used *von Rechtswegen*. By the seventeenth century it was customary to omit *von*, so that *wegen* became a postposition governing the genitive. As such it survives to the present day, chiefly in rather formal style: *des ungünstigen Klimas wegen*; hence also *des-*, *weswegen*. But, at the same time, *wegen* was used as a preposition proper, i.e. it was placed in front of its noun by analogy with other prepositions, and this became the more usual construction. In the dialects, which by this time had lost the genitive, *wegen* was construed with the dative; such usage is common in *Umgangssprache* everywhere and not infrequently occurs in literature. A colloquial *von wegen* with the dative is often heard in some districts; it is of respectable ancestry, formerly with the genitive: (Luther) *die Unschuld Davids, davon er sang dem Herrn, von wegen der Worte des Mohren.*

A formation comparable to the above is MHG *an . . . stat*, which survives in *an Eidesstatt*. Frequently, however, the genitive followed and the spelling *anstatt*, from the eighteenth century on, shows that the original noun and preposition had coalesced to give a new preposition, a development facilitated by the fact that *Stätte* had ousted *Statt* as the ordinary word for 'place'. By the seventeenth century, *anstatt* was being shortened to *statt*; both remain in common use today. Eng. *instead* is found in ME, but OE has *on . . . stede*, closer to the German. These prepositions obviously governed the genitive in the first instance, but as with *wegen*, the spoken language widely adopted the dative construction which is also not unknown in literature, cf. *stattdem* besides *stattdessen*.

As a preposition, 'along' was best expressed in the oldest language by *after*: OHG (Charm) *man gieng after wege* 'a man walked along a road'; this was traditional Germanic practice. Later on, adverbs based on *lang* 'long' developed into prepositions, like Eng. *along*. The first is the MHG adverb *langes*, *lenges* 'along' (originally a gen.sg. adjective) > NHG *längs*, which retains the adverbial sense until the eighteenth century, but afterwards occurs only as a preposition, usually with the dative: *Bäume wachsen längs dem Wege.* In the classical period another adverb *entlang*, of northern (Low German) provenance, appears: (Goethe) *rausche, Fluß, das Tal entlang*, though not until Campe's dictionary of 1807 was this newcomer "officially" admitted to the High German literary language. The word *entlang* has commonly retained its adverbial function to the present day, but it has also become a preposition (or postposition). In the consciousness of speakers, however, the two different functions are often not clearly felt. When appearing to govern the accusative as in *er ging den Weg entlang*, the phrase *den Weg* is properly speaking an accusative after the verb of motion, and *entlang* an adverb; see 'Adverbial accusative', p. 3. When governing the dative, e.g. *Bäume wachsen dem Wege entlang*, the construction is a secondary development of *an dem Wege entlang*, where *entlang* is, of course, purely adverbial. Older writers sometimes used *entlang* as a preposition proper, i.e. they put it before the noun, hence constructions of the type *entlang dem Wege*, *entlang den Weg*; even the genitive occurs: (E. T. A. Hoffmann) *entlang eines süß rauschenden Baches*. But such usage remained literary and is now unusual.

A MHG compound preposition *binnen* < *be*+*innen* (for the latter see p. 197), of Central German origin, becomes common in older NHG, generally in association with the dative. In the language of today it is purely temporal: *binnen kurzem* 'within a short time', but a relic of former spatial use is traceable in *Binnenland*. The MHG preposition *ûȝer* (p. 179) inspired a complementary formation in MHG *inner* 'inside' which survived in literature until the nineteenth century: (Storm) *inner des Hoftores*, but chiefly in southern writers: (Anzengruber) *inner vier Wänden*, (Pestalozzi) *inner vierzehn Tagen*. Notice (Logau) *inner Landes* 'inside the country', i.e. 'at home', as opposed to *außer Landes*. This preposition has now been replaced in the spatial sense by *innerhalb*, in the temporal sense by *binnen*.

Until modern times *gemäß* (OHG *gimâȝi*, MHG *gemæȝe*) remained exclusively an adjective associated with the dative (p. 24) and this usage is still possible: *eine mir gemäße Haltung* 'an attitude that suits my book'. But from the eighteenth century onwards, *gemäß* came to be felt as a preposition and such is its ordinary function today; it may now precede or follow: *gemäß der Vorschrift*, *der Vorschrift gemäß* 'according to rule'. A few other adjectives have evolved in the same way, e.g. *unweit*. Thus *unweit von dem Dorfe* was abbreviated to *unweit dem Dorfe*—but the positive adjective was not so treated, it remained *weit von dem Dorfe*. Now *unweit* was felt to be a preposition, and by analogy with other prepositions it is found with the genitive as well: *unweit des Dorfes*. We may here also note the recent adjectival adverbs in *-lich* which function solely as prepositions governing the genitive: *anläßlich des Jahreswechsels*, *hinsichtlich der vielen Probleme*. They are based on nouns (*Anlaß*, etc.) and for this reason, it is presumed, they govern the genitive.

A few prepositions were originally participles. The commonest of these is *während*. As a present participle *während* becomes prominent in Early NHG in prepositional phrases like (Zinkgref) *in währender Ehe*. It further appears in a genitive construction without a preposition, common in the seventeenth and especially eighteenth centuries: (Lessing) *währendes Krieges*, (Goethe) *währender Arbeit*. From such genitives, about the beginning of the eighteenth century, the preposition *während* arose through false division: *währender Arbeit* became *während der Arbeit*. The new preposition was regarded as governing now the genitive, now the dative. The present-day literary language prescribes the former, but as in all analogous cases, the unaffected colloquial very often prefers the dative in keeping with a marked trend to avoid the genitive (p. 19). It will be noticed that *während* is a word of bookish provenance. It is not improbable that the whole syntactical process outlined above was inspired by foreign models. A Latin ablative absolute construction like *vita durante* 'while life lasts', i.e. 'during life', led to similar things in French where *durant* eventually assumed the functions of a preposition. Needless to say, Eng. *during* and Dutch *gedurende* are naturalized forms of the same word and, like their prototype, used as prepositions. German writers may have felt a stylistic need to imitate these developments. A few past participles have taken the same course, e.g. *unbeschadet*, *ungeachtet*. These govern the genitive, most likely after the analogy of *ungeachtet* from *achten*+gen. Such usage dates from the sixteenth century.

Since the sixteenth century the genitive of certain nouns has acquired the function of a preposition governing the genitive, notably *angesichts*, *mangels*, *zwecks*, further *mittels*, also *mittelst* (cf. *nebst*, p. 181). The modern prepositional phrases *auf Seiten*, *von Seiten*+gen. are clearly of long standing as is shown both by the absence of the article and by the *n*-inflection of the dat.sg. This helped to isolate the phrases somewhat from the noun *Seite*, so that *Seiten* was free to develop into a preposition: (Felsenburg, from *D. W.*) *seiten meiner ist an euch . . . nicht das Geringste versäumt worden.* Later analogical *-s* was added to give *seitens*, the form used today.

The officialese of the chanceries created a fair number of prepositions, some of which survive. We consider three of these.

Late MHG *nâch lût*+gen. 'in consonance with' was almost at once reduced to *lût* > NHG *laut*. The new preposition was often used with the dative as well, and this practice underlines many clichés heard today, as *laut Bericht*, *laut Protokoll*, though to the modern user such phrases sound more like mechanical formulae than syntactical groups. Early NHG *in* or *aus Kraft*+gen. 'in *or* by virtue of' was, by the sixteenth century, being regularly reduced to *kraft*. About the same time *nach Vermöge*+gen. 'do.' (where *Vermöge* is a now extinct feminine noun related to *Vermögen* n.) was likewise shortened to *vermöge*. Both are found today in formal contexts: *kraft seines Amtes*, *vermöge seines Wissens*. One suspects foreign precedents for these developments. The latter examples, at any rate, recall French *en vertu de* (with *vertu* in its original meaning of 'strength'), *à force de*, cf. Eng. *in virtue of*, *by force of*.

The preposition *inmitten* developed in early modern times from the MHG adverbial *enmitten* 'in the middle' which goes back to OHG *in mittên* where *mittên* is the attributive dat.pl. of the adjective *mitti* 'middle', as in (Notker) *in mittên arbeiten* 'in the midst of tasks'. In accordance with its origin, the emergent preposition naturally took the dative: (Keiserberg) *in mitten dem paradeisz*. But, especially as *inmitten* inevitably came to be felt as meaning *in der Mitte*, it soon began to take the genitive as well. This case is the rule in the language of today: *wie ein Sommertag inmitten des schon vorgeschrittenen Herbstes*, though the older dative maintained itself sporadically for a long time: (Grillparzer) *inmitten dem Kind Italien und dem Manne Deutschland*.

The position of the preposition *gegenüber* is rather exceptional. It first appears in the eighteenth century as the result of the conflation of *über* in adverbial use with the simple preposition *gegen*, as follows: (Klopstock) *gegen dem hohen Golgatha über*, whence with preceding dative (Wieland) *der schönen Nymphe gegenüber*, in which position *gegen* and *über* amalgamate to give the new preposition. Today *gegenüber* may precede as well as follow: *gegenüber dem Laden*, *dem Laden gegenüber*, except when the meaning is 'in relation to, in respect of'; then the preposition most commonly follows its noun, often compulsorily, e.g. *er verhielt sich uns gegenüber recht reserviert*. It is noteworthy that in this combination *gegen* continues to govern the dative, its historically correct case; see next section. The word *gegenüber* is sometimes replaced by *vis-à-vis* borrowed from French in the eighteenth century. In the spoken language of some places it is preferred to *gegenüber* in many contexts, hence e.g. Austrian *vis-à-vis dem Geschäft* for more usual German *gegenüber dem Laden.*

In conclusion, we mention two prepositions which arose through ellipsis. The phrase *Trotz sei dem König* could become, by the sixteenth century, *trotz dem König*; similarly *Dank sei dem König* could become, by the eighteenth century, *dank dem König*. In the case of the former, at any rate, the connexion between preposition and original noun was lost, and *trotz* early came to be used with the genitive. This is the construction prescribed for the literary language, though the position of the original dative remains unchallenged in *trotzdem.*

gegen *versus* wider

The preposition *wider*, now used with the accusative, formerly took the dative as well: OHG (Otfrid) *nist liut . . . thaz widar in ringe* 'there is no people . . . that would wage war against them'. This dative became much less usual in MHG, until by the modern period the accusative is the case normally found, though the other is not unknown: (Goethe) *Gewand, das wider dem Leibe ruht.* In the contemporary language only the accusative is possible, though as a preverb *wider* may still be associated with the dative (see p. 30). The use of this preposition has, however, declined in the face of competition from *gegen*, see also p. 196. Today the simple preposition *gegen* (OHG *gegin*, also *gagan*, etc.) takes the accusative only; in the medieval period, on the other hand, it almost exclusively governed the dative: OHG (Notker) *alsô wazzerlôs erda gagen regene was ih gagen dir* 'as waterless earth to rain was I to thee', MHG (Helmbrecht) *waz die wunders mit ir kraft / worhten gegen der heidenschaft* 'what wonderful deeds they wrought with their strength against heathendom!' Meanwhile *gegen* (common in MHG, though not yet so in OHG) had been replacing *wider* and this process was accelerated at the beginning of modern times. In consequence, *gegen* also began to take the accusative as the case most usually governed at the time by *wider*. This ushered in a period of instability; Luther, for instance, wavers between the two cases. Subsequently, however, the accusative made great headway, though there are still occasional examples of the dative as late as the classical era: (Goethe) *ich will gegen ihnen halten.* It will be remembered that the dative always remains after the compound preposition *gegenüber*, see previous section. The dative is likewise found with *entgegen*, often employed as a stylistic alternative to *gegen*; thus *entgegen meinem Rat* may sound a trifle more emphatic than *gegen meinen Rat.* It most commonly follows its noun: *dem Strom entgegen.* In general, however, *entgegen* functions more typically as an adverb (preverb), but it is found as a genuine preposition from the earliest times: OHG (Ludwigslied) *reit her dara in Vrankôn ingagan Northmannon* 'he rode there into the (land of the) Franks against the Northmen'.

Whereas *wider* appears to be a primary preposition (one might compare *mit*), the origin of *gegen* is obscure, though it is of Germanic age.

Prepositions ordinarily used with accusative and dative

As a reflex of Indo-European practice, the primary prepositions *an*, *auf*, *hinter*, *in*, *über*, *unter*, *vor* and the secondary prepositions *neben*, *zwischen* govern the accusative when there is motion towards, the dative (as representative of the Indo-European locative) when rest at is implied: *er geht an das Ufer*, *er steht an dem Ufer.*

In a large number of instances, however, two conceptions are subjectively possible, and hence either accusative or dative may be felt appropriate. In the recent period there has been a marked tendency to codify usage in doubtful cases, and where this has taken place, older practice now appears incorrect. We note, to start with, that the dative often occurred where now only the accusative is admissible: (Lessing) *als hätte ich mein Studieren am Nagel gehangen*, (Herder) *so gelangen wir in einem Vorhof*, (Goethe) *er hatte sich in einigen Häusern eingeschlichen*, (Schiller) *auf dieser Bank von Stein will ich mich setzen*, (Uhland) *sie ward in heil'gern Sphären aufgenommen.* Conversely, the accusative may occur in older style where today only the dative is found, notably in the case of the common verbs *ankommen*, *einkehren*, *eintreffen*: (Heine) *daß ich . . . auf die Wartburg ankam*, (Chr. Weise) *allwo ich in ein Wirtshaus einkehrte*, (Kleist) *in unser Lager eingetroffen*;

similarly after the corresponding nouns, e.g. (Lessing) *nach seiner Ankunft in die Stadt.* After the prepositions *über* (see further 'The preposition *über*', p. 191) and *auf*, it is now usual to find the accusative in figurative contexts: *sie schüttelte den Kopf über das unartige Kind.* In Luther's Bible we read of the foolish man, *der sein Haus auf den Sand baute.* Today the dative seems commoner in literal contexts, the accusative more characteristic of metaphorical use: *wir haben Häuser auf dich gebaut*, i.e. 'we have pinned great faith in you'. Needless to say, the Biblical phrase is in ordinary use today, but generally in a figurative sense. One would otherwise, in practice, tend to build *auf (dem) Sande.*

Although present usage in these respects is much more regulated than it was, say, a couple of centuries ago, complete standardization has not yet been achieved, so that uncertainties and contradictions may still be encountered. Some idea of the hesitancy in these questions may be seen from the pages of *Der Große Duden, Stilwörterbuch.* For example, under 'einschließen' we read *jemand in ein Zimmer einschließen*, but *den Feind in einer Festung einschließen*, under 'verstecken' we find *das Kind versteckt sich hinter die Mutter*, but *du mußt dich vor ihm verstecken.* Actual practice is, fortunately, not as arbitrary as such examples suggest. Many good German speakers would as readily accept the alternative constructions in every case, i.e. *jemand in einem Zimmer einschließen*, etc. Others, claiming to be more discerning, would detect slightly varying shades of meaning, based on the fundamental concept that the accusative implies motion towards and the dative rest at. Thus *jemand in ein Zimmer einschließen* would be held to convey the idea of actually putting someone into a room to lock him up in, whereas *den Feind in einer Festung einschließen* would be interpreted as indicating that the enemy had already retreated to the stronghold so that all that needed to be done was to shut him in.

In certain cases both constructions may be found with recognized semantic differences, e.g. *sie schreibt auf die Tafel*, but *sie schreibt auf der Maschine* 'she types', *sie schreibt an die Tafel* (= *auf die Tafel*), but *sie schreibt an ihrem Buch* 'she is engaged in writing her book'. One would, however, use the dative in the sentence: *es steht auf (an) der Tafel geschrieben*, since the notion of rest at is complete.

English students will notice that the present-day grammatical conventions of German may not conform to what they—as native speakers of English—regard as logical. When we read, for instance,

(Heine) *die Haifische . . . bissen sich vor Wonne in den Schwänzen*, we instinctively feel that the dative is logically correct and that the accusative would be quite out of place. But German linguistic logic has decided otherwise. In the contemporary language, indeed, the accusative alone is permissible, witness such clichés as *in den sauren Apfel beißen, in die Augen beißen* (e.g. of smoke), *sich auf die Lippen, auf die Zunge beißen*. Other examples may appear equally surprising: *er macht einen Knoten ins Taschentuch, er stützt sich auf einen Stock, er kleidet seine Gedanken in schöne Worte*; here the accusative is obligatory, although the dative is amply attested in older style. And vice versa, the dative is sometimes the prescribed case where we may feel that only the accusative should be used: *das Flugzeug landet auf der Landebahn*, just as the well-known dative construction associated with *ankommen*, etc. (see above) strikes us as unexpected.

When referring to time, however, the prepositions govern one case only: *an, in, unter, vor* take the dative: *an einem Sonntag, in drei Tagen*, (local) *unter der Woche* 'during the week' (older than *während der Woche*, cf. Luther *unter der Stunde*), *vor zehn Monaten*, while *auf, über* take the accusative: (Luther) *Herodes auf seinen Jahrstag* "Herod on his birthday" / (Menge) 'Herodes an seinem Geburtstage', but still *auf meine alten Tage* 'in my old age' and general in the sense 'until': *wir verschieben es auf nächsten Samstag, über eine kleine Weile*.

The doublets von *and* für

The prepositions *vor* and *für* are closely related, and go back via MHG *vor(e)* and *für(e)* to OHG *fora* <**fura* and *furi* respectively. They are, then, differentiated forms of the same word, the former denoting rest at and therefore governing the dative, the latter denoting motion and taking the accusative: (Tatian) *sô liuhte iwar lioht fora mannon* "let your light so shine before men", *fiel . . . furi sîne fuoȥi* "fell down . . . at his feet". In the specialized sense 'for' only *furi* was used: (Tatian) *ouga furi ouga inti zan furi zan* "an eye for an eye and a tooth for a tooth".

This basic distribution of functions remained the same in the MHG period, but since then the form *vor* has, to all intents and purposes, replaced *für* except when the meaning is 'for'. But, wherever *vor* took the place of *für*, the case following remained unchanged. In this way *vor* came to govern the accusative as well as the dative, and so joined the class of prepositions regularly construed with both cases (see p. 188). Historically, it was the North and Centre which took the lead in this development, and here *vor* actually replaced *für* in all senses, as Dutch *voor*. The present, compromise position, largely the work of Adelung, was not generally reached until after the middle of the eighteenth century. Consequently, usage in the classical era was not yet fully regularized, and *für* still sometimes occurs where the new dispensation required *vor*. Consider Goethe's well-known lines: *ich ging im Walde / so für mich hin*. Inquire of a native speaker what *für mich hin* means. You will most likely be told, perhaps after some hesitation, that the phrase means 'alone' or 'not intending to do anything in particular'. Press the matter and you will see that your informant is unable to quote any parallel idiom, and he will admit that the words are unusual. The truth is that the real meaning of Goethe's words is not spontaneously apparent nowadays at all. What people may feel the words to mean is based on what they deduce from the present sense of *für*, i.e. 'for', supported by a vague association with expressions of the type *er spricht vor sich hin* 'he's talking to himself'. To Goethe *für mich hin* meant 'onwards, forwards', the literal meaning being 'before me (implying motion)'. It is a late example of a now lost traditional use of *für*, just as Luther has *für sich und hinder sich* 'forwards and backwards'; see *D. W.*, 4, col. 620.

As a further product of the instability of the pair *vor / für* in the classical era, the latter can occur in place of the former even when the dative is necessary: (Goethe) *für meinen Blicken sicher*, (Schiller) *und weinten für Schmerzen und Freuden*. Modern relics of this period of confusion are *vorerst*, *vorlieb* for correct, but now obsolete *fürerst*, *fürlieb*. In one type of petrified group, *für* continues to be used in its oldest sense: *Jahr für Jahr*, *Wort für Wort*. Here, however, the original meaning of the preposition is no longer apparent; this has no doubt been true of such groups for a long time and will account for the exceptional preservation of the old form. In this connexion one could contrast, e.g. *die Arbeit geht Schritt für Schritt weiter* with *er setzt Schritt vor Schritt*.

The preposition über

NHG, MHG *über* presupposes OHG **ubir*. But, in fact, the ordinary OHG form is the phonologically unexpected *ubar* (cf.

W. Braune, *Althochdeutsche Grammatik*). We conclude that the form *über* is due to the OHG adverb *ubiri* 'over'.

Beside OHG *ubar*, there occurs in Tatian and one or two other sources a form *obar*. It seems that these variants tended to have different functions. The former was used, typically, when motion was implied, the latter denoted rest at; they accordingly govern the accusative and dative respectively: (Tatian) *thie heilago geist quimit ubar thih* "the Holy Ghost shall come upon thee", *ni forlâzent in thir stein obar steine* "they shall not leave in thee one stone upon another". It is tempting to find in the differing uses of *obar* and *ubar* a typological affinity with OHG *fora* and *furi*, discussed in the previous section. But the evidence is too scanty to permit any firm decision, especially since *obar* does not continue into MHG. Indeed, in OHG itself, *obar* was not a common word, its meaning being more generally expressed by *oba*, also with the dative. This latter regularly passed into MHG as *ob*(*e*). There now arose an opposition characteristic of the whole MHG period: when rest is meant, 'over' is translated by *ob*(*e*) with the dative, but when motion is involved, then *über* with the accusative. Only at the beginning of modern times did this opposition break down, when *über* started to replace *ob*, which it has, by now, almost entirely supplanted.

As *über* extended its range at the expense of *ob*, a degree of contamination was inevitable, with the result that *über* now began to take the dative as well. In this way *über* joined the class of prepositions construed with the accusative or dative according to whether motion or rest is implied. On the other hand, *über* keeps, it would seem, a certain hankering after its traditional case, for it is occasionally found with the accusative when the dative would be expected. Consider the often-heard cliché *er ist über alle Berge*, or in the same vein *er ist über die Grenze*, though here *über der Grenze* is also possible, though less usual. The accusative has become particularly common after *über* in figurative contexts. In many cases the accusative is definitely secondary, e.g. *siegen über* now with the accusative, formerly with the dative, *über* having here obtruded into the sphere of *ob*—compare the verb *obsiegen*. When employed in the causal sense, where *über* has replaced *ob* in ordinary use, but has not evicted it entirely from high style, the dative is often found in older writings: (F. Schlegel) *wie muß man staunen über dem, was du sagst*. Nowadays one must put *über das*, *was du sagst*; in high style, where appropriate, *staunen ob* is still just possible. The foregoing applies to several other verbs, e.g. *sich freuen, klagen, lachen, trauern, weinen*. (For *ob*, see pp. 195 f.)

In dialect or near-dialect speech in southern Germany and Austria one may hear *ober* with the dative instead of *über* to denote rest at: *es hängt ober dem Tor*. This preposition appears in southern texts at the beginning of the modern period and, judging from its absence in MHG, it will be a new formation, perhaps suggested by *oberhalb* lit. 'upper side' (p. 182). This local form is sometimes met with in southern writers of note: (Hebel) *unter ihnen und ober ihnen*, (Stifter) *wenn die . . . Mondesscheibe ober ihr stand*.

The preposition zu

The preposition *zu* goes back to MHG, OHG *zuo*. In OHG, however, *zuo* is nearly always an adverb, the phonetically reduced *za, zi* being the normal forms of the preposition: (Wessobrunn Prayer) *tiuflun za widarstantanne* 'to withstand devils', (Charm) *Phol ende Wodan vuorun zi holza* 'P. and W. rode through a wood'. In MHG these forms are further reduced to *ze*: (Walther) *der unsern tôt ze tôde sluoc* 'who beat our death to death'. There is conflation with the dat.pl. of the definite article: (Nibelungenlied) *zen Burgonden* 'to the Burgundians' and with the indefinite article: (Dietmar) *der gedanke vil, die ich hin zeiner frouwen hân* 'the many thoughts I have for a lady'. The preposition is sometimes strengthened by the full form *zuo*: (Nibelungenlied) *dô sah man Gêrnôten . . . gân zuo z'im* 'then Gernot was seen going to him'. And now the use of *zuo* alone as a preposition begins to increase: (Nibelungenlied) *zuo den Burgonden* = *zen B.*, above, (Walther) *ich was von der sunnen / gegangen zuo dem brunnen* 'I had gone out of the sun to the well'. By the end of the MHG period *zuo* had replaced *ze* entirely, though traces of the latter may survive to this day in dialect, as Bavarian–Austrian *zaus* '(at) home' < MHG dial. **zûse*, i.e. *ze hûse*.

The sense of 'rest at a place' has been present in German from the beginning: OHG (Tatian) *Maria . . . stuont zi themo grabe* "Mary stood . . . at the sepulchre"; in MHG the commonly occurring type (Nibelungenlied) *zen Burgonden* often means 'in the land of the Burgundians'. There are considerable traces of such use in NHG. It is still familiar in association with town and city names in certain formal connexions, e.g. *die Deutsche Akademie der Wissenschaften zu Berlin*, and in a number of stereotype expressions such as *zu Tisch(e)*, see p. 92.

In a handful of instances from the older language the accusative appears instead of the dative, particularly before *sich* which in medieval German is accusative only (p. 67): OHG (Notker) *sîn nevo Alderih zuhta daz rîche ze sih* 'his grandson Alderich seized the kingdom'. But why the preposition *zu*, which judging by its Indo-European cognates basically denotes motion towards, should almost exclusively have been used with the dative, as good as never with the accusative, remains one of the riddles of German and Germanic grammar.

nach *and* nahe, nächst; fern

The preposition *nach* has only been distinguished from the corresponding adverb (or adjective) *nah(e)* 'near, near by' in the modern period. In the older language, i.e. OHG *nâh*, MHG *nâch*, *nâ*, the two were not formally differentiated. Although the use of *nâh* as a preposition is well established in the oldest recorded German, it is evidently a secondary development of the preliterary period, for in the other Old Germanic languages this word occurs only as an adverb (or adjective), as OE *nēah* whence the modern *nigh*. We note, however, that the OE comparative adverb *nēar* 'nearer' eventually becomes the modern preposition *near*. In German, *nach* usurped the role of *after*+dat., extinct since Early NHG; accordingly *nach* has always governed the dative.

The close relationship between preposition and adverb is again exemplified in the modern language where the adverb *nahe* 'near' may, in literary style, also occasionally function as a preposition; it then governs the dative: (fairy tale) *nahe dem Brunnen stand ein Baum*. To some extent its opposite *fern* has the same double function. The phrase *fern von* 'far from' may be abbreviated to *fern*, e.g. *fern (von) dem Trubel der Großstadt*, where the abbreviated form suggests higher style, as in *fern den Wirren der Zeit*; it may follow its noun: *der Heimat fern*. Cf. *unweit*, p. 184; see also p. 25.

Lastly, *nächst* has developed from an adverb into a preposition: *nächst seinem Bruder hat er dich am liebsten*.

Case after prepositions; a note on regional use

At the beginning of this chapter (p. 174), reference was made to constructions of the type *von die Frau*, sometimes heard in local speech. Indeed, in the pedestrian colloquial of many regions, such variations on standard use are regularly found. Thus, in Bavarian or Austrian German, the accusative may occur where only the dative or genitive is formally correct, e.g. *bei die Männer*, *seit letztes Monat* (neuter!), *wegen die Fliegen*. This is why Austrian menus regularly print *mit Heurige* 'with new potatoes'.

Traditional prepositions now obsolete or obsolescent

The traditional prepositions have proved themselves to be rather durable parts of the lexicon. All the same, a few of them have gone out of use or grown rare.

Early OHG *aȥ* 'at', which became extinct about the middle of the ninth century, has already been referred to (p. 176). It was replaced mainly by *za* (later variant *zi*), now *zu*. Another ancient preposition disappeared before the end of the ninth century; this was *ur*, later variant *ir* 'out of, outside, from': (Hildebrandslied) *ih wallôta sumaro enti wintro sehstic ur lante* 'I wandered sixty summers and winters outside the country', (Otfrid) *engil ir himile* 'an angel out of heaven'. It survives as a petrified relic, no longer understood, in a few compounds, e.g. *Ursprung*, *Urteil*; see also 'Dative after verbs compounded with a preposition (preverb)', p. 29. This preposition was replaced chiefly by OHG *ûȥ* > NHG *aus*.

The preposition *after*, commonly meaning 'after', continued in restricted use into the early modern period, when it was finally eclipsed by *nach*. In medieval German it governed the instrumental of the demonstrative: *after diu* 'after that', otherwise generally the dative: OHG (Baptismal Vow) *gilaubistû lîb after tôde* 'do you believe in life after death?', older NHG (Zinkgref) *after mir kommen meine Mitgenossen*. The word lived on as the first element in a considerable number of compound nouns. But most of these have now passed out of use as the literal sense of *after* was no longer apparent to the ordinary speaker. Its place was often taken by the transparent *nach*, thus *Afterwelt* 'posterity' succumbed to *Nachwelt*. A few examples linger on, in local use only, as *Aftermahd* 'second mowing (aftermath)', *Aftermieter* 'subtenant', beside the more general *Nachmahd*, *Untermieter*.

Throughout the medieval period the preposition OHG *oba*, MHG *ob(e)* 'on, over' remained in general use: OHG (Tatian) *gieng oba themo waȥȥare* "walked on the water", MHG (Helmbrecht) *mînen gart ob in wegte* 'my goad over them (I) swung'.

In modern times, however, *ob* has been superseded by other prepositions, most typically by *über* which, in the earlier period, had meant 'over' only when motion was implied. In NHG, *ob* survives in archaizing or poetic contexts. In its primary sense it is rare in the more recent language: (Keller) *ob dem Hause standen die schönen Sterne*, being usually found in a figurative sense: (Heine) *da weinten zusammen die Grenadier' / wohl ob der kläglichen Kunde*. A relic of the local sense remains, however, in geographical names: *Rothenburg ob der Tauber*. The word is also met with as the first element in a handful of compound nouns, e.g. *Obacht*, *Obdach*, and as a preverb in *obliegen*, *obsiegen*, *obwalten*.

The preposition *wider* 'against', having during the whole medieval period competed with *gegen*, has now largely disappeared: (Grimm, Märchen) *sie . . . warf ihn aus allen Kräften wider die Wand*, in recent editions often modernized to *gegen die Wand*. When used figuratively, *wider* is still possible: *der Glaubensbote wetterte wider die Verderbtheit der Menschen*, but normally *gegen die Verderbtheit*; in a few clichés *wider* is used exclusively: *wider Erwartung*. The word is well represented in compound nouns and adjectives: *Widerschein*, *Widersinn*, *widerspenstig*, *widerwillig*; here it is not interchangeable with *Gegen-*, contrast *Widerstand* and *Gegenstand*. See also '*gegen* versus *wider*', p. 187. And now a form of *gegen* itself must also be noticed among prepositions obsolescent in the modern language. This is *gen*, a shortening of Early NHG *gehn*. The latter continues MHG *gein*, a not unusual contraction parallel to *gegen*, < OHG *gegin*. Luther commonly uses this form to indicate motion towards, and this usage alone survives today. It is, however, rare, and generally employed with some Biblical allusion: *gen Himmel*. It appears that the contracted form came to be felt as a word different from *gegen*; this will account for its survival.

Another traditional preposition OHG *ab*(*a*), MHG *ab*(*e*) 'from' was usual until modern times: OHG (Hildebrandslied) *obana ab hevane* 'down from heaven', MHG (Hartmann) *er wirfet d'ougen abe mir* 'he turns his eyes from me'. This preposition survived longest in Swiss German, hence (Pestalozzi) *das Vieh ab der Weide zu holen*, but it is now extinct in literary German except in the petrified relic *abhanden* lit. 'from hands' i.e. 'lost'. It was replaced by *von*, e.g. *er wendet die Augen von mir*, *das Vieh von der Weide zu holen*. But *ab* is, of course, fully alive as an adverb (and preverb) and we need it, for instance, in a translation of the Hildebrand phrase above: *von oben herab vom Himmel.* Compare the following MHG sentence with an idiomatic modern equivalent: (Walther) *mit sînem bluote er ab uns twuoc / den ungefuoc* 'mit seinem Blute wusch er uns den Schaden ab' (see 'Origin of the primary prepositions', p. 175). It is a truism to state that a strict distinction between preposition and adverb cannot be made in all instances. Since the former arise out of the latter, it follows that at some point there will be half-way houses. It seems, for instance, that *ab* is on the way towards re-establishing itself as a preposition, at least in a limited sphere. Consider the phrases *ab Lager*, *ab Wien*, *ab Montag*. In the consciousness of the speaker the word *ab* has here the same function as, for example, the preposition in any of the following: *außer Fassung*, *mit Geld*, *ohne Mittel*, *wegen Hochverrat*. On the other hand, its adverbial character is undeniable in *ab nächsten Montag*.

Two adverbs, purely Germanic formations, with the basic meanings 'from inside, from outside' also took on the functions of prepositions during the Common Germanic period, and the words in question survived at least in the oldest stages of the derivative languages. In OHG they appear as *innan(a)*, *ûȥan(a)* and are commonly employed as prepositions: (Otfrid) *innan thînes herzen kust* 'within the purity of thy heart', *stuant ûȥana grabes* '[Mary] stood outside the sepulchre'. The MHG descendants *innen*, *ûȥen* may still be prepositions, but the adverbial use predominates. In the contemporary language *innen*, *außen* are solely adverbs, as prepositions they have been quite superseded by *innerhalb*, *außerhalb*; but see *binnen* (p. 184).

VIII · CONCORD

GENDER

General use of the masculine

DISCREPANCIES between natural and grammatical gender were present in older German as they are in the modern language. Inanimate objects are frequently masculine or feminine: *der wec* 'der Weg', *diu strâȥa* 'die Straße'. Conversely, animate beings are sometimes neuter: *daȥ kint* 'das Kind'; likewise the diminutives: *daȥ kintlîn* 'das Kindlein, Kindchen'.

Further discrepancies, doubtless an ancient trait also, occur as between masculine and feminine. For instance, the statement *die Katze ist ein Haustier* includes *der Kater*, the statement *der Hund ist ein Haustier* includes *die Hündin*. This, the so-called general use of the masculine, is of some practical concern as it is common in the predicative position. Contrast *die Närrin behauptet, daß . . .* 'the fool (i.e. the foolish woman) maintains that . . .' with *Marie, du bist ein Narr*, commoner than *Närrin* which sounds a little stilted in this position. But usage varies, and each case must be taken on its own merits. For instance, only *sie ist eine gute Schülerin* is possible, not *ein guter Schüler* which must refer to a schoolboy. On the other hand, one may say either *sie ist Architekt* or *Architektin*, where the former sounds very formal and not at all personal as does the latter, for the masculine is preferred in formal contexts. Thus, in an announcement of a lecture: *Referent — Frau Dr. Schulz*, but in a discussion on the lecture afterwards one would say, e.g., *die Referentin sagte . . . .* In entirely formal contexts the masculine is invariably used, e.g. on the back of an envelope: *Absender — Erika Schwarz*. Inconsistencies can arise where a noun has no feminine form: *sie ist ein Strohmann, unser Gast, ein starker Esser*. We have suchlike things in English: *she will be chairman*. And similarly in set expressions: *sie ist Herr der Lage* 'she is master of the situation'. The use of the adjective *weiblich* with purely masculine forms is also possible; it occurs most commonly in the plural: *weibliche Studenten* 'women students' as an alternative to *Studentinnen*, similarly *weibliche Mieter* = *Mieterinnen*. Stylistically, such usage is somewhat formal and implies a contrast with the masculine world.

It goes without saying that present-day usage does not necessarily coincide with older practice: MHG *siu was sîn vriunt* must now become *sie war seine Freundin*, though in other contexts only the masculine is possible: *meine Mutter ist kein Freund von Tabletten.*

Finally, the general use of the masculine extends to the pronouns: *aus den Männern klug werden? wenn einem der eigene Ehemann dauernd Rätsel aufgibt?*

Pronouns

Where there was a discrepancy between the natural and the grammatical gender, a pronoun was often used in the older language in the natural gender: (Otfrid) *thiz kint . . . ther blintêr ward giboranêr* 'this (male) child . . . who / which was born blind', (Nibelungenlied) *ein vil edel magedîn . . . Kriemhilt geheiȥen, si wart ein schœne wîp* 'a most noble maiden . . . named Kriemhild, she became a beautiful woman', *verbiut eȥ dînem wîbe, der mînen tuon ich sam* lit. 'forbid it to your wife, I'll do likewise to mine'. In recent German the principle of grammatical agreement has established itself as far as the more bookish relative pronoun is concerned. Whereas Goethe could switch over to the natural gender when he wrote *jenes Mädchen, das vertriebene, die du gewählt hast*, modern usage strictly demands the neuter: *das du gewählt hast*. Otherwise, the pronoun most commonly appears in the natural gender—in practice only the feminine is significant—not only in light style: *so ein prima Mädel! von ihr waren alle entzückt!* but equally in literary language proper: (Heine) *ich denk' an das tote Gretchen . . . doch die ist tot jetzund.* Correspondingly, the possessive adjective occurs typically in the natural gender: *Schwesterlein hat ihr neues Kleid an*, again older practice: MHG (Anon.) *sælic sî daȥ beste wîp / diu mich trœstet sunder spot. / ich bin vrô; dêst ir gebot* 'blessed be that excellent woman who sincerely consoles me. I am well contented; that is her command'. Strict grammatical concord in these matters is nowadays associated with special genres, for example in fairy tales: (Grimm) *da wollten die Zwerge es begraben, aber es sah noch so frisch aus wie ein lebender*

Mensch und hatte noch seine schönen roten Backen, or in technical style: (biology textbook) *das befruchtete Weibchen der Waldameise wirft nach dem Hochzeitsflug seine vier locker sitzenden Flügel ab.*

In older German, pronouns or attributes referring to two or more nouns of different gender appear, in accordance with ancient Germanic grammar, in the neuter: (Tatian) *Zacharias inti quena imo . . . sie wârun rehtiu beidu fora gote* "Z. and his wife . . . they were both righteous before God", (Hartmann) *guot spîse und dar nâch senfter slâf, diu wâren im bereit* 'good food and thereafter sweet sleep, these awaited him'. Feeling for this ancient usage was doomed to disappear with the loss of the distinctive neut.pl. inflexion during the late MHG period, but traces of the construction are still evident in the singular in a few contexts: *willst du einen Apfel oder eine Apfelsine? — keines von beiden.* With persons, however, the general use of the masculine is now normal: *kannst du dich noch an deine Großeltern erinnern? — an keinen von beiden.*

Articles

Here we note an exception to the rule of agreement between article and noun. It concerns diminutives. The regional diminutive *-l*, found in the South, forms neuters like other diminutive endings: South Ger. *es geht wie am Schnürl* = Standard Ger. *am Schnürchen.* With proper names, however, the natural gender asserts itself: *der Seppl* 'Joe', *die Liesl* 'Liz' (South German colloquial regularly uses articles before names, p. 97.) Sometimes, in North German colloquial, the diminutive ending *-chen* does not affect the gender of the word to which it is attached: *guten Tagchen* 'hello', *es wird eine Zeitchen dauern* 'it'll take a bit o' time'.

NUMBER

General and collective use of the singular

The general use of the singular, in the oldest period without any article, has always been a common feature of German, as of English: (Otfrid) *sô muater kindelîne duat* 'as a mother does for a child / wie die (eine) Mutter dem (einem) Kind tut'. Traditional pairs of nouns occurring in phrases like *von Haus und Hof, mit*

Kind und Kegel, über Stock und Stein preserve the oldest state of affairs, as Eng. *from father to son.*

Closely akin to the general use of the singular is its use as a collective: *Korn* '(single) grain; corn', *Haar* '(single) hair; head of hair'. A parallel development took place in English, but both languages then felt some need for differentiation as well. In English, 'corn' is mostly confined to the collective use, the single seed generally being the 'grain', while in German, particularly in spoken German, the plural *Haare* is very commonly used when the meaning is 'head of hair'.

Nouns plural in form but singular in meaning

In the Old Germanic languages, words meaning 'dwelling' may appear in the plural in cases where the sense is clearly singular. Presumably some such notion as 'the buildings' or 'the rooms' (which comprise the dwelling) underlies this usage. There are several examples in OHG: (Otfrid) *fuar si zi iro selidon* 'she went to her dwelling' (sg. *selida*), *fuar Krist zen heimingon* 'Christ went to his native district' (sg. *heimingi*), though this latter word is otherwise only used in the singular: *thie heiminges tharbent* 'those who are away from (lit. lack) their native land'. Stylistic criteria suggest that Otfrid's use of the plural was already then archaic. Nevertheless, an example occurs as late as Notker: *in dien inheimon* (in tabernaculo) 'in the tabernacle' (sg. *inheim*). Words denoting places may be similarly treated: (Otfrid) *in then gewon* 'in the district' (sg. *gewi*), *zen stetin filu wîhen* 'to the very holy city' (sg. *stat*), with a reminiscence still in place-names: *Amstetten, Heilstetten.*

As is well known, the festival names *Ostern, Pfingsten, Weihnachten* are plural in form, hence (saying) *weiße Weihnachten, grüne Ostern,* though the first may have a singular: *in diesem Jahr gab es keine weiße Weihnacht.* The plural names are, however, usually followed by a singular verb: *Weihnachten kommt,* (saying) *wenn Ostern und Pfingsten auf einen Tag fällt* (i.e. never); cf. also p. 203. These plural names appear to have arisen through association with the frequently used plural *Zeiten.* One use survives in the idiom *in alten Zeiten* 'in olden times'. In the earliest language, however, the plural can also occur when the reference is unambiguously to a single point of time: OHG (Otfrid) *quement noh thio zîti* lit. 'the times shall yet come' corresponding to the Vulgate 'venit hora' / "the hour cometh" (John iv. 23).

Abstract nouns used in the plural

In the oldest language, abstract nouns may occur in the plural in contexts where today the plural is either impossible or used in a different sense: (Otfrid) *helfâ* 'helpful deeds / hilfreiche Taten' (sg. *helfa*), NHG *Hilfe* having no plural; *mehti* 'mighty deeds / Großtaten' (sg. *maht*), NHG pl. *Mächte* meaning only 'powers'.

A notable feature of the oldest period was the frequent preference for the plural of abstract nouns when there was no plural sense: (Otfrid) *thio druhtines kunfti* 'the coming of the Lord / die Ankunft des Herrn' (sg. *kunft*) beside the logical singular in *sîn kunft ist . . . ungisewanlîcho* 'his coming is . . . unseen'. Further examples: (Notker) *waz sint toh nû mîne sculde* (cuius criminis) 'what indeed is now my guilt?', *nâh mînen unsculden* (secundum innocentiam meam) 'according to my innocence'; there is a relic of this plural in the modern idiom *sich etwas zu Schulden* (*zuschulden*) *kommen lassen*.

Such usage was clearly optional and it may be noted that Otfrid most often employs these forms in the rhyme. This is not to deny, however, that the plurals may well have contained some shade of meaning or, perhaps more likely, conveyed a stylistic nuance no longer recoverable. Certainly such things are found in various living languages. One might consider that the plural may have been felt to be more emphatic or more intensive than the plain singular. It is noteworthy that there was sometimes no feeling for the literal plural in these cases, witness the following sentence from Otfrid where the plural *kunfti* takes a singular verb: *ni firnimist thu . . . / . . . wanana thih rîne thie selbun kunfti sîne* 'you do not perceive whence his actual coming affects you'.

But this striking plural is, in practice, most often met with in prepositional phrases, some of which have every appearance of being traditional: (Muspilli) *in kihuctin* 'in the recollection / in der Erinnerung' (sg. *kihuct*, i.e. normalized *gihugt*), (Otfrid) *mit îlon* 'with haste / mit Eile' (sg. *îla*), *mit riwon* 'with regret / mit Reue' (sg. *riwa*), (Notker) *mit minnon* 'with love / mit Liebe (Minne)' (sg. *minna*). The construction has survived sporadically down to the present time: MHG *mit vröuden* 'with pleasure / mit Freude (or less usually *mit Freuden*)', NHG *zu Schanden*—a petrified form, hence the now common alternative orthography *zuschanden*, for *Schande* has otherwise no plural; cf. also *zu Schulden*, above.

Subject and verb

It is a commonplace of our grammar that a singular subject takes a singular verb and a plural subject a plural verb. But exceptions to this general rule are found at all periods, especially in earlier times before the more strict application of a logical grammatical code.

In older German a subject consisting of two or more singular nouns regularly took a singular verb if this came first: (Otfrid) *flôȥ thar ûȥ bluat inti waȥȥar* 'blood and water flowed out of it', (Nibelungenlied) *um si begunde sorgen wîp unde man* 'men and women sorrowed for her'. But when such a multiple subject preceded the verb, grammatical concord was the rule. An exception, however, occurs when the subject is formed by closely allied concepts; here the singular is regular: (Nibelungenlied) *vride unde suone sî iu von uns bekant* 'peace and reconciliation be announced to you from us'. The following lines illustrate both main rules: (Helmbrecht) *mich enlât mîn hûbe und mîn hâr / und mîn wol stânde gewæte / niht belîben stæte; / diu sint beidiu sô glanz, / daȥ* . . . 'my cap and my hair and my good clothing do not permit me to stay; they are all (lit. both) so fine that . . . '.

In modern usage grammatical concord is the rule, though a multiple subject formed by allied concepts may still take a singular verb: *wo Glück und Friede soll gedeihen, / muß Herz und Kopf beisammen sein*, (Münchhausen) *Angst und Besorgnis schwebte auf allen Gesichtern*, (Goethe) *so verrauschte Scherz und Kuß, / und die Treue so*; likewise in contemporary language: *Laune und Stimmung ist gut*; *ihm soll jetzt gerade der Prozeß und der Garaus gemacht werden*. The same tendency was once present in English: (Richard II) *sorrow and grief of heart makes him speak fondly*.

In older German a plural subject is occasionally found with a singular verb in circumstances which have not yet been clarified; in the majority of cases the verb precedes the subject: (Nibelungenlied) *dô stoup ûȥ dem helme . . . die viwerrôten vanken* 'then showered from the helmet . . . the fire-red sparks', (Luther) *und fiel des Tages vom Volk dreitausend Mann*. The practice could come in handy for rhyming purposes: (Wolfram) *an disen aht frouwen was / röcke grüener denne ein gras* 'on these eight ladies were suits greener than any grass'. There are parallels in older English: (Chaucer) *that neuer yet was herd so gret mervailles*, (Hamlet) *that spirit upon whose weal depends and rests the lives of many*.

In some cases, the conflict between singular and plural is not easily resolved; logic is often the loser. Luther translates *Dein ist das Reich und die Kraft und die Herrlichkeit* corresponding to our "Thine is . . .", see further 'Copula', p. 205. Such usage is a feature of everyday speech in both languages: *wo ist das Auto und das Rad?* 'where is the car and the bike?' The conflict between number is well illustrated in the case of collective nouns, which are a transitional category, singular in form but plural in meaning. In the older period, a collective noun often took a plural verb: (Wolfram) *gâhten zuo den kielen daȥ hungerc her* 'the hungry army hastened to the ships', (Luther) *das ganze Israel steinigten ihn, und verbrannten sie* ('them') *mit Feuer*. This is on all fours with Eng. *the government say*. There are examples where the first predicate is logically in the singular, but an additional predicate appears in the plural: (Luther) *die ganze Herde Säue stürzte sich von dem Abhang ins Meer, und ersoffen im Wasser*. These examples sound strange today; in the last one, for instance, Menge has *und ertrank in den Fluten*.

Further, a singular subject qualified by a genitive plural often took a plural verb: (Hartmann) *eȥ lâgen undern benken vil guoter knehte* 'there lay under the benches many good men', (Berthold) *ir gar lützel blîbent* 'very few [lit. little] of them remain', (Schiller, archaizing) *es leben selbst in unseren Landesmarken der Sassen viel*. This usage is still sometimes possible and, indeed, normal though the original genitive may have been replaced by other constructions: (by a preposition) *eine Reihe merkwürdiger Zwischenfälle* (or *von merkwürdigen Zwischenfällen*) *wurden nie aufgeklärt*, or (by a noun in apposition) *eine Menge Menschen waren dort* (but *eine Menschenmenge war dort*). Finally, the singular of certain pronouns can be thought of as a collective and occasionally, in older style, takes a plural verb: (Luther) *und hatten ein jeglicher Harfen und goldene Schalen voll Räuchwerks*.

Collective noun with plural pronoun

In the older language especially, a plural pronoun sometimes refers to a collective singular: (Luther) *alle die Menge des Hauses sollen sterben, wenn sie Männer worden sind,* (Goethe) *das junge Paar hatte sich nach ihrer Verbindung . . . nach Engagement umgesehen.* With this last example compare, in principle, Eng. *has everyone got their pen?* where 'correct' *has everyone got his or her pen?* is almost facetious. In this particular instance German, however, has no problem: *hat jeder seine Feder?* (See 'General use of the masculine', p. 199.)

A noun, singular in form, may acquire a plural meaning if qualified by such attributes as *kein* or *manch.* A pronoun referring to a noun so qualified can appear in the plural, especially in the older period: (Goethe) *ein echter deutscher Mann mag keinen Franzen leiden, doch ihre Weine trinkt er gern,* (Walther) *als ich gedenke an manegen wünneclîchen tac, / die sint mir enpfallen gar* lit. 'as I think of many a joyful day, they are quite lost to me'. But a (free) rendering into modern German goes: *voll Wehmut muß ich denken an manchen schönen Tag, der spurlos hingegangen.*

Copula

When the subject and predicate are nouns joined by the copula (the verb 'to be'), they generally have, in the nature of things, the same number: *der Mann ist Soldat, die Männer sind Soldaten.* Where in exceptional cases there is a difference in number, uncertainty may arise as to whether the copula should agree with the subject or the predicate. Usually the subject proves the stronger, but sometimes feeling associates the copula with the predicate: (Lessing) *der Termin, den man ihm setzt, sind acht Tage,* a sentence which would be quite normal today. The same problem occurs in English, and we sometimes make the copula agree with the predicate as in German: *die Hälfte waren Versager* 'half were duds', *zehn Mark ist zu viel,* cf. 'ten shillings is too much'. But, in practice, we do it rather less than the Germans; for instance, we must use the singular in translating Lessing's sentence above: 'the time he is given is eight days.'

Where the subject is a neut.sg. pronoun and the predicate in the plural, the copula regularly agrees with the latter: *alles, was wir dort zu hören bekamen, waren faustdicke Lügen.*

On the use of the neut.sg. pronoun in reference to nouns regardless of number or gender, e.g. *das sind meine Gründe,* see pp. 55, 71, etc. The same usage occurs, though rarely, with the relative pronoun: MHG (Nibelungenlied) *si heten dâ ir friunde zwelf küener man, / daz starke risen wâren* 'they had there of their friends twelve bold men, who were strong giants', Early NHG (Luther) *sieben Fackeln mit Feuer brannten vor dem Stuhl, welches sind die sieben Geister Gottes.*

IX · NEGATION

Emergence of nicht

IN the earliest OHG, the ordinary negative adverb was the particle *ni* inherited from Germanic. It stood before the verb: (Muspilli) *enti imo hilfa ni quimit* 'and help does not come to him'. The particle could be repeated before an indefinite pronoun, combining with it to give rise to a new word: *ni*+*iowiht* 'not anything' > *niowiht* 'nothing': (Wessobrunn Prayer) *dô dâr ni*(*o*)*wiht ni was* lit. 'nothing was not there then'.

By the nature of things, the use of the negative usually implies a certain emphasis; it is easier to say 'yes' than 'no'. Consequently one finds in various languages a tendency to strengthen the negative word. In OHG this was done by inserting *niowiht* lit. 'nothing' generally after the verb; it functioned as an adverb and meant something like 'by no means' or '(not) at all': (Otfrid) *ni zawêta imo es niawiht* 'he did not succeed in it (at all)'. In later OHG this use was common, and more so in MHG, by which time *niowiht* had been abbreviated via *niwiht* to *niht*, while *ni* was weakened *ne*, *en*, or simply *n*: (Nibelungenlied) *des enist mir niht ze muote* 'it is not my intention', *sine kunde's niht bescheiden* 'she could not describe it'. Side by side with such usage, however, many examples occur without the original particle: (Nibelungenlied) *unt wil du niht erwinden* 'and if you will not desist', *nu ist dir dîn schilt / mit swerten niht verhouwen; du lîst ermorderôt* 'now thy shield is not slashed with swords; thou liest murdered'. Clearly, the old particle is becoming redundant, *niht* is no longer an optional strengthener, but the bearer of the negative sense proper.

The rich literature of the thirteenth century shows that the process by which *niht* eliminated the old particle was to some extent bound up with syntactical matters. We mention some typical cases. In Classical MHG the original negative particle was used alone in connexion with the auxiliaries *dürfen*, *künnen* 'können', *mügen* 'mögen', *suln* 'sollen', *türren* 'to dare', *wellen* 'wollen', whenever the dependent infinitive was omitted: (Walther) *des enmac nû niht gesîn; ez enwil diu liebe frouwe mîn* 'now that cannot be; my dear lady does not wish it', (Hartmann) *der gerne biderbe wære, wan daz sîn herze enlât* '(one) who would gladly be serviceable, only his heart does not permit him'. Similarly *wizzen* 'wissen' with a dependent interrogative clause: (Walther) *ichn weiz, obe ich schœne bin* 'I do not know whether I am beautiful'. The particle also occurs alone in connexion with a subjunctive giving the sense 'unless': (Walther) *den lîp wil ich verliesen, si enwerde mîn wîp* 'I will die (lit. lose my life) unless she becomes my wife' (cf. p. 221). The particle further occurs by itself in short parallel clauses in parataxis: (Walther) *nun hân ich friunt, nun hân ich rât* lit. 'now I have not friend, now I have not help' (MHG *nun* = *nu* 'now'+*n* 'not').

But in the second half of the thirteenth century, *niht* spread to clauses like the above which had hitherto resisted its encroachments. The old particle now rapidly declined and by 1300 had virtually disappeared, leaving *niht* (NHG *nicht*) in sole possession of the field.

Parallels in French and English

It is noteworthy that in a neighbouring language, in French, a not dissimilar development took place. Thus, in the French *ne . . . pas* lit. 'not . . . (a) step', the word *pas* was originally introduced to strengthen the true negative *ne*. Even today the word *pas* is not used in certain cases: *je ne puis vous aider*; on the other hand, it is often the sole bearer of the negative idea: *pas du tout!* All this is reminiscent of the general situation in German before 1300. How far these phenomena may have resulted from syntactic borrowing from one language to another and, if so, which language was the giver and which the receiver, cannot now be ascertained if only for the fact that the genesis of the thing lies far back in the preliterary period of both languages. But mutual influences were certainly possible, not to say probable. It may be noticed, for example, that Old French used several synonyms for *ne . . . pas*, one of which was *ne . . . goutte* lit. 'not . . . (a) drop'. Otfrid whose home was Weißenburg (in Lorraine, now officially Wissembourg), not far from the linguistic frontier, several times uses *ni . . . drof*, where *drof* can hardly be anything else than a reduced form of *dropfo*, *tropfo* 'drop': *ni forihti thir, biscof! ih ni terru thir drof* 'fear not, bishop! I shall not harm you (one bit)'.

We may also compare developments in our own language. In OE the particle *ne* was the ordinary negative adverb. The use of *nōht* (= OHG *niowiht*) as a strengthening adverb was possible, though not usual. Then, in ME texts, the strengthening adverb, now become *nought*, subsequently weakened to *not*, comes to the fore and by the fifteenth century, the old particle was given up. Schematically we have: OE *ic ne secge*, ME *i ne seye* beside *i ne seye nought* > *not*, later only *i seye not* = *I say not*, where we reach, by identical means, the same stage as modern German *ich sage nicht*. But English went a step further. The principle of emphasis, inherent in the negative sentence, once more asserted itself, this time exploiting the auxiliary verb 'to do', and gave rise to the new construction *I do not* (> *don't*) *say*, general since about 1700, except in the case of auxiliaries: *I haven't*, *I cannot*—exceptions to some extent paralleled again, in principle, in French and earlier German.

Negative pronouns and adverbs

We saw above (p. 207) how the syntactical repetition of the particle *ni* led to the formation of a new indefinite pronoun (*iowiht* 'anything, aught', *niowiht* 'nothing, naught'); similarly *ioman* 'anybody', *nioman* 'nobody'. New adverbs also came into being in the same way: *io*(*mêr*) 'ever(more)', *nio*(*mêr*) 'never(more)'.

In the old period, the negative forms were more commonly used with a negated verb: (Muspilli) *daz ist allaz so pald, daz imo nioman kipâgan ni mak* 'all that (army) is so bold that nobody can withstand it', though positive forms sometimes occur: (Otfrid) *ni bist es io giloubo, selbo thu iz ni scouwo; / ni mahtu iz ouh noh thanne yrzellen iomanne* 'you will never believe it unless you see it yourself; you cannot yet describe it to anybody either'. In the middle period, however, the negative form becomes the rule after a negated verb: (Nibelungenlied) *done kunde niemen trœsten daz Sîfrides wîp* 'then nobody could comfort Siegfried's wife', *ern möhte sînen lieben sun lebenden nimmer gesehen* 'he could never see his beloved son alive (again)', (Helmbrecht) *ez enwelle et nieman rinder* 'unless anybody perchance wants cattle'. On the other hand, the positive forms are used in some constructions where modern feeling is for the negative, notably in subordinate clauses after *gebieten* and *wænen*: (Wolfram) *den gebôt si allen an den lîp, daz si immer ritters würden lût* 'she commanded them all on pain of death that they should never speak about a knight', (Helmbrecht) *ich wæne, ieman gesæhe / sô manegen vogel ûf hûben* 'I ween nobody (ever) saw so many birds (depicted) on a cap'.

The particle in the above construction shared the general decline of the old negative and finally disappeared; it was in any case redundant, the negative form of the pronoun or adverb being sufficient indication of the sense.

Double negative

Many of the examples already quoted show that, in earlier German, two negative words in the same sentence do not cancel each other out; on the contrary, they maintain or reinforce the negative idea. The same is true of older English. This was good Germanic style, as it still is good Slavonic (Russian *ya ničego ne vižu* 'I see nothing' lit. 'I of-nothing not see').

According to the rules of Latin grammar, however, two negatives in the same sentence are held to cancel each other out, and since the beginning of the modern period German grammarians, schooled in the Latin tradition, have successfully advocated this rule for their own language, too. Nevertheless, older practice may be noticed occasionally in the classical and other writers: (Goethe) *nirgends war keine Seele zu sehen*, (Schiller) *das disputiert ihm niemand nicht*, (Chamisso) *das ist kein Spielzeug nicht*. We cannot imagine English writers of this age and calibre lapsing into such solecisms. English grammarians, too, taught the Latin rule on negatives; clearly they were even more successful in winning acceptance for their views, for though the double negative was common in OE and ME, and still frequent in the Elizabethans, it was given up by the seventeenth century. In both languages, however, the old construction remains intact in dialect. In German, indeed, the construction is acceptable even when speaking a more standard type of language: *ich habe kein Geld nicht*. Such a sentence does not, anyway, automatically provoke a superior smile as does the sub-standard English *I haven't got no money* should it fall upon the wrong ears. In colloquial German the double negative may be regarded as a tolerable regionalism. This being so, we must not be surprised to encounter it now and then in writing; indeed, it sometimes slips into the most careful style: (W. Henzen) *Rankes Ausspruch*, *selbstherrschender und gewaltiger als Luther sei wohl nie ein Schriftsteller in keiner Nation aufgetreten, ist . . . nicht übertrieben.*

As a curiosity, we will mention that the double negative is a feature of Yiddish, which broke off from German proper in the later Middle Ages and subsequently evolved in Slavonic surroundings: *ikh hob keyn gelt nit*. Multiple negatives are likewise regular: *er hot mir keyn mol nit gezogt keyn wort* 'he never once said a word to me'. The influence of Slavonic would encourage this feature, but there is no reason not to suppose that it continues genuine Germanic practice.

Position of nicht

In contrast to the ancient negative particle *ni*, which always immediately preceded the verb, the new formation *nicht* may appear in various positions: (Tatian) *ni wâri dese fon gote, ni mohti tuon thes iowiht* 'wäre dieser nicht von Gott, er könnte nichts tun'. In the following we consider the position of *nicht* in the modern language.

The adverb *nicht* normally follows the verb: *ich weiß nicht*. If there is an object, the negative follows it in unemphatic order: *wir kennen diesen Bericht nicht*. But if emphasis is intended, the negative will be placed in other positions. One can say: *nicht wir kennen diesen Bericht*, where special attention is drawn to *wir*. In *wir kennen nicht diesen Bericht*, the negative may be attached either enclitically to *kennen* or proclitically to *diesen* or *diesen Bericht*, the nuances of emphasis varying accordingly; further emphasis may be obtained by stressing the negative. But there are exceptions to the over-all rule. Thus one says regularly *er hat die Absicht nicht*, i.e. placing the negative after the object, but one must say *er hat nicht die Absicht hinzugehen*, since *er hat die Absicht nicht hinzugehen* would be understood differently, *nicht* then going with *hinzugehen*.

The negative usually precedes the complement in structures like *ich bin nicht der Ansicht*, while *ich bin der Ansicht nicht*, being out of the ordinary, sounds perhaps jocular—or poetic. Similarly *das Dach ist nicht so schlecht*—emphatic is *nicht so schlecht ist das Dach* or *so schlecht ist das Dach nicht*—but Lessing has *das Dach ist so schlecht nicht*, which nowadays sounds unfamiliar in such a context; it would be more in place in poetry: (Chamisso) *der Kanzler spricht bedeutsam: 'Das ist die Meinung nicht'*.

The negative is commonly placed directly after the conjunction in a subordinate clause: *er schaute, ob kein Schiff käme*, but this does not apply if the subject of the clause is an unstressed word: *er schaute, ob es nicht käme*. Generally speaking, however, the negative is found before the word it specially qualifies: *er hat sich nicht deswegen aufgeregt, er hat sich deswegen nicht aufgeregt*. The nuances may be very slight: *keine Besserung ist zu erwarten, eine Besserung ist nicht zu erwarten*.

Exceptionally, in high style, *nicht* can precede its verb: (Menge) *nein, nicht schlummert und nicht schläft der Hüter Israels*.

Pleonastic negative

Pleonastic or redundant negatives have no doubt been in use sporadically from the beginning. The following are among the more typical examples.

A pleonastic negative may be found in the earlier modern period after comparatives: (Luther) *das Wort Gottes ist schärfer denn kein zweischneidiges Schwert*, and occasionally in the classical writers: (Goethe) *wir schweben in diesem Augenblick in einer größeren Gefahr, als ihr alle nicht seht*. This reminds one of the expletive *ne* in French, e.g. *il est plus riche qu'on ne le pense*. A pleonastic negative was further used after verbs with an inherent negative sense: (Luther) *hüte dich, daß du mit Jakob nicht anders redest*, (Schiller) *die Würde hindert, daß die Liebe nicht zu Begierde wird*. Similarly, too, after negative expressions of doubt: (Lessing) *ich zweifle nicht, daß sie ihr Versprechen nicht würde gehalten haben*, with which we may again compare French usage: *je ne doute pas qu'il n'y aille*. These redundant negatives are impossible today. The use after comparatives is puzzling to modern ears—the Germans have as much trouble with the French construction as we have—while in the other examples the pleonastic negative is nowadays felt to have logical negative force, with confusing results. On the other hand, a pleonastic negative is still common, though optional, in a subordinate clause introduced by *bevor* or *ehe* if the main clause contains a negative; when the subordinate clause precedes the main clause, the pleonastic negative is usual: *Sie können kein Geld erwarten, bevor / ehe die Ware (nicht) geliefert ist — bevor / ehe die Ware nicht geliefert ist, können Sie kein Geld erwarten*. Clauses introduced by *bis* show the same use of the negative: *bis du nicht dein Brot aufgegessen hast, darfst du keinen Kuchen haben.*

Litotes

Litotes or understatement is relevant here as far as MHG is concerned, where such commonly used terms as (*vil*) *selten* lit. '(very) seldom', or *lützel ieman* lit. 'hardly anybody' have acquired an entirely negative sense, i.e. 'never' and 'nobody': (Nibelungenlied) *den herren muoten selten deheiniu herzen leit* 'affairs of the heart never troubled the gentleman', (Kürenberg) *son weiȥ doch lützel ieman, wieȥ under uns zwein ist getân* 'so indeed nobody knows what has passed between us two'.

X · CLAUSE COMBINATION

CO-ORDINATION

CO-ORDINATE clauses may be placed together either with or without a connecting word. Connecting words are chiefly demonstrative pronouns or adverbs (or particles) or co-ordinating conjunctions.

Asyndesis

The placing together of clauses without a connecting word is termed asyndesis. It is a permanent feature of the language, though fashions change in this as in other respects. It was, for instance, an established feature of Old Germanic style that sentences having the same subject could be strung together without any repetition of the subject and without any connecting word, e.g. in the archaic diction of Muspilli: *denne varant engilâ uper dio marhâ, / wechant deotâ, wîssant ze dinge* 'then angels fly over the lands, wake the people, lead (them) to the judgement'. But nowadays, as in English, asyndesis throughout is felt to be too stark. In natural style a conjunction is now inserted before the final clause: *dann fahren die Engel über die Länder, wecken die Völker und führen* (*sie*) *zum Gericht*. Very often the subject is taken up again by a pronoun in the second clause: *sie wecken*, etc.

Demonstrative words, etc.

From the earliest times demonstrative pronouns and adverbs have acted as links between clauses: OHG (Physiologus) *sô heizzit ein tier* elevas, *daz ist ein helfant, ter hebit mihela verstannussida* 'then there is an animal called *elevas*, that is an elephant, he has great intelligence'. The demonstrative is here clearly not a relative, which would of course require subordinate word order. Here an example of connecting word and relative pronoun side by side: MHG (Berthold) *reht als alle die sternen des himels . . . , die habent alle samt ir lieht von der sunnen, diu uns dâ liuhtet* 'just as all the stars of heaven . . . , they all together have their light from the sun which shines upon us'. We may notice here that, in ordinary simple speech, the present construction is preferred to a relative clause: instead of *es gibt Leute, die nie zufrieden sind*, the spoken language will more often have *es gibt Leute, die sind nie zufrieden.* Both sentences correspond idiomatically to 'there are people who are never satisfied', English being in this instance unable to express the stylistic difference implicit in the German. Luther often employs the demonstrative in this way: *da erschienen ihnen Moses und Elias, die redeten mit ihm*, but such usage today sounds too colloquial for high style, hence (Menge) *es erschienen ihnen Mose und Elia und besprachen sich mit ihm.* On the other hand, the popular construction is usual in fairy-tale style: *es war einmal ein König, der hatte . . . .* Further examples of average use today: *Eierkuchen, die habe ich gern* 'I like pancakes'; *was ein rechter Bauer ist, der geht bei Wind und Wetter aufs Feld*; *es war so bitter kalt, deswegen sind wir zu Hause geblieben*; *er wird schon kommen, darauf können Sie sich verlassen.* Adverbs of time or place may have the same function, especially *da* is very common in this respect: *wir kommen in dem Dorf an, da ist weit und breit niemand zu sehen.* The particles *so, also* are often employed in a similar way: *die Plätze sind bereits ausverkauft, so (also) hat es keinen Sinn länger zu warten*, see also pp. 231 ff.

Several connecting words in the above categories have become subordinating conjunctions, as explained elsewhere in this chapter.

Co-ordinating conjunctions

An old German word for 'and' is OHG *ioh* which, though common enough in its time, becomes rare in the middle period (MHG *ioch*) and finally dies out in Early NHG. This West Germanic conjunction also figures in Gothic where *jah* is the standard word for 'and'. NHG *und*, MHG *unde*, OHG *anti* > *enti*, or (usually) *inti*, (rarely) *unti*, also occurs from the beginning. It seems to have originally had an adversative sense, cf. the etymologically related Greek *antí* 'against', Latin *ante* 'in front of', and its Old Norse cognate *en* has the meaning 'but'. However, no trace of such a meaning is identifiable in German, where in the oldest records the word may alternate with *ioh*: (Otfrid) *thû scalt beran einan alawaltendan / erdun ioh himiles inti alles lîphaftes* 'you shall bear one who will rule supremely earth and heaven and all life'. Incidently, this repetition of the conjunction before each phrase is traditional, the modern practice of confining the conjunction to the last clause is apparently a subsequent development, though going back to the Middle Ages: MHG (Walther) *ich sach, swaȥ in der werlte was: / velt, walt, loup, rôr unde gras* 'I saw what was in the world: field, wood, leaf, reed and grass'.

In the older period the conjunction *und* may occur where there are no connexions with a previous clause. Effectively, then, sentences can begin with a functionless *und*: MHG (Berthold) *nu lât eȥ iuch erbarmen, daȥ sich got über iuch erbarme, daȥ sô manic mensche von unglouben verdampt wirt. Unde der mâne bezeichent unglouben* . . . 'now let it cause you to have pity, that God may have pity on you, that so many men are damned through disbelief. And the (inconstant) moon signifies disbelief . . . '. Such practice continues down to Luther, but the excessive use of functionless *und* in the Bible is attributable to the original, as also in the Authorized Version. The use of *und* is standard with concessive clauses: *die Anschaffung zusätzlicher Arbeitskräfte würde, und wäre es nur für eine begrenzte Zeit, unser Budget zu sehr belasten.* This construction is first recorded early in the MHG period: (Milstatt Genesis) *ich hetes nie enbiȥȥen und hete siȥ ê niht gezzen* 'I should never have had a bite of it if she hadn't eaten it first'.

The conjunction *auch*, for which 'also' is but one possible translation, often connects two clauses: *sein Angebot war an und für sich nicht verlockend, auch wollte man damals keine Geschäfte mit ihm abschließen.* As a further development, the conjunction acquires consecutive force: (Schiller) *in den schwedischen Kriegsgesetzen war die Mäßigkeit befohlen, auch erblickte man in dem schwedischen Lager weder Silber noch Gold.*

The conjunction *auch* often occurs together with *und*, when it plays an emphasizing role: *ich kenne ihn und auch seine Schwester* or *und seine Schwester auch*; but *auch* alone must be equally common, at least in spoken style: *ich kenne ihn, auch seine Schwester*, etc. Similarly *weder Heizung noch Licht*, (*und*) *auch kein Wasser.* Such usage is ancient: OHG (Otfrid) *zi nuzzi grebit man . . . îsîne steina, ouh tharazua fuagi silabar ginuagi* 'for a useful purpose they mine . . . crystals, and thereto add silver in plenty'; *ouh* often occurs with *ioh* 'and': (Otfrid) *ioh sint ouh filu kuani* 'and are also very courageous'. Out of this emphasizing function arose the use of *auch* in a way which adds nothing new to the preceding clause but which instead draws attention to part of it or to something implied in it: *niemand hier hat Geld, auch er nicht.* In some contexts, indeed, *auch* has acquired the meaning 'even', being synonymous with *selbst* or *sogar*, though in these cases the word ceases to be a conjunction: *auch ein Wurm krümmt sich* 'even a worm will turn'. It very commonly appears in connexion with conditional clauses when it imparts something of a concessive sense: *auch wenn* or *wenn auch alle Stricke reißen* 'even if the worst comes to the worst'. The same use is possible with indefinite relative pronouns and adverbs: *was auch geschieht, ihm kann nichts passieren*; *wo er sich auch aufhält, die Polizei wird ihn zu finden wissen.*

As we see, the uses of *auch* and *und* sometimes overlap. In this connexion we notice that in Old Norse *auk* > *ok* is the standard term for 'and'. The OE form is *ēac*, whence old-fashioned *eke*. All these forms are of course etymologically identical; they are related to the verb *eke* lit. 'augment'.

Until the turn of the eighteenth century *beides . . . und*, older *beide . . . und*, served as correlative conjunctions, just like Eng. 'both . . . and'. It is evident that the use of the pronoun is secondary. 'I saw both man and boy' was in the first place 'I saw both: man and boy', hence the pronoun originally varied for gender (pp. 83 f.). But during the modern period this construction was replaced by a newcomer *sowohl . . . als* (*auch*). During the initial stage of the evolution of the new construction, both elements retained their full sense as particles of comparison: (Luther) *denn man wird sehen, daß solche Weisen doch sterben, sowohl als die Toten und Narren umkommen.* The redundant addition of *auch* is optional.

The form of the disjunctive conjunction NHG, MHG *oder* 'or', OHG *odar*, more usually MHG *ode*, OHG *odo*, older *edo, eddo, edho*, will be due to the influence of *weder*, perhaps also of *aber*, with which it is not infrequently associated, e.g. *oder aber er gibt es au* . The word corresponds to OE *oþþe*, but not to the modern *or* which is a special contraction of *other* dating back to ME.

To distinguish alternatives sharply, the correlatives *entweder . . . oder* are used just like 'either . . . or'. Eng. *either* derives from OE *ǣgþer*, older *ǣghwæþer* = OHG *iogahwedar* (p. 83). Ger. *entweder* goes back to the MHG pronoun *eintweder* 'one of two'; the origin of the prefix *eint-* remains problematic, but it will contain *ein* 'one'. The construction is seen to be comparable in principle to that of the other correlatives 'both . . . and', thus *ich brauche entweder eine Tasse oder eine Schale* originally meant 'I need one of the two: a cup or a bowl'. In High German the construction is only known from the middle period, but the prototype occurs in Old Low German: (Heliand) *duod êndihweðar, wanod ohtho wahsid* 'does one of the two, wanes or waxes'.

The adversative conjunction NHG, MHG *aber* 'but, however', OHG *abar*, is a development peculiar to High German; the term is cognate with Gothic *afar* 'afterwards'. These words are etymologically affiliated to OHG *after*, OE *æfter* 'after', Gothic *aftra* 'again'. German substantially preserves the original sense in the adverbial use of *aber* 'again', formerly common, but now surviving only in the literary word *abermals* and in the (mainly literary) expressions of the type *Hunderte und aber Hunderte* or *Aberhunderte*. As a conjunction, however, *aber* has moved away from its original meaning; its present adversative sense is found in the earliest records. This sense is, as a rule, rather strong nowadays and, accordingly, the frequent occurrences in Luther's Bible where *aber* has virtually no adversative character sound remote to modern ears: *da aber Jesus ihre Gedanken sah, sprach er* "and J. knowing their thoughts said". We may contrast Menge's contemporary idiom: *weil nun J. ihre Gedanken durchschaute, sagte er*.

The conjunction *jedoch* 'however, yet' goes back to Late OHG (Williram) *dero allero flîʒ, doh er* diversis modis *sih skeine, er ist iedoch mîn* cibus *unte mîn* delectatio 'the zeal of them all, though it appear in different forms, is yet my sustenance and my delight'.

Close in meaning to *aber* and *jedoch* is the common conjunction *nur* 'only', MHG *newære*, OHG *niwâri* lit. 'were (it) not'. It has been in use since the old period: (Williram) *daʒ du niet anderes ne meines newâre mîna minna* 'that you have nothing else in mind only my love'. In meaning, *nur* overlaps with *allein* and, in the modern period, this word too may be found as a conjunction. It has never been particularly prominent and is little used today. Perhaps it is most familiar in the often-quoted line from Faust: *die Botschaft hör' ich wohl, allein mir fehlt der Glaube.*

The conjunction *vielmehr* 'rather' has been in use since Early NHG: (Luther) *und fürchtet euch nicht vor denen, die den Leib töten und die Seele nicht mögen töten. Fürchtet euch aber vielmehr vor dem, der Leib und Seele verderben mag in der Hölle.*

Since the old period, a special conjunction has been employed to express a contrast between some word in its own clause and a word in a preceding negative clause: OHG (Otfrid) *ni fand in thir ih ander guat suntar rôȥagaȥ muat* lit. 'I did not find in thee other good but a wretched mind', MHG (Mystics) *niht ûȥe sunder alleȥ inne* 'not outside, but all inside'. The NHG form *sondern* is due to contamination from Low German, cf. OLG *an sundron*: (Luther) *das Kind ist nicht gestorben, sondern es schläft.* This conjunction is not prominent in MHG; it was at this period pushed into the background by now obsolete *wan(e)*, p. 231: (Rother) *sie ne heten vrowede nieht, wane vrost unde naȥ* 'they did not have any comfort, but frost and wet'. MHG *sunder* was, however, common as a preposition (p. 178).

The conjunction NHG, MHG *noch*, OHG *noh* 'and not, nor' has been conjectured to have arisen from *ni . . . ouh* 'not . . . also'. It is, at any rate, quite distinct from the adverb *noch* 'still, yet', originally 'and now' from *nu* 'now' and the prehistoric enclitic *-h* 'and'. The conjunction *noch* linked negative to negative, hence the correlation *noch . . . noch* 'neither . . . nor'. Such use continued into the nineteenth century. Examples: OHG (Wessobrunn Prayer) *dat gafregin ih mit firahim . . . dat ero ni was noh ûfhimil, | noh paum . . . noh pereg ni was . . . noh sunna ni scein* 'this I learnt from men that there was no earth nor heaven above, there was no tree . . . nor mountain . . . nor did the sun shine', MHG (Walther) *ioch meine ich niht die huoben noch der hêrren golt* 'and I do not mean the estates or the gold of noblemen', NHG (Luther) *es ist keine Sprache noch Rede, da man nicht ihre Stimme höre*, (Schiller) *wer nimmt's auf sich, den König zu belehren? noch Sie noch ich*, (Uhland) *das Schwert ist nicht zu schwer noch leicht.* Occasionally the negative is omitted before the first part of a correlation: MHG (Walther) *dem sint die engel noch die frouwen holt* 'neither angels nor women regard him with favour', NHG (Wieland) *er schwor, in Wasser noch in Luft ihr jemals zu begegnen.* In modern style, *noch* survives as the second element in the correlation *weder . . . noch*, but is otherwise extinct, having been replaced by *und* (or *auch*) *nicht.*

In the negative correlation *weder . . . noch*, the first word goes back to OHG *nihwedar*: (Notker) *dâr neweder ist ze heiȥ noh ze kalt* 'there it is neither too hot nor too cold', originally 'neither (of the two): too hot nor too cold', since *nihwedar* was in the first place a pronoun. It only gradually came into use as a conjunction, cf. MHG *eintweder* (p. 217). The construction is still rare in the old period, but becomes common in MHG when it competes seriously with the older *noch . . . noch*. Having now the character of a conjunction in close association with the negative *noch*, the form could be shortened to *weder*: MHG (Helmbrecht) *weder hier noch anderswâ* 'neither here nor elsewhere', and this form was generalized: NHG (Luther) *sammelt euch aber Schätze im Himmel, da sie weder Motten noch Rost fressen*. Under the influence of *noch . . . noch*, the synonymous parallel *weder . . . weder* arose in NHG. It enjoyed a certain vogue, but disappeared during the nineteenth century. The construction is doubtless best remembered today in the quotation from Faust: *bin weder Fräulein weder schön*.

The conjunction *indessen* 'nevertheless' has developed from an original temporal sense; its older modern form is *indeß*: (Luther) *da das Jesus hörte, sprach er . . . Indeß kamen die Jünger Johannes zu ihm* "then", i.e. while he was talking. This conjunction goes back to OHG *innan des* and has occasionally been used as a subordinating conjunction too. The parallel formation *unterdessen* is now only used as an adverb 'meanwhile', but formerly appeared as a co-ordinating, occasionally as a subordinating conjunction. Neither of these words is prominent; they are certainly not used by ordinary speakers, who may not even know their meanings.

SUBORDINATION

Subordinate clauses may be joined to a main clause either with or without a connecting word. Connecting words are the subordinating conjunctions.

Asyndesis

Dependent assertions can be joined to a main clause asyndetically, i.e. without a conjunction: *die Schwierigkeit war, ich hatte kein Geld*; *es ist besser, wir gehen jetzt*; *Sie sehen doch ein, er hat kaum eine Chance*; *ich bin der Ansicht, die Frau kann nichts dafür*. This type of asyndesis is especially favoured in the spoken language, and is doubtless ancient.

Conditional clauses may be construed without a conjunction, the word order being sufficient indication: OHG (Otfrid) *bistu Krist guato, sage uns iȥ gimuato* 'if you are the good Christ, please tell us so', MHG (Nibelungenlied) *welt ir mir niht gelouben . . . , sô muget ir selbe hœren Kriemhilde klagen* 'if you do not wish to believe me . . . , you can yourself hear K.'s wailing'. The construction is, of course, still commonplace: *kommt sie heute nicht, kommt sie morgen.* It will be noticed that the word order is that of the direct question; presumably then such clauses were, in fact, originally direct questions.

In the types of sentence illustrated above there is, of course, no formal mark of subordination. It is the logical dependence of one clause on another which makes matters explicit. In other examples, the subordinate nature of the clause is apparent from the subjunctive mood of the verb. As we know (p. 136) the subjunctive has, in the modern period, been extensively used as a formal indicator of indirect statement, and not least in clauses construed without a conjunction: (Goethe) *doch ist es immer besser, man reise in der Jugend,* (Schiller) *meinst du, du seist nachher weniger ehrlich?* Very often the dependent clause is linked by an anticipatory *da(r)-* in the main clause (p. 58): *wir hatten damit gerechnet, er würde erst morgen kommen.* Such a construction is part and parcel of the present-day literary language, though a *daß*-clause, it is true, is more typical and also the ordinarily spoken form: *daß er erst morgen kommen würde.*

In addition to the present indicative in conditional clauses (above), a present subjunctive is by no means rare in MHG: (Nibelungenlied) *gedenket iuwer triuwe . . . , gesende iuch got von hinnen* 'be mindful of your fealty . . . , if God sends you hence'. Conditional clauses in the past can naturally also be construed without a conjunction. Here the verb is traditionally in the preterite subjunctive, which may become the pluperfect subjunctive in Modern German (p. 126), e.g. MHG (Kudrun) *und sæhe eʒ niht her Hartmuot, ir wære ir houbet dâ benomen* 'und hätte es Herr H. nicht gesehen, es hätte ihr den Kopf gekostet'.

In a construction related to the conditional, medieval German used the negative subjunctive in a subordinate sentence without a conjunction in order to denote an exception to a statement made in the main clause (cf. p. 209): OHG (Ludwigslied) *sô duon ih, / dôt ni rette mir iʒ* 'so I shall do, unless death prevents me', MHG (Nibelungenlied) *waʒ wære mannes wünne . . . , eʒ entæten schœne meide* 'what would a man's joy be . . . if it wasn't for pretty maids?' In MHG these clauses often contain *dan(ne), den(ne)* 'then':

(Hartmann) *swaȥ lebete in dem walde, eȥ entrünne danne balde, / daȥ was zehant tôt* 'whatever (creature) lived in the wood was dead at once, unless it ran away quickly'. The construction was distinctive enough to be used even when the subjunctive form had fallen together with the indicative: (Nibelungenlied) *mîn houbet wil ich vliesen, ir enwerdet mîn wîp* 'I will lose my head, unless you become my wife'. But it could not survive the eclipse of the traditional negative (about 1300), except by using *dan(ne)*, *den(ne)*. In this form, but only used after a main clause containing a negative, the construction continued: (Luther) *er sollte den Tod nicht sehen, er hätte denn zuvor den Christ des Herrn gesehen.* Examples are still met with in the classical period: (Goethe) *kommt man hin, um etwas zu erhalten, / erhält man nichts, man bringe denn was hin.* But, generally speaking, the construction was replaced in the modern period by clauses with *wenn nicht*, hence Goethe's phrase in more modern idiom would be: *wenn man selbst nichts hinbringt.* In one phrase, however, the construction survives to this day and is still usual in literary style: *es sei denn (daß)*, which regularly developed (as above) from MHG *eȥ ensî (daȥ)* commonly used as the equivalent of 'unless, except for'. We could slightly paraphrase Goethe's words and put: *es sei denn, man bringe selbst etwas hin.* That would be acceptable written form today.

The conjunction daß

The conjunction *daß* has arisen from a special application of the nom.acc.neut. of the demonstrative pronoun. It is therefore identical with *das*, the difference in spelling being an arbitrary convention not older than the sixteenth century. Medieval German uses *daȥ* for both, just like Eng. *that*.

The evolution of the conjunction began as follows. The pronoun originally, long before the first written records, belonged to the main clause, but referred to the contents of the following clause which had the character of a dependent assertion, e.g. *ich sage das: er kommt.* Later, though still in the preliterary period, *das* came to be regarded as appertaining not the main, but to the subordinate clause. It then ceased to be a pronoun and turned into a conjunction. German shares this construction with the other West Germanic languages, and also with North Germanic. The Old Norse form, however, is *at* instead of the expected *þat*; it is assumed that the initial consonant has been lost in this unstressed word. The conjunction remains in use in all languages derived from Old Norse, including Faroese. But in this language, in addition, the pronoun meaning 'that' is commonly employed in precisely the same way as we assumed it was used in prehistoric times before it became a conjunction. Thus in Faroese one can have, as in other languages: *eg sigi at hann kemur* 'I say that he comes', but one can also have: *eg sigi tað: hann kemur* 'I say that: he comes', where the pronoun bears a strong demonstrative stress. History is repeating itself.

When *das* became a conjunction its connexions with the demonstrative were inevitably broken. As a conjunction it did not inflect and could be attached to other cases, e.g. *ich erinnere mich noch dessen, daß wir öfters beisammen waren.* It can, of course, be attached to *da*(*r*)-, e.g. *man kann den Ausfall in der Produktion damit begründen, daß keine Nachlieferung an Rohstoffen stattfand.* Ger. *daß* has a wide range of functions comparable to its English congener 'that', understandable in view of their common origin, but there are divergencies as well.

We note the ancient and modern use of *daß* in the sense 'because, since / weil, denn, da': MHG (Nibelungenlied) *alrêst begunde im danken diu minneclîche meit, / daz er . . . sô rehte hêrlîchen streit* 'only then did the lovely maid (begin to) thank him for having fought so magnificently'; modern German would be *dankte ihm dafür, daß* (p. 58), NHG (Luther) *weil sich dein Herz erhebet, daß du so schöne bist* "because of thy beauty". In the contemporary language, this use remains rare and is confined to high style: (Menge) *Rahel weint um ihre Kinder und will sich nicht trösten lassen, daß sie nicht mehr da sind.* Mention may also be made of the traditional use of *daß* to mean 'since / seit (dem)': *es ist noch keine Stunde, daß er hier gewesen ist,* MHG (Helmbrecht) *diu wîle dûhte im ein jâr, / daz er niht enroubte* 'the time since he had last committed a robbery seemed like a year to him'. In literary style, a wish may be expressed by *daß* with the subjunctive: (Schiller) *o daß sie ewig grünen bliebe, / die schöne Zeit der jungen Liebe.* Older use may no longer be idiomatically possible: MHG (Walther) *daz alle krâ gedîen, / als ich in des gunne* 'möge es doch allen Krähen ergehen, wie ich's ihnen wünsche' (Böhm).

From the earliest times, *daß* has been used to introduce a consecutive clause. It was still common in the writings of the classical period: (Schiller) *der Advokat zitterte, daß ihm die Zähne klapperten.* It is later found mainly in poetry: (von Fallersleben) *wir singen frisch und wohlgemut, / daß Feld und Wald erklingen.* But it is also heard in some spoken German, in the South at any rate, and may appear in print: (magazine) *sie klopfte den Teppich, daß der Staub nur so flog.* The commoner conjunction today is *so daß*, also going back to OHG, though it was then much less usual; it did not, in fact, become at all general until the modern period. The first occurrences are in translated matter where *sô daz* renders Latin *ita ut*: (Tatian) *bigonda predigon sô thaz her ni mohta gân in thie burg* (coepit praedicare ita ut non posset) 'began to preach so that he could not go into the city'.

On *daz* in final clauses, see p. 132.

daß *preceded by a preposition*

The oldest example of the conjunction *daß* preceded by a preposition is *ohne daß*, which goes back to Late OHG *âne daz* shortened from *âne daz daz* where the first *daz* is the pronoun governed by *âne*, the second one the conjunction. The original meaning was, however, 'only, except', the modern sense not occurring until the eighteenth century. Luther wrote (1546): *Salomo . . . wandelte nach den Sitten seines vaters David, On das er auff den Höhen opfferte.* But the sense is the opposite of what the conjunction means today, so an edition for the modern reader must perforce adjust the reformer's vocabulary: *S. . . . wandelte nach den Sitten seines Vaters D., nur daß er auf den Höhen opferte.* Next in order of appearance are *auf daß*, *bis daß*, both found in the middle period. The former belongs to Late MHG, becoming very usual in Early NHG when it was commonly employed by Luther. But it is not used much nowadays (see p. 133). MHG *biz* can appear without *daz* and *bis* is the usual form today, though *bis daß* is known from poetry at least: (patriotic song) *bis daß das Auge bricht.* MHG *biz* (*daz*) eventually replaced an older *unz*, still the commoner conjunction in MHG; *unz* is cognate with Eng. *until.*

A purely modern example is (*an*)*statt daß*, the short form being secondary (p. 183). This conjunction is a creation of the eighteenth century. It will be noticed that (*an*)*statt*, which governs the genitive (or dative), is here simply placed before the conjunction, after the analogy of *ohne daß*, etc. As in the case of *ohne daß*, the conjunction *(an)statt daß* can also be construed with the infinitive: *ohne daß / (an)statt daß sie ihre Arbeit machte, ging sie in der Stadt spazieren* or *ohne / (an)statt ihre Arbeit zu machen, ging sie* etc. (pp. 154 f.). Two other examples, *außer daß* and *während daß*, appear in the same century. The normal forms today, however, are *außer*, *während*. Whether the first is an abbreviated form is not clear. At any rate, the preposition *außer* sporadically developed into a conjunction in the medieval language: (Tatian) *nio in altare, ûzar sîn namo skal sîn Johannes* (nequaquam, sed vocabitur Joannes) "not so, but he shall be called John". The conjunction *während*, on the other hand, is definitely shortened from *während daß* which in turn represents an only slightly older *während dessen* (or *dem*) *daß*.

indem, nachdem

Other cases of the demonstrative pronoun have combined with a preposition to form a conjunction (cf. *indessen, unterdessen*, p. 220). The important conjunction *indem*, which in the modern language has developed subtle shades of meaning, is not older than Early NHG. Basically, it is a temporal conjunction: (Luther) *indem er aber gedachte, siehe, da erschien ihm ein Engel des Herrn im Traum* "but while he thought on these things". This conjunction was preceded in the early medieval language by the similarly constructed *innan diu* or *in diu* for *in diu daz*. In the same way NHG *nachdem*, MHG *nâch deme* was preceded by OHG *nâh diu (daz)*, though here there was actual continuity, the form *deme* replacing *diu* as the latter gradually went out of use. In the case of this word, too, the temporal sense is the primary one. Nevertheless, its use as a causal conjunction is old: (Luther) *da sprach Israel zu Joseph: ich will nun gerne sterben, nachdem ich dein Angesicht gesehen habe, daß du noch lebest* "now let me die, since I have seen thy face, because thou art yet alive". And likewise Notker's *nâh tiu* translates Latin *quia* 'because, since'. This shift from temporal to causal is exactly paralleled in the case of *seit* (below).

damit

Final *damit*, now the main final conjunction, has been in use since the twelfth century. In origin, it is the demonstrative *damit*, which was, naturally, also employed as a relative (p. 247). It was from relative use, where *mit* had the instrumental meaning, that the conjunction arose. Many examples still testify to its origin: (Luther) *was kann der Mensch geben, damit er seine Seele wieder löse?* It is known that *damit* is here meant to be the final conjunction 'in order that', but taking the sentence as it stands, without reference to the original, one would be equally justified in regarding *damit* as a relative 'with which'—which gives substantially the same sense. See further p. 133.

doch

In addition to co-ordinating functions, mostly still familiar from contemporary German, *doch* 'though' could, in the oldest language, also act as a subordinating conjunction: (Otfrid) *nist man, thoh er wolle, thaȥ gumisgi al gizelle* 'there is no man who could count the multitude, even if he wished to'. This conjunction was replaced in MHG by *swie*, though *doch* may be used beside it (p. 235).

CONJUNCTIONS FROM ADVERBS

Most conjunctions are, in fact, adverbs adapted for the purpose of combining sentences. They may have simply a co-ordinating function (cf. p. 214) or, with the development of the principle of grammatical subordination, they have often come to function as subordinating conjunctions. The more significant of these are considered below.

da, †do

NHG *da* incorporates two older words: an adverb of place MHG *dâ*, OHG *dâr* 'there' and an adverb of time MHG, OHG *dô* 'then'. Both belong to the demonstrative stem. The former is a very old formation with the local *r*-suffix, cf. *hier* (p. 50). The latter is most probably the acc.fem.sg. of the demonstrative pronoun (Gothic *þō*) giving a literal meaning 'that', some such word as 'time' being understood; cf. the etymology of *dann* (below).

Both words had, from the earliest records, a well-established subordinating function: OHG (Otfrid) *thô Krist in Galilea kwam, wart thaȥ thô mâri* lit. 'when Christ came into Galilee, that then became known' ('his fame spread abroad'), MHG (Helmbrecht) *welt ir hœren . . . wie Troye wart besezzen, / dô Pârîs der vermezzen / dem künege ûz Kriechen nam sîn wîp* 'do you want to hear . . . how Troy was besieged when daring Paris stole the Greek king's wife?' But *dâ* was more typically used as a relative (p. 244).

By the close of the middle period these two words were generally confused owing to a widespread change of *â* to *ô* which took place in the spoken language over much of the High German area. Some Early NHG writers have therefore exclusively or predominantly *do*, but others, following the literary tradition, commonly put *da*, and this form was eventually confirmed as the recognized standard regardless of origin. This is not to say that the two words had not already, to some extent, drawn together semantically before they were confused phonetically. The form *dâ* had, in fact, made incursions into the territory of *dô*. Thus, in medieval German, *da(r)nach* had a temporal sense: OHG (Notker) *sô Dioterih . . . Ôtaccheren . . . sâr dara nâh ersluog* 'when Theoderic shortly afterwards slew Odoacer'. Furthermore, the relative use of *dâ* in connexion with a noun which denoted a period of time made this form the equivalent of a temporal conjunction, hence: (Nibelungenlied) *ze einen sunewenden, dâ Sîvrît ritters namen gewan* 'at a solstice when Siegfried received the title of knight', where *dâ* has the meaning and function of *dô*, cf. in the same text: *daz was in einen zîten, dô vrou Helche erstarb* 'that was at a time when the Lady H. died'.

As a temporal conjunction, NHG *da* has now been very largely replaced in the living language by *als* or *wie*. Luther still prefers the older usage: *da nun Joseph vom Schlaf erwachte, tat er, wie ihm des Herrn Engel befohlen hatte*. A limited use of *da* in this function continued in literature: (Schiller) *da der Griechen Schiffe brannten, / war in deinem Arm das Heil*, (Münchhausen) *wenige Minuten später, da ich gerade dem General Elliott die Sache erzählte*. Today this use is generally felt to be poetic or old-fashioned and stilted, but in the South the construction may survive in dialect or in colloquial close to dialect, e.g. (Austrian) *es ist schon spät gewesen, da er nach Haus gekommen ist*.

WO

The NHG conjunction *wo* goes back to MHG *wâ, swâ*, OHG *sô hwâr sô* 'wherever'. From the basic local sense a number of new meanings were developed. Thus a hypothetical use arose and this lives on in *wo nicht*, *womöglich*, standard expressions alternating with *wenn nicht*, *wenn möglich*. But the conjunction survives best in the regional speech of the South, as follows. From the local emerged a purely temporal sense: *wo ich noch jung war, bin ich oft in den Bergen geklettert*. This development can be traced in the medieval language: (Walther) *swâ ein edeliu frouwe . . . zuo vil liuten gât* 'wherever *or* whenever a noble lady goes to a company of people'. The conjunction may have causal character: *wo er gekommen ist, kann ich ihm den Brief geben*. It regularly introduces a contrast: *warum tust du das, wo du (doch) weißt, daß ich's nicht mag?* It is noticeable that the meanings of the colloquial examples correspond to secondary meanings evolved by the standard conjunction *da*, in origin a local adverb also.

dann, denn

The modern forms *dann* 'then' (in the full temporal sense) and *denn* 'than; then (in weakened temporal sense); because, since' were not distinguished until the early part of the eighteenth century. Previously, each form could have any of the above meanings. In the same way Eng. *than* and *then* are ultimately identical. In dialect German, *denn* is the northern form, *dann* is general in the South, their medieval ancestors being *danne*, *denne*, the latter rare in OHG. These forms themselves are extensions of OHG *dana* 'from here, hence'; *-na* is an element signifying 'from', while *da-* has been etymologized as the ablative of the demonstrative pronoun, the ablative having the sense 'from' and also being the case of comparison (p. 31).

In OHG, *danne*, *denne* is either a temporal adverb '(from) then (on)', a subordinating conjunction 'whenever' (see next section) or a conjunction after comparatives: (Notker) *ter was rîchero danne der brûoder* 'he was richer than his brother'. In later MHG another word *wan* may also appear after comparatives (see below), but *danne*, *denne* remained the usual conjunction until the seventeenth century when it yielded to *als* and *wie*. Luther's form was *denn* and this was still fairly common in the classical period. Today it is usual in the literary cliché *denn je*, e.g. *stärker denn je*, and for obvious reasons in *denn als* 'than as'. Apart from these, it may be still occasionally introduced for stylistic effect: (tourist brochure) *stille Winkel, weltverloren und die Andenken an altväterlichen Brauch und Arbeitsgang reicher bewahrend denn anderswo.*

During the modern period *denn*, before the eighteenth century also in the form *dann*, has been regularly used as a co-ordinating conjunction 'because'. Following a conventional definition, *denn* is most commonly equated with the English conjunction *for*. This is misleading to the extent that *denn* is a much more usual word than *for*. It is also the reason why Germans, when speaking English, often make excessive use of this conjunction; and vice versa. In the present function *denn, dann* replaced MHG *wan*(*de*), see †*wan* causal. The replacement happened as follows. There was, in MHG, besides causal *wan* an entirely unrelated *wan* 'than', a recent formation (see †*wan*, †*niwan*) which seriously competed with the older *danne, denne*. Towards the end of the middle period, the latter regained ground and almost drove the competitor out of use. Success did not stop at that. Thanks to confusion between comparative and causal *wan* brought about by homophony, *danne, denne* began to replace causal *wan* as well, so that by the beginning of the modern period the latter, too, had largely fallen into disuse.

wann, wenn

In the oldest period *danne* (previous section) occurred as a subordinating conjunction: (Otfrid) *thanne ir betôt, duet iȥ kurzlîchaȥ* 'whenever you pray, make it brief'. In MHG, this conjunction was replaced by *swenne, swanne* from OHG *sô hwanne sô* 'when(so)ever', a development comparable to the relative use of indefinites (p. 246): (Helmbrecht) *die lûhten sô mit glanze, / swenne er gie bî dem tanze* 'they [the buttons] shone with such brightness whenever he danced'. By a further shift, the conjunction may refer to a single occasion: (Walther) *hêrre, waȥ si flüeche lîden sol, / swenne ich nû lâȥe mînen sanc* 'Lord, what curses will she have to bear, when I now cease my song'. In such examples, *swenne* came near to the meaning 'if', for which the standard medieval conjunction was *ob* (p. 239) and this word maintained its leading position until the end of the middle period. But the potential competitor remained. Meanwhile, in the fourteenth century, *swenne, swanne* was regularly reduced to *wenn, wann*. At length the latent opposition to the old conjunction broke through, for in Early NHG *wenn, wann*, in company with *so* (p. 232), is seen to be replacing *ob* in conditional clauses. Like *denn, dann*, both forms were used indiscriminately, though in the dialects *wenn* is typically the northern, *wann* the southern variety. In the literary language, the use of the two forms side by side continued for longer than was the case with *denn, dann.* Instances are common in the classical period and persisted well into the nineteenth century. But since then *wenn* alone has been used as the standard form. It can, of course, be either temporal or conditional: *wenn er zurückkommt, werde ich es ihm sagen* 'when *or* if he comes back'. On the whole, the language tolerates this ambiguity, though an unequivocal conjunction 'if' is to hand, see *falls*. Finally, *wenn* can still be used in its original indefinite sense: *wenn ich in Deutschland war, mußte ich deutsch sprechen* 'whenever I was in Germany', though admittedly *immer wenn* or *wenn immer ich in Deutschland war*, etc. would be more usual wording.

NHG *wann* remains to be mentioned. This word is, in standard use today, only employed as an interrogative adverb: *wann kommst du? sage mir wann du kommst.* As such, it goes back to MHG *wanne, wenne*, OHG *hwanne, hwenne*, with the same meaning. It is thus not directly connected with the conjunction *wenn*, †*wann.*

†wan *causal*

The oldest causal conjunction in German is *danta*. But this word only occurs in the oldest glosses where it renders Latin *ideo* or *quia*. It was replaced by *hwanta*: (Tatian) *sliumo giengun ûf, wanta sie ni habêtun erda tuifî* "forthwith they sprung up, because they had no deepness of earth". In origin, *hwanta* was an interrogative pronoun 'why?'; the same development is seen in French *car* 'because, for' from Latin *quare* 'why?'. This remained the usual conjunction in MHG: (Hartmann) *wande sî mir dô tâten michel unreht, dô wart mîn leit manecvalt* 'for they did me grave wrong, great was my grief'; more commonly, however, the form is shortened to *wan*: (Walther) *wan kumet er dar, dêswâr er wirt ertœret* 'because if he comes there, in truth he will turn completely deaf'. At the end of the middle period, this word yields to *denn, dann*, and dies out in Early NHG: (Aventin) *den armen ist mer zu glauben dan den richen, wan es ist gar ein sprichwort.* In view of its origin, the clause introduced by *hwanta* was, in the beginning, a main clause. Under the influence of *sîd* 'since' (see *seit*), subordinate order is sometimes found after *hwanta*: (Muspilli) *ni ist in kihuctin himiliskin gote, / wanta hiar in werolti after ni werkôta* '(the soul) is not remembered by heavenly God, because here in the world (it) did not act accordingly'. And similarly into Early NHG.

†wan, †niwan

Etymologically distinct from *wan* causal (previous section) is *wan* 'except, but, than', of disputed origin; cf. Behaghel, iii, p. 328. We assume shortening from *niwan*: OHG (Notker) *wir nehabin andrin chuninch newan den Rômcheiser* 'we have no other king than Caesar', MHG (Nibelungenlied) *im enkunde niht gevolgen wan Kriemhilde man* 'none could follow him except Kriemhild's husband', (Walther) *niemer niemen / bevinde daz, wan er und ich* 'may no one ever find that out, but he and I'. This conjunction was extensively used in MHG with the function of *sondern* (see p. 219). In the meaning 'than', *wan* naturally competed with the old-established *danne, denne*. The ultimate result, as explained above (p. 229), was the replacement of *wan* of whatever origin; it barely survived into Early NHG: (Luther, non-Biblical) *dieser spruch ist heller wan die Sonne*, (variant *wen*) *sehen nichts wen gutes an den creaturen*; his normal usage is *heller denn, nichts denn.*

so

The conjunction *so* has naturally much in common with its English counterpart. It has had from the beginning, in both languages, co-ordinating and subordinating functions.

Co-ordinating *so* is the idiomatic equivalent of 'then' after temporal or conditional clauses introduced by *wenn*, e.g. *wenn ich Ihnen nicht schreibe, so unternehmen Sie nichts weiter*; *wenn du die nötigen Werkzeuge hast, so kannst du die Arbeit machen.* In some areas, at any rate, this *so* is replaced by *dann*, and either conjunction can, of course, be omitted altogether. The construction is traditional: MHG (Helmbrecht) *swenne er gie bî dem tanze, / sô wart er . . . vil minneclîche an gesehen* 'whenever he danced, loving eyes were cast upon him'. In other cases temporal *so* alternates with *da*, e.g. *es dauerte nicht lange, so (da) kam sie zurück.*

Subordinating *so* can also have a temporal function: MHG (Kürenberg) *der tunkele sterne der birget sich; / als tuo du, frouwe schœne, sô du sehest mich* 'the dim star hides itself; so do you, fair lady, whenever you see me'. Here *sô* has the meaning of *swenne* and, like it (p. 229), develops into a conditional conjunction: (Walther) *dû kundest al der werlte fröude mêren / s ôduz ze guoten dingen woldes kêren* 'you could have added to the joys of the world, if you had dedicated it [i.e. your art] to good things'. In Early NHG, conditional *so* becomes extremely common, as can be seen in Luther: *und so dich jemand nötiget eine Meile, so gehe mit ihm zwei*; *was hülfe es dem Menschen, so er die ganze Welt gewönne und nähme doch Schaden an der eigenen Seele?* This use, however, soon passed its zenith and *wenn* rapidly took over. The construction may still occur in the classical period: (Schiller) *wir träumen, so wir glauben, unsere Ideen und Empfindungen von außen zu empfangen*, but it is no longer found today except in the phrase *so Gott will*, an archaism comparable to the even more archaic *ob Gott will* (p. 239). The most recent formula is, of course, *wenn Gott will.*

The temporal function of subordinating *so* was not necessarily lost as a result of the development just outlined. For example, the use seen in OHG (Otfrid) *sô si in ira hûs giang, thiu wirtun sia êrlîcho intfiang* 'when she entered the house, the woman of the house received her with reverence', is still found, occasionally, in Early NHG: (Luther) *so er danck gesagt hat dem Vatter, brach ers.*

In the medieval language, the conjunction was regularly used to express a comparison: OHG (Tatian) *sô mih santa ther fater, sô santa ih iuwih* 'as the father sent me, so I sent you', MHG (Anon.) *mich dunket niht so guotes noch so lobesam / sô diu liehte rôse und diu minne mînes man* 'nothing seems to me so good and so praiseworthy as the bright rose and the love of my husband'. Compare further: OHG (Ludwigslied) *sô lange sô wili Krist* 'as long as Christ wills', MHG (Walther) *sô wîp sô man* 'woman as well as man'. A concessive sense may be present: OHG (Ezzo) *die sternen . . . vil luzel liehtes pâren, sô berhte sô sie wâren* 'die Sterne gaben nur wenig Licht, so hell sie auch waren'.

See also the next section.

also, als

In origin, *also* was a strengthened or emphatic form of *so* (previous section) and had the same basic uses; it arose as OHG *alsô* 'entirely so'. The form may be preferred for emphatic reasons:

(Luther) *und es geschah also* "and it was so". In the eighteenth century *also* is provided with the meaning 'therefore', in which sense it seems to be short for *und also* a calque on Latin *itaque* (Behaghel, iii, pp. 67 f.). Since this is now the only living meaning of the word, the contemporary language no longer offers the alternative Luther had: Menge puts *und es geschah so*. The title of Nietzsche's book *Also sprach Zarathustra* is thus seen to be a conscious archaism.

MHG *alsô* came to be used in unstressed positions as well. It was then often reduced to *alse*, *als*, whence the modern *als*. Eng. *as* is similarly a reduced form of *also*, OE *eallswâ*.

Reference has been made in the foregoing section to the use of *so . . . so* to express a comparison. From the end of the OHG period there was a tendency to replace *sô* in this construction by the longer *alsô*: MHG (Walther) *alsô diu sunne schînet / durch ganz geworhtez glas, / alsô gebar diu reine Krist, diu magt und muoter was* 'as the sun shines through finished glass, so did that pure one, who was maid and mother, give birth to Christ'. The full form *alsô* was then, as set out above, frequently weakened to unstressed *alse*, *als*. In a comparison, the first conjunction could also still be *sô*: (Walther) *wære er sô milt als lanc* 'were he as generous as he is long', and this arrangement prevailed. It continued in ordinary use into the eighteenth century: (Goethe) *ein so armes Mädchen als ich bin*. Nowadays, however, the combination *so . . . als* is only poetic: (Hauptmann) *so Gatte als Brüder*. In the more recent language *als*, as a conjunction of comparison, survives in the combination *sowohl . . . als (auch)*, further in comparison clauses, and also in such related uses as: *er wies sich als deutscher Staatsbürger aus*; *Pearse war als Toter politisch bedeutender denn als Lebender*. To some extent phrases of the type *so bald* (*schnell*, etc.) . . . *als möglich* and *so viel* (*wenig*) . . . *als* are still in use, but normally *wie* has replaced *als* in this function, here as in other cases (see below).

Although *als* has lost ground to *wie*, it gained a new function as the usual conjunction found after a comparative adjective. Presumably the new role somehow arose from the old one. A solitary instance occurs in classical MHG: (Walther) *daz er gesæhe ie grœzer gebe, / als wir ze Wiene haben . . . enpfangen* 'daß er jemals größere Geschenke gesehen habe, als wir in Wien erhalten haben'. Not until the fifteenth century do further examples appear; in the next century they become numerous and *als* quickly supersedes its rival *denn*. Furthermore, *als* was now regularly found after negatives: (Goethe) *ich sehe nichts als einen schwarzen Pudel*, likewise after *kein*: (Schiller) *ich trage kein Lehen als des Reiches*, but in this latter case the language of today prefers *außer*. Since the eighteenth century *als* in the present function has faced competition from *wie* (p. 236). One of the results has been the creation of the double form *als wie*: (Goethe) *und bin so klug als wie zuvor*. This form is not permissible in good style today; it has sometimes been adopted by the spoken language but is regarded as substandard.

In the modern language *als* occupies a prominent position as a temporal conjunction 'when'. It refers to a definite time in the past: *als ich voriges Jahr in Deutschland war, mußte ich deutsch sprechen*, thus contrasting with indefinite *wenn* (p. 230). The use of *als* as a temporal conjunction first appears in Late OHG, an older construction having the simplex *sô* (p. 232). Temporal use of *als* is well attested in MHG: (Nibelungenlied) *daz sol sîn getân, / als wir nun komen widere* 'that shall be done when we return'. But only very rarely is it used to denote a definite time in the past: (Nibelungenlied) *als der künic Gunther die rede vol gesprach, / Hagene der küene den guoten Rüedegêren sach* 'when king G. finished speaking, H. the bold caught sight of good R.', the usual medieval conjunction in this role being *dô*. However, in the fifteenth century *als* begins to take over the function of *dô*, or *da* as it was soon to become. Luther makes some use of it: *als nun Jesus an dem galiläischen Meer ging, sah er zwei Brüder*, but he prefers *da*. Shortly afterwards, *als* makes rapid progress to become the modern standard. Meantime its use with the present tense has died out; today *wenn* is required: *das wird getan werden, wenn wir wiederkommen*.

In the older language *als* regularly kept its modal function: MHG (Helmbrecht) *sprich ein wort nâch unserm site, / als unsere vordern tâten* 'speak a word in our manner, as our forefathers did', (folksong) *es ist ein Reis entsprungen / aus einer Wurzel zart, / als uns die Alten sungen*. This function is now performed by *wie*, i.e. modernizing: *wie uns die Alten sangen*. Today *als* with a past tense can only mean 'when'.

A comparison clause may be introduced by *als*: (Helmbrecht) *vater unde muoter sprang, / als in nie kalp erstürbe* 'father and mother ran as if they had never lost a calf'. The construction is still possible, especially in literary style: *als wäre ihnen nie ein Kalb verendet.* In the contemporary language *als ob, als wenn* are commoner than *als*, and are more generally used in speaking. See also p. 240.

†sam

The MHG conjunction *sam(e)* goes back to OHG *sama, samo*, which had arisen from the identical adverb 'likewise, similarly', ultimately one with the pronoun *samo* 'the same' (p. 73).

This conjunction was still prominent in Classical MHG: (Walther) *vinster sam der tôt* 'black as death', (Hartmann) *alsô volleclîchen / sam Jôben den rîchen* '(he tempted her) as thoroughly as Job the rich', *doch tete si sam diu wîp tuont* 'but she did as women do'. Very often the sense is 'as though': (Helmbrecht) *si fuoren sam si wolden toben* 'they rode as though they were going mad'. A strengthened form *alsam* is also common: (Walther) *eȥ smecket alsam eȥ balsmen sî* 'it smells as though it were balm'. After Early NHG the conjunction gave way to *alsô* (*alse, als*); in the sense 'as though' its place was taken by *als* (*ob*) (pp. 232, 240).

wie

MHG *swie* 'as' goes back to OHG *sô hwio sô*, in origin a generalizing relative adverb. In the earlier period *swie* is only used to introduce clauses, a use which is still current: (Walther) *tuo mir swie dû wellest* 'tue an mir wie du magst' (on NHG *wie* from MHG *swie*, see below). MHG *swie* is the commonest concessive conjunction: (Hartmann) *swie tump ich sî, / mir wonet iedoch diu witze bî* 'however inexperienced I may be, I still have my wits about me'. In this function it may be supported by *doch*, which was itself a concessive conjunction in the old period (p. 226): (Walther) *dâ gienc eins keisers bruoder und eins keisers kint / in einer wât, swie doch die namen drîge sint* 'there an emperor's brother and an emperor's child strode in one garment, although the names are three'. Concessive use of *wie* is also possible in the modern period, especially in association with *wohl*, a pattern already well established by the beginning of the modern era: (Luther) *aber wiewohl er sie kannte, kannten sie ihn doch nicht.* The same conjunction is used by Menge at this point in his contemporary version.

During the course of the fourteenth century *swie* in common with other adverbs, e.g. *swâ*, or pronouns, e.g. *swer*, gave up the initial *s*. Since the end of the Middle Ages *wie* figures not only in its traditional role of clause opener, but also as a conjunction connecting parts of a clause. In this new function *wie* was usurping the place of *als*. Luther uses both terms: *sein Haupt aber und sein Haar war weiß wie Wolle, als der Schnee, und seine Augen wie eine Feuerflamme*. Gradually *wie* became more general in this function and has now replaced *als* except in the cases mentioned on p. 233.

Not only in the above function has *wie* extended its range in the modern period. It has supplanted subordinating *als* in its modal sense: *wie ich an dem Hause vorbeiging, hörte ich einen Lärm* 'as I was passing' (cf. p. 234). It has, furthermore, advanced at the expense of *als* in the temporal sense. True, this use has not made much impress on the literary language, though it has sometimes occurred in writing: (Friedjung) *wie nun die Klammern dieser Regierung morsch wurden, setzten die konservativen ungarischen Magnaten alles daran* 'when now'. But this use is firmly entrenched in the spoken language of many districts: *wie er dort war, hat er mit meinem Vater gesprochen*.

Since the eighteenth century *wie* can occur after comparatives: (Klopstock) *mehr wie die Erden, die quollen*, (Tieck) *fabelhafter wie alles*. But such usage soon disappeared from literary texts and is not admitted in the standard language today, except perhaps to avoid repetition of *als*, e.g. *das Deutsche erweist sich als altertümlicher wie das Niederländische*. Even though the standard insists on *als*, regional and substandard speech regularly employs *wie*, e.g. *ich bin stärker wie er*.

On the double form *als wie*, see p. 234.

It is apparent that the foregoing usages, where NHG *wie* continues MHG *swie*, are not directly connected with the NHG conjunction *wie* 'how', e.g. *ich möchte wissen, wie es ihm jetzt geht*. In this case, NHG *wie* goes back through MHG to OHG *hwio*, identical with the adverb 'how': (Helmbrecht) *welt ir nû hœren . . . von frouwen Helchen kinden / wie die wîlen vor Raben / den lîp in sturme verloren haben* 'do you wish to hear . . . about Lady Helche's children, how they in days of yore before Ravenna lost their lives in battle?' We may notice that this conjunction can traditionally have the meaning 'that': (Schiller) *er gestand mir auch, wie er itzt selbst einsähe*, (Luther) *es kam ein erlogen Geschrei aus, wie Antiochus sollte tot sein*. How this usage arose can be seen from borderline cases: MHG (Walther) *er seit mir danne wie daȥ rîche stê verwarren* 'he told me how *or* that the kingdom was distracted'.

nun

NHG *nun*, MHG *nû(n)*, OHG *nû* 'now' is, of course, a most venerable item of vocabulary, one which goes back to Indo-European times, cf. Latin *nunc*, Greek *nŷn* 'do.' As the literary form, *nun* has been obligatory since the seventeenth century, but *nu* is still widespread in colloquial German. In the twelfth century, MHG *ie* 'ever' and *zuo* 'to' united to give *iezuo* 'now', whence NHG *jetzt*. This neologism has throughout the centuries extended its scope at the expense of the traditional word. But in one sphere it has made no progress: it has not evolved a subordinating function. This remains the preserve of the older term. As a reflex of a West Germanic innovation, *nû* appears in the earliest German as a temporal and causal conjunction: OHG (Otfrid) *wir . . . birumês mit redinu in zwîfalteru frewidu, / nû wir thaȥ wîȥi mîden ioh himilrîhhes blîden* 'we . . . are with reason doubly pleased now that we shall escape punishment and enjoy heaven', MHG (Kudrun) *ich wil dir volgen, nû si sô schœne sî* 'I will follow you as she is so beautiful'. In MHG *nû daȥ* also occurs: (Gottfried) *nû daȥ diu maget und der man den tranc getrunken* 'after the maid and the man (had) drunk the potion'. We remark that Eng. *now* (*that*) is no longer temporal, only causal. In NHG the construction became less usual, though it is still possible in literary style: *nun er reich ist, hat er Freunde*. In popular language this would be *jetzt da er reich ist*, in southern colloquial *jetzt wo*.

ehe, bevor

NHG *ehe* represents MHG *ê* and is often so pronounced; the medieval form regularly arose from OHG *êr* 'before, ere', originally a comparative adverb 'earlier, rather' (< †rathe 'early') (p. 180).

In MHG, *daȥ* or *danne* may be added: (Nibelungenlied) *si fuoren zweinzec mîle, ê daȥ eȥ wurde naht* 'they travelled twenty leagues before night fell', (Walther) *ê danne ich lange lebte alsô, / den krebȥ wolte ich ê eȥȥen rô* 'before I lived for long in such a state I would rather eat crayfish raw'.

Until the seventeenth century *bevor* was used solely as an adverb, substantially synonymous with *ehe*, hence an old expression *ehe und bevor*. But then it becomes interchangeable with *ehe* as a conjunction also and is now the commoner word. Indeed, in some places *bevor* is the only word used in the spoken language, as, for example, in Vienna; in Berlin both are heard. Meanwhile the adverb *bevor* has died out, not having been used since the eighteenth century.

We recall that, in English, *before* has entirely supplanted *ere*, except in poetry.

seit(dem), sintemal

NHG *seit*, MHG *sît*, OHG *sîd* 'since' is a basically temporal conjunction developed from a comparative adverb 'later' (p. 180). Eng. *since*, ultimately from OE *siþþan* < *sīþ* 'seit'+*þan* (demon. pron., presumably an old ablative) has evolved a causal sense in addition to the original temporal one. A like development was commonplace in MHG: (Hartmann) *du enweist ouch rehte waȥ du tuost, / sît du benamen ersterben muost* 'you do not realize either what you are doing, since you must die in any case'. The conjunction *daȥ* may be added: (Walther) *sît daȥ nieman âne fröude touc, / sô wolte ouch ich vil gerne fröude hân* 'since no one without good cheer is worth anything, I for my part would therefore much like to have good cheer'. The causal sense survives in Early NHG but was afterwards replaced by *da*, so that today *seit* is again a purely temporal conjunction as it was in the oldest period.

The form *seitdem* came into use in the modern period. It seems to go back to MHG *sît dem mâle daȥ* 'since the time that' (cf. *sintemal*), but *seitdem* is only temporal, not causal; it is entirely synonymous with *seit*. Though it may be heard in conversation, it is more generally seen on the printed page.

A by-form of MHG *sît* was *sint*, still kept in some dialects. The phrase *sint dem mâle* (*daȥ*) acquired the force of a causal conjunction. Luther uses it: *da sprach Maria zu dem Engel: wie soll das zugehen, sintemal ich von keinem Manne weiß?* By the eighteenth century this conjunction was generally regarded as too clumsy for serious use. Though no longer a living word in the proper sense, it is nevertheless still quite well known and sometimes used jocularly or ironically.

CONJUNCTIONS FROM OTHER PARTS OF SPEECH

ob

NHG *ob* goes back via MHG *ob(e)* to OHG *oba*, *ubi*, oldest *ibu*, clearly cognate with Eng. *if*.

Throughout the recorded period *ob* has been employed to introduce dependent interrogative clauses: OHG (Otfrid) *ni bin ih ouh thes wîsi, ob er thes lîbes scolo sî* 'ich bin auch nicht sicher, ob er mit dem Leben bezahlen soll'. Closely related to the foregoing are the conditional clauses and, in the medieval language, these too were introduced by the same conjunction: OHG (Hildebrandslied) *ibu dû mî ênan sagês, ik mî dê ôdre wêt* 'if you name me one, I shall know the others', MHG (Helmbrecht) *ob dû getrûwest geleben / des ich dir hân ze geben, / sô sitz und twach dîne hende* 'if you believe that you can live from what I have to give you, then sit down and wash your hands'. But in Early NHG, owing to competition from *so* (p. 232) and *wenn*, *wann* (p. 229), this use declines and subsequently becomes rare. It is still occasionally found in the classical period and even later: (Chamisso) *ob es in unsrer Macht und billig ist, / wird gerne dir bewilligt dein Begehr*. By now, however, it is extinct, except in the traditional phrase *ob Gott will*, still known to some people. The main conditional conjunction today is *wenn*.

Formerly *ob* was extensively used in concessive clauses, which are of course derived from conditional clauses: OHG (Notker) *ube ih anderro sachôn beroubôt pin, mînero chunnôn nemahta mih nioman beroubôn* 'even if I am robbed of my other things, no one could rob me of my knowledge'. Often the conjunction is preceded by *und*: MHG (Mystics) *und ob si iȥ hœren, sô widerstên si ime mit hertikeit ires herzen* 'even though they hear it, yet they oppose it with the hardness of their hearts', Early NHG (Luther) *und ob ich albern bin mit Reden, so bin ich doch nicht albern in dem Erkenntnis*. But *wenn* was already spreading to these clauses as well, hence in Luther's hymn: *und wenn die Welt voll Teufel wär . . . so fürchten wir uns nicht so sehr*. This is a regular construction today. The older conjunction, however, continued in high style: (Schiller) *ob uns die See, ob uns die Berge scheiden, / so sind wir eines Stammes doch und Bluts*. It may still be imitated: *ob Freund, ob Feind*, even *ob Bub, ob Mädel*.

As the concessive force of *ob* diminished, it became necessary to add other words to emphasize the concessive nature of the clause.

In this way *auch* was at one time used: (Schiller) *ob auch das Roß sich schäumend bäumt . . . nicht rast' ich.* Other emphasizing words are *gleich, schon, wohl.* Nowadays these words are united with *ob*, hence *obgleich, obschon, obwohl*, the last being commonest. However, these are felt to be conjunctions in their own right with the meaning 'although'. They have been in existence since the sixteenth century, but in older style the qualifying words were often separated: (Luther) *du . . . hast dein Herz nicht gedemütigt, ob du wohl solches alles weißt.* This order is still common in the eighteenth century: (Münchhausen) *ob ich nun gleich dieses Mal mit heiler Haut davonkam.* The classical writers sometimes use it: (Goethe) *ob ich schon weiß, daß er vor Nacht nicht kommt, / vermut' ich ihn doch jeden Augenblick.* The combination *obzwar* was formerly not uncommon, but is today rather rare: (M. Giustiniani) *obzwar das Phänomen bisher bloß am Uran beobachtet wurde.* The conjunction *wenn* here competes to some extent with *ob*. Thus *wenn auch* has replaced *ob auch* (above): *er könnte es nicht machen, wenn er es auch wollte.* We may compare further *wenngleich, wennschon* 'although'. In medieval German especially, other conjunctions could be used in concessive clauses, see *doch*, †*sam*, *so*, *wie*.

Likewise connected with conditional clauses are the comparison clauses introduced by *als ob*, known since MHG: (Walther) *ors, als ob eȥ lember wæren, / vil maneger dan gefüeret hât* 'gar mancher hat da Streitrosse weggeführt, als ob es Lämmer wären'. Later *wenn* came to be used in these clauses, too, hence today alternatively *als wenn* (or *wie wenn*) *es Lämmer wären.* The older construction was MHG (*al*)*sam* or *als* (pp. 234 f.), the latter being still possible: *als wären es Lämmer.*

weil

In Late OHG the combination *die wîla* (*sô*) could be employed to introduce a temporal clause. Here *die wîla* is an accusative of extent of time (*hwîla* 'Weile'): (Notker) *wanda al die wîla sô wir in demo lîchâmin pin, so wellen wir geellindôt fone gote* 'for all the while we are in the body we wish (to be) estranged from God'. The construction continues in MHG, where *daȥ* may be appended: (Hartmann) *die wîle daȥ er leben sol, / sô stât unser sache wol* 'as long as he lives we shall be all right'. The construction is known in Early NHG: (Luther) *und dieweil Mose seine Hand emporhielt, siegte Israel.* It then declines, but Lessing could still write: *dieweil es noch Zeit ist.* The word may be abbreviated to *weil* in the modern period: (Luther) *weil es dir wohl gehet, ist er dein Geselle,* (Schiller) *verschieb's nicht länger die erliegende Natur zu erstärken, weil die Lebensflamme noch brennt.* Eng. *while* was similarly abbreviated from older *the while.* Neither of the foregoing usages is productive in the standard language today, having been replaced by *während,* but they are familiar from proverbs: *man muß das Eisen schmieden, dieweil es heiß ist,* or from quotations: (Usteri) *freut euch des Lebens, weil noch das Lämpchen glüht.* A by-form *derweil* is well known from Uhland's poem: *will mir die Hand noch reichen, / derweil ich eben lad.* This word, furthermore, is fully alive in regional German, at least in the South: *derweil die Kinder sich spielen, können wir unseren Kaffee trinken.* The form *dieweil* also survives in some spoken German.

In contemporary German *weil* is only used as a causal conjunction 'because, since, for'. This sense developed out of the meaning 'as long as', e.g. 'I can't leave as long as the visitors are here' can soon become 'I can't leave because the visitors are here'. This meaning emerged at the end of the middle period, but only in the latter part of the modern period did it become fully established. Older causal conjunctions are *denn,* †*wan.*

falls

Since the sixteenth century the phrases *auf den Fall daß* and *im Fall(e) daß* have been employed in literature to introduce a conditional clause; the conjunction proper *daß* may be omitted, cf. Eng. *in case.* Of these only *im Falle daß* is usual today. Towards the end of the seventeenth century a genitive form *falls* appears. The existence of these conjunctions is thoroughly justified in view of the ambiguity of *wenn* (p. 230) and *falls* at any rate may be heard and seen in contexts where English would have 'if'. There is, however, no indication of *falls* seriously dislodging *wenn* 'if', though such a development would not be surprising.

trotzdem

The rise of NHG *trotz* has been discussed on p. 187. After 1800 the combination *trotzdem* came to function as a conjunction 'although'. The connecting force would lie initially in the demonstrative *dem*. It was used with *daß*, which could subsequently be omitted, and this is normal style today: *trotzdem er tot ist, dauert sein Einfluß fort*. The form *trotz* (*daß*) has also been used in literature, but is now not usual in written work. But one can hear *trotz daß* now and again: (rambling conversation) *trotz daß der Arzt gekommen ist und mir Medizin verschrieben hat, ist das Fieber weiter gestiegen*.

RELATIVE CLAUSES

Asyndetic relative clauses

The asyndetic ('unlinked') relative clause, that is to say, a relative clause not linked to the main clause by a relative word (pronoun or particle), is presumed to be the earliest type of relative clause known to the Germanic languages. Such clauses are not infrequent in the German of the earliest period: (Otfrid) *in droume sie in zelitun then weg sie faran scoltun* 'in a dream they told them the way they should go'. Clauses of this sort are, of course, a commonplace in English. But it may be noted that, in ancient German, a relative word could be omitted even when it would have been the subject of its clause: (Otfrid) *er sâr in thô gisagêta thia sâlida in thô gaganta* 'he at once told them the good fortune which had befallen them', i.e. like Shakespeare's *youth's a stuff will not endure*. After the OHG period, asyndetic relative clauses occur but rarely, though the construction survived into modern times: (Luther) *den ersten Fisch du fehist, den nimm* 'take the first fish you catch'.

In conclusion we note a commonly used type of asyndetic clause containing the verbs *heißen* or *sich nennen*, e.g. *drunten liegt ein Dorf, heißt* (*nennt sich*) *Unteraichwald*. The construction is old: OHG (Physiologus) *ein sclahda naderôn ist, hêizzet* vipera 'there is a species of adder which is called viper'.

Relative pronouns

A relative pronoun occurs in the earliest texts; it is *der, diu, daz*, i.e. the present-day *der, die, das*. The following are examples from the Mondsee Matthew: *sê dîne gungirun tuoant daz sie ni môzun tuoan in fêratagum* (ecce discipuli tui faciunt quod non licet facere sabbatis) "behold thy disciples do that which is not lawful to do upon the sabbath day", *hwelîh iuwêr ist der man der ein scâf habêt* (quis erit ex vobis homo, qui habeat ovem unam) "what man shall there be among you that shall have one sheep", *sê mîn sunu den ih gachôs* (ecce puer meus, quem elegi) "behold my servant whom I have chosen".

One is bound to ask, however, whether the syntax of a translated work could have been influenced by the original. The OHG Matthew is certainly no slavish interlinear version. Nevertheless, it is a fact that the German relatives in the text correspond exactly to those in the Latin. Maybe they were not entirely idiomatic, or at least their occurrence was dependent on the original, as the following example could suggest: *enti aer antwurta demo za imo sprah, quadh* (at ipse respondens dicenti sibi, ait) "but he answered and said unto him that told him". Here the original has no relative pronoun, its participle constructions have no parallel in German and must be rendered freely. It is reasonable to suppose that we here have an idiomatic translation, and we see that the German uses the asyndetic construction, lit. 'and he answered the one to him spoke, said'.

At all events, it is evident that at this time the relative pronoun had by no means established itself so firmly as it did in the later language.

From demonstrative to relative pronoun

The OHG relative pronoun *der, diu, daʒ* is formally identical with the demonstrative pronoun; it is, in fact, the demonstrative cast in a new role. We consider again the essential part of the last example *antwurta demo za imo sprah*, in natural English 'answered the one who spoke to him'. The asyndetic clause appears as the complement of the demonstrative pronoun *demo*; here *demo* clearly belongs to the main clause. But should the main and subordinate clauses both require the same case, it becomes possible to regard the demonstrative as belonging to the subordinate clause: (Otfrid) *thô liefun sâr thie nan minnôtun meist* 'then ran at once they who loved him most'. Sentences of this sort were the starting-point for the conversion of the demonstrative into a relative pronoun. And this economic construction (where the demonstrative and relative are effectively united in one word) remained for a long time in very common use: MHG (Walther) *êr unde guot hât nû lützel ieman, wan der übele tuot* 'nobody now has honour and wealth, except he who does evil', *si bienen die si wolten, / unt niht den si solten* 'they excommunicated those whom they wanted to and not him whom they should have'. Luther employs it: *wer ist die hervorbricht wie die Morgenröte?* or *habt ihr nicht gesehen den meine Seele liebet?* However, he can use the modern construction as well: *wer ist die, die aufgehet aus der Wüste wie ein gerader Rauch?*

Today this usage survives in such a traditional phrase as *Ehre dem Ehre gebührt*; in the present-day language, however, *dem* is felt to be a relative 'to whom'. Hence the modern punctuation of Luther's examples above: *wer ist, die hervorbricht wie die Morgenröte? habt ihr nicht gesehen, den meine Seele liebet?* Otherwise the construction is still living particularly when the pronoun is in the nominative: *ich meine, die so argumentieren, übersehen zweierlei*; *der mir gefällt ist zu groß*. This succint mode of expression may be preferred to the cumbersome *die(jenigen), die*, etc., not only in conversation, but also in good literary style, hence (Goethe) *ach, der mich liebt und kennt, / ist in der Weite*, while in modernizing Luther's *selig sind, die da hungert und dürstet nach der Gerechtigkeit* (where *die* is accusative as part of the impersonal construction, p. 170), Menge writes *selig sind, die nach der Gerechtigkeit hungern und dürsten.*

Conversion of the demonstrative pronoun into a relative also took place in OE: (Andrew) *þæt is se ilca ealwalda god þone on fyrndagum fæderas cūþon* 'that is the same all-ruling God which in days of yore our fathers knew' (*þone* = Ger. *den*). At an early date the neut.sg. *þæt* came to be used regardless of the gender or number of its antecedent, and by the ME period such usage had become general, hence the Modern English invariable relative *that.*

From demonstrative to relative adverb

The transformation of the demonstrative pronoun into a relative was paralleled in the case of the demonstrative adverbs OHG *dâr* 'there', *dara* 'thither', *dannân* 'thence', similarly in compounds *dârinne* 'therein', etc.: (Otfrid) *nist in erdrîche, thâr er imo io instrîche / noh winkil under himile, thâr er sich generie* 'there is nowhere on earth, where he will ever escape from him, nor any corner under heaven, where he will save himself', *thu giangi thara thu woltôs* 'you went where you wished'. This usage continued throughout the Middle Ages: (Walther) *sô lise ich bluomen dâ rîfe nû lît* 'then I shall pick flowers where hoar frost now lies'. It is still normal with Luther: *ihr sollt euch nicht Schätze sammeln auf Erden, da sie die Motten und der Rost fressen, und da die Diebe nach graben und stehlen.* But afterwards competition from *wo* (see 'From interrogative to relative', below) becomes serious, though the use of *da* survived into the classical period: (Goethe) *du findest dich vor einem Gewölbe, da wohl zwanzig Stufen hinabgehen.*

Attraction

The close association of the demonstrative and the emerging relative pronoun in the OHG period gave rise to the feature called attraction. Where a main and a subordinate clause require different cases, the subordinate clause nevertheless frequently adopts the case required by the main clause. In other words, the demonstrative in the main clause is strong enough to attract the relative into its own grammatical case: (Otfrid) *thes thigit worolt ellu thes ih thir hiar nu zellu* 'for this all the world is pleading, which I am here now telling you' (*thiggen*+gen., *zellen*+acc.). By a similar attraction the pronoun in the subordinate clause often follows the case of an antecedent which is not a demonstrative: (Exhortatio) *hlosêt ir . . . rihtî dera calaupa dera ir in herzin cahuctlîho hapên sculut* 'hear . . . the rule of the faith which you are to have in memory in your hearts', and this in spite of the original (audite . . . regulam fidei quam in corde memoriter habere debetis). But the main tendency, nevertheless, is for the relative pronoun to take the case required by its own clause: (Notker) *taz mag man wola sehen an dero* sphaera, *diu* in cella Sancti Galli noviter *gemachôt ist* 'that one can see on the globe which was recently made in the monastery of St. Gall', and this is the normal state of affairs in the later language. Attraction is, however, still occasionally found in MHG: (Nibelungenlied) *aller mîner êren, der muoz ich abe stân, / triuwen unde zühte, der got an mir gebôt* 'all my honours, I must forsake them, responsibilities and duties, which God gave me' (*abe stân*+gen., *gebieten*+acc.).

From interrogative to relative

It often happens that there is a natural affinity between an interrogative and a relative clause, e.g. in OHG: (Monsee

Matthew) *inu ni lârut ir hwaʒ David teta*, or the same in OE: (West Saxon Gospels) *ne rǣdde ge þæt hwæt David dyde* (non legistis quid fecerit David) "have ye not read what D. did?". Or compare the MHG lines: (Helmbrecht) *hie wil ich sagen waʒ mir geschach, / daʒ ich mit mînen ougen sach* 'here I will recite what befell me, what I saw with my own eyes'. A consequence of this close affinity has been a tendency for the interrogative pronoun (always a strong and vivid pronoun) to usurp the functions of a relative. This becomes evident in eleventh-century English and such relatives have been competing with the older *that* ever since: *a man who works*, (now substandard) *a thing what works*. It is possible that the impetus to this development came from outside, since the use of the interrogative as a relative first occurs in translations from Latin. The same tendency is manifest, though only to a very limited extent, in translated texts in OHG: (Tatian) *thû nû ni habês mit hiu scefês* "thou hast nothing to draw with". But this particular usage did not spread. When, many centuries later, simple interrogative pronouns appear as relatives in German, the genesis of this development is to be found in native sources, firstly as a result of natural affinity, and secondly arising out of phonetic changes, as follows.

In early OHG *hwer* 'who' and *hwelîh* 'which' preceded and followed by *sô* function as indefinite relative pronouns: *sô hwer sô* 'who(so)ever', *sô hwelîh sô* 'which(so)ever'. By the ninth century the second *sô* is generally omitted, the usual forms now being *sô wer, sô welîh*, which by the end of the OHG period had been reduced to *swer, swelih* > MHG *swer, swelch*: (Helmbrecht) *swer volget guoter lêre / der gewinnet frum und êre, / swelch kint sînes vater rât / ze allen zîten übergât, / daʒ stât ze jungest an der scham* 'whoever follows sound teaching, that one wins profit and honour, which-ever child at all times neglects its father's advice, that one will come to shame in the end'. Similarly with adverbs, e.g. OHG *sô hwara (sô)* 'whithersoever' > MHG *swar*: (Walther) *swar ich zer werlte kêre, dâ ist nieman frô* 'wherever in the world I turn, no one is happy (there)'. In such sentences the indefinite relative refers to the demonstrative in the main clause and comes close in function to a definite relative. In some cases, the two relatives approch so closely that the possibility of confusion arises: (Hartmann) *dar an begunde er suochen / ob er iht des funde / dâ mite er swære stunde / möhte senfter machen* 'he began to look there (to see) if he could find anything with which he might make unhappy hours more pleasant', *dâ zuo liebte er ouch sî / swâ mite er mohte* 'he for his part sought to gain her affection by what means he might'. Then, in the fourteenth century, the initial *s* of the indefinite relatives was lost so that they became formally identical with the interrogatives, thus: *swer*, *swelch* > *wer*, *welch*; *swâ*, also *swô* > *wo*. It is now, therefore, formally speaking, the interrogative pronoun which, through confusion with the (definite) relative pronoun, begins in certain positions to assume the functions of this relative. Particularly the adverb *wo* intruded into the position hitherto held by *da*. The two relative adverbs compete for some four centuries, until about 1800 *wo* is established as the accepted norm (see 'From demonstrative to relative adverb', p. 244). Similarly Hartmann's *dâ mite* and *swâ mite* (above) develop into *damit* and *womit*, which, having become semantically identical, compete for a while until *womit* supersedes its rival.

In the same way the neuter interrogative *was* has ousted the older relative *das* in a number of positions, e.g. when the antecedent in the main clause is a pronoun referring to something indefinite. Compare these MHG sentences with their modern translations: (Helmbrecht) *eʒ ist wâr daʒ ich iu lise* 'es ist wahr, was ich euch lese', (Berthold) *alleʒ daʒ ich gesach* 'alles was ich sah'. The spread of *was* at the expense of *das* may be compared to the struggle between *wo* and *da*. Luther's usual word is *das*, e.g. *auf daß erfüllet würde, das da gesagt ist durch die Propheten*, but he also uses the new relative: *alles, was darinnen ist*. Subsequently *was* becomes ever more frequent, the older word dying out in this function in the classical period: (Tieck) *vieles . . . das ich jetzt selbst ganz vergessen habe*.

In the spoken German of many areas *was* has replaced *das* in all positions: *das Ding, was ich gekauft habe*, and has become a solecism in educated speech, too. In parts of central Germany it has come to be used regardless of the gender and number of its antecedent: *Leute, was viel Geld haben*, i.e. a parallel to our own substandard 'people what have a lot of money'.

welch

Early in the fifteenth century another interrogative pronoun appears as a relative. This is *welch*, at first adjectival in function:

(Jostes) *ein bild des vaters, in welchem bild*. . . . This was a new construction, unknown to older German. It was a creation of chancery style, most likely in imitation of French *lequel* or Latin *qui*, originating in the Netherlands towards the end of the thirteenth century. It is recorded in Low German before occurring in High German. Eng. *which* (etymologically identical with Ger. *welch*) developed as a relative about the same time. It is clear that the already established relative pronoun (*der*, *die*, *das*) could not be employed adjectivally since it was also used demonstratively as well as functioning as the definite article—in English it would have been confused with the demonstrative adjective *that*. Soon *welch* was being used as a relative pronoun proper: (Luther) *die Werke des Fleisches . . . Saufen, Fressen und dergleichen, von welchen ich euch zuvor habe gesagt*; *denn ein Weib hatte von ihm gehört, welcher Töchterlein einen unsauberen Geist hatte*. This relative is not, of course, descended from the indefinite pronoun, but its spread must have been encouraged by the existence of the generalizing relative which did derive from *swelch*: (Luther) *welche ich lieb habe, die strafe und züchtige ich*.

In the modern period *welch* gained ground rapidly. The classical authors made free use of it and in the nineteenth century it almost drove *der* out of the written language. But all the same it hardly made any impression on the ordinarily spoken language and, with the return to a more natural written style in this century, *welch* has receded very much into the background. Its use is, however, prescribed to avoid an accumulation of homophones: *die, welche die Nachricht brachten*. Today the word has a rather stilted, old-fashioned ring. It therefore has its uses in pastiche, and jocularly too, as in the often-heard *ich bin derjenige, welcher* 'I'm the one in question'. Somewhat in the same vein—with a play upon meanings: *Frage: Gibt man in der Sowjetunion Trinkgelder? Nimmt man welche? Antwort: Man gibt keine, und man nimmt keine. Mit einer Ausnahme: Ausländer geben welche, und Kellner oder ähnliche Leute, welche oft mit Ausländern zusammenkommen, nehmen welche.*

das — welches — was

A relative word may refer not only to a noun or pronoun in the main clause, it may refer to the whole main clause itself. In the early period *das* was, of course, the only possible relative pronoun in such a case, but at the beginning of the modern period *welches* begins to replace it, *das* finally dying out in the classical period. The new relative becomes very prominent in the eighteenth century, but just at this time another competitor comes to the fore in the shape of the relative *was*, a word with some basis in the spoken language, which after the beginning of the nineteenth century establishes itself as the norm. Not surprisingly, all three relatives are found in Goethe's writings: *ich habe sie mit bewaffneter Hand angefallen, das in Florenz unerhört sei—jene sind reizend, diese schmerzstillend, welches auf eins herauskommt—heute kann ich dir schon Hoffnungen machen, was ich vorgestern noch nicht konnte.*

Relative particles

We have already ('From demonstrative to relative adverb', p. 244) referred to the use of relative adverbs, which are naturally uninflected, and may represent any grammatical case or number. All such invariable words may be termed relative particles.

In the oldest German, especially in Otfrid, *the* is in use as an inherited relative particle; it is apparently a demonstrative pronoun in origin, belonging to the stem of *der*. Examples: (Otfrid) *in doufe the unsih reinôt* 'in baptism which purifies us', *in berge the er mo zeinti* 'on a mountain which he showed him', *widar thie thih* (= *the*+*ih*) *waltu* 'against those over whom I rule' (*waltan*+ gen.). The same particle was in common use in OE: (Aelfric Gloss) *sē þe brȳde hæfþ, sē is brȳdguma* "he who hath the bride is the bridegroom". The particle survived until the beginning of ME, by which time, however, it had become confused with the definite article. Henceforward, its place was taken by *þæt* 'that' (see 'From demonstrative to relative pronoun', p. 243). In Late OHG, *the* gave way to an old competitor, another uninflected relative, in origin the adverb of place *dâr* 'there'.

The development of the demonstrative adverb *dâr* 'there' into a relative adverb 'where' has already been noticed (p. 244). This stage was also reached in OE: (Saxon Chronicle) *on þære byrig þǣr se cyning ofslægen læg* 'in the castle where the king lay slain'. But in German the line of development went much further, *dâr* assuming the functions of a relative particle in the fullest sense: (Tatian) *thia thâ truogun gistuontun* (hi autem qui portabant steterunt) "they that bare him stood still", (Otfrid) *ther thâr was in wâni* 'the one of whom it was believed' lit. 'the one there (i.e. where) was in belief'. The construction survives to a certain extent in later German: (Nibelungenlied) *die dâ torsten vehten, die lâgen alle erslagen* 'those who dared to fight, they all lay slain', (Luther) *die da saßen am Ort und Schatten des Todes, denen ist ein Licht aufgegangen.*

Parallel to *da* is the use of *wo* in the present-day colloquial of various regions, notably in Alemannic, where it is the normal relative word: *Leute, wo viel Geld haben* 'people who have a lot of money'. When standing for a dative, the relative use of *wo* is very widespread in spoken German, also in the speech of the educated, and frequently appears in writing: *die, wo das Herz noch jung ist* (= *die, denen* . . .) 'those who are still young in heart'.

Chiefly characteristic of the MHG period is the remarkable use of the conjunction *und* as a relative particle. The first attestations, it is true, date from Late OHG: (Vienna Genesis) *in elliu diu und er tete, sô hete er guote site* 'in all that which he did he behaved correctly', but the idiom only becomes prominent in the middle period: (Nibelungenlied) *ich mane iuch der genâden und ir mir habt gesworn* 'I remind you of the fealty which you have sworn to me', (Mystics) *an dem êrsten anblicke unde du die sêle an sihst* 'in the first moment in which you look upon the soul'. The importance of the construction can be gauged from the fact that at the same time in Old Norse a parallel use of *ok* 'and' (p. 217) is widely found, especially in literary texts translated from German. The use of *und* as a relative particle continued throughout the middle period, finally petering out in the seventeenth century. Its origin is still obscure.

Lastly, the conjunction *sô* has been in use as a relative particle. The first occurrences are sparse, but usage becomes prominent in the sixteenth century—there are many instances in Luther's Bible—subsequently declining, but persisting until recent times: OHG (Notker) *tô neteta er ze êrest nîeht uber daz, sô demo cheisere lîeb was* 'then he at first did nothing but was pleasing to the emperor' lit. 'nothing above that as [i.e. which] was pleasing', MHG (Nibelungenlied) *waz sint diu leit der schœnen Kriemhilt, sô du hast geseit* 'what are the misfortunes of the fair K. which you have mentioned?', (Luther) *alle Juden, so in Ägyptenland wohnen,* (Keller) *das Dutzend Bücher, so der alte Herr besaß, immer wieder durchzulesen.* English uses *as* in the same way: *handsome is as handsome does*, but the construction is now common only in substandard speech: (Eliza Doolittle) *what I say is, them as pinched it done her in.* It is clear that the English construction arose out of the correlative use of *as*, cf. *such men as do that sort of thing*, where *as* has the value of *who.* The German construction would arise in the same way; for an early example (in the Low German area) cf. Old Saxon (Heliand) *sulike gesîðos, sô he im selbo gicôs* 'such followers as he himself chose (for himself)'.

Strengthened relatives

In OHG the relative pronoun may be strengthened by any of the following particles: *sô*, *the*, *thâr*.

The first is very rare: (Otfrid) *zi selben sancte Petre, ther sô giang in then sê* 'to St. P. himself, who walked into the sea'. The second is met with occasionally: (Tatian—here old *th* is shifted to *d* in enclitic position) *iogewelîhhemo, therde habêt wirdit gigeban* (omni habenti dabitur) "unto everyone that hath shall be given". But the third is very common and remained in frequent use until modern times. In the older language there was a marked tendency to use *thâr* pleonastically, which doubtless contributed significantly to the spread of the construction: (Tatian) *bithiu wanta thû ni giloubtus mînên wortun, thiu thâr gifultu werdent in iro zîti* (pro eo quod non credidisti verbis meis quae implebuntur in tempore suo) "because thou believest not my words, which shall be fulfilled in their season". In later German the particle loses its final *r*: (Berthold) *wie sælic die sint, die dâ reinez herze tragent* 'how blessed are they who bear a pure heart', (Luther) *Gnade sei mit euch und Friede von dem, der da ist, und der da war, und der da kommt, und von den sieben Geistern, die da sind vor seinem Stuhl.* To a limited extent the construction is current today, e.g. *Menschen, die da glauben* can occur in certain contexts when it has a somewhat more elevated tone than the usual *Menschen, die glauben*, though the speaker does not now analyse *da* as a relative, but as a demonstrative emphasizing the predicate. The particle *da* may equally be used with the indefinite relative: (Luther) *wer da hat, dem wird gegeben werden*; it may also occur after another relative particle: (Luther) *und hast versucht die, so da sagen, sie seien Apostel.*

Strengthened relatives occur locally in colloquial German. The type *der wo* is heard in Franconian: *Leute, die wo viel Geld haben.* In Austrian the pronoun may be strengthened by the (invariable) relative *was* (see p. 247): *Leute, die was viel Geld haben.* The particles are enclitic.

Relative with 1st or 2nd person

The demonstrative pronoun *der* has, of course, always referred to the 3rd person, and this remained so when the word became a relative pronoun as well. But there was sometimes a need for a relative pronoun which could refer to the 1st or 2nd person, not necessarily in the spoken language, but for those whose business it was to translate from Latin. These translators could, as they often did, transpose the Latin words mechanically into German like (Tatian) *ich bim Gabriel thie aȥstantu fora gote* (ego sum G. qui adsto ante dėum). Such a literal rendering most likely sounded odd to German ears. This we would infer from the opening words of the OHG translations of the Lord's Prayer, five of which have come down to us. The oldest, from St. Gall, written before 800, begins *fater unsêr thû pist in himile* (pater noster qui es in caelis) and the other versions all follow this pattern, just like the Wessobrunn Prayer: *cot almahtîco du himil enti erda gaworahtôs* 'God Almighty, who wroughtest heaven and earth'. It very much looks as though contemporary German could not use the demonstrative idiomatically as a relative in this position. Evidently the relative was implicit in the personal pronoun because in the Tatian version of the Lord's Prayer it is found strengthened by *thâr* (see 'Strengthened relatives', p. 251): *fater unser thû thâr bist in himile.* Rare examples of this same usage occur in MHG: (Mystics) *mit dir du eine krône bist aller êren* 'with thee who art a crown of all honours', (Vorauer Sündenklage) *Maria du dâ bist wâriu muoter* 'Mary who art a true mother'. The construction is also attested for the 1st person: (Otfrid) *thaȥ bin ih, giloubi mir, ih hiar sprichu mit thir* 'I am he, believe me, who here speaks with thee'.

It is not until the Early NHG period that there occur sufficient examples of relative constructions involving the 1st and 2nd persons to show clearly the tendencies in the language. By this time the relative *der* had established itself. It is found, though more rarely, with the 1st or 2nd person of the verb: (Sachs) *mich Armen, der nicht vil vbrigs hab*, (Murner) *ohnerachtet* ('despite the fact that')

... *ihr Männer seyd, die uns zur Nothwendigkeit gemacht habt.* This usage occurs sporadically in the later literature: (Goethe) *ich, der mit Euch rede,* (Kleist) *ihr seid die beiden einzigen, die mich davor retten könnt.* But, more commonly, the verb is in the 3rd person. This is because, in the overwhelming majority of instances, the relative *der* refers to a 3rd person when it naturally governs a verb in the 3rd person, which then came to be used analogically for the other persons. In many cases, of course, the 1st and 3rd persons of the verb were identical, and this will have facilitated the development. The construction survived into the nineteenth century. Examples: (Sachs) *dw vngetrewer poser* ('böser') *gaist, der wenig geit* ('gibt') *und vil verhaist,* (Luther) *ich Johannes, der auch euer Bruder und Mitgenosse an der Trübsal ist,* (Heine) *ich, der sonst die Signatur aller Erscheinungen begreift.*

The present construction, where the relative is qualified by the 1st or 2nd person pronoun, goes back to about 1500. Sachs knows it: *solt wir also abzihn mit schanden, die wir vor almal sint pestanden*; it is usual with Luther: *Gott sprach zu Mose: Ich werde sein, der ich sein werde* "I am that I am", *ach Gott, der du bist ein Gott der Geister des Fleisches.* By the eighteenth century this had become the most general construction.

Relative in literary style

We have already noticed that the relative *welch* has always been essentially a book word only, in fact a stylistic alternative to *der*: (Luther) *die Gerechtigkeit, die vor Gott gilt, welche kommt aus Glauben in Glauben,* (Münchhausen) *sie haben unstreitig, meine Herren, von . . . Sankt Hubertus, nicht minder von dem stattlichen Hirsch gehört, der ihm einst im Walde aufstieß, und welcher das heilige Kreuz zwischen dem Geweihe trug.* Scheffel paraphrased Luther's old-fashioned *wer ist, die hervorbricht wie die Morgenröte?* with *wer ist die, welche hervortritt wie die aufgehende Morgenröte?* Yet in spite of intense cultivation in literature, this relative has remained rather an empty word. Today it is generally avoided in good style, only occasionally can it be found used to achieve a special effect: (Rilke) *wir alle fallen . . . / und doch ist Einer, welcher dieses Fallen / unendlich sanft in seinen Händen hält*; here the unexpected *welcher* seems to direct the attention back to the antecedent, emphasizing it in a way that the banal *der* cannot.

In older German there were, as we know, other relative words as well. Given this state of affairs, it was but natural that then, too, stylistic considerations should play a part in the choice of relatives: (Luther) *tut wohl denen, die euch hassen; bittet für sie, so euch beleidigen und verfolgen.* Meanwhile the range of choice has become narrower. Nevertheless, the old relatives occasionally appear, especially in verse: (Bürger) *die Saat, so deine Jagd zertritt.* Rückert places the old beside the new in the verse *der Stuhl ist elfenbeinern, darauf der Kaiser sitzt; / der Tisch ist marmelsteinern, worauf sein Haupt er stützt.* Many stylists of the recent period use the type *der da* which nowadays strikes a distinctive note or conveys something of an emotional effect: (Eichendorff) *schläft ein Lied in allen Dingen, / die da träumen fort und fort.* Menge modernizes Luther: *wer ist diese, die da hervorglänzt wie das Morgenrot?* But we must not forget to add that, in the modern language, *da* is no longer felt to belong to the relative pronoun (p. 251).

Average use today

As a result of developments outlined above, average use today prefers *der* as the normal relative pronoun and *was* when the antecedent is a whole clause.

When the pronoun is preceded by a preposition and does not refer to a person, it may often be replaced by *wo(r)-*, e.g. *herzlichsten Dank für die Charakteristik, in der* (or *worin*) *Sie mir eine so generöse Einschätzung zuteil werden lassen.* There is some stylistic difference, the construction with *wo(r)-* being rather more formal; the spoken language therefore usually has the pronoun: *dort siehst du das Pony, von dem ich erzählt habe.* When, however, the antecedent of the relative is a whole clause, the use of *wo(r)-* is, in general, obligatory in correct style: *Galilei machte das Pendel viermal so lang, wodurch er die Schwingungszeit verdoppelte*; the construction *durch was* may occur, but is substandard. It is to be observed, however, that certain prepositions cannot be combined with *wo(r)-*, so that in such cases a pronoun must always be used: *hier ist mein Wörterbuch, ohne das ich unmöglich auskommen kann*; *diese Firma zahlt gut, weswegen* (p. 183) *sie immer genug Arbeitskräfte bekommt.* There are, furthermore, occasional instances where a combination with *wo(r)-* is morphologically possible, but idiomatically impossible. One can have either *ich erkannte den*

Fehler, an dem unser Versuch scheiterte or *woran unser Versuch scheiterte*, but only *es war ein Tag, an dem die Sonne schien*, although *wo die Sonne schien* would be a normal alternative.

On the replacement of pronouns by adverbs, see p. 58. On prepositions not combining with adverbs, see p. 54.

XI · WORD ORDER

As even a beginner soon notices, German word order is to a large extent a matter of the position of the verb, in particular of the finite verb, which can come first, second, or at the end of its clause or sentence. It will be convenient to consider these positions in turn.

Finite verb first

Since the earliest records, the finite verb has been found in the initial position in questions when there is no interrogative word: *hast du Zeit?* Likewise in the syntactical development of such sentences seen in conditional clauses (p. 221): *hast du Zeit, so werden wir bleiben.* Further, in wishes: *möge der Versuch ihm gelingen! könnte ich nur schlafen!* also in concessive clauses of the type *sei es auch jetzt noch so kalt, es wird bald wärmer* and, of course, in the hortative: *gehen wir*, and the imperative: *geh, geht, gehen Sie*, the last example historically the pres.subj. (p. 130); otherwise in such use the subject is placed first: *Gott behüte.* But in the medieval language the verb could be placed first; relics survive in the Austrian *pfüat di Gott* (= *behüte dich Gott*) 'goodbye', also in *Grüß* (*dich*, etc.) *Gott*, a greeting widely used in the South.

In OHG the verb frequently appears in the initial position in independent statements: (Monsee Matthew) *see, quimit der brûtigomo* (ecce, sponsus venit) 'behold, the bridegroom comes', (Tatian) *was thô zît nâh sehsta* (hora erat quasi sexta) "it was about the sixth hour", and equally in the poetry, this order being especially prominent in Otfrid: *fialun sie thô framhald* 'they then fell down (on their knees)', *loug ther wênego man* 'the wretched man lied'. The verb in this position doubtless had stylistic value; compare the alternating word order in these lines from Muspilli: *muor varswilhit sih, swilizôt lougiu der himil, / mâno vallit, prinnit mittilagart, / stên ni kistentit, verit denne stûatago in lant* 'the marsh land devours itself, the heaven is hot with flame, the moon falls, the earth burns, no stone remains standing, then the day of retribution comes'. But by the middle period this practice had ceased and the verb in such statements now had to come second as in the modern language: *siehe, der Bräutigam kommt*, etc.

So German early lost a traditional construction. But it will be remembered that the employment of *dô* and later of *eȥ* > NHG *es* (p. 56) as sentence openers meant that the verb could still be the first significant word in the sentence. Then, in later MHG, the verb again begins to appear in the initial position proper, especially in connexion with the verb *sprechen*. This idiom is common in Luther: *spricht Simon Petrus zu ihnen: 'ich will hin fischen gehen'*. Other verbs follow suite and the construction takes on an archaic, folksonglike flavour, hence (Goethe) *sah ein Knab' ein Röslein stehn . . . lief er schnell, es nah zu sehn*. It must have early acquired considerable stylistic value in literary work. That such usage was essentially a development of the written language is confirmed by the fact that a separable preverb remains compounded with its verb, a feature entirely absent from the spoken language: Early NHG (Ackermann) *zu reste ist gegangen meines heiles sunne: auf geet sie nimmermere*, NHG (A. Miegel) *aufflog ein jubelnder Bogenstrich . . ., anhub die Fiedel zum drittenmal*. The construction has sometimes in recent German prose fiction appeared as a literary mannerism, but forming no integral part of a real tradition, something like Eng. *came the dawn*.

Initial position of the verb is not unknown in the modern colloquial language. It may occasionally be heard in dramatic narrative: *kommt da plötzlich jemand hereingeschneit*. In fact, the construction is quite usual in exclamatory statements. But here it will be of different origin, for an exclamation such as *ˈist sie nicht gescheit!* 'my word, she *is* clever!' can be no more than a modification of the interrogative *ist sie nicht gescheit?* The question expects the answer 'yes', of course, and the difference between the two sentences in actual speech is one of intonation. As soon as the new pattern was established, corresponding positive exclamations became possible, i.e. synonymous *ˈist sie gescheit!* Other everyday examples: *ˈhast du Glück!* 'you *are* lucky!', *ˈwar das eine Hetze!* 'that *was* a rush!', *ˈhat er ausgesehen!* 'what a sight he looked!'. In another common colloquial type, initial position with an emphatic nuance arises as follows: *dort sind gute Äpfel—können Sie welche mitnehmen*, similarly *die sagen das bloß*—machen sie aber nicht.

We notice also initial position in emphatic commands: *gehst du raus!* 'out with you!', *wirst du Ruhe geben!* 'be quiet!' (cf. pp. 107, 113). We have already mentioned (p. 130) the exceptional development of *sind Sie* as a colloquial alternative to *seien Sie*. The new form falls into line with the other polite imperatives, e.g. *kommen Sie*, where the subjunctive (as distinct from the indicative) origin of the form is no longer spontaneously apparent. But it seems to have also been reinterpreted as an example of emphatic word order (as above): at any rate an analogical, equally substandard *bist du so gut* (standard *sei so gut*) is frequently heard.

Initial position is normal in NHG in connexion with *doch*, e.g. *hatte ich doch Glück*, more emphatic, more exciting than *ich hatte Glück*. Literary examples go back to the beginning of the modern epoch: (Heine) *vertraust du dich doch sorglos / täglich dem wilden Meere*, (Luther) *ist doch niemand in deiner Freundschaft, der also heiße*. Initial position is also found in *weiß Gott* (MHG *weiȥ got*), whence *weiß der Teufel*, etc. Finally, in sentences with *mögen*, e.g. *mag es immerhin schneien*; *mag es noch so schneien, wir gehen trotzdem hin*.

Finite verb second

It is probable that, in Germanic, the finite verb most usually appeared in the second position. It is, at any rate, in accordance with an immemorial tradition that the finite verb in German takes the second place in statements which form a main clause: *wir kamen gestern an, gestern kamen wir an*. Theoretically, any part of the sentence can take the first place: *auf den Bergen liegt Schnee, am folgenden Tag fand die Verhandlung statt*. Not infrequently an inseparable word group or a subordinate clause comes first: *in den Lehrerberuf einsteigen möchte ich nicht*; *nachdem ich fertig war, ging ich ins Bett*. The finite verb takes the second place in dependent clauses which have no conjunction: *ich meine, er muß jeden Augenblick erscheinen*. What we really have here is, of course, two main clauses in juxtaposition, the regular word order of main clauses remaining unchanged.

The conjunctions *aber*, *allein* (p. 218) 'but', *sondern, denn, oder* are not regarded as forming part of a clause and therefore do not modify the word order: *aber er sagte*, etc. The conjunction *und* is also usually so treated; exceptionally, however, it may cause inversion of subject and verb at all periods of the language: OHG

(Notker) *sie mugen iro ougun ûf ze liehte erheven, unde sint sie den fogelen gelîh* 'they can raise up their eyes to the light and they are like the birds', MHG (Walther) *dô tagete eȥ und muoste ich wachen* 'then it dawned and I awoke'. There are many examples in Luther: *du bist allerdinge schön, meine Freundin, und ist kein Flecken an dir*, where inversion has obvious rhythmic value; it is also used for variation: (Matt. vii. 25) *und ein Gewässer kam*, (vii. 27) *und kam ein Gewässer*. The grammarians campaigned against this inversion, so that in later literature examples are much rarer: (Goethe) *gewichen bin ich her ans Licht, / und sollt' ihr weiter mich nicht treiben*. For some decades now, however, inversion has again been more usual, especially in some official and business styles: (recent report) *dank dem Fortschritt der Medizin ist die Sterblichkeit stark gesunken, und nimmt die Bevölkerungszahl entsprechend schnell zu*. Other conjunctions may be optionally regarded as part of the clause, in which case they affect the word order. These are *doch, jedoch, entweder*, e.g. *entweder kommt er morgen oder . . .* or *entweder er kommt morgen oder . . .*, there being no essential stylistic difference between the two constructions.

A few particles *auch, bereits / schon, kaum, nicht* refer either to the whole clause, in which case they are treated as independent elements affecting the word order, or else they can refer to a certain word with which they then form a single syntactic unit and thus have no influence on the order of words. Contrast *auch trank er übermäßig* 'in addition he drank immoderately' with *auch er trank übermäßig* 'he, too, drank immoderately', or *den meine ich nicht* 'I don't mean that one' with *nicht den meine ich* 'it's not that one I mean'.

In medieval German, the temporal adverb *thô, dô* 'then' can function as a sentence opener, the verb formally taking second place: OHG (Tatian) *thô antwurtita imo ther seocho* (respondit ei languidus) 'the sick man answered him'; this adverb is constantly used in MHG heroic epic: (Nibelungenlied) *dô sprach der junge Gîselher* 'Young G. said', (Kudrun) *dô wolten's niht getrouwen die von Sturmlant* 'the men of S. wouldn't believe it'. Less usually, the local adverb *thâr, dâr* appears with the same function: (Otfrid) *thâr was ein man fruatêr* 'there was a wise man'. In English, of course, this latter construction has become very general; in German, however, *es* has now assumed the role of unambiguous sentence opener (p. 56).

Finite verb at the end in main clause

In OHG the finite verb of a main clause is sometimes located at the end: (Charm) *suma hapt heptidun, suma heri lezidun* 'some fastened bonds, some held up the army', (Hildebrandslied) *sunufatarungo iro saro rihtun* 'son and father got their equipment ready', *forn her ôstar giweit* 'long ago he journeyed east'. Such attestations in the oldest original writing together with the fact that final position occurs in other Old Germanic languages prove that we are dealing with a syntactical feature of high antiquity. Poetry is the main province of this construction, but occasional examples in prose are not lacking: (Isidor) *Jacob dher hôho fater bauhnendo quhad* 'Jacob the patriarch beckoning said', (Tatian) *mîn tohter ubilo fon themo tiuvale giweigit ist* (vexatur) 'my daughter is evilly tormented by the devil', (Notker) *taȥ ouga al sihet unde al bechennet* 'the eye sees everything and recognizes everything'. How far these and other sporadic occurrences in the prose of a later age are attributable to Latin influence may sometimes be a moot point. But in poetry, especially in the old-world diction of the popular epic, the construction continues as genuine German: MHG (Nibelungenlied) *Kriemhilt in ir muote sich minne gar bewac* 'in her heart K. quite renounced love', *daȥ volc si allenthalben kapfen an began* 'on all sides the people stared (began to stare) at them'. This poetic device, so handy for rhyming, is found throughout the modern period, being particularly common from the eighteenth century on: (Luther) *groß Macht und viel List / sein grausam Rüstung ist*, (Goethe) *ein Veilchen auf der Wiese stand, / gebückt in sich und unbekannt*, (Schiller) *und herein mit bedächtigem Schritt / ein Löwe tritt*, (Uhland) *der Jüngling spricht's, ihn Kraft durchdringt, / das Schwert er hoch in Lüften schwingt*. The very large number of instances found in unbroken sequence down the centuries shows that modern usage is not to be regarded as casual poetic licence on the part of individual authors, but that it forms an integral part of an ancient tradition.

Definitely independent of the above tradition are certain occurrences in prose. The most striking examples are seen in parallel clauses beginning with *je . . . je*, where the (regular) final position of the verb in the first clause is imitated for reasons of symmetry in the second: (Luther) *je edler das Gliedmaß ist, je mehr die andern ihm helfen sollen*—modern idiom requires in the second clause *umso* (or *desto*) *mehr sollen die andern ihm helfen.* Examples continue into the early nineteenth century: (Wieland) *je mehr sie ihn besah, je mehr sie Reize fand.* The construction is a replica of medieval *sô . . . sô*: MHG (Walther) *sô ich ie mêre zühte hân, / sô ich ie minre werdekeit bejage* 'the more decency I have, the less esteem I find'. Notice the parallelism in the proverbial *wes Brot ich esse, des Lob* (or *Lied*) *ich singe.*

Final position may also exceptionally occur after the synonyms *anders* 'otherwise' and *sonst*: (Luther) *man fasset auch nicht Most in alte Schläuche; anders die Schläuche zerreißen*, (Lessing) *sonst er doch einiges Geld bekommen hätte.* But this feature has disappeared today.

It goes without saying that second position becomes final position also in sentences like *die Glocke läutet*; for the purpose of classification such examples are naturally referred to the second position, as in *die Glocke läutet hell.*

Position of finite verb in subordinate clause

The basic rule that the finite verb in a subordinate clause comes at the end is an outstanding characteristic of modern German syntax. Since such order is exceptional in a main clause, and even then confined to poetry, final position of the verb has become the hallmark of subordination. It rests upon a very old tradition, one which was already predominant in OHG: (Notker) *alle die* astronomiam *chunnen, die bechennent, taz* aequinoctialis zona *den himel rehto in zwei teilet, unde fone iro ze dien ûzerostên* polis *îowederhalb ebenfilo ist* 'alle, die Astronomie können, erkennen, daß die äquinoktiale Zone den Himmel genau in zwei Teile teilt, und daß von ihr zu den äußersten Polen auf jeder Seite dasselbe ist'. Poetic style is freer, but on the whole the general structure is usually the same: (Muspilli) *doh wânit des vilo. . . . gotmanno, / daz Elias in demo wîge arwartit werde. / Sô daz Eliases pluot in erda kitriufit, / sô inprinnant die pergâ* 'but many servants of God believe that Elias will be wounded in the combat. When Elias' blood drips onto the earth, then the mountains will burst into flame.'

On the other hand, the present rule which lays down absolutely that the verb must come last in the subordinate clause is a creation of the modern literary language, and dates from about the middle of the seventeenth century. And yet this rigid rule is, in actual fact, more a matter of theory than of practice, for another part of the clause may still, under certain conditions, follow the verb. These conditions are, in the main, the dictates of style, the written language being variable within itself and having other canons than the colloquial of everyday. Furthermore, what is necessary in the modern language will often be at variance with what was preferred in times gone by. A few pages of Luther's Bible suffice to show that, in his day, a part of the clause more often followed the subordinate verb than is usual in any written German at the present time. All the same, it is permissible to classify together all subordinate clauses in which at least one element follows the verb. We shall do this and give some account of the history of word order in such subordinate clauses.

It often happens, in older style, that an infinitive follows the finite verb. The infinitive may then stand at the end of the clause: (Luther) *die wol mugen mit krieg die welt erfullen*, (Schiller) *und was von allen deinen Schätzen / dein Herz am höchsten mag ergötzen*. Some instances recall forms of spoken German heard locally to this day, like the following relative clause from Goethe's letters: *von der du wirst gehört haben* stylistically comparable to 'who you will have heard of'. The infinitive is often followed by a further part of the clause: (Luther) *bis daß er sollte hervortreten vor das Volk*. These things are amply quotable from medieval sources, too: MHG (Berthold) *wan eht si ir liebeȥ kint solte an sehen* 'but that she should only look upon her dear child', OHG (Notker) *tîe unsih lêrênt habên rehte site* 'who teach us to have right morals'.

The past participle of the verb may follow the finite part: OHG (Tatian) *fon sô welichero suhti was bihabet* "of whatsoever disease he had" lit. 'was held' (tenebatur), MHG (Berthold) *den daȥ alter an im hæte gemaht* 'which age would have done to him', NHG (Luther) *alle aber, die geläubig waren geworden*, (Lessing) *daß er in der letzten Hälfte des zwölften Jahrhunderts muß sein verfaßt worden*, (Schiller) *wenn seine Gewalt nicht wäre gebrochen worden*. This last example reminds us that the spoken language of today may still employ this order: a phrase such as *wenn das nicht wäre geschrieben worden* can often be heard in the speech of persons of all classes. Where there are two participles, the finite verb may appear between them: (Luther) *nachdem wir geboren sind gewesen.* This order, too, will have had its roots in contemporary oral usage, for it is widely found in dialect and substandard speech at the present time: *ich weiß, wie das gemacht ist worden.* In sentences where the infinitive replaces the past participle, e.g. *ich habe ihm nicht helfen können*, both infinitives come after the finite verb: *er weiß, daß ich ihm nicht habe helfen können*; a phrase closely attached to an infinitive will not be separated from it: (Schiller) *wie ich nun werde zu Werk gehen müssen.* This practice constitutes a formal exception to the rule that the finite verb in a subordinate clause must come last. In the spoken language, locally, the finite verb can appear between the infinitives: *er weiß, daß ich ihm nicht helfen habe können.*

The finite verb may precede its predicate as follows: OHG (Notker) *tîe imo . . . newâren gevolgig* 'who were not obedient to him', MHG (Berthold) *daʒ sie wæren wîse* 'that they might be wise', NHG (Luther) *Simon, der da heißt Petrus.* This order is common when the predicate is followed by some complement: (Luther) *welches sind die Gebete der Heiligen.* Indeed, if the complement is long, this order may be regarded as regular: (Luther) *welcher ist der treue Zeuge und Erstgeborene von den Toten und Fürst der Könige auf Erden.* Modern examples are much less usual: (Goethe) *daß er würde der Spiegel deiner Seele.*

There are cases where the subject follows the verb: (Luther) *daß sich bewegten die Grundfesten des Gefängnisses.* This usage survives as poetic licence: (Uhland) *bis sich hebt am letzten Rand / ein Palast im Morgenschimmer.*

The finite verb is, in a number of cases, followed by an object: OHG (Notker) *die in sînen zîten wândon des sûonetagen* 'who in his times were expecting the day of judgement', MHG (Mystics) *alse diu sunne an sich ziuhet den fiuhten luft* 'as the sun draws to itself the damp air', Early NHG (Luther) *daß ihr nicht widerstreben sollt dem Übel.* This order may be expected if the object is particularly long or if it takes a complement: (Luther) *bis er ausbaute sein Haus und des Herrn Haus und die Mauer um Jerusalem her*; *die nicht haben das Siegel Gottes an ihren Stirnen.* This order is also common if the object is associated with a relative clause: (Luther) *da ich mich aber wollte erkundigen der Ursache, darum sie ihn beschuldigten.* Examples from the classical period: (Goethe) *daß ich nicht sehen kann das Volk! daß ich nicht . . . ausdrücken kann, mein Bester, die Empfindungen, die mein Herz bestürmen!* The indirect object may be similarly treated: MHG (Landrechtbuch) *daz er den himel ûf slüzze allen den, die den fride hielten*, Early NHG (Luther) *daß wir Antwort geben denen, die uns gesandt haben.*

Most commonly of all, the finite verb may be followed by a prepositional group: OHG (Notker) *daz sî micheli nîeht nehabet wider dero micheli des himiles* 'that it has no size compared with the size of heaven', MHG (Berthold) *daz sie êre unde guot haben unz an ir tôt* 'that they may have honour and wealth until their death', NHG (Luther) *wo sie nicht Buße tun für ihre Werke* "except they repent of their deeds", (Gryphius) *daß der Kaiser Frieden gemacht habe mit dem König von Schweden.* Indeed, in the medieval language, it is almost as common to find a prepositional group after the verb as to find it in front, without it being possible to account, in precise terms, for one or the other. Considerations of emphasis, the character of the prepositional group, e.g. its length, whether a necessary adjunct of the verb or not, and finally doubtless also personal predilection, all can have played a part.

After Early NHG, instances in literature become rare, but the spoken language continued the old freedom, as is indicated by modern colloquial examples. All over the German-speaking world today, in dialect and in more standard forms of the language, prepositional groups are quite often heard after the verb: *ich erzähle dir gleich, was ich gehört habe bei Müllers*; *sagen Sie mir bitte, wieviel Sie ausgeben wollen für das Geschenk*; *er behauptet, daß nichts mehr übrig bleibt davon.* The style is casual, but not vulgar. It crops up perennially in the essays of younger school children. It was characteristically the *Stürmer und Dränger* who restored this word order to its lost literary status. It often represents natural speech: (Schiller) *auch liegt ihm Edelreich hart an mit ihren Vorwürfen und Klagen.* This order remained the exception, of course, but by virtue of its being exceptional, it could be used for stylistic effect: (Goethe) *ich ahnete ganz leise, was für ein Schauplatz das noch werden sollte von Seligkeit und Schmerz.* This usage then dies down in literature, but never disappears entirely. It is, in fact, fairly common today in various styles: (novelette) *daß sie eifersüchtig waren auf ihre Nebenbuhlerinnen*, (biography) *die wie sie eingeschlossen lebten in kärglich beleuchteten Zellen.* It is not infrequently employed to simplify the word order of the sentence generally, as, for example, when a relative clause has to be accommodated: (Behaghel) *seit ich . . . den ersten Spatenstich getan habe zu dem Gebäude, das nun endlich unter Dach gekommen ist.* Rhythmic and stylistic factors may only be apparent when the clause is considered in connexion with the rest of the sentence: (story) *er weiß, daß er die Welt für immer verläßt, daß er nie wieder die Berge sehen wird, die Wache halten an seinem Grab.*

The infinitive with *zu* is of itself almost the equivalent of a subordinate clause: *dort steht der Mann, der mich bat ihn zu besuchen.* Not unexpectedly, such a construction often follows the verb, in the medieval texts regularly so: OHG (Notker) *samasô du newizzist dien zeantwurtenne* 'as you do not know how to answer them', MHG (Mystics) *daz wir wünschen nach gotes willen ze sîn* 'that we wish to be according to God's will'. Similarly Luther: *als er hatte aufgehöret zu reden.* This order has continued down to the present time, especially when the infinitive takes a complement: (Hebel) *daß dieser wünschte in ein Armenspital gebracht zu werden.* If, on the other hand, the link between finite verb and infinitive is particularly close, as when the nature of the former presupposes the latter, the infinitive construction regularly precedes: (Luther) *da auch die Heiden nicht von zu sagen wissen*, (Hebel) *alsdann sich ihrer zu bemächtigen suchen.* This order is often found when the infinitive takes a short complement: *was man gefunden zu haben glaubt*, but equally common and more popular in tone: *was man glaubt gefunden zu haben.* Apart from the foregoing, examples occur where the infinitive precedes the finite verb simply in consonance with the general tendency to put the latter at the very end: (Luther) *daß er auch von dem Herrn, eurem Gott . . . abzufallen gelehret . . . hat.* Such usage is not unusual later: (Chamisso) *das ich anzusehen mich geschämt hätte*, but it is nowadays felt to be undesirably stilted.

Position of the infinitive

The infinitive is normally placed at the end of the main clause. This general rule has obtained since the beginning of the records: OHG (Notker) *tune maht nieht mit einero dohder zewena eidima machôn* 'you can't make two sons-in-law with one daughter', MHG (Berthold) *dar umbe möhten wir doch gerne ze dem himelrîche komen* 'therefore we should very much like to get to heaven'. But the older language was more tolerant of exceptions than the modern literary language where word order has been rigidly codified. Modern spoken German, on the other hand, preserves many of the freedoms of the older period.

The infinitive may sometimes be followed by its object: OHG (Williram) *er scal ane imo selbemo bedûhan des lîchamen gluste* 'he shall mortify in himself the lusts of the body'. This usage is well known to Luther: *ich will halten die Gebote meines Gottes*, and especially when the object is extensive: *ich bin kommen, zu rufen die Sünder zur Buße und nicht die Gerechten.* The infinitive is occasionally followed by an adverb: (Luther) *dein Vater . . . wird dir's vergelten öffentlich.* But chiefly prepositional groups are found after the infinitive: OHG (Notker) *taȥ mag man wola sehen an dero* sphaera 'one can well see that on the globe', MHG (Berthold) *welt ir nû genesen von dem êwigen tôde* 'if you wish to escape eternal death', Early NHG (Luther) *wie lange soll ich sorgen in meiner Seele und mich ängstigen in meinem Herzen täglich?* This usage was revived in the literature of *Sturm und Drang*: (Goethe) *ihr sollt wieder haben alles, was euch gebührt,* (Schiller) *der Abt muß . . . Rechenschaft ablegen über die seiner Hut anvertrauten Seelen.* Examples are often found in modern style: *die Lehrer sind zu bemitleiden wegen ihrer schweren Aufgabe*; *Herrn Paucker habe ich zu danken für bibliographische Hinweise.* This order is a common feature of spoken style: *sie konnte sich nicht fassen vor Glück*; *sie müssen ja so müde sein von der langen Fahrt*; *ich möchte nur noch eins hier hereinstellen in die Ecke*; *man kann ihm nicht helfen dabei*; *was können wir herausbringen davon?*

In subordinate clauses, the finite verb has first call on the final position, so that here, in average use, the infinitive precedes the finite verb: *Martin sagte, daß ich kommen sollte.* For exceptions see pp. 262, 265. The same applies when there are two infinitives: *ich befürchte, daß er sitzen bleiben wird*, but substandard *daß er wird sitzen bleiben* is heard in uneducated speech; cf. also p. 263. In former times, word order in these cases could vary a great deal; an example from Luther gives an idea of the possibilities: *wenn aber mein Herr König mit seinen Vätern entschlafen ist, so werden ich und mein Sohn müssen Sünder sein.*

Position of the past participle

Like the infinitive, the past participle is normally placed at the end of the main clause. This has been general practice since the earliest records: OHG (Notker) *sâr des anderen iâres wart Thioterih ferloren* 'the very next year Theoderich died', MHG (Berthold) *in habent die engel wol sehstic hundert iâr an gesehen* 'the angels have been looking at him, indeed, for sixty hundred years'. But as with the infinitive, the older language and the spoken style of today admit more exceptions than the modern literary language. In particular, prepositional groups often come after the participle: MHG (Berthold) *du hâst gesündet an got* 'you have sinned against God', Early NHG (Luther) *ich habe meinen König eingesetzt auf meinen heiligen Berg*. Again it was the *Stürmer und Dränger* who rehabilitated this word order in literature: (Schiller) *ich habe's ihm gesagt mit einem heiligen Eide*. It has since remained in use in imitation of the spoken language: (Raabe) *das Lachen ist teuer geworden in der Welt*, or for rhetorical effect: (G. Schwab) *die alten Götter verlangten Blut und Tränen, und damit ist der Boden Italiens getränkt von Anbeginn*, or simply to stop the participle getting too far away from its auxiliary: (notice) *die Gedenkfeier wird veranstaltet vom Germanistischen Institut der Universität unter Mitwirkung der Deutschen Bücherei*. Examples from the spoken language: *man ist ausgeschaltet von allem*; *wir waren entsetzt über sein Benehmen*; *ich bin einverstanden damit*.

If an infinitive is present in the main clause, the participle today is placed in front of it: *wir werden es bis dahin geschafft haben*. In the medieval language, however, the infinitive not infrequently preceded: OHG (Tatian) *ni mag burg werdan giborgan* (non potest civitas abscondi) 'a city cannot be hidden', MHG (Sermon) *si möhte wol hân gesprochen* 'she could well have said'.

In subordinate clauses, the finite verb occupies the final position so that here the past participle must precede the finite verb: *sie sagt, daß er es getan hat*. For exceptions see pp. 262–3.

The past participle is often used without a finite verb. In this function it is often moved forward, usually to the first place in its clause, for stylistic reasons: (Luther) *ein Buch, geschrieben inwendig und auswendig, versiegelt mit sieben Siegeln*, (Kleist) *und ging, völlig ausgesöhnt mit seinem Schicksal, fort*, (Schiller) *ich traf ihn am Abend, niedergesunken unter Kugelgepfeife*. This order is current in modern style: *angetrieben vom roten Tuch*; *gestützt auf die bisherigen Erfahrungen*. It is common in structures such as *das Städtchen, eingebettet in sanfte Hügel, ...*; *die Arbeit, bezogen auf den gegenwärtigen Stand der Forschung*. ... Indeed, this order is now regular in formal contexts: *Festschrift für N.N., dargebracht von Freunden und Schülern, herausgegeben von X.Y.Z., erschienen 1965*, similarly *Elegie, geschrieben auf einem Dorffriedhof*.

Position of the present participle

The present participle, like the other nominal parts of the verb, usually comes last in its clause: OHG (Notker) *taȝ urlub kab imo Zeno, sîn lant ioh sîne liute ze sînên triuwôn bevelehendo* 'Z. gave him permission, commending to his care his land and subjects', MHG (Berthold) *sælic sint, die reines herzen sint, wan sie werdent got sehende* "blessed are the pure in heart, for they shall see God", Early NHG (Luther) *es waren aber Juden zu Jerusalem wohnend*. In modern style, the participle may, for convenience, be placed at the beginning of its clause: (news-sheet) *aufbauend auf die freundschaftliche Begegnung zwischen Vertretern der beiden Städte* . . . . It goes without saying that the ordinary colloquial makes no use of such constructions involving the present participle; they are now purely literary.

From paratax to hypotax

In the foregoing sections we have seen how the modern literary language has laid down stricter rules of word order than were customary in medieval times and that they sometimes conflict with the living spoken style. In so far as these stricter rules concern the all-important matter of the position of the finite verb in subordinate clauses, there can be little doubt that the influence of Humanistic Latin played a part. It is true that German had, from the beginning, known and largely preferred this word order as a genuinely native structure, but that it should come to be adopted exclusively must have been due to the literary activity of an *élite* steeped in Latin.

A trend towards a clear-cut distinction between main and subordinate clauses in terms of word order appears strongly in Early NHG, and feeling in this matter developed rapidly. It is noteworthy that Luther's final revision of his Bible not infrequently shows a modification of the word order in favour of the emerging standard: (1522) *da er aber horet von Jhesu, sandt er die Elltisten der Juden zu yhm, vnd batt ynh, das er keme, vnd macht seynen knecht gesund*, but (1546) *da er aber von Jhesu höret, sandte er die eltesten der Jüden zu jm, vnd bat jn, das er keme, vnd seinen Knecht gesund machet.*

In medieval German, paratax, i.e. the use of separate sentences one after another without grammatical subordination, was the more typical form of composition. Consider these lines from one of the great stylists: (Wolfram) *sîn lîp was klâr unde fier. / ûf dem plâne am rivier / twuoc er sich alle morgen. / er enkunde niht gesorgen, / ez enwære ob im der vogelsanc. / diu süeze in sîn herze dranc. / daz erstracte im sîniu brüstelîn. / al weinde er lief zer künegîn. / sô sprach si 'wer hât dir getân? / du wære hin ûz ûf den plân.' / er enkunde es ir gesagen niht, / als kinden lîhte noch geschiht. / dem mære gienc si lange nâch. / eines tages sî in kapfen sach*, etc. etc. 'he was handsome and majestic. On the meadow by the river he washed every morning. He had no cares but for the song of the birds above him. The sweetness went to his heart. That burst his little breast. Weeping he ran to the queen. So she said "Who has hurt you? You went out to the meadow." He couldn't tell her, as is often the case with children. She thought long about the matter. One day she saw him gazing. . . .'

Not much prose was written in German in the Middle Ages. Though it is all heavily indebted to Latin models, paratax remained, by comparison with present standards, a noticeable feature. But towards the beginning of modern times, German came to be used extensively in administration and began to assume a more complicated hypotactical character. The nature of this development can also be seen in Luther's work in those instances where he later preferred subordination to paratax: (1522) *vnd es ware umb die dritte stund, vnd sie creutzigeten yhn* (similarly in the Greek original, and in the Vulgate), but (1546) *vnd es war umb die dritte stunde, da sie jn creutzigten.* The written language continued to develop in this direction and now shows considerably greater preference for hypotax than was usual in Luther's day. The difference may be readily gauged by comparing the Reformer's Bible with the translation by Menge, which is entirely in the idiom of the present day. We take an example. Matt. ii. 12 is construed in the Greek as a single, hypotactical sentence, of which the

Vulgate offers a very literal translation: et responso accepto in somnis ne redirent ad Herodem, per aliam viam reversi sunt in regionem suam. This passage Luther breaks up as follows: *und Gott befahl ihnen im Traum, daß sie sich nicht sollten wieder zu Herodes lenken. Und zogen durch einen andern Weg wieder in ihr Land.* Today, such paratax seems clumsy. Menge puts: *weil sie hierauf im Traum die göttliche Weisung erhielten, nicht wieder zu Herodes zurückzukehren, zogen sie auf einem anderen Wege in ihr Heimatland zurück.*

Compound verbs with separable prefix (preverb)

The traditional positions of the separable preverb in a main clause may be illustrated by the following medieval examples: MHG (Walther) *starken liuten wæt erȝ houbet abe* 'it blows strong people's heads off / kräftigen Leuten bläst er den Kopf ab', *si sehent mich niht mêr an in butzen wîs* 'they no longer look at me as though I were a scarecrow'. According to the basic canon of NHG grammar, however, the separable word must in all cases go to the end, and it consequently very often finds itself at some distance from the verb: (magazine) *diese Entwicklung spiegelt den Wandel in den Beziehungen der Völker, wie er sich in unserem Jahrhundert vollzogen hat, wieder.* Rigid application of this rule led to ponderous sentences where the reader has half forgotten the verb by the time the separable word appears: (Kleist) *er . . . setzte seine Reise mit dem Rest der Koppel, halb und halb ungewiß, ob nicht doch wohl wegen aufkeimender Pferdezucht ein solches Gebot im Sächsischen erschienen sein könne, nach Leipzig, wo er auf die Messe wollte, fort.* Today, directness is more typical of acceptable style, so that the separable word is frequently brought nearer to its verb: (learned article) *nachträglich weist mich Güterbock noch hin auf den noch heute in der Türkei gebräuchlichen, schweren zweirädigen Karren, türkisch 'kagni', mit Scheibenrädern, der sehr urtümlich mutet.* This trend has become most marked in the last few decades. Other examples: (literary history) *hier knüpfen wir an die Romantik an mit ihrem schwärmerischen Hang zum deutschen Mittelalter,* (history book) *doch fahren wir erst fort in der skizzenhaften Schilderung der Geschichte des Landes Mitanni,* (serial story) *ich reiße mich gewaltsam los von diesem Augenblick und den tausend Erinnerungen.* A teacher in a Berlin secondary school recently suggested that the sentence *am folgenden Tag fanden im Senat Verhandlungen über die Bestrafung der Catilinarier statt*, written in a pupil's essay, should be amended to *am folgenden Tag fanden im Senat Verhandlungen statt über die Bestrafung der Catilinarier.*

This contemporary development springs from the cardinal principle of syntax that words belonging to each other will tend to come together. The question of priorities is, of course, the problem. In the present case, it may be stated that the spoken language has never tolerated the excesses of the written language. Indeed, the colloquial varies considerably even from the moderate style nowadays customary in writing. Examples: *sie baut vor auf ihre Art*; *stehen Sie mit an hier?* 'are you queueing up here as well?', (local) *zieh dir aus die Jacke, wenn's zu warm ist*, (advertisement, in imitation of the colloquial) *seid schlau, lernt beim Bau—fragt nach bei der Fachgemeinschaft Bau.* This natural, and hence vivid order may be appropriate for high style: (epic) *steig hinauf auf die Mauer, Urschanabi! Geh einher auf der Mauer von Urak, der stark umfriedigten Stadt!* just like Luther: *tritt her von der Höhle Amana!*

Incapsulation

The attributive adjective is preceded by its complement: *ein mir unverständliches Ergebnis*; *jener in ganz Deutschland wohlbekannte Artist.* This construction, which may be termed incapsulation, arose at the beginning of modern times in the officialese of the chanceries. In many examples several adjectives and their complements are used before a single noun. Such long periods were felt to be elegant and often appear in classical literature: (Lessing) *o des unschuldigen, friedlichen, mit dem Mantel der christlichen Liebe alle Mängel bedeckenden, nur aus Gefälligkeit widersprechenden Mannes!* This style remains an integral part of the modern literary tradition, being especially prevalent in writing of a technical nature: (textbook) *für das anfangs wegen seines Fleisches geschätzte und außerdem schon frühzeitig verehrte Tier.* Needless to remark, the construction has never formed part of the ordinarily spoken language.

Dative and accusative

The indirect (dative) object traditionally precedes the direct (accusative) object: OHG (Isidor) *gab dhuo got Moysi êwa* 'then

God gave Moses the law'. This is still normal practice today: *ich gebe dem Gepäckträger den Koffer.* But this order is sometimes disturbed. The accusative may be put first to bring it into closer contact with something which has preceded: (Luther) *da das Volk das sah, verwunderte es und pries Gott, der solche Macht den Menschen gegeben hat.* This kind of thing can be heard in conversation any day: *was soll ich mit den vielen Koffern machen? Gib den großen Koffer dem Gepäckträger, die beiden kleinen nehmen wir selber.* Special emphasis may also change the order, e.g. the dative may be emphasized by putting it second: *ich widme dieses Buch seinem Andenken.* Or sentence rhythm may require this order: *er widmete das Buch dem Andenken seiner treuen Freunde.*

Inflexions and word order

It is obvious that German word order is freer than English. To start with the simplest of examples: the English sentence 'the Indian hunts the tiger' can be given in German as either *der Inder jagt den Tiger* or *den Tiger jagt der Inder.* In English, such modification of the order would reverse the sense, but in German ambiguity is excluded thanks to the inflexions: *der Inder* must be the subject and *den Tiger* must be the object regardless of position. If, now, we wish to translate 'the woman sees the cat', we notice that only *die Frau sieht die Katze* is possible, for in this case German is on all fours with English, *die* as much as 'the' being invariable for nominative and accusative, and thus not able to distinguish a subject from an object. In such cases the sense is determined by a basic rule of sequence: subject—verb—object. It may be noted here that in OHG the fem.sg. article distinguishes nom. *diu*, acc. *dia*, whence MHG nom. *diu*, acc. *die.* It follows that medieval German could use free order with these forms: OHG (Notker) *wir wiȥen, daȥ tia erda daȥ waȥer umbegât,* but in NHG the subject must come first: *wir wissen, daß das Wasser die Erde umgibt.*

We recall, however, that even if the subject and object are not distinguished by an inflexional form, free order is nevertheless still possible in German if the sense remains unambiguous: *die Frau malt die Tür* can therefore be changed to *die Tür malt die Frau.* English word order, on the other hand, has become too rigid to permit such inversion as a rule. Where subject and object are different numbers, the verb of course makes matters clear: *die ostgermanischen Sprachen vertritt das Gotische.*

The significance of variable word order is discussed in the next section.

Emphatic word order

Where variation of the basic sequence (subject—verb—object) is allowed, emphatic word order becomes possible: *Lebkuchen esse ich gern*, where attention is immediately drawn to the object standing first, as also in the examples in the section above. This order is very usual in all styles: *ˈden Tag vergesse ich nicht* 'I'll never forget that day', *Brot für alle hat die Erde*; *leid tun mir alle, die Albanisch treiben müssen* 'I'm pretty sorry for . . . '. The degree of emphasis may, however, be very slight: *Spaten und Eimer können wir hier lassen, die anderen Sachen schaffen wir fort*, hardly different from *wir können Spaten und Eimer hier lassen*. In written style, such order may be preferred more for reasons of sentence rhythm than for true emphasis: *besondere Freude machte mir Dein Brief, da er soviel Interessantes enthielt*. The dative object may be similarly treated: *einem Narren kann man kein ungebautes Haus zeigen*; *mir erzählst du das?*

Other parts of the sentence may likewise be emphasized by being placed first. Adverbs and prepositional groups commonly occur initially: *hier brütet ein Vogel*; *auf der Wiese weiden Kühe*. As before, emphasis may be but slight, and in writing especially, this order may be chosen for stylistic convenience: *von der Mitte des Plafonds hängt eine Lampe herunter, die den ganzen Saal hell erleuchtet*. In the same way, an infinitive may stand first or be moved forward as far as possible: *ausgehen darf sie schon, nur arbeiten darf sie noch nicht*; *selber schreiben möchtest du können und wüßtest vielleicht, was? leuchtende Beispiele, denen nachzueifern ich nicht gewillt bin!* In fact, nominal forms of verbs often appear in the opening position, again for reasons of emphasis or style: *wir haben es bisher nicht gemacht — aber gemacht werden muß es!* (learned article) *geschrieben worden ist sie* (the manuscript), *wie die Forschung jetzt allgemein anerkannt, in Zürich, kurz nach 1300*. Whole phrases are regularly transposed: *daß er nicht zahlen konnte, wußte man schon lange*; *ob ich nächste Woche Zeit dafür haben werde, kann ich dir heute noch nicht sagen.*

The above principles have applied at all periods of the language, e.g. OHG (Notker) *taȝ urlub kab imo Zeno* 'Z. gave him permission', (Williram) *gesêret habest tu mir mîn herza* 'you have wounded my heart', MHG (Berthold) *ûf ertrîche sehen wir in alle tage in sînem gewalte* 'on earth we see him every day in his might'.

Emphasis is not only obtained by moving words to the front; it may also be obtained, though less usually, by sending them to the end. One can say: *bei Schwarz muß alles immer schnell gehen*, but one can also say and achieve equal, if not greater emphasis: *alles muß immer schnell gehen bei Schwarz*. On a most unseasonable summer's day, this remark was overheard: *die Ostsee wird noch zufrieren im Sommer*. Other examples: *ich lasse mich nicht aus dem Konzept bringen von ihr*; *komisch daß du so ordentlich bist — bei deiner Mutter* 'considering what your mother is like'. These examples are not to be separated from those on pp. 264f., 267 where prepositional groups come at the end without necessarily implying emphasis, though they could do so and this would be brought out in the spoken word by the stress. Conversely, the above examples need not be emphatic; the last one, incidentally, could not be construed in any other form without altering the sense.

It sometimes happens that this sort of emphatic order in German corresponds to non-emphatic order in English—we ignore here the possibilities of emphatic stress on a given word which are the same in both languages. Thus *jetzt* is emphatic by position in the sentence *wir trinken Kaffee jetzt*, but 'we'll take coffee now' is non-emphatic; idiomatically the latter is Ger. *wir trinken jetzt Kaffee*. By the same token, *in England* is emphatic by position in *Lebensmittel sind billiger in England*; non-emphatic order would be *Lebensmittel sind in England billiger*, idiomatically equivalent to 'food is cheaper in England'.

Occasionally the subject of the sentence is moved back to the final emphatic position: *zu diesen Zeiten unterrichten die Kinder die Studenten* 'at these times the students (as opposed to the regular teachers) teach the children'. Examples are not unusual in literary style: (historical novel) *als dann der Sonnenwagen am östlichen Rand des Horizonts aus den Fluten stieg, ertönten auf allen Schiffen der Griechen die Hörner*.

Stylistic variation

We have discussed above some of the factors which determine word order and have seen that considerable variations are possible in spite of certain formal rules. This situation is naturally exploited for stylistic effect at all levels. We take a few examples: (Erika Mann) *das konnte jeder sehen, daß heute noch was setzen würde an Wind und Wetter. Stoffel war sehr einverstanden gewesen mit diesem Gespräch, denn er hätte um keinen Preis fortmögen vom Blaubergsee,* (Giustiniani) *sie ist gebannt von ihrem Traum, von ihrer Armut gepeinigt, überanstrengt von harter Arbeit,* (political slogan) *die Republik schützen, Freundschaft halten dem Freund, keine Chance geben dem Feind!* (Menge) *seht, er kommt mit den Wolken, und sehen werden ihn die Augen aller, auch die, welche ihn durchstochen haben, und wehklagen werden um ihn alle Geschlechter der Erde*; Luther's words here are: *siehe, er kommt mit den Wolken, und es werden ihn sehen alle Augen, und die ihn gestochen haben, und werden heulen alle Geschlechter der Erde.*

Naturally enough, these things are seen in poetry. One simple stanza from Uhland may suffice to illustrate a freedom of word order by no means felt to be undue licence; on the contrary, the changing word order is the very life breath of the verse: *er hat ihn erstochen im dunklen Hain / und den Leib versenket im tiefen Rhein; / hat angelegt die Rüstung blank, / auf des Herrn Roß sich geschwungen frank.*

Questions of word order are also considered on p. 17 (position of genitive), p. 39 (postpositive adjective), p. 211 (position of negative).

Word order in English

The word order of OE is comparable to that of OHG, both languages being heirs to the same tradition. The OE material is, however, much more extensive than the OHG and some of it is older. It follows that the evidence of OE can be of value in explaining the OHG background, and for this reason Behaghel constantly refers to OE and quotes extensively from it in his discussion of early German word order. But the break up of the OE inflexional system and the loss of literary continuity owing to the Norman invasion destroyed many features which OE had in common with German. When, in its ME form, the language reappears after the French interregnum, the syntax is seen to be closer to that of modern English than to the purer Germanic language of the Anglo-Saxons.

INDEX OF AUTHORS OR WORKS

OLD HIGH GERMAN

Ambrosian Hymns	*c.* 800
Baptismal Vow	Early 9th century
Benedictine Rule	*c.* 800
Charms	(various)
Exhortatio ad plebem christianam	Second half of 8th century
Ezzos Gesang	First half of 11th century
Hamelburger Markbeschreibung	9th century
Hildebrandslied	Mid-8th century
Isidor: *Contra Judaeos*	Second half of 8th century
Ludwigslied	881/2
Monsee Matthew/Fragments	*c.* 800
Muspilli	*c.* 830
Notker	d. 1022
Otfrid: *Evangelienbuch*	*c.* 870
Petruslied	*c.* 900
Physiologus	11th century
Samaritan Woman	*c.* 900
St. Gall Paternoster	Late 8th century
Tatian: *Evangelienharmonie*	*c.* 830
Vienna Genesis	Late 11th century
Wessobrunn Prayer	Second half of 8th century
Williram	d. 1085

MIDDLE HIGH GERMAN

Beheim, M. von: *Gospels*	1343
Berthold von Regensburg	d. 1272
Crane	after 1250
Dietmar von Aist	*fl.* 1180
Freidank	*fl.* 1230
Gottfried von Straßburg	*fl.* 1210
Hartmann von Aue	*c.* 1160–*c.* 1220
Heinrich VI	1165–97
Helmbrecht	*c.* 1265
Kudrun	*c.* 1230
Kürenberg, Der von	*fl.* 1160
Lamprecht	*fl.* 1130
Landrechtbuch	*c.* 1280
Milstatt Genesis	Second half of 12th century
Minnesinger	13th–14th century
Morungen, H. von	d. 1222
Mystics	13th–14th century
Neidhart von Reuenthal	*c.* 1180–*c.* 1250

NEW HIGH GERMAN

PRINTED IN GREAT BRITAIN
AT THE UNIVERSITY PRESS, OXFORD
BY VIVIAN RIDLER
PRINTER TO THE UNIVERSITY